Relational Identities and Other-than-Human Agency in Archaeology

Relational Identities and Other-than-Human Agency in Archaeology

EDITED BY

Eleanor Harrison-Buck
and Julia A. Hendon

UNIVERSITY PRESS OF COLORADO

Louisville

Published by University Press of Colorado
245 Century Circle, Suite 202
Louisville, Colorado 80027

ASSOCIATION
of UNIVERSITY
PRESSES

The University Press of Colorado is a proud member of
the Association of University Presses.

The University Press of Colorado is a cooperative publishing enterprise supported, in part,
by Adams State University, Colorado State University, Fort Lewis College, Metropolitan
State University of Denver, Regis University, University of Colorado, University of Northern
Colorado, Utah State University, and Western State Colorado University.

ISBN: 978-1-60732-746-2 (cloth)
ISBN: 978-1-64642-135-0 (paperback)
ISBN: 978-1-60732-747-9 (ebook)
DOI: https://doi.org/10.5876/9781607327479

Library of Congress Cataloging-in-Publication Data

Names: Harrison-Buck, Eleanor, editor. | Hendon, Julia A. (Julia Ann), editor.
Title: Relational identities and other-than-human agency in archaeology / edited by Eleanor
    Harrison-Buck and Julia A. Hendon.
Description: Boulder : University Press of Colorado, [2018] | Includes bibliographical
    references and index.
Identifiers: LCCN 2017054090| ISBN 9781607327462 (cloth) | ISBN 9781646421350 (pbk) |
    ISBN 9781607327479 (ebook)
Subjects: LCSH: Social archaeology—Case studies. | Agent (Philosophy)—Case studies. |
    Material culture—Philosophy. | Archaeology—Philosophy.
Classification: LCC CC72.4 .R456 2018 | DDC 930.1—dc23
LC record available at https://lccn.loc.gov/2017054090

The University Press of Colorado gratefully acknowledges the generous support of the College
of Liberal Arts and the Center for the Humanities at the University of New Hampshire
toward the publication of this book.

The financial support provided by a Research and Professional Development grant from
Gettysburg College is gratefully acknowledged.

Cover photograph by Justin Kerr.

Contents

Relational Identities
and Other-than-Human
Agency in Archaeology

1

Archaeologists who engage in relational personhood and other-than-human agency, often characterized as a relational or ontological archaeology (Alberti 2016; Watts 2013a), variously identify as post-humanist, (neo-)materialist, non-representationalist, or realist, among other labels. Bruno Latour's (1993, 2013) work has been hugely influential among this diverse body of scholarship, recently labeled the "new ontological realism" (Gabriel 2015) or, alternatively, the "new materialist" archaeology (Thomas 2015). Generally speaking, these scholars reject the classic "humanist" divides, such as culture-nature, human-animal, and animate-inanimate (Watts 2013b:16). In studies of relational personhood, this so-called post-humanist approach is not anti-human but rather considers personhood more broadly to include both human and other-than-human beings, such as animals, plants, spirits, and inanimate things (Thomas 2002; Fowler 2004, 2016).

Some of the most prominent "problem domains" in studies of ontological archaeology involve agency and personhood. There is a long history of attention given to studies of relational personhood in archaeology (Brück 2001; Fowler 2004, 2016; Thomas 2002; Gillespie 2001; Wilkinson 2013, 2017, among others) and in recent years a burgeoning of literature focused specifically on object-based agencies, biographies, and itineraries (Gosden and Marshall 1999; Hodder 2012; Joyce and Gillespie 2015b; Knappett and Malafouris 2008; Mills and Walker 2008; Olsen 2010; Webmoor

An Introduction to Relational Personhood and Other-than-Human Agency in Archaeology

ELEANOR HARRISON-BUCK
AND JULIA A. HENDON

DOI: 10.5876/9781607327479.c001

3

and Witmore 2008, among others). This volume provides a global perspective on these two interrelated "problem domains"—agency and personhood—and adds to a growing body of archaeological literature that explores the regional variability and intricacies of agency and how this ontological status informs relational personhood (for other recent contributions, see Buchanan and Skousen 2015; Watts 2013a).

Agency is closely related to animacy—"an ontology in which objects and other nonhuman beings possess souls, life-force and qualities of personhood" (Brown and Walker 2008:297). Here we note the important point that agency and personhood (and therefore animacy) are not synonymous. In other words, while all things have the potential for agency, not all agents (including humans) are necessarily persons. As Hill (this volume) notes, while many things have agency—the ability to act—not all of them possess the capacity for reciprocity where social identity is a mutually constituted relationship, which defines personhood in many societies (Ingold 2006; see also Pauketat and Alt, this volume). While some gloss agency and animacy as the same, the studies presented here and elsewhere highlight important distinctions between these two terms that are not just semantic (Ingold 2013:248; Zedeño 2013:121). Timothy Ingold (2013:248) suggests that agency and animacy "pull in opposite directions," with the former referencing the intention of humans and nonhumans and the latter involving attention, vitalism, growth, and becoming. Ingold (2013:248) concludes that the term "agency" is tied to cognitivism and should be replaced with animacy, which he defines as non-discursive or bodily experienced knowledge (cf. Budden and Sofaer 2009; Harrison-Buck, this volume). While many of the contributions in this volume deal explicitly with animacy, the term strictly references a being with a life force—a quality associated with personhood—and is not applicable to every agent, namely non-persons. In this volume we maintain the term "agency" because it allows contributors to appropriately characterize a broader array of actors, not just social beings but also the asocial entities.

The terms "other-than-human" and "nonhuman" are used interchangeably in the literature and in this volume to refer to relational (social) beings, such as animals, plants, objects, and spirits. Terms like "other-than-human" or "nonhuman" distinguish between biologically human beings and other beings. We recognize that in many ways such terms are problematic in that they perpetuate a false subject-object divide that does not accurately portray the shared ontological status between human and nonhuman beings (sensu Ingold 2013:247). Some, like Benjamin Alberti and Yvonne Marshall, question whether we can overcome this and other forms of "hypocrisy" in our theorizing of relational ontologies (Alberti and Marshall 2009), echoing the sentiments of Eduardo

Viveiros de Castro (2002) who suggests that "other peoples' ontological commitments (their worlds) have been converted by anthropology into epistemologies (worldviews)" (Alberti and Marshall 2009:346). While the contributors of this volume are encouraged to explore ontological difference in their case studies, they also recognize the interpretative challenges and acknowledge that our modes of inquiry in archaeological anthropology are deeply rooted in Western ontologies and epistemologies. Despite these limitations, the wealth of ethnographic data on Amerindian and North Eurasian ontologies demonstrates the need for more expansive (sensu Hviding 1996) and non-anthropocentric views of who (or what) is a socially recognized person. Such studies emphasize to archaeologists working in these and other areas of the world the importance of considering the ontological status of nonhuman agency and personhood in our archaeological reconstructions of past societies, regardless of whether they are considered "animistic."

NONHUMAN AGENCY IN ARCHAEOLOGY

Nonhuman agency in the context of relational personhood is not a human projection of imagination onto things but rather a condition of being alive in the world (Ingold 2006:10). In its simplest form, *agency* is the capacity to act (Hill, this volume; Robb 2010:493), but definitions of agency vary considerably in a range of contexts (see Dobres and Robb 2000 for examples). In recent years the focus has turned to object-based agency, and in such cases agency "denotes the power of objects to shape human behavior and influence change" (Zedeño 2013:121; see also Brown and Walker 2008:297; Pauketat 2013:27). Studying the agency of nonhumans has also gained recent scholarly attention, expanding on material agency to include animals, organisms, and other tangible and intangible phenomena (Buchanan and Skousen 2015; Pauketat 2013; Watts 2013a). By expanding our understanding of agency to include nonhuman social actors, some advocate a *symmetrical* process in the construction of personhood (Malafouris 2013; Witmore 2007). The "principle of symmetry" suggests that personhood is not necessarily restricted to one type of entity (i.e., living biological human beings), and nonhumans "should not be regarded as ontologically distinct [from humans], as detached and separated entities, a priori" (Witmore 2007:546).

Current theoretical approaches to nonhuman agency in archaeology have been inspired by the writings of numerous scholars, including Bruno Latour (1993) and Karen Barad (2007), who consider all phenomena relational because in their studies of science and metaphysics "there is no a priori distinction to be made between social and natural-biological relations in the first place" (Wilkinson 2013:419; for further discussion, see also Martin 2013 and contributions in Descola and Pálsson 1996). Although interest in understanding relations between all sorts of social actors has increased in recent decades, an anthropological recognition of nonhuman social actors can be traced back to the pioneering works of A. Irving Hallowell. Hallowell (1960) coined the term "other-than-human persons" to more accurately capture the scope and texture of Ojibwa ontology and worldview. In more recent scholarship, Timothy Ingold's (1986, 2000, 2010, 2011) ecological phenomenology and his characterizations of an animic ontology (Ingold 1998, 2006), Morten Pedersen's (2001) studies of North Asian indigenous ontologies, as well as Philippe Descola's (1996) socialized naturalism and Eduardo Viveiros de Castro's (1998, 2004) perspectivism among Amerindian (Amazonian) groups have been influential in bringing the question of the ontological status of nonhuman agents as persons to the forefront of anthropological debate.

This volume explores the benefits and consequences for both archaeological theorizing and interpretation when we consider other-than-human agents as social actors who possess a life force—animacy—and qualities of personhood capable of producing change in the world (Alberti and Bray 2009; Brown and Walker 2008; Fowler 2016; Harrison-Buck 2012, 2015; Hendon 2010, 2012; Skousen and Buchanan 2015; Swenson 2015; Watts 2013b). To avoid homogenizing nonhuman agency and personhood as an identity formation, contributors in this volume examine these processes through a series of case studies in different temporal, geographic, and cultural contexts. Most of the studies presented in this volume deal with societies that are traditionally characterized as "animistic" or "totemic"; however, nonhuman agency and relational personhood are also invoked in modern contexts and are not necessarily restricted to any one type of society (see further discussion below on "Relational Personhood").

NARROWING THE DIVIDE: RELATIONAL OBJECT-BEINGS AND THE SPACES IN BETWEEN

Among the many other-than-human persons that exist in the world, objects and their roles as social actors are perhaps of greatest interest to archaeologists. While the archaeological contexts presented in this volume vary substantially, these studies all share the fundamental premise that "intentionality and reflexive consciousness are not exclusive attributes of humanity but potentially available to all beings of the cosmos" (Fausto 2007:497; for further discussion and critique of humanism in archaeology, see Thomas 2002). Although for many of us it might be difficult to envision objects as animate subjects, a number of anthropologists have led the way in firmly defending their "personhood" (Hodder 2012; Miller 2005; Olsen 2003, 2007; Webmoor and Witmore 2008).

Shifting our focus to objects has narrowed the perceived divide between humans (subjects) and nonhumans (objects). Severin Fowles (2010:25) worries that in our efforts to narrow the subject-object divide, we risk overlooking the "more complicated world of relations in which, packed between the multitudes of self-evident things, are crowds of non-things, negative spaces, lost or forsaken objects, voids or gaps—absences, in other words, that also stand before us as entity-like presences with which we must contend." Similarly, Marisa Lazzari (2003, 2005) notes that archaeologists' desire to make things visible and our quest to uncover the "real" meaning behind the symbolic or metaphorical thing is linked with the Western tendency to divide subjects and objects. This perspective echoes a broader postmodernist critique of the interpretative (representationalist) approach to personhood that dominated the post-processual movement, where the human body and the individual were given primacy (Skousen and Buchanan 2015:3). Lazzari (2003) and others advocate an alternative ontology that considers both the seen and the unseen in knowledge building and emphasizes "the relational nature and mutual constituency of both the subject and the object" (Lazzari 2003:200).

Studies of personhood by social psychologists and anthropologists lead us to suggest that Fowles's "non-things," much like Lazzari's "unseeable" domains, are not voids or empty spaces but are filled with the relational dialogues and intersubjective experiences that are central to how humans come to consider nonhumans as persons (Brill de Ramírez 2007; Gillespie and Cornish 2010; Hendon 2010; Miller 1987; Robb 2010). To explore the dialogic and intersubjective nature of this space, some insist we must adopt "an interpretive approach that can address communications and relationships that are not constrained by the articulation of human language and reason" (Brill de Ramírez 2007:24). Case studies presented in this volume advocate such an approach, whereby intersubjectivity does not reside solely in the mind and dialogic activity is not restricted to language. Craft making, bundling, censing, hunting, divination, dreaming, trance states—these are among the many forms of dialogic, intersubjective experience that simultaneously engages bodily experience and an embodied mind. Such activities produce a range of identities and "conversive" relationships (sensu Brill de Ramírez 2007), which seek connections between (human and nonhuman) persons and the cosmos, as opposed to a strictly discursive perspective, which tends to divide and categorize aspects of the world (see also Budden and Sofaer 2009).

Such conversive relations are similar to non-discursive experiences, involving repeated, intimate engagements with tools, materials, objects, and places that create opportunities for more materially mediated interactions (see Budden and Sofaer 2009). Yet conversive relations go beyond simply a non-discursive, bodily performed experience; they are generative actions that bind intangible relational beings, create personhood, and produce an animate ontological status in an object-body. It is the co-creative (re)productive process that is crucial for generating the movement and life force in a relational being (see Harrison-Buck, this volume). Intersubjectivity captures important aspects of the relationships, identities, and interdependencies that are continually formed through this conversive relationship (Harrison-Buck 2015; Hendon 2010). Through the interplay of subject and object, body and mind, both conversive "dialogue" and intersubjectivity create a web of shared significance and meanings (Jackson 1998) that are "constituted and reconstituted through historical action" (Hendon 2010:28). Elsewhere, Julia Hendon (2010:27–28) describes this "web of human sociality" as "communities of practice in which learning takes place and knowledge is constructed." Lynn Meskell (2005:2–3) refers to this interplay of cultural construction, praxis, and object biographies as "material habitus."

Ian Hodder (2012) suggests that human-object relationships gradually develop into intentional configurations that are actively negotiated and, as such, are inherently unstable. This idea of instability and ongoing change is a central component of Ingold's (2007) idea of meshwork where relationships, whether human or nonhuman, are in a constant state of flux and ongoing movement. More recent studies of movement (for objects, specifically) describe this circulation as an itinerary—the string of places and the nodes where these object-bodies come to rest before moving on (Joyce and Gillespie 2015b). This itinerant meshwork involves objects as well as persons, places, animals, and other nonhuman agents, which together form groupings that are variously referred to as nodes (Joyce and Gillespie 2015a), knots (Ingold 2007), bundles (Pauketat 2013; Zedeño 2008), or assemblages (Deleuze and Guattari 1987; Harris 2013; Jones 2011; Jones and Alberti 2013). These entangled meshworks and bundled assemblages form a relational field that is "constantly moving, gaining and losing parts, and becoming articulated with other assemblages" (Skousen and Buchanan 2015:5). There are many physical expressions of this ontological meshwork in which bundles of knowledge are learned and passed on. Storytelling is one example, and another involves the bundling and transfer of sacred objects—a widely shared practice found throughout the Americas (Pauketat 2013; Zedeño 2008). These and other examples are presented in this volume and shed light on how the numinous comes to reside in an object-body, its movement through the world, and the nature of its agency as a relational person.

RELATIONAL PERSONHOOD

Personhood—"a state of being a person" (Fowler 2004:7)—is often described as *relational* (Brück 2004, 2005; Fowler 2004, 2008, 2010, 2016; Hutson 2010). In this definition of personhood, identity is partible, permeable, or both, what Marilyn Strathern (1988) coined the "dividual" who, as opposed to the individual, is not tied to a single human body. Rather, the dividual is composed of fractal or divisible parts that are contextual and shifting in nature (Fowler 2004:7; see also Fowler 2002, 2016; Thomas 2002). Chris Fowler (2004:20–21) keenly observed that "dividuals" are not without self-awareness or individuality; these aspects simply represent less important elements of the relational self. In a more recent publication, Fowler (2016) reiterated this message, cautioning scholars to resist polarizing relational versus bounded types of persons, as this creates a "closed" and universalized ontology and paints groups as internally consistent and without contradiction, often falsely dichotomizing Western and non-Western cultures (see also recent discussions by Fowles 2013; Harris and Robb 2012; Harrison-Buck, this volume; Wilkinson 2013).

Cognitive scientists argue that we are all relationally constituted at birth (Pina-Cabral 2016). Human beings are inherently social and their personhood is shaped by intersubjective bodily experience, making the opposition between Western individual and non-Western dividual a moot point (see Harrison-Buck, this volume). Yet despite what cognitive science and cultural anthropology say about relational personhood, Marshall Sahlins (2011:14) argues that most scholars base their studies on the singular individual rather than placing the emphasis on the intersubjective (inherently social) being as a site of analysis. In this volume contributors recognize that intersubjectivity is a fundamental and indispensable condition of all personhood and that it is from here that we discover our individual selves and learn appropriate ways of being in the world in which we live and move about. In any society, personhood is not a static or fixed category but an ongoing engagement—conversive—and mutually constituted.

The diverse set of case studies presented in this volume covers a range of cultural, geographical, and historical contexts. Yet they all address how mutually constitutive conversive relations involve generative acts that together produce things in the world, which include both human and nonhuman entities (for further discussion of these shared aspects, see Harrison-Buck, this volume). As inherently co-creative and conversively responsive, the status of relational persons is contingent on both ongoing movement (agency) and reciprocal engagements (mutual constitution) with other relational entities (Hill 2011:409; Ingold 2006:12). For the Pueblo in the American Southwest, Severin Fowles (2013:157) describes this relationship as a complex *interdependency* rather than a simple "cause-and-effect" relationship—"a nonmodern cosmology ... in which human doings and the cosmos are consistently read in light of one another." In this and other instances, humans, plants, spirits, animals, and objects are all potentially persons and are among the many receptacle-bodies where the numinous comes to reside, sometimes remaining dormant until an interaction occurs with another relational being, bringing it to life.

PRACTICING PERSONHOOD: RESPONSIVE RELATEDNESS AND EMBODIED EXPERIENCE

Relational personhood is a condition of being alive in a world that, as Graham Harvey (2006:12) notes, is "a community of persons not all of whom are human." This results in a distinct way of knowing the world that emphasizes one's reciprocal relationship with it. Nurit Bird-David (1999:S68–S69) has described this as a two-way conversation of "responsive relatedness"—perceived as "mutually responsive changes in things in-the-world and at the same time in themselves" (see also Alberti and Bray 2009; Harvey 2006; Ingold 2006). For instance, in some societies hunters regard animals as other-than-human persons and view their success in the hunt as an animal's willingness to sacrifice itself, contingent on their close relationship with the animal being hunted (Hill 2011 and this volume; see also Brown and Emery 2008; Fausto 2007; Ingold 1996, 2000; McNiven 2010, 2013; Pedersen 2001). In these instances, hunters often follow specific protocols for killing and eating animals that are associated with rituals of self-sacrifice.

A two-way relationship between humans and animal persons that requires special attention resembles Bird-David's (1999) "responsive relatedness," discussed above. This kind of empathetic concern for another sentient being (human, animal, or otherwise) is directly related to an intersubjective relational ontology as an embodied experience and is akin to Fowles's (2013:158) notion of *sympathy*, where "ecology and morality meet." Centered on bodily feelings, a relational ontology involves a conscious awareness of one's positioning and activity in the world as a reciprocal and relational being. It is heavily reliant on human physiology and bodily sensation (Furst 1997; Harrison-Buck

2015; Houston and Taube 2000; Houston et al. 2006; Ingold 2006, 2010; López Austin 1988; Pauketat 2013). People enmeshed in a relational ontology "turned, not to theological pronouncements and speculations to verify their ideas, but to experience—to what can be seen, touched, heard, and smelled" (Furst 1997:2–3). Many studies have characterized these distinct ways of knowing the world as physical aspects of spirituality and ritual practice traditionally associated with animistic and totemic societies (Bird-David 1999; Houston and Taube 2000; Houston et al. 2006; Insoll 2011; López Austin 1988; McNiven 2010; Molesky-Poz 2006; Pauketat 2013; Pedersen 2001; Stross 1998; Tedlock 1982). Rather than a set of religious beliefs, Jean Molesky-Poz (2006:154–68) describes this as a "theology of experience" and as "ways of living [one's] beliefs" (Molesky-Poz 2006:45)—a shared embodied experience that engages both the body and the mind.

Lynn Meskell (2005) notes that the lived experience both shapes the material world and is shaped by materiality (see also Malafouris 2013). Yet she also emphasizes the role of immateriality and its specific relationship with "embodied practices in the spheres of magic and making" (Meskell 2005:3). As an embodied practice, material agency is more than just about enchanting objects and animating the inanimate. Alfred Gell (1999:179) suggests that the enchantment of objects is a technical process whereby "magic" serves as a dialectical method for dealing with uncertainty and is inherently linked to the notion of knowledge and rational technical solutions. Although Gell's approach has been critiqued for offering a "coolly detached formalism [to] enchantment" (Fowles 2013:156), one could argue that this kind of dialectical reasoning is present when groups look to sacred materials, such as bundles, for help in solving a problem. Among the Blackfoot tribes in native North America, Maria Nieves Zedeño (2008:368) notes: "[The most powerful bundles] are generally attributed to actions of the supreme beings who transferred a bundle to a human . . . [and when] called upon by the bundle holder for help on a particular matter, [the object-persons] act in concert to concede what is being asked of them. In this process, object-persons transfer their power to one another and to the bundle holder, who can in turn complete the ritual."

Instructions for how bundles are to be assembled, used, or transferred to other humans often are delivered through visions or dreams. The dialectical methods used to obtain answerability in the world can vary considerably. In some cases, ritual practitioners seek knowledge by "listening to the movements in their bodies," often in the blood and breath, or by casting seeds, by reading fire, or through music and dance (Molesky-Poz 2006:158–59; Tedlock 1982:50). These are not one-way pronouncements of systematized doctrine but two-way meta-sensory communication that is constituted through ongoing movement with mindful and bodily attentiveness. Being a part of this communication signals personhood—a constitution of being in a relational field that fuels movement in a "world of perpetual flux" (Ingold 2006:12).

While the material and cosmic levels may appear as a stark dichotomy, it is precisely between these two planes that relational beings stand (e.g., Molesky-Poz 2006:156). Timothy Pauketat (2013:32–33) describes this liminal space between structure and agency (mind and body) as the "phenomenal relationships between things, substances, and other intangible qualities . . . that engage the senses—sight, sound, smell, taste, and touch—in ways that lend them agentic or transformative power." In many studies of material agency, the sensuous qualities of the fetishized object or substance are highlighted. While these qualities should certainly not be ignored, equally important as the object (or body) itself is its embodied (mind-body) participation in an "unfolding dialogue" with other relational beings (sensu Jordan 2001:101). The intersubjective relationships of this embodied experience impart animacy and are an unfolding dialogue in that they are always in a process of being made, spawning life and energizing potent forces to move about the universe (see Ingold 2007, 2011, 2013). According to Susan Berry Brill de Ramírez (2007:22), "Such intersubjective communications between diverse persons (be they animate or inanimate—human, animal, plant, rock, star, etc.) occurs [sic] in relationally based interactions that are neither discursively nor dialogically oppositional, but conversively co-creative." In other words, the interdependent nature of these "doings" (sensu Fowles 2013) forms ongoing conversive relationships that not only bring one another into existence but then require "a mutual promise to care for one another" throughout life (Molesky-Poz 2006:76, discussing the relationship between Maya Daykeepers and their sacred bundles).

In a system of relational personhood, conversive relationships are a fluid "meshwork" (sensu Ingold 2007). These ever-changing identities are partible, permeable, or both and not necessarily fixed to a particular object- or human-body (Fowler 2004). In this way, there may be many receptacles or thresholds where the numinous comes to reside and interact with other human and nonhuman persons. The spirit *thing* is irreducible to a specific object or particular place but provides them with a special "interior quality" (Pedersen 2001:415). This is not a tangible *thing* but a (sympathetic) feeling or concern that draws a person to a particular thing and marks the beginning of an unfolding conversive relationship between subject and object—perhaps something approximating what "thing theorist" Bill Brown (2001:4) describes as the object/thing dialectic where "the thing really names less an object than a particular subject-object relation." It is this subject-object relationship that distinguishes the special things from the countless other things that go unnoticed.

And what of the things that do not seem to house any animate life or practice any personhood? These are the things that go unnoticed, or what Morten Pedersen (2001:415–16) calls the "asocial entities"—"the small grey stone and a piece of peeled wild onion" that, for some unexplained reason, are devoid of any "mutual animistic relations." These asocial entities might sit right next to the more remarkable things one is drawn to. Clearly, these are no ordinary *things*. Yet like humans, not all things or, rather, relations are created equal. To be sure, some things are more powerful than other things. The notion of hierarchy applies to the chosen things assembled in cache offerings and also in sacred bundles. For instance, among the Blackfoot tribe, Zedeño (2008:368) observes a clear hierarchy in which "a bundle's relative power stems from its specific origin or 'pedigree.'" The same might be said for a valued heirloom piece that is curated and later placed as a central component of a dedicatory cache—a social practice that constitutes a hierarchy of selective memories that bind people and things through time and space (for some examples, see Joyce 2000; Joyce and Gillespie 2015b; Mills and Walker 2008).

CAN NONHUMANS BECKON AN EVENT?

While studies of nonhuman agency have elevated objects to the status of social actors, they are often still treated as "pre-discursive matter dressed over with meaning" (Nanoglou 2009:187; see also Butler 1993). As Bjørnar Olsen (2007:580) observes, "Things may be social, even actors, but [they] are rarely assigned more challenging roles than to provide society with a substantial medium where it can inscribe, embody and mirror itself." For instance, Gell's (1998) semiotic theory of personhood has been criticized for placing objects in a subordinate role to humans. As Holbraad notes, Gell "[treats] objects *as if* they were persons" and masks the "irreducible sense [that] objects just *are* people" (Holbraad 2009:434, emphasis in original; see also Alberti and Marshall 2009). Julia Hendon (2010) has noted that Gell's distinctions represent an unwillingness on his part to take his ideas to their logical conclusion. Similarly, Ingold (2000:97) concludes that the positioning of objects in the relational field is what imbues them with power, but humans are often at the foci of that power.

So, how autonomous are objects? Can they operate as relational beings independent of humans? Or is this simply a human projection of imagination onto "things"? It is difficult for most Western thinkers to accept that consciousness is not universally exclusive to human beings and that the notion of person-hood—the reciprocal qualities of relational beings—can be bestowed on animals, plants, spirits, and objects. Yet as we will see in the chapters presented in this volume, seals *required* that their bodily remains be treated in specific ways by human hunters (Hill, this volume) and objects like jade plaques held the capacity to *speak* and do "lively" things (Looper, this volume), while implements like grinding tools could potentially *cause* sickness to those who mistreated them (Hendon, this volume). It seems clear that agency is not necessarily initiated or directed by humans but that nonhumans can also beckon an event. This invariably leads to an interdependent relationship that requires an appropriate form of reciprocal engagement, which in some cases can leave material traces detectable in the archaeological record.

THE RELATIONAL MATTERS OF BEING AT HAND

The above introduction situates personhood and nonhuman agency in archaeological theory and practice, but we leave it to the contributors of this volume, through their case studies, to more fully cross-examine these ideas regarding agency and materiality in various cultural contexts. Each chapter in this volume examines material culture and particular sets of relationships, practices, actions, materialities, epistemologies, and ontologies of other-than-human agency and personhood that create, embody, and enact complex social worlds. We examine these diverse processes through a series of case studies in different temporal and cultural contexts that cover a wide geographic range, including Australia, Africa, Europe, and the Americas. While the cultures and archaeological contexts presented in this volume vary substantially, these studies all consider other-than-human agency and personhood in the archaeological record and the potential impacts of these social actors.

Erica Hill (chapter 2) examines other-than-human social actors among the proto- and early historic Yup'ik and Inupiaq Eskimo of Alaska and the coastal region of the Bering Sea, where a variety of creatures possessed personhood, lived socially, and acted as agents in these enculturated landscapes. Using zooarchaeological evidence and oral narratives, Hill explores the intersection of agency and personhood in Eskimo relations with animals and some of the other-than-human beings that inhabited this complex social world. Importantly, the Eskimo differentiated between agency and personhood, and those differences had implications for human behavior in the course of hunting, traveling, and foraging. Knowledge and practice of these "ritual" behaviors was part of everyday life, and engagement with other-than-human entities was not limited to shamans—all persons conversively engaged in this unfolding and reciprocal relationship.

Meghan Howey in chapter 3 also focuses on the proto- and early historic Contact period in the Americas, examining European-derived kettles that were interred in the burials of the Mi'kmaq of northeastern North America. This practice emerged in the Maritimes during a liminal stage of social alterity, which occurred in the midst of the early colonial encounters of the sixteenth and early seventeenth centuries. Europeans frowned on the "senseless" burial of copper kettles, but to the Mi'kmaq these materials were more than functional utilitarian objects. Howey concludes that copper kettles had unique sensory qualities and were selectively included as grave goods because they held an animating spirit the Mi'kmaq referred to as *mntu*, which existed throughout the universe. Animated with *mntu*, European-origin kettles were referred to as "relatives" who embodied conditions of personhood. Howey explores the complexities of the colonial encounter in the Maritimes using a combination of ethnohistoric and archaeological data and concludes that this European object was turned into a Mi'kmaq relation as a crucial means for navigating the afterworld during a time of devastatingly high death rates as a result of the introduction of European disease. These powerful other-than-human agents empowered the Mi'kmaq when they returned to a world of their own in the afterlife.

In chapter 4, Timothy Pauketat and Susan Alt examine other-than-human agency in the process of Mississippianization in and around the great American city of Cahokia between ca. AD 900–1100. Their analysis takes a genealogical approach to reconstructing the Cahokian way of life in which maize agriculture, pottery production, and mound building were not merely technological developments or material consequences of Mississippianization but rather entangled "rhizomes"—active and enmeshed agents in the Mississippianization of people. These "agentive" raw materials, through their engagement with other organisms, substances, and phenomena such as water and fire, "territorialized" people (sensu Deleuze and Guattari 1987). Pauketat and Alt conclude that the Mississippianization process and Cahokia's rapid transformation from a large village into a planned city was not the result of a singular development but constituted a "poiesis"—an entanglement of relational nodes that involved "ongoing co-mediation between human and other-than-human organisms, substances, and phenomena."

In chapter 5, Maria Nieves Zedeño, Wendi Field Murray, and Kaitlyn Chandler discuss the agency of birds as other-than-human persons and suggest that the exchange of bird feathers was part of an inalienable-commodity–inalienable continuum among native groups in the North American Plains region. In aboriginal value systems across the Plains, certain feathers from birds such as eagles, woodpeckers, meadowlarks, and waterfowl were highly prized for their magical and cosmological power and were often included as elements in sacred bundles. Likewise, both native and European dyes were prized for their brilliant colors and were considered holy and transformative in their use as paint on feathers and quills, all of which were included in bundles. Similar to the copper kettles discussed by Howey (this volume), European dyes came to be highly valued for their spiritual power and sought after by native groups in trading activities with Europeans at the time of contact. These and other examples presented by Zedeño and colleagues exemplify what they describe as the inalienable-commodity–inalienable continuum, in which certain objects, such as European dyes, could easily transition from one to the other throughout their route of circulation or what some might refer to as the object's biography or "itinerary" (see Joyce and Gillespie 2015b).

Chapters 6 (Looper) and 7 (Hendon) deal specifically with native notions of object-based agency and personhood in ancient Mesoamerica. In chapter 6, Matthew Looper explores the interrelated visual communication systems of Maya hieroglyphic writing and pictorial art as a means of accessing these perspectives. He presents a detailed analysis of the iconography as well as the text/image relationships of an incised shell plaque from the western Maya region to illustrate the very complex manner in which the textual and pictorial record communicates agency. His analysis suggests that for the ancient Maya, the mechanism through which the agency of these objects is activated is intimately connected to the acts of writing and reading as well as to the associations of vital breath with speech. Looper observes that the Maya ascribed agency not only to breath and speech but also to the medium of wind and sound, such as the thunderous roar of a human breath or a gust of wind blown through a conch shell trumpet. A broader implication of Looper's study is the recognition that agency depends upon both discourse and materiality to achieve its social effects and that this can take place independent of the human body (for a related example, see Harrison-Buck 2012:66–67).

Looper's study indicates that, as in many other cultures, a nonhuman appearance did not disqualify an object, organism, or substance from being an agent in ancient Mesoamerica. Hendon (chapter 7) comes to a similar conclusion in her study of tools as other-than-human agents. Implements, such as spindle whorls used for weaving and groundstone used for grinding activities, tend to be understood strictly in terms of their functionality (textile and food production, respectively). Hendon explores a robust ethnographic data set, as well as visual scenes in Postclassic and Contact period codices, to re-conceptualize tools not strictly in terms of functional technology but as sets of relationships between tools and people that embody a relational ontology and fundamental core of Mesoamerican personhood. As extensions of the self, tools embody extra-somatic essences or "soul" parts of those who use them and are persons themselves in that they recursively shape the personhood of those who use them. Hendon concludes, therefore, that tools are both agents and persons because they act back or reciprocate through the kinds of actions they are repeatedly engaged in over time, and those actions contribute to social memory (see also Hendon 2010, 2012).

In chapter 8, Ian McNiven examines the agency and personhood of marine transport canoes among the Torres Strait Islanders. The status of canoes as object-beings began with the felling of the trees that produced these vessels and was elaborated through the use of decorative elements, such as paint, shells, streamers, and feather adornments, and through "magical" acts, such as the beating of a canoe with bunches of grasses. According to McNiven, the material and conceptual elaboration of canoes constituted an animic process of socialization that expresses four interdependent constituents—anthropomorphism, zoomorphism, intentionization, and predatorization. He concludes that by transforming the tree (associated with land, anchoring, and heaviness) into a canoe hull (associated with the sea, mobility, and lightness), the canoe was deemed a domesticated or socialized (versus wild) entity. These acts embody the canoe with elements, namely, lightness and speed, deemed successful among persons (human or otherwise).

Ann Stahl, in chapter 9, explores personhood and the agency of objects in the Banda area of west-central Ghana. She examines African villages that date between the fourteenth and nineteenth centuries, focusing on the remains of bangles, rings, beads, and other objects typically classified as "ornaments." Stahl argues that this label masks the agency of these efficacious objects and interprets design elements not just in terms of their visual or "symbolic" meaning but also as cues that prompted efficacious action. During the course of their circulation or "object itinerary" (sensu Joyce and Gillespie 2015a), such ornaments configured well-being as forms of protection and healing through their actions on bodies and as bundled offerings at shrines. Stahl concludes that ornamenting a human or nonhuman body (such as a shrine context) was not merely a representational act "but an ontologically significant practice" that produced subjects (infants, children, emerging adults, and so on) and formed personhood through techniques of the subject as "marked" and "bundled" assemblages (sensu Keane 2008). Stahl's detailed analysis is couched in the broader changing historical context of West Africa that impacted

African ornamentation as "technologies of personhood" as a result of centuries of Saharan and later Atlantic trade involving intercontinental entanglements with Europeans.

In chapter 10, Joanna Brück and Andrew Jones examine the occurrence of fossils in British Early Bronze Age burials and critique traditional assumptions of personhood that rely on grave goods as status indicators of the interred. As neither prestige goods nor indices of status, fossils prompt a reconsideration of such Western-based models that, as Brück and Jones note, "presuppose that the human self is set apart from (and is superior to) the natural world, including inanimate objects." Instead, they suggest that Bronze Age people may have seen fossils as crafted objects from long ago rather than as simply "natural" specimens. They cite the presence of crafted fossil skeuomorphs (artifacts made to resemble fossils) that lends support to this idea. The material response among Bronze Age inhabitants suggests a shared intersubjectivity whereby fossils and crafted fossil skeuomorphs served as recursive indices of once-living beings, perhaps in reference to cosmogonic origins. As relational and cosmologically charged beings linked to earlier ancestral periods, these "natural" and crafted objects were fitting accompaniments for deceased ancestors. Brück and Jones conclude that the fossils and other various elements of the grave assemblage constitute an expression of relational personhood that conflates the nature-culture divide and "[situates] the person in narratives of belonging and genealogy."

In the final chapter of the volume (chapter 11), Eleanor Harrison-Buck examines contemporary theories of agency and personhood and the use of relational perspectives in archaeology. In recent years, relational personhood has replaced interpretative approaches that are aimed at decoding the "symbolic" meaning of the object-body and their context(s). Grounded in Western epistemology, such representational approaches are heavily focused on context and the interpretative meaning of an object-body, which are problematic because they tend to ignore other perspectives (Alberti et al. 2013; Skousen and Buchanan 2015). Harrison-Buck reviews archaeological and ethnographic case studies, including those presented in this volume, that demonstrate the regional and contextual variability of agency and relational personhood worldwide. One shared theme she explores is agency and personhood as a generative and mutually constituted process, as opposed to fixed or universal categories. She addresses an overarching critique of the so-called new ontological realism (Gabriel 2015; Thomas 2015), which generally rejects the classic "humanist" divides, such as culture-nature, human-animal, and animate-inanimate (Watts 2013b:16). Despite attempts to eradicate Cartesian dualisms, she argues that the wholesale rejection of cognitivism has to some extent perpetuated a mind/body split in current scholarship on relational ontology in archaeology.

CONCLUDING THOUGHTS

Shifting our perspective of the world to a "meshwork" of intricate relational fields (sensu Ingold 2006) provides archaeologists with an epistemic practice that allows alternative ontologies to emerge in our theorizing but is only successful when taken seriously. Elsewhere, Linda Brown and William Walker note, "In using terms such as 'ascribed,' 'beliefs,' or 'symbolic constructs' to describe the agency of nonhuman persons and things, we dismiss [these alternative] ontologies while running the risk of overlooking the 'real' material implications of interactions with these active agents" (Brown and Walker 2008:297–98). Taking nonhuman agency and relational personhood seriously means defining the ontological inconsistencies and variation and how these social (or asocial) beings operationalize in the local landscape. By viewing humans and other-than-humans as co-equal persons in the world, we recognize a greater diversity of conversive participants and are forced to reconsider our interpretive approaches to archaeology that are steeped in colonialist perceptions of discursive forms of hegemonic communication, which have traditionally dominated the field of anthropology (Brill de Ramírez 2007:24–25).

In many of the chapters in this volume, the theoretical framework relies on ethnographic data and addresses the relevance of local knowledge in our archaeological interpretations. In this way, the volume elevates indigenous theory to the level of other theoretical paradigms in the field of anthropology. That said, it remains questionable whether being on par with the scientific community (and writing and publishing about one's culture) is necessarily an emancipatory ideal for the indigenous community (Kumoll 2010:84). As anthropology can never be entirely extricated from its colonial roots and fully escape its Western modes of inquiry, the hypocrisy and paradox of this field remains a problem that may never be resolved, particularly for indigenous scholars (Alberti and Marshall 2009; Hereniko 2000; Nicholas 2010). In truth, it is debatable whether destabilizing Western intellectual traditions in any way directly benefits indigenous communities (but see Lazzari and Korstanje 2013). However, most scholars, including the contributors to this volume, would probably agree that listening to the indigenous communities and considering their ontological and epistemological frameworks has strengthened their interpretations and benefits anthropology. Without critical revision, we risk perpetuating what Bird-David (1999:S68) describes as a "twofold vicious cycle." Anthropologists become guilty of trying to save indigenous peoples from derogatory images of *primitivity* and, in turn, attempt to rehabilitate popular views of these "non-Western" cultures by casting them in a new light of economic and political complexity that is more sophisticated, at least by our own standards. Postmodern epistemology has left us with a harsh dichotomy that in some ways has only furthered the vast ontological divide between the "West and the rest"—the very thing post-colonial scholars have been working so hard to dismantle. Skirting this divide and finding a "way out" is the challenge the contributors of this volume take up in an effort to move the ontological project forward in archaeology.

REFERENCES CITED

Alberti, Benjamin. 2016. "Archaeologies of Ontology." *Annual Review of Anthropology* 45 (1): 163–79. https://doi.org/10.1146/annurev-anthro-102215-095858.

Alberti, Benjamin, and Tamara L. Bray, eds. 2009. "Animating Archaeology: Of Subjects, Objects, and Alternative Ontologies." Special Section. *Cambridge Archaeological Journal* 19 (3): 337–43. https://doi.org/10.1017/S0959774309000523.

Alberti, Benjamin, Andrew M. Jones, and Joshua Pollard, eds. 2013. *Archaeology after Interpretation: Returning Materials to Archaeological Theory.* Walnut Creek, CA: Left Coast.

Alberti, Benjamin, and Yvonne Marshall. 2009. "Animating Archaeology: Local Theories and Conceptually Open-Ended Methodologies." *Cambridge Archaeological Journal* 19 (3): 344–56. https://doi.org/10.1017/S0959774309000535.

Barad, Karen. 2007. *Meeting the Universe Halfway: Quantum Physics and the Entanglement of Matter and Meaning.* Durham, NC: Duke University Press. https://doi.org/10.1215/9780822388128.

Bird-David, Nurit. 1999. "'Animism' Revisited: Personhood, Environment, and Relational Epistemology." *Current Anthropology* 40 (S1): S67–S91. https://doi.org/10.1086/200061.

Brill de Ramírez, Susan Berry. 2007. *Native American Life-History Narratives: Colonial and Postcolonial Navajo Ethnography.* Albuquerque: University of New Mexico Press.

Brown, Bill. 2001. "Thing Theory." *Critical Inquiry* 28 (1): 1–22. https://doi.org/10.1086/449030.

Brown, Linda A., and Kitty F. Emery. 2008. "Negotiations with the Animate Forest: Hunting Shrines in the Guatemalan Highlands." *Journal of Archaeological Method and Theory* 15 (4): 300–337. https://doi.org/10.1007/s10816-008-9055-7.

Brown, Linda A., and William H. Walker. 2008. "Prologue: Archaeology, Animism, and Nonhuman Agents." *Journal of Archaeological Method and Theory* 15 (4): 297–99. https://doi.org/10.1007/s10816-008-9056-6.

Brück, Joanna. 2001. "Monuments, Power, and Personhood in the British Neolithic." *Journal of the Royal Anthropological Institute* 7 (4): 649–67. https://doi.org/10.1111/1467-9655.00082.

Brück, Joanna. 2004. "Material Metaphors: The Relational Construction of Identity in Early Bronze Age Burials in Ireland and Britain." *Journal of Social Archaeology* 4 (3): 307–33. https://doi.org/10.1177/1469605304046417.

Brück, Joanna. 2005. "Homing Instincts: Grounded Identities and Dividual Selves in the British Bronze Age." In *The Archaeology of Plural and Changing Identities*, ed. Eleanor Casella and Chris Fowler, 135–60. London: Kluwer. https://doi.org/10.1007/0-306-48695-4_7.

Buchanan, Meghan E., and B. Jacob Skousen, eds. 2015. *Tracing the Relational: The Archaeology of Worlds, Spirits, and Temporalities: Foundations of Archaeological Inquiry.* Salt Lake City: University of Utah Press.

Budden, Sandy, and Joanna Sofaer. 2009. "Non-discursive Knowledge and the Construction of Identity: Potters, Potting, and Performance at the Bronze Age Tell of Sz'azhalombatta, Hungary." *Cambridge Archaeological Journal* 19 (2): 203–20. https://doi.org/10.1017/S0959774309000274.

Butler, Judith. 1993. *Bodies That Matter: On the Discursive Limits of "Sex."* New York: Routledge.

Deleuze, Gilles, and Felix Guattari. 1987. *A Thousand Plateaus: Capitalism and Schizophrenia.* Trans. B. Massumi. Minneapolis: University of Minnesota Press.

Descola, Philippe. 1996. "Constructing Natures: Symbolic Ecology and Social Practice." In *Nature and Society: Anthropological Perspectives*, ed. Philippe Descola and Gísli Pálsson, 82–102. New York: Routledge. https://doi.org/10.4324/9780203451069_chapter_5.

Descola, Philippe, and Gísli Pálsson, eds. 1996. *Nature and Society: Anthropological Perspectives.* New York: Routledge. https://doi.org/10.4324/9780203451069.

Dobres, Marcia-Anne, and John E. Robb, eds. 2000. *Agency in Archaeology.* London: Routledge.

Fausto, Carlos. 2007. "Feasting on People: Eating Animals and Humans in Amazonia." *Current Anthropology* 48 (4): 497–530. https://doi.org/10.1086/518298.

Fowler, Chris. 2002. "Body Parts: Personhood and Materiality in the Manx Neolithic." In *Thinking through the Body: Archaeologies of Corporeality*, ed. Yannis Hamalakis, Mark Pluciennik and Sarah Tarlow, 47–69. London: Kluwer/Academic. https://doi.org/10.1007/978-1-4615-0693-5_3.

Fowler, Chris. 2004. *The Archaeology of Personhood: An Anthropological Approach.* London: Routledge.

Fowler, Chris. 2008. "Fractal Bodies in the Past and Present." In *Past Bodies: Body-Centered Research in Archaeology*, ed. Dusan Borić and John Robb, 47–57. Oxford: Oxbow Books.

Fowler, Chris. 2010. "Relational Personhood as a Subject of Anthropology and Archaeology: Comparative and Complementary Analyses." In *Archaeology and Anthropology: Understanding Similarities, Exploring Differences*, ed. Duncan Garrow and Thomas Yarrow, 137–59. Oxford: Oxbow Books.

Fowler, Chris. 2016. "Relational Personhood Revisited." *Cambridge Archaeological Journal* 26 (3): 397–412. https://doi.org/10.1017/S0959774316000172.

Fowles, Severin M. 2010. "People without Things." In *An Anthropology of Absence: Materializations of Transcendence and Loss*, ed. Mikkel Bille, Frida Hastrup, and Tim Flohr Soerensen, 23–41. New York: Springer Science + Business Media. https://doi.org/10.1007/978-1-4419-5529-6_2.

Fowles, Severin M. 2013. *An Archaeology of Doings: Secularism and the Study of Pueblo Religion.* Santa Fe, NM: School for Advanced Research Press.

Furst, Jill Leslie. 1997. *The Natural History of the Soul in Ancient Mexico.* New Haven, CT: Yale University Press.

Gabriel, Markus. 2015. *Fields of Sense: A New Realist Ontology.* Edinburgh: Edinburgh University Press.

Gell, Alfred. 1998. *Art and Agency: An Anthropological Theory.* Oxford: Oxford University Press.

Gell, Alfred. 1999. *The Art of Anthropology: Essays and Diagrams.* London: Berg.

Gillespie, Alex, and Flora Cornish. 2010. "Intersubjectivity: Toward a Dialogical Analysis." *Journal for the Theory of Social Behaviour* 40 (1): 19–46. https://doi.org/10.1111/j.1468-5914.2009.00419.x.

Gillespie, Susan D. 2001. "Personhood, Agency, and Mortuary Ritual: A Case Study from the Ancient Maya." *Journal of Anthropological Archaeology* 20 (1): 73–112. https://doi.org/10.1006/jaar.2000.0369.

Gosden, Chris, and Yvonne Marshall. 1999. "The Cultural Biography of Objects." *World Archaeology* 31 (2): 169–78.

Hallowell, A. Irving. 1960. *Ojibwa Ontology, Behavior, and World View.* New York: Columbia University Press.

Harris, Oliver J.T. 2013. "Relational Communities in Prehistoric Britain." In *Relational Archaeologies: Humans, Animals, Things*, ed. Christopher Watts, 173–89. London: Routledge.

Harris, Oliver J.T., and John Robb. 2012. "Multiple Ontologies and the Problem of the Body in History." *American Anthropologist* 114 (4): 668–79. https://doi.org/10.1111/j.1548-1433.2012.01513.x.

Harrison-Buck, Eleanor. 2012. "Architecture as Animate Landscape: Circular Shrines in the Ancient Maya Lowlands." *American Anthropologist* 114 (1): 64–80. https://doi.org/10.1111/j.1548-1433.2011.01397.x.

Harrison-Buck, Eleanor. 2015. "Maya Religion and Gods: Relevance and Relatedness in the Animic Cosmos." In *Tracing the Relational: The Archaeology of Worlds, Spirits, and Temporalities*, ed. Meghan E. Buchanan and B. Jacob Skousen, 115–29. Foundations of Archaeological Inquiry. Salt Lake City: University of Utah Press.

Harvey, Graham. 2006. "Animals, Animists, and Academics." *Zygon* 41 (1): 9–20. https://doi.org/10.1111/j.1467-9744.2006.00723.x.

Hendon, Julia A. 2010. *Houses in a Landscape: Memory and Everyday Life in Mesoamerica*. Durham, NC: Duke University Press.

Hendon, Julia A. 2012. "Objects as Persons: Integrating Maya Beliefs and Anthropological Theory." In *Power and Identity in Archaeological Theory and Practice: Case Studies from Ancient Mesoamerica*, ed. Eleanor Harrison-Buck, 82–89. Foundations of Archaeological Inquiry. Salt Lake City: University of Utah Press.

Hereniko, Vilsoni. 2000. "Indigenous Knowledge and Academic Imperialism." In *Remembrance of Pacific Pasts: An Invitation to Remake History*, ed. Robert Borofsky, 78–91. Honolulu: University of Hawaii Press.

Hill, Erica. 2011. "Animals as Agents: Hunting Ritual and Relational Ontologies in Prehistoric Alaska and Chukotka." *Cambridge Archaeological Journal* 21 (3): 407–26. https://doi.org/10.1017/S0959774311000448.

Hodder, Ian. 2012. *Entangled: An Archaeology of the Relationships between Humans and Things*. Malden, MA: Wiley-Blackwell. https://doi.org/10.1002/9781118241912.

Holbraad, Martin. 2009. "Ontology, Ethnography, Archaeology: An Afterword on the Ontography of Things." *Cambridge Archaeological Journal* 19 (3): 431–41. https://doi.org/10.1017/S0959774309000614.

Houston, Stephen D., David Stuart, and Karl A. Taube. 2006. *The Memory of Bones: Body, Being, and Experience among the Classic Maya*. Austin: University of Texas Press.

Houston, Stephen D., and Karl A. Taube. 2000. "An Archaeology of the Senses: Perception and Cultural Expression in Ancient Mesoamerica." *Cambridge Archaeological Journal* 10 (2): 261–94. https://doi.org/10.1017/S095977430000010X.

Hutson, Scott R. 2010. *Dwelling, Identity, and the Maya: Relational Archaeology at Chunchucmil*. Lanham, MD: Altamira.

Hviding, Edvard. 1996. "Nature, Culture, Magic, Science: On Meta-Languages for Comparison in Cultural Ecology." In *Nature and Society: Anthropological Perspectives*, ed. Philippe Descola and Gísli Pálsson, 165–84. New York: Routledge.

Ingold, Tim. 1986. *The Appropriation of Nature: Essays in Human Ecology and Social Relations*. Manchester: Manchester University Press.

Ingold, Tim. 1996. "The Optimal Forager and Economic Man." In *Nature and Society: Anthropological Perspectives*, ed. Phillipe Descola and Gisli Palsson, 25–44. New York: Routledge.

Ingold, Tim. 1998. "Totemism, Animism, and the Depiction of Animals." In *Animals, Anima, Animus*, ed. Marketta Seppälä, Jari-Pekka Vanhala, and Linda Weintraub, 181–207. Pori, Finland: Pori Art Museum.

Ingold, Tim. 2000. *The Perception of the Environment: Essays on Livelihood, Dwelling, and Skill*. London: Routledge. https://doi.org/10.4324/9780203466025.

Ingold, Tim. 2006. "Rethinking the Animate, Re-Animating Thought." *Ethnos* 71 (1): 9–20. https://doi.org/10.1080/00141840600603111.

Ingold, Tim. 2007. *Lines: A Brief History*. London: Routledge.

Ingold, Tim. 2010. "Footprints through the Weather-World: Walking, Breathing, Knowing." *Journal of the Royal Anthropological Institute* 16: S121–S139. https://doi.org/10.1111/j.1467-9655.2010.01613.x.

Ingold, Tim. 2011. *Being Alive: Essays on Movement, Knowledge, and Description*. London: Routledge.

Ingold, Tim. 2013. "The Maze and the Labyrinth: Reflections of a Fellow-Traveler." In *Relational Archaeologies: Humans, Animals, Things*, ed. Christopher Watts, 245–49. London: Routledge.

Insoll, Timothy. 2011. "Animism and Totemism." In *The Oxford Handbook of the Archaeology of Ritual and Religion*, ed. Timothy Insoll, 1004–16. New York: Oxford University Press. https://doi.org/10.1093/oxfordhb/9780199232444.001.0001.

Jackson, Michael. 1998. *Minima Ethnographica: Intersubjectivity and the Anthropological Project*. Chicago: University of Chicago Press.

Jones, Andrew M. 2011. *Prehistoric Materialities: Becoming Material in Prehistoric Britain and Ireland*. Oxford: Oxford University Press.

Jones, Andrew M., and Benjamin Alberti. 2013. "Introduction: Archaeology after Interpretation." In *Archaeology after Interpretation: Returning Materials to Archaeological Theory*, ed. Benjamin Alberti, Andrew M. Jones, and Joshua Pollard, 15–42. Walnut Creek, CA: Left Coast.

Jordan, Peter. 2001. "The Materiality of Shamanism as a 'World View': Praxis, Artefacts, and Landscape." In *The Archaeology of Shamanism*, ed. Neil S. Price, 87–104. London: Routledge.

Joyce, Rosemary A. 2000. "Heirlooms and Houses: Materiality and Social Memory." In *Beyond Kinship: Social and Material Reproduction in House Societies*, ed. Rosemary A. Joyce and Susan D. Gillespie, 189–212. Philadelphia: University of Pennsylvania Press.

Joyce, Rosemary A., and Susan D. Gillespie. 2015a. "Making Things out of Objects That Move." In *Things in Motion: Object Itineraries in Anthropological Practice*, ed. Rosemary A. Joyce and Susan D. Gillespie, 3–19. Santa Fe, NM: School for Advanced Research Press.

Joyce, Rosemary A., and Susan D. Gillespie, eds. 2015b. *Things in Motion: Object Itineraries in Anthropological Practice*. Santa Fe, NM: School for Advanced Research Press.

Keane, Webb. 2008. "The Evidence of the Senses and the Materiality of Religion." *Journal of the Royal Anthropological Institute* 14 (Supplement s1): S110–S127. https://doi.org/10.1111/j.1467-9655.2008.00496.x.

Knappett, Carl, and Lambros Malafouris, eds. 2008. *Material Agency: Toward a Non-Anthropocentric Approach*. New York: Springer Science + Business Media. https://doi.org/10.1007/978-0-387-74711-8.

Kumoll, Karsten. 2010. "Indigenous Research and the Politics of Representation: Notes on the Cultural Theory of Marshall Sahlins." In *Beyond Writing Culture: Current Intersections of Epistemologies and Representational Practices*, ed. Olaf Zenker and Karsten Kumoll, 69–88. Oxford: Berghahn Books.

Latour, Bruno. 1993. *We Have Never Been Modern*. Cambridge, MA: Harvard University Press.

Latour, Bruno. 2013. *An Inquiry into Modes of Existence: An Anthropology of the Moderns*. Trans. Catherine Porter. Paris: Editions La Decouverte.

Lazzari, Marisa. 2003. "Archaeological Visions: Gender, Landscape, and Optic Knowledge." *Journal of Social Archaeology* 3 (2): 194–222. https://doi.org/10.1177/1465303003002004.

Lazzari, Marisa. 2005. "The Texture of Things: Object, People, and Landscape in Northwest Argentina (First Millennium AD)." In *Archaeologies of Materiality*, ed. Lynn Meskell, 126–61. Malden, MA: Blackwell. https://doi.org/10.1002/9780470774052.ch6.

Lazzari, Marisa, and Alejandra Korstanje. 2013. "The Past as a Lived Space: Heritage Places, Re-emergent Aesthetics, and Hopeful Practices in NW Argentina." *Journal of Social Archaeology* 13 (3): 394–419. https://doi.org/10.1177/1469605313487616.

López Austin, Alfredo. 1988. *The Human Body and Ideology: Concepts of the Ancient Nahuas*. Trans. Thelma Ortiz de Montellano and Bernard Ortiz de Montellano. Salt Lake City: University of Utah Press.

Malafouris, Lambros. 2013. *How Things Shape the Mind: A Theory of Material Engagement*. Cambridge, MA: MIT Press.

Martin, Andrew M. 2013. *Archaeology beyond Postmodernity: A Science of the Social*. Lanham, MD: Altamira.

McNiven, Ian. 2010. "Navigating the Human-Animal Divide: Marine Mammal Hunters and Rituals of Sensory Allurement." *World Archaeology* 42 (2): 215–30. https://doi.org/10.1080/00438241003672849.

McNiven, Ian. 2013. "Between the Living and the Dead: Relational Ontologies and the Ritual Dimensions of Dugon Hunting across Torres Strait." In *Relational Archeologies: Humans, Animals, Things*, ed. Christopher Watts, 97–116. New York: Routledge.

Meskell, Lynn, ed. 2005. *Archaeologies of Materiality*. Malden, MA: Blackwell. https://doi.org/10.1002/9780470774052.

Miller, Daniel. 1987. *Material Culture and Mass Consumption*. Oxford: Basil Blackwell.

Miller, Daniel. 2005. "Materiality: An Introduction." In *Materiality*, ed. Daniel Miller, 1–50. Durham, NC: Duke University Press. https://doi.org/10.1215/9780822386711-001.

Mills, Barbara J., and William H. Walker, eds. 2008. *Memory Work: Archaeologies of Material Practices*. Santa Fe, NM: School for Advanced Research Press.

Molesky-Poz, Jean. 2006. *Contemporary Maya Spirituality: The Ancient Ways Are Not Lost*. Austin: University of Texas Press.

Nanoglou, Stratos. 2009. "Animal Bodies and Ontological Discourse in the Greek Neolithic." *Journal of Archaeological Method and Theory* 16 (3): 184–204. https://doi.org/10.1007/s10816-009-9069-9.

Nicholas, George, ed. 2010. *Being and Becoming Indigenous Archaeologists*. Walnut Creek, CA: Left Coast.

Olsen, Bjørnar. 2003. "Material Culture after Text: Remembering Things." *Norwegian Archaeological Review* 36 (2): 87–104. https://doi.org/10.1080/0029365031000650.

Olsen, Bjørnar. 2007. "Keeping Things at Arm's Length: A Genealogy of Asymmetry." *World Archaeology* 39 (4): 579–88. https://doi.org/10.1080/00438240701679643.

Olsen, Bjørnar. 2010. *In Defense of Things: Archaeology and Ontology of Objects*. Lanham, MD: Altamira.

Pauketat, Timothy R. 2013. *An Archaeology of the Cosmos: Rethinking Agency and Religion in Ancient America*. New York: Routledge.

Pedersen, Morten A. 2001. "Totemism, Animism, and North Asian Indigenous Ontologies." *Journal of the Royal Anthropological Institute* 7 (3): 411–27. https://doi.org/10.1111/1467-9655.00070.

Pina-Cabral, João. 2016. "Brazilian Serialities: Personhood and Radical Embodied Cognition." *Current Anthropology* 57 (3): 247–60. https://doi.org/10.1086/686300.

Robb, John. 2010. "Beyond Agency." *World Archaeology* 42 (4): 493–520. https://doi.org/10.1080/00438243.2010.520856.

Sahlins, Marshall. 2011. "What Kinship Is (Part One)." *Journal of the Royal Anthropological Institute* 17 (1): 2–19. https://doi.org/10.1111/j.1467-9655.2010.01666.x.

Skousen, B. Jacob, and Meghan E. Buchanan. 2015. "Introduction: Advancing an Archaeology of Movements and Relationships." In *Tracing the Relational: The Archaeology of Worlds, Spirits, and Temporalities*, ed. Meghan E. Buchanan and B. Jacob Skousen, 1–17. Salt Lake City: University of Utah Press.

Strathern, Marilyn. 1988. *The Gender of the Gift: Problems with Women and Problems with Society in Melanesia*. Berkeley: University of California Press. https://doi.org/10.1525/california/9780520064232.001.0001.

Stross, Brian. 1998. "Seven Ingredients in Mesoamerican Ensoulment: Dedication and Termination in Tenejapa." In *The Sowing and the Dawning: Termination, Dedication, and Transformation in the Archaeological Record of Mesoamerica*, ed. Shirley B. Mock, 31–39. Albuquerque: University of New Mexico Press.

Swenson, Edward. 2015. "The Materialities of Place Making in the Ancient Andes: A Critical Appraisal of the Ontological Turn in Archaeological Interpretation." *Journal of Archaeological Method and Theory* 22 (3): 677–712. https://doi.org/10.1007/s10816-014-9202-2.

Tedlock, Barbara. 1982. *Time and the Highland Maya*. Albuquerque: University of New Mexico Press.

Thomas, Julian. 2002. "Archaeology's Humanism and the Materiality of the Body." In *Thinking through the Body: Archaeologies of Corporeality*, ed. Yannis Hamilakis, Mark Pluciennik, and Sarah Tarlow, 29–45. London: Kluwer/Academic. https://doi.org/10.1007/978-1-4615-0693-5_2.

Thomas, Julian. 2015. "The Future of Archaeological Theory." *Antiquity* 89 (348): 1287–96. https://doi.org/10.15184/aqy.2015.183.

Viveiros de Castro, Eduardo. 1998. "Cosmological Deixis and Amerindian Perspectivism." *Journal of the Royal Anthropological Institute* 4 (3): 469–88. https://doi.org/10.2307/3034157.

Viveiros de Castro, Eduardo. 2002. "O nativo relativo." *Mana* 8 (1): 113–48. https://doi.org/10.1590/S0104-93132002000100005.

Viveiros de Castro, Eduardo. 2004. "Exchanging Perspectives: The Transformation of Objects into Subjects in Amerindian Ontologies." *Common Knowledge* 10 (3): 463–84. https://doi.org/10.1215/0961754X-10-3-463.

Watts, Christopher, ed. 2013a. *Relational Archaeologies: Humans, Animals, Things*. New York: Routledge.

Watts, Christopher. 2013b. "Relational Archaeologies: Roots and Routes." In *Relational Archaeologies: Humans, Animals, Things*, ed. Christopher Watts, 1–20. New York: Routledge.

Webmoor, Timothy, and Christopher L. Witmore. 2008. "Things Are Us! A Commentary on Human/Things Relations under the Banner of a 'Social' Archaeology." *Norwegian Archaeological Review* 41 (1): 53–70. https://doi.org /10.1080/00293650701698423.

Wilkinson, Darryl. 2013. "The Emperor's New Body: Personhood, Ontology, and the Inka Sovereign." *Cambridge Archaeological Journal* 23 (3): 417–32. https://doi.org/10 .1017/S0959774313000541.

Wilkinson, Darryl. 2017. "Is There Such a Thing as Animism?" *Journal of the American Academy of Religion* 85 (2): 289–311.

Witmore, Christopher L. 2007. "Symmetrical Archaeology: Excerpts of a Manifesto." *World Archaeology* 39 (4): 546–62. https://doi.org/10.1080/00438240701679411.

Zedeño, Maria Nieves. 2008. "Bundled Worlds: The Roles and Interactions of Complex Objects from the North American Plains." *Journal of Archaeological Method and Theory* 15 (4): 362–78. https://doi.org/10.1007/s10816-008-9058-4.

Zedeño, Maria Nieves. 2013. "Methodological and Analytical Challenges in Relational Archaeologies: A View from the Hunting Ground." In *Relational Archaeologies: Humans, Animals, Things*, ed. Christopher Watts, 117–34. New York: Routledge.

2

Following the lead of ethnographers working in the Arctic, Subarctic, and Amazonia, archaeologists have recently directed their attention to identifying and describing relational ontologies in the past. These ontologies are generally animist in orientation, assigning agency—and sometimes personhood—to a host of other-than-human actors, including animals, ostensibly "inanimate" objects, spirits, ancestors, and the dead (Betts et al. 2015; Watts 2013). Agency has been defined broadly as the "causal consequences" objects have on human activity, including the performance characteristics of material things (Brown and Walker 2008:298). Dobres and Robb (2000) argued that agency is critical to the understanding of material culture, social reproduction, and the construction of both group and individual selves. They identified variables relevant to the study of agency in the past, such as intentionality, operative scale, and role in social change. Their work addressed personhood tangentially, suggesting that the social constitution of the subject in terms of gender, age, race, and class was relevant to the exercise of agency (Dobres and Robb 2000:8–9, 11). More recently, Robb (2010:494) has revisited agency, defining it as "the socially reproductive quality of action within social relationships" mediated and contextualized by material things.

Robb (2010) focused on agency as a social phenomenon enacted through intersubjective practice. This perspective is linked to recent archaeological approaches that privilege personhood. Robb's "agents" overlap with

Personhood and Agency in Eskimo Interactions with the Other-than-Human

Erica Hill

DOI: 10.5876/9781607327479.c002

how "persons" are generally defined in relational ontologies; that is, persons are agential beings constituted through socially (i.e., relationally) situated actions. Personhood is conditioned by corporeal experience and by variables such as age, sex, gender, and social status. Social interactions and processes contribute, in tandem with embodiment, to the construction of the person. Temporal and spatial factors—history and geography—frame experience and structure engagements with the world, including social relations with other persons and encounters with agents. Persons share common experiences of space, things, and actions (Bird-David 1999:S72) within the social realm. As a relational process, therefore, personhood is "culturally contingent, historically specific, and internally unstable" (Finlay 2014:1192).

Agency, in the sense I employ it here, is a necessary but insufficient capacity that defines persons. In the simplest terms, all persons are agents, but not all agents are persons. Relational ontologies may attribute agency to, for example, figurines (Hendon et al. 2014), Native American bundles (Zedeño 2008), architecture and landscape features (Brown and Emery 2008; Harrison-Buck 2012; Herva 2009; Sillar 2009), and animals such as fish (Losey 2010), dogs (Laugrand and Oosten 2007; Losey et al. 2011), bears (Betts et al. 2015; Losey et al. 2013), and sea mammals (Hill 2011, 2013; McNiven 2010, 2013). All of these agents are animate and capable of action, but not all of them are persons.

The person may be constituted and dissolved in multiple forms throughout the life course as identity markers develop, shift, recede, or disappear. Human burial practices and cemetery organization have been especially productive avenues of research (e.g., Janik 2011). Cemeteries provide multiple, often contemporaneous examples of how personhood was—or was not—materialized. Categories of person may be inferred though body placement, quantity and quality of offerings and grave goods, evidence of grave reopening, and proximity to others. When and to what extent infants and children possess agency and become persons, for example, varies, indicating that personhood is a process (Finlay 2014:1196–98; Janik 2000) rather than a prediscursive phenomenon, as I discuss below in reference to Inupiaq Eskimo "wild babies."

Paying close attention to the specifics of bodily experience, skeletal features, grave goods, and interment—whether human or nonhuman—can inform us about how persons were categorized and personhood was constructed in the past. Such an approach can be employed at multiple scales—that of the community, for example, in the study of cemeteries (e.g., Janik 2000), and at the level of the individual. An osteobiographical approach (Boutin 2012) has been employed effectively in archaeological studies of personhood and may be useful in the interpretation of both humans and animals (e.g., Losey et al. 2011).

Evidence of care for humans or nonhumans with injuries or disabilities, for example, may inform us about the experience of such conditions, as well as about the ontological status of the deceased (Rivollat et al. 2014; Tilley 2015; Tilley and Oxenham 2011). Two recent studies of physically compromised individuals—a probable male suffering from chondrodystrophic dwarfism (Tilley 2015) and a child with Down syndrome (Rivollat et al. 2014)—found that the deceased were given normative funerary treatment, with no apparent evidence of stigmatization or spatial isolation from others. Such treatment contrasts with burial evidence for the segregation or differential treatment of children, possibly as incomplete or non-persons, in many cemeteries (Finlay 2000; Scott 2001).

Losey and colleagues (2011) have argued for the status of dogs and wolves as persons based on their burial treatment by hunter-gatherers in the Lake Baikal region. Not all wolves were buried in cemeteries, indicating that a specific wolf was somehow significant, perhaps identified as a particularly capable protector based on its position encircling a human head. In a similar vein, Argent (2010) has interpreted the Pazyryk horse burials as evidence that some—but not all—horses were recognized and honored for who they were or what they had done.

Bendrey (2014) has recently reported on the remains of a goat with evidence of a healed fracture. The severity of the injury would have prevented the animal from grazing and foraging with herd members, indicating that humans chose to care for the animal rather than cull it. While Bendrey does not argue that the goat was considered a person, this case study demonstrates the potential of approaches that combine fine-grained osteological analysis with an appreciation for how cultural and archaeological contexts can inform us about relations among humans and nonhumans.

In this chapter I explore the linked concepts of personhood and agency in the North American Arctic. I suggest that Eskimo of Alaska and Chukotka (figure 2.1) recognized a number of beings and "objects" as agential—capable of action and generating causal consequences. In addition, *some* of those agents were capable of interacting with each other and with humans as persons. Distinguishing between the two was a skill essential to daily life, whether the activity was risky, such as hunting or traveling, or relatively safe, such as dancing or scraping seal skins. Through analysis of oral narratives, imagery, and archaeological deposits, I describe how proto- and early historic Eskimo living along the Bering Sea coast differentiated between persons and agential non-persons. This exploration contributes to broader discussions of hunter-gatherer ontologies and, more specifically, to what Jordan (2008) has advocated as the study of "northern mind."

FIGURE 2.1. *Map of the Bering Sea region.*

RELATIONAL ONTOLOGIES AND THE HUNTER-GATHERER PAST

Influenced by Ingold (e.g., 2000a) and by broader academic trends in anthrozoology, or human-animal studies, researchers have recently drawn attention to differences between hunter-gatherer and agro-pastoralist modes of human-animal interaction (Oma 2010; Orton 2010; Russell 2002). Ingold (1987, 2000b, 2002, 2006) has persuasively argued that cosmology or worldview, human-animal interactions, and subsistence mode are entangled phenomena—that humans, animals, and the landscape itself are dynamic "constituents of the dwelt-in world" (Ingold 2000c:42). Ingold explicitly refutes the idea that "some distinctive hunter-gatherer world-view" exists (Ingold 2000b:42) while recognizing significant differences in the ways members of hunter-gatherer, pastoralist, agrarian, and industrial societies perceived the environment and engaged the world (Ingold 2000a, 2006:13).

Certainly, the acts of hunting and gathering present humans—and other animals—with very different challenges and opportunities than domestication and pastoralism. But hunter-gatherer and pastoralist ontologies are also variable, reflecting the particulars of history and geography and producing culturally distinct "meshworks" of social phenomena (Ingold 2006:13). Fijn (2011:45; see also Oma 2007, 2010) explicitly rejects Ingold's broad characterization of pastoralism as a productive mode in which humans dominate their subjugated flocks. She has suggested that Mongolian herders take an animist perspective of the world, considering their horses, sheep, and goats to be persons and subjects with whom herders engage in relations of mutual respect. While acknowledging that such subject-object relations obtain in some herding societies, Fijn (2011:45–47) sees animist hunters and gatherers of the Arctic as better analogs to the Mongolian herders she studies than many other pastoralist peoples.

While animism appears to be a perspective that many hunter-gatherer and some herding societies share, the relational particulars differ. The remainder of this chapter explores those particulars—specifically, distinctions between agents and persons—among proto- and early historic Eskimo of the Bering Sea coast. Such distinctions were critical in animist societies populated by multiple types of persons and non-persons. Personhood, in contrast to agency, is an embodied social phenomenon enacted and reproduced through praxis and engagement in intersubjective relations. For a person, whether human or other-than-human, social relations with other persons are rule governed and dependent upon a shared understanding of interpersonal etiquette.

The proto- and early historic Eskimo landscape was a crowded one, inhabited not just by human and other-than-human persons but also by *non-persons*—agents whose actions had real, often serious consequences for others. Since these agential non-persons obeyed no rules and belonged to no society, they were unpredictable and therefore potentially dangerous. The successful navigation of daily life amid such a multitude of beings required the differentiation of agents from persons and of one type of person from another. Accurate identification of an agent or person was a prerequisite for appropriate action. In the case of agential non-persons, action could involve avoidance or violence; engagement with other persons could also involve avoidance or violence, but, in addition, it could involve communication, negotiation, and reciprocal action.

ESKIMO PERSONS

For historic period Eskimo, as for many other small-scale societies, negotiation and reciprocity were behaviors essential to the constitution of the social person, the *personne morale* of Mauss (1985), who existed within a network of roles and obligations. Such persons were linked by kinship and marriage to both the living and the dead (Praet 2013). Among nineteenth-century Eskimo, most humans, many animals, and some things were persons. They all possessed agency, a necessary but insufficient condition of personhood. Some agential beings were not persons. Wild babies, for example, were known for horrific acts of cannibalism, but their behavior—uncontrolled, insatiable consumption—identified them as lacking personhood. Such agential non-persons violated taboos, acted in unpredictable ways, and were incapable of respect for others. In contrast, persons possessed awareness (Fienup-Riordan 2009) and behaved according to the strictures of their species.

Relations between "real" Eskimo persons and other-than-human persons such as prey animals were built upon the shared values of reciprocity, respect, empathy, and restraint (Fienup-Riordan 2007). These values were enacted and experienced intersubjectively, in social arenas governed by rules and involving pre- and proscribed behaviors (i.e., "taboos"). The Eskimo experience of the personhood and agency of themselves and others proceeded from specific social personae as constituted by the intersections of sex/gender, age, kin group, disability, capacity, skill, and status as a spouse or parent. The nature of personhood shifted throughout the life course (Finlay 2014; Fowler 2004) and was conditioned by activity, location, and the presence or absence of other persons. Embodied experience of personhood was therefore highly contextualized both spatially and temporally.

Adult Inupiaq and Yup'ik men and women, specifically husbands and wives engaged in hunting and sewing, related to prey animal persons in distinct, though complementary ways. While men generally hunted seals, walrus, and whales, women's behavior determined whether they were successful. Women's thoughts and actions during the hunt, their treatment of animal bodies, and the skill and attention they devoted to sewing garments made from animal skins and hides directly influenced an animal's willingness to "give itself" to a hunter. Whales came to women who shared with others, refrained from quarreling and troublesome thoughts (Bodenhorn 1990), and constructed beautifully sewn clothing (Chaussonnet 1988). Shamans, whaling captains (*umialiit*), and their wives carried additional burdens of leadership, taking roles as community representatives to members of animal societies. Relations among men, women, and prey animals therefore differed depending upon the specific intersections of the gendered body with age and skill set, as well as upon season, activity, and status in the community.

Physical form—the bodies of human, seal, walrus, and whale persons—structured experience. Nineteenth-century Eskimo analogized an animal's skin to a coat and a beak or muzzle to a mask (Fienup-Riordan 1994:59), which could be taken on and off to facilitate transformation. The outer form determined the perspective of the person, similar to the "mimetic empathy" of the Yukaghir described by Willerslev (2007). Animal persons, like human persons, had preferences, tendencies, and capacities that humans might learn to know and recognize. In contrast to humans, however, an individual animal usually represented a type of person rather than a unique combination of attributes like a human person (Ingold 1987:247; see also Willerslev 2007:2074). Yup'ik Eskimo considered beluga whales to be peaceful and hard-working. Spotted seals were ill-tempered, while ringed seals were gentle and sensitive (Fienup-Riordan 1994:60–61). Knowing the preferences and personalities of prey animals—and the rules of etiquette their hunting required—was critical to the survival of all persons, whether human or animal.

In a Siberian Yupik story (Dolitsky 2000:21–22), a hunter who could not take any animals is given advice by a polar bear in exchange for assistance. The polar bear was naked and freezing, having lost a fight with another bear. The hunter covers him with clothing made of bear skin and helps him by killing the quarrelsome bear. In gratitude, the bear explains why the hunter is unsuccessful: his dirty clothes are driving away prey animals, plus his wife is combing her hair at the same time she sews clothing, thus violating a hunting taboo. According to the bear, "It's because of that grime that you can't hunt well. The animals are afraid of the stench of your clothing." This reference to scent likely concerns seals, who had a particular dislike of filth and slovenliness (Søby 1969–70).

While prey animals were generally known for their preferences and behaviors as a species rather than as individuals, a hunter might encounter an animal one-on-one. Under such circumstances, he might deal with the animal as an individual, just as the hunter dealt with the polar bear. In oral narratives recounting this sort of interaction, an element of reciprocity or exchange is usually present, as when an old man protects a reindeer from a wolf in exchange for a back scratcher (Dolitsky 2000:48). Negotiation and exchange are also central to encounters with orcas (i.e., killer whales) on both sides of Bering Strait. Orcas near the village of Naukan, Chukotka, encountered a party of hunters with a whale and began dragging them into a cave, despite attempts by the hunters to negotiate with them "in their own language." The hunters escaped only after one of them tossed his earrings into the sea as a gift (Dolitsky 2000:136). This way of dealing with orcas is also known in Southwest Alaska, where orcas will share blubber and meat with humans in exchange for beads (Fienup-Riordan 2011:73–79).

These examples illustrate how human and animal persons interact and negotiate to survive. While the rules of animal persons may not be the same as those of human persons, they are nevertheless internally consistent and predictable. They can be learned by humans, as recounted in the story of a boy who lives with seals (or salmon) for a year. The story is known in multiple versions in the North Pacific and describes how a boy learns to see the world from a seal perspective. What the boy sees as a skylight is, from a human perspective on the other side of the ice, a seal breathing hole. When the boy encounters human hunters, he sees them as a seal does, wearing the evidence of their disrespectful behavior—a man who drinks too much water wears a bucket on his head (Fienup-Riordan 1990, 2007).

This exchange of perspectives, termed Amerindian perspectivism (Viveiros de Castro 1992, 1998; see also Willerslev 2004, 2007), is associated with human-animal transformation, a phenomenon still observed in Alaska villages (Cassady 2008). Such an exchange is made possible by the persistence of personhood—known as *inua* among Inupiat or *yua* among Central Yupiit (Fitzhugh and Kaplan 1982; Hill 2011, 2012)—despite physical form. The shared "soul substance" facilitates communication between types of persons and enables them to coexist. The human person must know the pre- and proscriptions for engaging with other-than-human persons—know what to do and how to do it, as when the hunter threw earrings to the orca. Such actions—on both sides of the interpersonal equation—materialized social rules founded on reciprocity.

Gift exchange and reciprocity are only possible among persons because only persons have the capacity to engage in social behaviors and observe rules. In other words, only those agents who are also persons are part of the Eskimo social world. In Eskimo ontologies, the largest category of person is composed of humans and some—but not all—nonhuman animals, which are perhaps best described as "other-than-human persons," following Hallowell (Hallowell 1960; Hill 2011, 2012). Almost all prey animals, including seals, whales, walrus, and caribou, were seen as persons, which is consistent with the idea that hunting is a social act, an engagement between members of two societies for mutual benefit. This perspective is derived from Brightman's definition of personhood as a form of "human-like subjectivity" (Brightman et al. 2012:2) defined in part through social action. Jordan has described it as "unfolding dialogue" (Jordan 2001:101) constituted through behavior and interaction.

Significantly for archaeology, this "dialogue" is enacted through patterned behavior involving the treatment of specific animal bones or body parts, such as the heads of bears (Jordan 2003, 2008) or the bladders of seals (Fienup-Riordan 1990, 1994). "Structured deposits" such as caches of seal bones on Nunivak Island (figure 2.2) materialize exchange relationships between human and animal societies. Nineteenth-century ethnohistoric documents indicate that seals, like beluga and other species of sea mammals, required their bodies and remains to be treated in specific ways by human hunters. Taboos governed all actions related to hunting, butchering, and consuming seals. Additional proscriptions structured speech, song, and even thoughts about prey animals. These taboos were a code of etiquette for social interaction between humans and prey, outlining what was—and was not—proper behavior or discourse.

Hunters took prey in ways that showed respect to the animal person, for example, by providing seals and whales with drinks of water once they had been hauled onto the ice. The animal's *inua* remained in the body and was aware of its treatment throughout the process of butchery. Through the 1800s in Southwest Alaska and Nunivak Island, the heads and bladders of seals were retrieved and cared for until the annual Bladder Festival, when the bones and bladders would be returned to the shoreline or pushed through the ice so the seals might return the following year (Himmelheber 2000:134–36).

The remains of seals and other animals, such as beluga and caribou, are archaeologically recoverable evidence of how Yup'ik and Inupiaq Eskimo interacted with other-than-human persons (Hill 2011, 2012, 2013). Caches of bones, sometimes with hunting gear or evidence of fire, are distinctive features that occur on both sides of Bering Strait. Though such caches are often described as "ritual" or "structured" deposits, the evidence from Alaska and Chukotka suggests that they might be more productively interpreted as reciprocal acts of gift giving that materialize the rules of etiquette between human and sea mammal persons. Caching of seal bones is thus the human observance of mutually agreed-upon rules for handling seal remains. Although this practice is documented from the nineteenth century, the structured deposition of animal bones has been going on for several hundred years in the Bering Sea region (Hill 2011).

A massive feature at a site on Cape Krusenstern (figure 2.3) was composed of an estimated 1,000 seal skulls and measured 5 m in diameter and approximately 50 cm thick, dating to around AD 500 (Giddings and Anderson 1986)—significantly larger and older than the smaller caches described here from the nineteenth century. Differences in the size, composition, and configuration of caches indicate that relations with other-than-human persons may

FIGURE 2.2. *Seal "burials" on the coast of Nunivak Island, 1927. Structured deposits of seal bones, especially skulls, resulted from the intentional acts of hunters returning the remains of seals to the sea. In exchange for proper treatment of their bones, seals would continue to "give" themselves to hunters. Courtesy, Henry B. Collins Collections, National Anthropological Archives, Smithsonian Institution, Washington, DC. NAA inv no. 1420803.*

FIGURE 2.3. *Seal skull feature associated with Ipiutak House 30 at Cape Krusenstern, Northwest Alaska. Originally published in Giddings and Anderson (1986:131, fig. 82). Courtesy, Douglas D. Anderson.*

have occurred at a number of different scales—that of the individual hunter and his wife as well as of the household, kin group, and community. The time depth also suggests that interpersonal relations—and relational ontologies themselves—have deep histories among the Eskimo. Such histories counteract the tendency to create timeless hunter-gatherer pasts differentiated only by economy and environment (Janik 2011; Sassaman 2000).

AGENTIAL NONPERSONS

Both archaeological and ethnohistoric evidence indicate that sea mammals possessed agency and personhood. They, like several other types of entities

(Burch 1971; Fienup-Riordan 1994, 2011), possessed "awareness" and could affect the lives of human persons. Encounters with them could be dangerous unless respect was shown and etiquette observed. However, some entities inhabiting the Eskimo landscape possessed agency but were not persons. These beings existed alone, beyond the bounds of human and animal communities (see Grønnow 2009 for examples from Greenland). They lacked the capacities for sociality and reciprocity, which defined personhood in the proto- and early historic Eskimo context. "Wild" or "cannibal" babies were one kind of agential non-person encountered by Yupiit and Inupiat beyond the bounds of the village.

Oral narratives on both sides of Bering Strait are replete with stories of wild babies—also called "big-mouth" or "monster" babies (e.g., Anderson 2005:112–13; Bergsland 1987:168–73; Fienup-Riordan and Kaplan 2007:64–83; Lantis 1990). Such babies were usually the product of some violation of a taboo—someone forgot to do something and, as a result, a big-mouth baby was born, usually by the expedient of eating its way out of its mother's body. As cannibals, these babies existed beyond the bounds of the social. Persons could not speak to or reason with them. The only way to deal with wild babies was to avoid, escape, or kill them. As late as the 1960s, specific lakes and places on the tundra were known to be inhabited by such babies, and people avoided hunting or traveling through those areas (Burch 1971).

Cannibal babies possessed agency—they had the capacity to act in meaningful and intentional ways—but they were not considered persons in the Eskimo ontological system. This excerpt from one version of the story, told by Inupiaq Simon Paneak (Bergsland 1987:169), describes the unpredictable and bizarre behavior of a wild baby, which has just eaten its mother: "The little baby no longer stayed by its mother, but jumped out through the skylight. And whatever belongings those people had, their dogs or themselves, it tried to get at, in order to eat them. Whenever it touched something, it's said, the little baby tore it to pieces—it had sharp teeth, it's said. As soon as it touched something with its mouth, it would bite a piece off. And it was bouncing . . . That little baby's only way of moving was to bounce."

Wild babies could be overcome by quick thinking, often informed by the wisdom of elders. In Paneak's version of the story, an orphaned boy remembered the advice of his grandmother and prevented the baby from following the villagers as they escaped. This and other versions end by noting the subsequent achievements of the boy, who became a leader and expert hunter.

Wild baby stories convey information not only about personhood and agency but also about proper behavior, including attention to elders and observance of taboos. The boy's success as a hunter indicates that his courage and respect for the rules earned him the approval of both human and animal persons. In contrast, wild babies obey no rules for living, as Inupiat (literally, "real" people) do; they respect no taboos or standards of behavior and refuse to negotiate or communicate. Reciprocity is *not* part of their behavioral repertoire; they are alone and asocial. As cannibals and insatiable consumers, they violate fundamental rules of Eskimo life—they consume the flesh of family members and eat voraciously without sharing.

Inupiat and Yupiit also recognized other beings as agents without personhood. Like wild babies, these beings were dangerous to persons. Their behavior generally included some element of uncontrolled consumption or an insatiable appetite. Disembodied hands, mouths, and heads (Anderson 2005:186–91) are frequent agents, such as the *itqiirpak*, a huge hand with mouths on each finger that devours noisy children. Another Yup'ik creature is the *meriiq*, which sucks the blood from one's big toe when that person has forgotten to procure water (Fienup-Riordan 1994:85). Some stories describe the behavior of humans, often adult men, who become cannibals or mistake something inedible for food. Two examples from Selawik, Northwest Alaska, describe men who refuse to eat what their wives have cooked—rejecting the society of their families—and instead consume their own children (Anderson 2005:241–44) or confuse rocks with (edible) blubber (Anderson 2005:245).

Wild babies, agential body parts, and some humans, while agents, either never had or lost their capacity to be persons. Their behavior is unpredictable and dangerous and usually features some act related to cannibalism or excessive appetite. These entities violate fundamental rules governing food consumption and sharing and fail to respond as a person would to reasonable speech or action. While these creatures have agency, they have somehow—often through the violation of a taboo by a human person—either given up their personhood or never had it to begin with.

CONCLUSION

The reciprocal social relations between human and other-than-human persons described in this chapter comprise what Mauss called a *total social phenomenon* (Mauss 1966 [1925]:1); that is, the principle of reciprocity between humans and other persons was woven into the very fabric of daily action and formed part of human social structure. In this view, interactions with other-than-human persons are as essential to the constitution of society as humans themselves. Such a view requires an expansion of our understanding of the social—it requires us to extend "sociality" to include relations with and among nonhuman persons. An accurate reconstruction of the past also requires understanding how age, sex, status, and a host of other variables constituted the person. Relational ontologies, such as the one described above, involved interactions not just between the human and other-than-human but among different *kinds* of human and other-than-human persons. Those humans who failed to behave properly and fulfill the obligations of kinship and marriage could lose their status as persons, as evidenced by their behavioral excesses. Differences between human persons—hunters and seamstresses, for example—structured interactions with prey animals and were dependent upon variables that included sex, activity, season, expertise, and marriage status.

This broader understanding of what constitutes the person implicates the practice of archaeology more broadly, extending the purview of the discipline to encompass those categories of "things" archaeologists have traditionally considered to be objects rather than agential subjects. By including other kinds of agents in our understanding of the complex social worlds of the past, our reconstructions of indigenous ontologies become more nuanced and multidimensional. As this chapter has shown, the conceptual domain of "agent" may include human persons; entities without personhood, such as cannibals or wild babies; and other-than-human persons, such as figurines (Hendon et al. 2014), animals (Hill 2011, 2013), and geographic features (Hill 2012).

Simply characterizing an indigenous ontology as "relational" actually tells us very little about the experience—the dwelling-in-the-world—of specific persons. Required is a culturally specific exploration of who was (and was not) considered a person; how personhood was constructed, acquired, or lost; and what rules or values governed relations among persons. Hunters in the Bering Sea region enacted their relationships with whales and walrus in ways quite distinct from the ways hunters of dugong did so in the South Pacific. Animal bladders and skulls were the loci of *anima* in the Bering Sea (Hill 2011), while Torres Strait Islanders privileged the ribs and ear bones of their prey (David and Badulgal 2006; McNiven and Feldman 2003).

Distinguishing between personhood and agency is a valuable endeavor because it defines not only what was considered appropriate social behavior but also what was not. Uncontrolled consumption and failure to share defined personhood by being antithetical to the ways "real people" acted in the early historic Eskimo past. Wild babies and hunters-turned-cannibals were agents, fully capable of action. But their actions violated the rules of sociality and reciprocity. Mere action denoted agency; action tempered by social rules defined persons. The distinction made here between agency and personhood departs from Robb's (2010) definition of agency as socially situated action. Early historic period Eskimo recognized non-social agents. Such agents were capable of intentional actions, such as cannibalism, and could effect change but lacked the capacity for reciprocity and sociality. In other words, while both agents and persons could *act*, only persons could *interact*.

This chapter is intended not to identify a distinct "hunter-gatherer perspective" that characterized forager societies—even Arctic forager societies but rather to describe a specific relational perspective and locate it in place and time. How Eskimo of Alaska and Chukotka defined personhood has changed as a result of factors that include geography and degree of interaction with other ethnic groups. Contact with Chukchi herders, Russian traders, and Athabascan speakers required redefinition of ontological domains. Similarly, daily and seasonal rounds, migration, displacement, and large-scale changes in settlement patterns brought human persons into contact with new and unfamiliar agents, such as the entities associated with specific places (Burch 1971) or embodied in geographic features (Hill 2012).

For Yupiit and Inupiat, personhood appears to have been a matter of degree rather than an absolute state. Human persons could retreat from society by refusing to share or, like the *qivittut* among Greenlandic Inuit (Grønnow 2009), by leaving their camps and villages to live by themselves. Grief, trauma, and loss could cause human persons to abandon friends and family, placing themselves beyond the bounds of the social in both ontological and geographic terms. Loss of personhood could also occur during life-cycle transitions, illness, and death. These liminal periods reconfigure social status, leaving human persons potentially vulnerable. If personhood is a fundamentally social phenomenon, as argued here, processes and events that radically affect a society's social structure are simultaneously threats to its members' ontological status.

The study of personhood and agency in the past offers archaeologists opportunities to explore perspectives on the world that may differ radically from their own. Commonplace finds such as animal remains, figurines, and burial offerings take on new meaning once notions of personhood and agency expand to include the other-than-human. The landscape itself, like the arctic tundra, transforms from an apparently natural environment to one crowded with animals and entities pursuing their own social lives. Such a perspective on the world has tremendous potential to—paraphrasing Ingold (2006)—astonish and so reanimate thought.

ACKNOWLEDGMENTS

I am grateful to Doug Anderson, who kindly granted permission to reproduce his 1961 photo of the seal skull pile at Cape Krusenstern. I also acknowledge Daisy Njoku at the National Anthropological Archives, who assisted me with copies of archival materials and photographic permissions.

REFERENCES CITED

Anderson, Wanni W. 2005. *The Dall Sheep Dinner Guest: Iñupiaq Narratives of Northwest Alaska.* Fairbanks: University of Alaska Press.

Argent, Gala. 2010. "Do the Clothes Make the Horse? Relationality, Roles, and Statuses in Iron Age Inner Asia." *World Archaeology* 42 (2): 157–74. https://doi.org/10.1080/00438241003672633.

Bendrey, Robin. 2014. "Care in the Community? Interpretations of a Fractured Goat Bone from Neolithic Jarmo, Iraq." *International Journal of Paleopathology* 7: 33–37. https://doi.org/10.1016/j.ijpp.2014.06.003.

Bergsland, Knut, ed. 1987. *Nunamiut Unipkaaŋich / Nunamiut Stories.* Barrow, AK: North Slope Borough Commission on Iñupiat History, Language, and Culture.

Betts, Matthew W., Mari Hardenberg, and Ian Stirling. 2015. "How Animals Create Human History: Relational Ecology and the Dorset–Polar Bear Connection." *American Antiquity* 80 (1): 89–112. https://doi.org/10.7183/0002-7316.79.4.89.

Bird-David, Nurit. 1999. "'Animism' Revisited: Personhood, Environment, and Relational Epistemology." *Current Anthropology* 40 (S1 supplement): S67–S91. https://doi.org/10.1086/200061.

Bodenhorn, Barbara. 1990. "'I'm Not the Great Hunter, My Wife Is': Iñupiat and Anthropological Models of Gender." *Études/Inuit/Studies* 14 (1–2): 55–74.

Boutin, Alexis T. 2012. "Crafting a Bioarchaeology of Personhood: Osteobiographical Narratives from Alalakh." In *Breathing New Life into the Evidence of Death: Contemporary Approaches to Bioarchaeology,* ed. Aubrey Baadsgaard, Alexis T. Boutin, and Jane E. Buikstra, 109–29. Santa Fe, NM: School for Advanced Research Press.

Brightman, Marc, Vanessa Elisa Grotti, and Olga Ulturgasheva. 2012. "Animism and Invisible Worlds: The Place of Non-Humans in Indigenous Ontologies." In *Animism in Rainforest and Tundra: Personhood, Animals, Plants, and Things in Contemporary Amazonia and Siberia,* ed. Marc Brightman, Vanessa Elisa Grotti, and Olga Ulturgasheva, 1–27. New York: Berghahn.

Brown, Linda A., and Kitty F. Emery. 2008. "Negotiations with the Animate Forest: Hunting Shrines in the Guatemalan Highlands." *Journal of Archaeological Method and Theory* 15 (4): 300–337. https://doi.org/10.1007/s10816-008-9055-7.

Brown, Linda A., and William H. Walker. 2008. "Prologue: Archaeology, Animism, and Non-Human Agents." *Journal of Archaeological Method and Theory* 15 (4): 297–99. https://doi.org/10.1007/s10816-008-9056-6.

Burch, Ernest S., Jr. 1971. "The Nonempirical Environment of the Arctic Alaskan Eskimos." *Southwestern Journal of Anthropology* 27 (2): 148–65. https://doi.org/10.1086/soutjanth.27.2.3629237.

Cassady, Joslyn. 2008. "'Strange Things Happen to Non-Christian People': Human-Animal Transformation among the Iñupiat of Arctic Alaska." *American Indian Culture and Research Journal* 32 (1): 83–101. https://doi.org/10.17953/aicr.32.1.14257q67g57mr66k.

Chaussonnet, Valérie. 1988. "Needles and Animals: Women's Magic." In *Crossroads of Continents: Cultures of Siberia and Alaska*, ed. William W. Fitzhugh and Aron L. Crowell, 209–26. Washington, DC: Smithsonian Institution Press.

David, Bruno, and Mura Badulgal. 2006. "What Happened in Torres Strait 400 Years Ago? Ritual Transformations in an Island Seascape." *Journal of Island and Coastal Archaeology* 1 (2): 123–43. https://doi.org/10.1080/15564890600870828.

Dobres, Marcia-Anne, and John E. Robb. 2000. "Agency in Archaeology: Paradigm or Platitude?" In *Agency in Archaeology*, ed. Marcia-Anne Dobres and John E. Robb, 3–17. London: Routledge.

Dolitsky, Alexander B., ed. 2000. *Tales and Legends of the Yupik Eskimos of Siberia*. Juneau: Alaska-Siberia Research Center.

Fienup-Riordan, Ann. 1990. "The Bird and the Bladder: The Cosmology of Central Yup'ik Seal Hunting." *Études/Inuit/Studies* 14 (1): 23–38.

Fienup-Riordan, Ann. 1994. *Boundaries and Passages: Rule and Ritual in Yup'ik Eskimo Oral Tradition*. Norman: University of Oklahoma Press.

Fienup-Riordan, Ann. 2007. "Compassion and Restraint: The Moral Foundations of Yup'ik Eskimo Hunting Tradition." In *La nature des esprits dans les cosmologies autochtones / Nature of Spirits in Aboriginal Cosmologies*, ed. Frédéric Laugrand and Jarich Oosten, 239–53. Université Laval, QC: Les Presses de l'Université Laval.

Fienup-Riordan, Ann. 2009. "*Cat Tamarmeng Ellangqertut / All Things Have Awareness*." In *Gifts from the Ancestors: Ancient Ivories of Bering Strait*, ed. William W. Fitzhugh, Julie Hollowell, and Aron L. Crowell, 226–39. Princeton, NJ: Princeton University Art Museum.

Fienup-Riordan, Ann. 2011. *Qaluyaarmiuni Nunamtenek Qanemciput / Our Nelson Island Stories: Meanings of Place on the Bering Sea Coast*. Seattle: University of Washington Press.

Fienup-Riordan, Ann, and Lawrence Kaplan, eds. 2007. *Words of the Real People: Alaska Native Literature in Translation*. Fairbanks: University of Alaska Press.

Fijn, Natasha. 2011. *Living with Herds: Human-Animal Coexistence in Mongolia*. Cambridge: Cambridge University Press. https://doi.org/10.1017/CBO9780511976513.

Finlay, Nyree. 2000. "Outside of Life: Traditions of Infant Burial in Ireland from Cillin to Cist." *World Archaeology* 31 (3): 407–22. https://doi.org/10.1080/00438240009696929.

Finlay, Nyree. 2014. "Personhood and Social Relations." In *The Oxford Handbook of the Archaeology and Anthropology of Hunter-Gatherers*, ed. Vicki Cummings, Peter Jordan, and Marek Zvelebil, 1191–203. Oxford: Oxford University Press.

Fitzhugh, William W., and Susan A. Kaplan. 1982. *Inua: Spirit World of the Bering Sea Eskimo*. Washington, DC: Smithsonian Institution Press.

Fowler, Chris. 2004. *Archaeology of Personhood: An Anthropological Approach*. New York: Routledge.

Giddings, J. L., and D. Douglas Anderson. 1986. *Beach Ridge Archeology of Cape Krusenstern: Eskimo and Pre-Eskimo Settlements around Kotzebue Sound, Alaska*. Washington, DC: National Park Service.

Grønnow, Bjarne. 2009. "Blessings and Horrors of the Interior: Ethno-historical Studies of Inuit Perceptions Concerning the Inland Region of West Greenland." *Arctic Anthropology* 46 (1–2): 191–201. https://doi.org/10.1353/arc.0.0027.

Hallowell, A. Irving. 1960. "Ojibwa Ontology, Behavior, and World View." In *Culture in History: Essays in Honor of Paul Radin*, ed. Stanley Diamond, 19–52. New York: Columbia University Press.

Harrison-Buck, Eleanor. 2012. "Architecture as Animated Landscape: Circular Shrines in the Ancient Maya Lowlands." *American Anthropologist* 114 (1): 64–80. https://doi.org/10.1111/j.1548-1433.2011.01397.x.

Hendon, Julia A., Rosemary A. Joyce, and Jeanne Lopiparo. 2014. *Material Relations: The Marriage Figurines of Prehispanic Honduras*. Boulder: University Press of Colorado.

Herva, Vesa-Pekka. 2009. "Living (with) Things: Relational Ontology and Material Culture in Early Modern Northern Finland." *Cambridge Archaeological Journal* 19 (3): 388–97. https://doi.org/10.1017/S0959774309000572.

Hill, Erica. 2011. "Animals as Agents: Hunting Ritual and Relational Ontologies in Prehistoric Alaska and Chukotka." *Cambridge Archaeological Journal* 21 (3): 407–26. https://doi.org/10.1017/S0959774311000448.

Hill, Erica. 2012. "The Nonempirical Past: Enculturated Landscapes and Other-than-Human Persons in Southwest Alaska." *Arctic Anthropology* 49 (2): 41–57. https://doi.org/10.1353/arc.2012.0021.

Hill, Erica. 2013. "Archaeology and Animal Persons: Toward a Prehistory of Human-Animal Relations." *Environment and Society: Advances in Research* 4 (1): 117–36. https://doi.org/10.3167/ares.2013.040108.

Himmelheber, Hans. 2000. *Where the Echo Began and Other Oral Traditions from Southwest Alaska.* Trans. Kurt Vitt and Ester Vitt. Fairbanks: University of Alaska Press.

Ingold, Tim. 1987. "Hunting, Sacrifice, and the Domestication of Animals." In *The Appropriation of Nature: Essays on Human Ecology and Social Relations,* ed. Tim Ingold, 243–76. Iowa City: University of Iowa Press.

Ingold, Tim. 2000a. "From Trust to Domination: An Alternative History of Human-Animal Relations." In *The Perception of the Environment: Essays on Livelihood, Dwelling, and Skill,* ed. Tim Ingold, 61–76. New York: Routledge. https://doi.org/10.4324/9780203466025.

Ingold, Tim. 2000b. "Hunting and Gatherering as Ways of Perceiving the Environment." In *The Perception of the Environment: Essays on Livelihood, Dwelling, and Skill,* ed. Tim Ingold, 40–60. New York: Routledge. https://doi.org/10.4324/9780203466025.

Ingold, Tim, ed. 2000c. *The Perception of the Environment: Essays on Livelihood, Dwelling, and Skill.* New York: Routledge. https://doi.org/10.4324/9780203466025.

Ingold, Tim. 2002. "Humanity and Animality." In *Companion Encyclopedia of Anthropology,* 2nd ed., ed. Tim Ingold, 14–32. London: Routledge.

Ingold, Tim. 2006. "Rethinking the Animate, Re-Animating Thought." *Ethnos* 71 (1): 9–20. https://doi.org/10.1080/00141840600603111.

Janik, Liliana. 2000. "The Construction of the Individual among North European Fisher-Gatherer-Hunters in the Early and Mid-Holocene." In *Children and Material Culture,* ed. Joanna Sofaer Derevenski, 117–30. New York: Routledge.

Janik, Liliana. 2011. "Why Does Difference Matter? The Creation of Identity among Prehistoric Fisher-Gatherer-Hunters of Northern Europe." In *Structured Worlds: The Archaeology of Hunter-Gatherer Thought and Action,* ed. Aubrey Cannon, 128–40. London: Equinox.

Jordan, Peter. 2001. "The Materiality of Shamanism as a 'World-View': Praxis, Artefacts, and Landscape." In *The Archaeology of Shamanism,* ed. Neil S. Price, 87–104. London: Routledge.

Jordan, Peter. 2003. *Material Culture and Sacred Landscape: The Anthropology of the Siberian Khanty.* Walnut Creek, CA: Altamira.

Jordan, Peter. 2008. "Northern Landscapes, Northern Mind: On the Trail of an Archaeology of Hunter-Gatherer Belief." In *Belief in the Past: Theoretical Approaches to the Archaeology of Religion,* ed. David S. Whitley and Kelley Hays-Gilpin, 227–46. Walnut Creek, CA: Left Coast.

Lantis, Margaret. 1990. "The Selection of Symbolic Meaning." *Études/Inuit/Studies* 14 (1–2): 169–89.

Laugrand, Frédéric, and Jarich Oosten. 2007. "Bears and Dogs in Canadian Inuit Cosmology." In *La nature des esprits dans les cosmologies autochtones / Nature of Spirits in Aboriginal Cosmologies*, ed. Frédéric Laugrand and Jarich Oosten, 353–85. Université Laval, QC: Les Presses de l'Université Laval.

Losey, Robert J. 2010. "Animism as a Means of Exploring Archaeological Fishing Structures on Willapa Bay, Washington, USA." *Cambridge Archaeological Journal* 20 (1): 17–32. https://doi.org/10.1017/S0959774310000028.

Losey, Robert J., Vladimir I. Bazaliiskii, Sandra Garvie-Lok, Mietje Germonpré, Jennifer A. Leonard, Andrew L. Allen, M. Anne Katzenberg, and Mikhail V. Sablin. 2011. "Canids as Persons: Early Neolithic Dog and Wolf Burials, Cis-Baikal, Siberia." *Journal of Anthropological Archaeology* 30 (2): 174–89. https://doi.org/10.1016/j.jaa.2011.01.001.

Losey, Robert J., Vladimir I. Bazaliiskii, Angela R. Lieverse, Andrea Waters-Rist, Kate Faccia, and Andrzej W. Weber. 2013. "The Bear-able Likeness of Being: Ursine Remains at the Shamanka II Cemetery, Lake Baikal, Siberia." In *Relational Archaeologies: Humans, Animals, Things*, ed. Christopher Watts, 65–96. New York: Routledge.

Mauss, Marcel. 1966 [1925]. *The Gift: Forms and Functions of Exchange in Archaic Societies*. Trans. Ian Cunnison. London: Cohen and West.

Mauss, Marcel. 1985 [1939]. "A Category of the Human Mind: The Notion of Person, the Notion of Self." In *The Category of the Person: Anthropology, Philosophy, History*, ed. Michael Carrithers, Steven Collins, and Steven Lukes, trans. W. D. Halls., 1–25. Cambridge: Cambridge University Press.

McNiven, Ian J. 2010. "Navigating the Human-Animal Divide: Marine Mammal Hunters and Rituals of Sensory Allurement." *World Archaeology* 42 (2): 215–30. https://doi.org/10.1080/00438241003672849.

McNiven, Ian J. 2013. "Between the Living and the Dead: Relational Ontologies and the Ritual Dimensions of Dugong Hunting across Torres Strait." In *Relational Archaeologies: Humans, Animals, Things*, ed. Christopher Watts, 97–116. New York: Routledge.

McNiven, Ian J., and Ricky Feldman. 2003. "Ritually Orchestrated Seascapes: Hunting Magic and Dugong Bone Mounds in Torres Strait, NE Australia." *Cambridge Archaeological Journal* 13 (2): 169–94. https://doi.org/10.1017/S0959774303000118.

Oma, Kristin Armstrong. 2007. *Human–Animal Relationships: Mutual Becomings in Scandinavian and Sicilian Households 900–500 BC*. Oslo Arkeologiske Series no. 9. Oslo: Oslo Academic Press.

Oma, Kristin Armstrong. 2010. "Between Trust and Domination: Social Contracts between Humans and Animals." *World Archaeology* 42 (2): 175–87. https://doi.org/10.1080/00438241003672724.

Orton, David. 2010. "Both Subject and Object: Herding, Inalienability, and Sentient Property in Prehistory." *World Archaeology* 42 (2): 188–200. https://doi.org/10.1080/00438241003672773.

Praet, Istvan. 2013. "The Positional Quality of Life and Death: A Theory of Human-Animal Relations in Animism." *Anthrozoos: A Multidisciplinary Journal of the Interactions of People and Animals* 26 (3): 341–55. https://doi.org/10.2752/175303713X13697429463510.

Rivollat, Maïté, Dominique Castex, Laurent Hauret, and Anne-Marie Tillier. 2014. "Ancient Down Syndrome: An Osteological Case from Saint-Jean-des-Vignes, Northeastern France, from the 5–6th Century AD." *International Journal of Paleopathology* 7: 8–14. https://doi.org/10.1016/j.ijpp.2014.05.004.

Robb, John. 2010. "Beyond Agency." *World Archaeology* 42 (4): 493–520. https://doi.org/10.1080/00438243.2010.520856.

Russell, Nerissa. 2002. "The Wild Side of Domestication." *Society and Animals* 10 (3): 285–302. https://doi.org/10.1163/156853002320770083.

Sassaman, Kenneth E. 2000. "Agents of Change in Hunter-Gatherer Technology." In *Agency in Archaeology*, ed. Marcia-Anne Dobres and John E. Robb, 148–68. London: Routledge.

Scott, Eleanor. 2001. "Killing the Female: Archaeological Narratives of Infanticide." In *Gender and the Archaeology of Death*, ed. Bettina Arnold and Nancy L. Wicker, 3–21. Walnut Creek, CA: Altamira.

Sillar, Bill. 2009. "The Social Agency of Things? Animism and Materiality in the Andes." *Cambridge Archaeological Journal* 19 (3): 367–77. https://doi.org/10.1017/S0959774309000559.

Søby, Regitze Margrethe. 1969–70. "The Eskimo Animal Cult." *Folk: Dansk Etnografisk Tidsskrift* 11–12: 43–78.

Tilley, Lorna. 2015. "Accommodating Difference in the Prehistoric Past: Revisiting the Case of Romito 2 from a Bioarchaeology of Care Perspective." *International Journal of Paleopathology* 8: 64–74. https://doi.org/10.1016/j.ijpp.2014.10.003.

Tilley, Lorna, and Marc F. Oxenham. 2011. "Survival against the Odds: Modeling the Social Implications of Care Provision to Seriously Disabled Individuals." *International Journal of Paleopathology* 1 (1): 35–42. https://doi.org/10.1016/j.ijpp.2011.02.003.

Viveiros de Castro, Eduardo. 1992. *From the Enemy's Point of View: Humanity and Divinity in an Amazonian Society*. Trans. Catherine V. Howard. Chicago: University of Chicago Press.

Viveiros de Castro, Eduardo. 1998. "Cosmological Deixis and Amerindian Perspectivism." *Journal of the Royal Anthropological Institute* 4 (3): 469–88. https://doi.org/10.2307/3034157.

Watts, Christopher, ed. 2013. *Relational Archaeologies: Humans, Animals, Things*. New York: Routledge.

Willerslev, Rane. 2004. "Not Animal, Not *Not*-Animal: Hunting Imitation and Empathetic Knowledge among the Siberian Yukaghirs." *Journal of the Royal Anthropological Institute* 10 (3): 629–52. https://doi.org/10.1111/j.1467-9655.2004.00205.x.

Willerslev, Rane. 2007. *Soul Hunters: Hunting, Animism, and Personhood among the Siberian Yukaghirs*. Berkeley: University of California Press. https://doi.org/10.1525/california/9780520252165.001.0001.

Zedeño, Maria Nieves. 2008. "Bundled Worlds: The Roles and Interactions of Complex Objects from the North American Plains." *Journal of Archaeological Method and Theory* 15 (4): 362–78. https://doi.org/10.1007/s10816-008-9058-4.

3

The indigenous peoples of the Maritimes were the first in northeastern North America to encounter colonial Europeans, having sustained interactions with Basque whalers/fishers and, soon after, French traders starting at the turn of the sixteenth century (Hornborg 2008; Martin 1975; Prins 2002; Reid 1995; Whitehead 1993). During the time of earliest contact, ca. AD 1500 to 1630, the Mi'kmaq and Maliseet experienced a near-constant influx of foreigners and their goods, including copper kettles. Their interactions with Europeans and their material objects produced diverse personhoods, social relations, and communities (Miller 2005:286). In this chapter I examine some of the subjectivities arising from their interactions with foreign goods (Joyce 2014; Mullins 2011). Specifically, I examine how the Mi'kmaq actively socialized one particularly significant European-origin good, the kettle, within the context of their preexisting value systems and well-established relational ontology, wherein objects were not only allowed but expected to possess purposeful agency (Brown and Walker 2008:297). In such an ontological perspective, humans do not form the sole exemplars of personhood (Alberti and Bray 2009:338).

To the Mi'kmaq, the entire universe was filled with an animating spirit called *mntu*; during the early colonial encounter, kettles were readily incorporated into this relational ontology. I explore how kettles, in the context of the social alterity of colonial contact, became the other-than-human relations of the Mi'kmaq that

Dead Kettles and Indigenous Afterworlds in Early Colonial Encounters in the Maritimes

Meghan C.L. Howey

DOI: 10.5876/9781607327479.c003

held the unique ability and specific responsibility to create an afterworld that was at once exclusively indigenous yet also a world prepared for a potential breach by Europeans.

I offer this case study to highlight the importance of conducting archaeologies that consider seriously in their reconstructions other-than-human agency and the potential this agency has for transforming social, economic, and ideological material realities (Harrison-Buck and Hendon, this volume). The case of the Maritimes also allows us to appreciate that colonial encounters provide a particularly salient venue for this exploration, as contact draws people into spaces where they experience and confront different object and thought worlds. In encounter, people are drawn into social alterity (*sensu* Taussig 1993). They are faced with the undeniable rawness of alterity—the "impossible but necessary, indeed everyday affair" of having to "register both sameness and difference, of being like and of being Other" (Taussig 1993:129). In circumstances of colonial contact, communities must negotiate their interdependent reciprocal relationships with human and nonhuman agents, which now include myriad new nonhuman agents previously not experienced and unincorporated into their relational worlds (Taussig 1993; Swenson 2015). Alterity creates openings for the activation of new, potent nonhuman agents and demands the definition of the primacy of these relationships by the human communities relating to them (Brown and Walker 2008:297).

EARLY COLONIAL ENCOUNTERS IN THE MARITIMES

The Maritimes are part of Wabanaki, or the "land of the dawn," which runs along the Atlantic seaboard from the Gaspe Peninsula in Quebec to southeastern Massachusetts (Brooks and Brooks 2010:12; figure 3.1). The Maritimes occupy the northeastern extent of this landscape and formed the traditional homelands of the Mi'kmaq and Maliseet. The name Mi'kmaq derives from their greeting *nikmaq*, meaning "my kin friends." The Basque, the French, and eventually the British would refer to the Mi'kmaq by various other names, including Souriquois, Tarentines, and Gaspesiens. Europeans adopted the Mi'kmaq name for the Maliseet, *mali'sit*, which translates to something akin to "they don't talk like we do." The Maliseet referred to themselves as *wukastuk kewiuk* in reference to the St. John River[1] (for more on terminology, see Hornborg 2008; Prins 2002; Whitehead 1993).

The position of the Maritimes brought the indigenous peoples living there into early encounter with Europeans. The Mi'kmaq were the first peoples in Wabanaki drawn into contact, meeting Europeans as they came down the

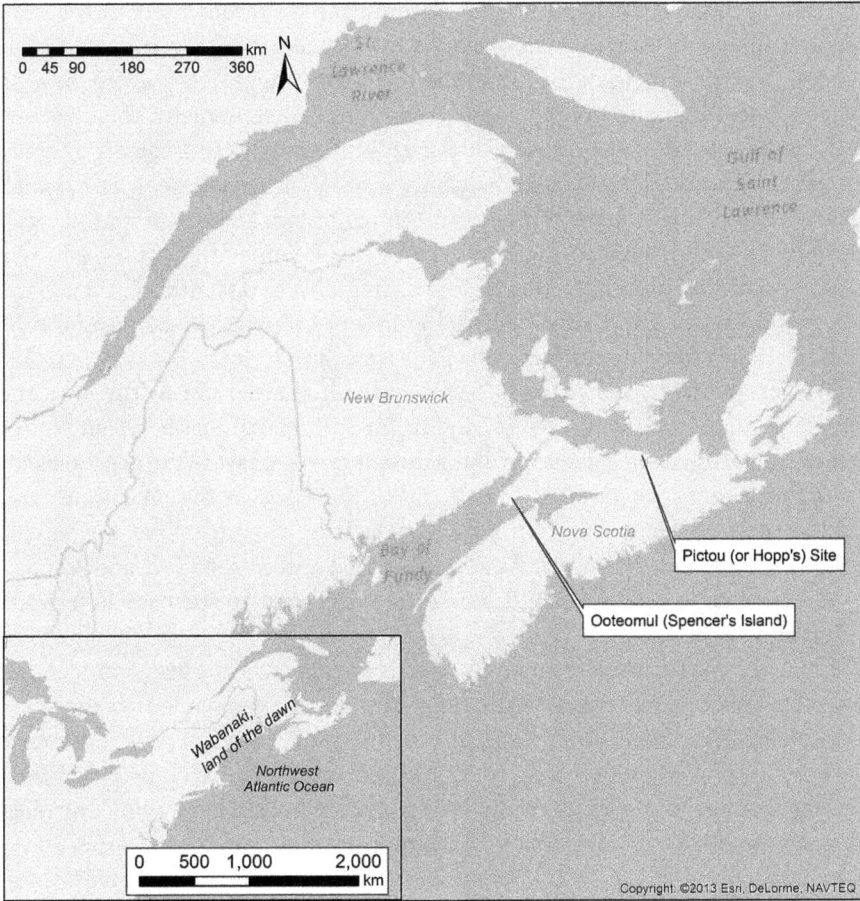

FIGURE 3.1. *General location of Wabanaki and a closeup of the Maritimes, which occupy the northeastern extent of Wabanaki. The Canadian provinces, including the Pictou site and Ooteomul, Kluskap's Kettle (Spencer's Island), are indicated.*

Atlantic seaboard because they were moving further and further afield as their fishing practices exhausted marine resources in their own waters in the northeast Atlantic of Europe during the fourteenth and fifteenth centuries (Roberts 2007). In the late fifteenth century, John Cabot landed on Cape Breton and brought confirmation of the rich fishing grounds of the Grand Banks back to Europe (Whitehead 1993:9).

The abundant marine resources of the northwest Atlantic waters of the Maritimes attracted more early European explorers. The Basque voyaged into the Maritimes and established whaling and fishing stations there in the early 1500s (Innis 1940; Kurlansky 1997). Like the Basque, the French came to this area as voyagers in the 1500s, but their interests quickly expanded beyond fishing into the fur trade, religious conversion, and settlement; they became the dominant colonial presence in the region during the sixteenth and seventeenth centuries (Prins 2002; Salisbury 1996; Whitehead 1993). The British began developing a larger presence in the region, including competing with the French in fur trade in the later part of the seventeenth century, and ultimately came to dominate the region during the eighteenth century (Paul 2000; Reid 1995). The British ushered in an era of increased adversarial colonial relations after this time as well (Paul 2000; Reid 1995).

While marine resources drew Europeans' initial attention to the area, the fur trade came to be a dominant conduit for cultural contact between Native Americans and Europeans there and across the Northeast (Wagner 1998:430). Informal trading for furs began as early as the 1520s in the Maritimes and on the coast of Maine (Salisbury 1996:452). After the mid-1500s, formalized trading accelerated along the Atlantic seaboard and in the Gulf and Estuary of St. Lawrence when demand for fancy furs began to increase in Europe (Fitzgerald et al. 1993).

From the outset, the Mi'kmaq were active agents in European contact, taking a particularly active role in the fur trade. The Mi'kmaq adopted the small European sailing boat, the shallop, and used it to sail the Gulf of St. Lawrence and the Gulf of Maine as far south as Massachusetts. The Mi'kmaq used their sailing abilities to establish themselves as Native middlemen who controlled the movement and introduction of European trade goods into other indigenous communities for years before Europeans themselves made significant contacts with tribal populations inland around 1610 (Bourque and Whitehead 1985). While the Mi'kmaq capitalized on a close engagement with Europeans in economic trade, this engagement also exposed them early and rapidly to European diseases against which they had no immunity. Estimates are that during the sixteenth century, the Mi'kmaq experienced a loss of at least 75 percent of their population as a result of foreign diseases; losses at this level continued well into the seventeenth century (Prins 2002:54).

SOCIAL ALTERITY, NEW WORLD PEOPLE, AND COPPER KETTLES

During the sixteenth and early seventeenth centuries, Mi'kmaq and colonial Europeans were becoming something that had never existed before: "New World People" (Reid 1995:74). Exactly what this would look like and what it meant was not yet clear. It was a time, then, of identity formation; Self and Other were intertwined in a "third space" (*sensu* Bhabha 2004). This third space held a material grip on the bodies and minds of both indigenous and European peoples (Gosden 2004:3). This material grip was manifest in the practice of the fur trade whereby the exchange of material goods became *the* mode by which contact with other human beings was mediated (Reid 1995:74). The exchange of material goods was important for facilitating economic relationships, but it did not become such a critical conduit for intercultural interaction on this basis alone. Exchange became the mode for contact because it provided a tangible way of navigating the uncertainties of alterity that lay at the heart of both Mi'kmaq and European experience during early colonial encounters (Reid 1995:74; see also Fitzgerald et al. 1993; Rubertone 1989; Salisbury 1996; White 1999).

Copper/copper-colored kettles were one of the most essential items in the trade networks established between Europeans and the Mi'kmaq and, indeed, among indigenous peoples across Wabanaki (Martin 1975; Trigger 1987; Turgeon 1997; van Dongen 1996). As exchange began in the 1500s, Europeans quickly recognized a widespread demand for copper kettles among Maritime and other northeastern indigenous groups (Groce 1980:108). Initially, they responded to this demand by trading high-quality iron-banded "red copper" kettles they had access to as products used in their home countries (Fitzgerald et al. 1993). As demand accelerated over during the 1500s, high-quality copper kettles were replaced in trade repertoires with a less complex, more economical rolled-rim variety with folded-over copper alloy lugs, often made of brass. These kettles are referred to as "trade kettles" (Ehrhardt 2005:73; Fitzgerald et al. 1993; Turgeon 1997). Figure 3.2 shows an example of a French-origin standardized trade kettle. Trade kettles were standardized in form and mass-produced in Europe specifically to supply the marked demand for kettles among indigenous communities in North America (Bradley 1987; Howey 2011; van Dongen 1996).

The popularity of the kettle was rooted in copper's preexisting highly charged value among the indigenous peoples of Wabanaki. Native copper had been used from the Archaic period (ca. 8000–800 BC) onward in potent symbolic ways, and copper's color was cognitively linked to a "metaphysics of light" (Childs 1994; Ehrhardt 2005; Hamell 1983; Miller and Hamell 1986). As European copper came to Wabanaki in the form of something novel and virtually irreproducible—kettles—it came to be invested with statutory and symbolic power exceeding even the power of native copper in prehistory (Turgeon 1997:9–10).

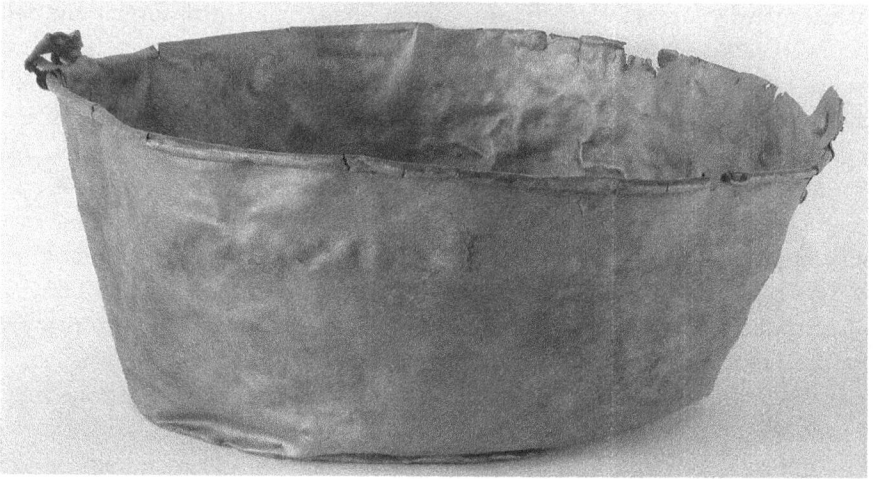

FIGURE 3.2. *Image of a standardized copper trade kettle used by the French during early contact (ca. seventeenth century). This well-preserved kettle was excavated at the Place Royale in Quebec City, which Samuel de Champlain began constructing in 1608. Marc Gadreau 2005, © Ministère de la Culture et des Communications, Quebec.*

The trade kettle's origin with the "Other" who had entered the social, economic, and ideological spheres of Maritime and northeastern indigenous communities, combined with its material connection to a native medium that had held symbolic significance for millennia prior to colonialism, fueled kettles' primary place in early contact trade (see also Howey 2011). Throughout early colonial contact, kettles, understood by Europeans as utilitarian cooking items, were not acquired by indigenous groups for this function. Instead, the demand for kettles was driven by their frequent and central incorporation into symbolically, ceremonially, and socially charged activities—most notably, indigenous burial practices.

Prior to contact, across the Maritimes and the Northeast, burials were furnished with very few durable grave goods (Brenner 1988; Crosby 1988; Whitehead 1993). During early contact, burial practices shifted and indigenous internments became furnished with copious amounts of grave goods, including large quantities of European-origin goods (and some native ones). These materially rich post-contact burials have come to be referred to as "copper-kettle burials" because some combination of whole or fragmentary European-made copper/brass kettles and other artifacts made from these metals permeated almost all of the burials (Petersen et al. 2004:2). Kettle burials occurred over a large portion of northeastern North America between ca. 1500 and 1680 (Brenner 1988; Gibson 1980; Loren 2013; Petersen et al. 2004; Trigger 1987). However, copper-kettle burials are best known from the Maritimes where they occurred first and featured kettles as the most elaborate of all grave goods.

Thirteen copper-kettle burial sites dating to the Protohistoric period (ca. AD 1500–1630) have been recorded in Nova Scotia and New Brunswick in Mi'kmaq traditional homelands (Whitehead 1993). The inclusion of kettles in Maritime indigenous graves during the Protohistoric period was so common that it formed one of the primary driving forces behind the persistent demand for kettles in trade exchanges, starting with the Basque and then with the French (Martin 1975:114). The Mi'kmaq sought kettles from European traders to replace the many that had been buried as ceremonial grave goods (Martin 1975:114).

ANIMISM AND AFTERWORLDS: MI'KMAQ COPPER-KETTLE BURIALS

For the Mi'kmaq, the entire universe is filled with an animating spirit called *mntu*. Mi'kmaq foundational cosmology understands everything in the world as imbued with sentient life and everything as related, expressed in the traditional phrase *msit no'kmaq*, "all my relations" (Robinson 2014:673–74). During early colonial encounters, I suggest that both elements of this long-established ontology—animate spirit and encompassing relatedness—were extended to European-origin kettles. The permeation of kettles across Protohistoric burials among the Mi'kmaq reflects kettles' embodiment as other-than-human relatives with souls and developed conditions of personhood.

KETTLE INCLUSION PATTERNS AT BURIAL SITES

Most of the copper-kettle burial sites recorded in Mi'kmaq territory in Nova Scotia and New Brunswick are known because they were unearthed in the late 1800s and early 1900s by landowners and interested locals or through accidental discovery; the unsystematic nature of these explorations has left a somewhat sketchy archaeological record of these sites (Whitehead 1993).[2] The extant evidence does suggest that kettles were included in Mi'kmaq copper-kettle burials in two ways: (1) as whole or partial kettles that were damaged, sometimes extensively, and (2) as intact kettles with little to no damage (Harper 1956, 1957; Martin 1975; Smith 1886; Whitehead 1993).

The best-recorded copper-kettle burial complex in the Maritimes comes from the Hopps or Pictou site in Nova Scotia, dug and published by local

TABLE 3.1. Summary of distribution of kettle/kettle-derived objects at Hopps site. Table derived from Harper 1956:appendix A, 1957. Note, Burial Pit 1 was dug in two sections in 1955 and Burial Pit 2 was dug in three strata in 1956.

Hopps (Pictou) site (ca. AD 1550–1630)

Burial Pit #	Section or Stratum	Whole Kettle	Kettle-Derived Object	Kettle/Kettle Object Description
1	1	YES	NO	3 intact inverted kettles; beneath each a black humus layer with human bones, including skull parts
1	2	YES	NO	4 inverted, crushed kettles; one lay over black humus layer (but with no bones)
2	Lowest Stratum	YES	YES	3 to 4 bodies lay on grave floor lined with kettle-derived copper sheeting 10 inverted, crushed kettles scattered throughout stratum (but not in contact with human bones)
2	Second Stratum	YES	NO	2 inverted copper kettles; one lay over human skull parts and several long bone fragments; the other lay over black humus layer (but with no bones)
2	Third Stratum	NO	NO	Ash layer from fire, no goods or bodies

teacher and avocational archaeologist J. Russell Harper (Harper 1956:appendix A, 1957 [see figure 3.1 for site location]). While this is the best recorded of the copper-kettle burials, the excavations occurred over only a few days and their expedient nature must be taken into account. Also, excavation focused only on burials and grave goods; there is no information about the nature or distribution of non-burial activities at the site. Excavations identified two burial pits. Although no age/sex data are available from the interments, both burial pits included numerous kettles and kettle-derived objects. The deposits contained both damaged and intact kettles. Table 3.1 provides a summary of kettle and kettle-derived object distribution in these two pits.

In what Harper designated as Section 1 of Burial Pit 1, three intact copper kettles were "placed with their bottoms upward" (inverted) on a painted animal skin, and beneath each kettle was a black layer of decayed organic material that contained human remains, including skull parts (Harper 1956:40–41; see table 3.1). Section 2 of Burial Pit 1 had six kettles, all of which were mutilated and inverted. Only one had a black layer under it. For the most part, these damaged kettles were not in contact with human remains (Harper 1956:42; see table 3.1).

In Burial Pit 2, Harper identified three distinct strata (Harper 1957:13). The lowest, or first, stratum was found to be lined with deconstructed kettle sheet metal and birch bark. It contained skeletal remains of three or four people and a compact mass of grave goods (Harper 1957:14; see table 3.1). This mass of grave goods included eight copper kettles that were inverted and "crushed or completely smashed" (Harper 1957:14; see table 3.1). In the second stratum were two inverted, intact copper kettles that both covered human remains and kept the earthen fill of the grave from touching the human remains (Harper 1957:16; see table 3.1). The uppermost, or third, stratum had the remains of two fires (Harper 1957:16).

A number of discrete patterns to the inclusion of kettles are apparent from these two burial pits. First, all kettles, whether intact or damaged, were inverted. Of the five intact whole kettles recovered across the two burial pits, four were inverted over human bones and one may have been (table 3.1). Of the fourteen damaged kettles recovered across the two burial pits, thirteen were not in contact with human remains (table 3.1). It appears that damaged kettles were kept out of contact with human remains while intact kettles were placed purposefully in direct contact with the bodies, including over the skull in one case (Burial Pit 1) (table 3.1).

A review of less well-recorded copper-kettle burial sites in the Maritimes confirms that both intact and damaged kettles were included in burials and that the practice of inverting kettles was common. These other burial finds also show a similar pattern of placing intact kettles in direct contact with bodies and damaged ones away from any human remains, although poor archaeological recording renders it hard to make conclusive determinations. For instance, at one copper-kettle burial recovered in the late 1800s on the Tabusintac River in New Brunswick, multiple undamaged kettles were found and recorded as "bottom up" and placed over human remains (Smith 1886:14–15); details beyond that are not provided. Another burial locale, known only from the description of the landowner in the 1930s, was said to have washed out of the Salmon River in Nova Scotia with a copper kettle overturned on the skull of a male burial, but there is little other information (Whitehead 1993:29). At the Northport site in Nova Scotia, a burial was accidentally discovered in the 1970s eroding out of a bank on private property, and four kettles were found inverted over a flexed inhumation burial (Whitehead 1993:41). Analysis of these kettles found the largest to be undamaged and the three smaller ones to have been cut and crushed (Whitehead 1993:45). Where each kettle was located specifically in relation to the body is not provided in site records, as the burial was found already eroding out of its original location. It seems reasonable to infer that the largest kettle, which is undamaged, was over the body while the other, smaller kettles, all damaged, were associated grave goods not in contact with the human remains, but there are not enough details to confirm such patterning.

LIVING KETTLES, DEAD KETTLES

Father Le Clercq, a missionary to the Mi'kmaq on the Gaspe Peninsula in the mid-seventeenth century, was told that kettles were included with a recently deceased individual to "bear him company and do him service in the Land of the Souls" (Le Clercq 1910 [1691]:302–3). Kettles could bear humans company because the Mi'kmaq had extended their foundational cosmology to include kettles during the early contact period. Kettles were living, animate beings; they possessed a life force, or "soul," and conditions for personhood (Zedeño 2008:363).

The complex animate life (and afterlife) of kettles is illuminated further in an exchange between a group of Mi'kmaq and Jesuits recorded by Nicolas Denys (1908 [1672]), a French aristocrat who became an explorer, colonizer, politician, and chronicler in Acadia from 1632 to 1672. Denys reported that the French disliked the fact that the Mi'kmaq put so many trade goods, especially kettles, in their burials and that they very much wanted to "disabuse" the Mi'kmaq of this practice. In one effort to dissuade this practice, the Jesuits (whom the Mi'kmaq often referred to as the robes) forced a group of Mi'kmaq to open a grave so they could show them how wasteful it was to place goods, including kettles, in burials. Denys relays the following response from the Mi'kmaq when they saw the many decayed burial goods items:

> There was there among other things a kettle, all perforated with verdigris. An Indian having struck against it and found that it no longer sounded, began to make a great cry, and said that some one wished to deceive them. "We see indeed," said he "the robes and all the rest, and if they are still there it is a sign that the dead man has not had need of them in the other world where they have enough of them because of the length of time that they have been furnished them. But with respect to the kettle," said he "they have need of it since it is among us a utensil of new introduction, and with which the other world cannot yet be furnished. Do you not indeed see," said he, rapping again upon the kettle, "that it has no longer any sound, and that it no longer says a word, because its spirit has abandoned it to go to be of use in the other world and to the dead man to whom we have given it?" (Denys 1908 [1672]:440).

One of the things this scene helps us understand is why some kettles were mutilated before their inclusion in burials. Damaging kettles by cutting and smashing them would have ruined their ability to make sound. In this scene, we see that if a kettle no longer makes a sound, its spirit has been released; it is only through this release that the deceased can be provided with this spirit of the kettle for use in the afterlife (Martin 1975:116). Such mutilation of kettles prior to inclusion in burials reflects, then, their ceremonial slaying. This treatment of kettles among the Mi'kmaq aligns with what Pauketat (2013:33–34) has suggested was important across much of Native North America: that "the qualities of things engage the senses, sight, sound, smell, taste, touch in ways that lend them agentic or transformative powers" and that "such things may have been understood by indigenous people as Witnesses, imbued with power and able to connect the living to the gods."

Another key aspect of this vignette is that the Mi'kmaq man concluded that the kettle was needed in the afterlife by the deceased more than were the other grave goods because the kettle was newly introduced in the world of the living and therefore the afterworld did not yet have it. By concluding that the afterworld was not yet furnished with European-made kettles, the man indicated clearly that the Mi'kmaq, even as they were engaged in the process of becoming "New World People" with an identity that involved Europeans, nevertheless still understood the afterworld to be an *exclusively* Mi'kmaq place. As kettles were slain and included in burials, these Mi'kmaq relations were freed to cross over from the living world to the exclusively Mi'kmaq afterworld, becoming present in the fundamentally Mi'kmaq next life.

While the afterworld was envisioned as free of colonial presence, the inclusion of undamaged kettles in physical contact with Mi'kmaq bodies was done to prepare the afterworld in case of future colonial encroachment. Through intimate contact with whole kettles, the irreproducibility of kettles and their origin with Europeans was transcended. What had been the foreign-derived statutory and symbolic power of kettles in this life was relayed directly through the act of physical contact to the Mi'kmaq dead for the next life. I suggest that these undamaged kettles had to remain alive (intact) to transfer their life force to the Mi'kmaq dead; the European-origin power transferred through this contact would remain with the Mi'kmaq in the afterworld even as they left Europeans themselves behind. Unlike the experience of early colonial encounters during the Protohistoric period in their earthly life, then, in this afterlife the Mi'kmaq would already have with them European-origin knowledge and power as a resource to protect them from future breaches of their indigenous space. This explains, I suggest, why we see such a protective placement of intact kettles—directly on the bodies and often covering the heads of the dead, shielding them in the transference and crossing over.

INVERTED WORLDS, INVERTED KETTLES

As noted, despite the unreliable nature of the archaeological recording of the copper-kettle burial sites, a striking commonality is that when kettles were included in burials (both damaged and undamaged) they were inverted rather than upright in their "normal" or "usable" position. For many societies, death reflects an inversion of the living world. Among the Mi'kmaq during early contact, death as an inversion may explain in part the inversion of kettles in graves. However, there were added layers of meaning to the inversion of kettles at a time when the world of the living for the Mi'kmaq was also being inverted before their eyes by Europeans—the very people who brought with them not only copper kettles but also deadly diseases. As mentioned, Mi'kmaq population losses were rapid and substantial in the Protohistoric period. The massive rate of loss certainly inverted their world, but the real thrust of the inversion, I suggest, came from the death patterns of these losses: it was Mi'kmaq leaders who interacted with colonists as well as children who experienced disproportionate rates of death from European diseases (Hornborg 2008:6). During early contact across the region, children formed roughly 70 percent of burials (Petersen et al. 2004).

With children dying at such fast rates in the sixteenth and early seventeenth centuries, the Mi'kmaq world was literally being "placed bottoms upward"; the normal cycle of life, death, and generational turnover was wholly upended during early contact. Moreover, community leaders were no longer present in this "New World" to help navigate the grief as well as the practical implications of this demographic crisis.

Kettles only work as cooking pots if they are upright; inverting them eradicates the utilitarian function instilled in them by Europeans. I suggest that when the Mi'kmaq inverted the kettles they included with their dead, they were furthering the transformation of kettles from European goods into their own relations. The Mi'kmaq encountered kettles in the "New World" during the early colonial period, but they did not activate them as other-than-human relations for assistance in this context; rather, they incorporated them into *msit no'kmaq* to accompany, protect, and serve their leaders and, more solemnly, their children, their next generation, now in the next world.

Aspects of Mi'kmaq mythology provide added salience to kettles' inclusion in Protohistoric burials. In particular, the departure narrative of Kluskap[3] provides important evidence for understanding kettles as animate other-than-human Mi'kmaq relations emergent within the social alterity of early colonial encounters. Kluskap is a multifaceted figure in Mi'kmaq cosmology. He is an essential culture hero and archetype of virtuous human life for the Mi'kmaq (Robinson 2014:674). In the Mi'kmaq creation story Kluskap is not the creator but the fourth level of creation, after the act of creation itself, the creation of the Sun, and the creation of Mother Earth; he is the "First One Who Spoke" (Augustine 2014:27). Chief Stephen Augustine, recalling the version of Kluksap's creation he heard from his grandmother, shares that "he is created from a bolt of lightning that hits the surface of Mother Earth. He is made of the elements of the earth: feathers and bone and skin and dirt and grass and sand and pebbles and water. An eagle comes to Kluskap with a message from the Giver of Life, Grandfather Sun and Mother Earth. The eagle tells Kluskap that he will be joined by his family, who will help him understand his place in this world" (Augustine 2014:27). His grandmother, nephew, and mother then arrive; "as each member of his family arrives, Kluskap asks his fellow beings—the animals, the fish, and the plants—to sustain the Mi'kmaq peoples" (Augustine 2014:28).

Kluskap holds an incredibly complicated position in Mi'kmaq religious belief systems, and he can even appear contradictory at times, as both hero and trickster (for more on Kluskap, see Reid 2013). There are, however, consistencies in his prominence across Mi'kmaq myths: Kluskap, as seen in the story of his creation shared by Chief Augustine, played a key role in the creation of the Mi'kmaq world and helped situate the Mi'kmaq as harvesters of that world (Reid 2013:34). Also, in various myths Kluskap prophesizes the coming of Europeans; he is the figure in Mi'kmaq cosmology who gives primordial meaning to colonial contact (Reid 2013:34). Yet it was colonial contact that drove this foundational figure to depart from the Mi'kmaq world. While there are variants to the myth of his departure, in general these myths see Kluskap grow dissatisfied with the colonists: "He was not able to cope with the white invaders who came into his domain" (Reid 2013:18). He tells the Mi'kmaq: "I am going to leave you. I am going to a place where I can never be reached by a white man" (Reid 2013:18). He then turns his kettle upside down and departs. His inverted kettle becomes an island; the Mi'kmaq continue to call this island Ooteomul, meaning Kluskap's Kettle, which is in Nova Scotia and today is called Spencer's Island (see figure 3.1) (Hornborg 2008:84). Figure 3.3

FIGURE 3.3. *Photograph of Ooteomul (see figure 3.1 for this island's geographic location). Photograph from Property #1 on Flickr Creative Commons: https://www.flickr.com/ photos/manager_2000/4854193299/in/photolist-asSfWq-asPCXn-asPBJK-7DTrd9-4X W2No-8p1dis-8BJTaa-8BMYnG-8BJTzB-8p1cAL-97So9u-8BJUcB-8BJTYX-8BJSHF -8oX1xV-6Uxbzj-prpZcQ-6Ut8FT-6ML4ev-6MQgu9-549MYd-5gdCgK-7DTrco-7DPA sX-7DPAtB.*

provides a photograph of this island, which shows its remarkable similarities with an overturned trade kettle.

What Kluskap is described as doing before leaving the Mi'kmaq is what we see occurring repeatedly in early colonial Mi'kmaq burials—he inverts a kettle and eradicates its utilitarian, European function. Inverted kettles in burials offered a re-inversion of the Mi'kmaq world in the next one—and that world would be, just as Kluskap himself was, viscerally Mi'kmaq both before and after Europeans. The fact that Kluskap inverts his kettle before being able to go to a place where he "can never be reached by a white man" reaffirms how even as the Mi'kmaq adapted to the context of contact with Europeans, they still envisioned and actively planned for an exclusively indigenous afterworld.

Kettles—ceremonially mutilated, purposefully left whole, and inverted— came to fill a role no other object could for the Mi'kmaq: the ability to create an afterworld that was both exclusively indigenous but knowledgeable about and prepared for Europeans. The multifaceted ways kettles were incorporated in burials addressed the impossible but necessary task of mimesis that often occurs in the face of the social alterity of colonialism (as described by Taussig 1993)—of being at once same and alter, being fundamentally indigenous yet actively prepared for colonial encroachment.

With Kluskap's inverted kettle turning into the island Ooteomul, the kettle, this irreproducible European-origin object, became primordially linked to the Mi'kmaq homelands (figure 3.3). Such tethering of myth to the physical landscape is an essential practice among many non-Western indigenous societies, wherein the physical landscape is not a backdrop for life but rather it and its varied features are "continually woven into the fabric of social life" (Basso 1996:110). Kluskap's journey, his continued presence in Mi'kmaq traditions, and his gifting of the kettle back from Europeans to the Mi'kmaq homeland all form an important part of the Mi'kmaq's creation and maintenance of their "symbolically interactive, topographically bounded, aesthetically effective, and meaningfully holistic landscape" (Dillehay 2007:318).

The primordial kettle inversion by Kluskap and its transformation into a piece of homeland further emphasizes the complicated biography of kettles. Kettles acquired significance in part because they connected to preexisting symbolic value systems around native copper, but they gained additional significance because of their European origin, form, and sensory qualities that could not be reproduced by the Mi'kmaq. Kettles, forming newly socialized goods that were not wholly indigenous and not wholly European, were prominently incorporated into Protohistoric burial practices wherein they were transformed fully into other-than-human Mi'kmaq relations responsible for bringing the Mi'kmaq to an afterworld free from colonialism but yet prepared for it. As kettles traveled with the Mi'kmaq to the next world, Kluskap's Kettle ensured that the Mi'kmaq remained always connected to the place where they in fact began—their Maritime homeland (figure 3.3).

CONCLUSION

Copper-kettle burials are a practice that emerged in the distinct context of the social alterity and liminality of early colonial encounters in the Maritimes during the sixteenth and early seventeenth centuries. During this period the Mi'kmaq had to grapple with the reality of being increasingly entrenched in a colonial world, but this could not negate the notion of humanity contained in being Mi'kmaq (Reid 1995:89). We can understand this complex duality of alterity expressed in the multifaceted inclusion of kettles in their burials. The Mi'kmaq extended their long-established relational ontology, one based on a world imbued with sentient life and encompassing relatedness, to these irre-producible European-origin goods. In doing this, the Mi'kmaq transformed kettles into objects that disavowed colonial reality and replaced it with the materialization of indigenous desires (Bhabha 2004 [1994]:130).

For the Mi'kmaq, kettles became relatives who could help them achieve their desire for a next world free from but fully prepared for colonial encroachment (both same and alter). Yet the Kluskap myth suggests that the next world was, in fact, back where they began, where Kluskap inverted his original kettle, tethering the Mi'kmaq to their place of origin and tying them deeply to their homeland. Looking again at this island as shown in figure 3.3, the fusion of topography, homeland, toponym, cosmology, and, ultimately, Mi'kmaq survivance is both undeniable and compelling. As explicated by Ojibwe scholar Gerald Vizenor (1998:15), survivance, "in the sense of native survivance, is more than survival, more than endurance or mere response; the stories of survivance are an active presence." During the Protohistoric period, kettles as *msit no'kmaq* were part of this active presence for the Mi'kmaq; they were other-than-human agents that helped the Mi'kmaq go forward in the return to a world of their own.

The practice of including copious amounts of grave goods, especially items supplied to the Mi'kmaq through trade, such as kettles, agitated colonial Europeans because it clashed with their market-based understanding of how to value and use material goods and conflicted with their Christian beliefs about burials and the afterlife; together, this undermined their sense of reality and order. Indeed, there were "few Indian customs which exercised the French as much as this one did" (Martin 1975:114). But since the inclusion of kettles in graves actually contributed to the demand for kettles in trade, Europeans overlooked this practice from a practical standpoint during the early colonial encounter, even though it clashed with their worldview (Martin 1975; Turgeon 1997). Nicolas Denys, whose account I referenced above, explains further that while the French often wanted to remove items from the Mi'kmaq graves that they thought were wasted, they never dared to do so, "for this would have caused hatred and everlasting war, which it was not prudent to risk since it would have ruined entirely the trade we had with them" (Denys 1908 [1672]:439).

The concept of other-than-human agency can seem beyond the mate-rial, making it feel hard to approach in archaeological frameworks. This and the other case studies presented in this volume are aimed at transcending this sense of limitation and helping us understand that nonhuman relations have significant potential to transform material realities. In the case of the Mi'kmaq, they were willing to engage the French in everlasting war if the lat-ter disturbed the kettles included in burials; not respecting the material reality and physical presence of nonhuman relations carried significant ramifications. While the French failed to understand Mi'kmaq reasoning, they nevertheless were compelled to recognize the relational ontology of the Mi'kmaq to avoid war and maintain trade relations. Kettles as relations who assisted the dead in the afterworld formed an ontological perspective that effectively drove the emergent, materially based market economy of the sixteenth- and early seventeenth-century Maritimes.

As suggested by this case study, other-than-human agency is not an abstract concept; it has clear material components, both in terms of the essential import of the materiality of the objects endowed with this agency and in the ways this agency can impact and even direct key cultural institutions, such as the economy. This may be especially powerful and clear in cases of colonial encounter. In these spaces, people are drawn into alterity and so confronted with the "impossible but necessary, indeed everyday affair" of having to "register both sameness and difference, of being like and of being Other" (Taussig 1993:129). Here, as communities grapple with myriad previously un-experienced human and nonhuman agents, they turn to these foreign goods and transform them into new relations capable of creating the subjectivities necessary to navigate the impossibly incongruent but unavoidable tasks of alterity. Recognizing other-than-human relations in past societies does not require us to leave the material. Rather, the material is imbued deeply in these relations, and conducting archaeologies that recognize them will ultimately provide more robust pictures of past social, economic, and ideological developments.

NOTES

1. The French sometimes called the Maliseet "Étchemins," likely a reference to their canoe skills on the St. John River. This term also encompasses the Passamaquoddy of Maine.

2. I do not include any pictures of the bodies or goods from sites to respect the fact that they have largely been repatriated.

3. Kluskap has various spellings, including Glooscap and Gluscabe.

REFERENCES CITED

Alberti, Benjamin, and Tamara L. Bray. 2009. "Introduction to Special Section Animating Archaeology: Of Subjects, Objects, and Alternative Ontologies." *Cambridge Archaeological Journal* 19 (3): 337–43. https://doi.org/10.1017/S095977430 9000523.

Augustine, Chief Stephen. 2014. "Mi'kmaq Creation Story." In *Dawnland Voices: An Anthology of Indigenous Writing from New England,* ed. Siobhan Senier (Mi'kmaq section ed. Jamie Battiste), 27–28. Lincoln: University of Nebraska Press. https://doi.org/10.2307/j.ctt1dgnjj2.6.

Basso, Keith H. 1996. *Wisdom Sits in Places: Landscape and Language among the Western Apache.* Albuquerque: University of New Mexico Press.

Bhabha, Homi K. 2004 [1994]. *The Location of Culture,* 2nd ed. London: Routledge.

Bourque, Bruce J., and Ruth H. Whitehead. 1985. "Tarrentines and the Introduction of European Trade Goods in the Gulf of Maine." *Ethnohistory* 32 (4): 327–41. https://doi.org/10.2307/481893.

Bradley, James W. 1987. *Evolution of the Onondaga Iroquois: Accommodating Change, 1500–1655.* Syracuse: Syracuse University Press.

Brenner, Elise M. 1988. "Sociopolitical Implications of Mortuary Ritual Remains in 17th-Century Native Southern New England." In *The Recovery of Meaning: Historical Archaeology in the Eastern United States,* ed. Mark Leone and Parker Potter, 147–82. Washington, DC: Smithsonian Institution Press.

Brooks, Lisa T., and Cassandra M. Brooks. 2010. "The Reciprocity Principle and Traditional Ecological Knowledge: Understanding the Significance of Indigenous Protest on the Presumpscot River." *International Journal of Critical Indigenous Studies* 3: 11–28.

Brown, Linda A., and William H. Walker. 2008. "Prologue: Archaeology, Animism, and Non-Human Agents." *Journal of Archaeological Method and Theory* 15 (4): 297–99. https://doi.org/10.1007/s10816-008-9056-6.

Childs, Terry S. 1994. "Native Copper Technology and Society in Eastern North America." In *Archaeometry of Pre-Columbian Sites and Artifacts,* ed. David Scott and Pieter Meyers, 229–53. Los Angeles: Getty Conservation Institute.

Crosby, Constance. 1988. "From Myth to History, or Why King Philip's Ghost Walks Abroad." In *The Recovery of Meaning: Historical Archaeology in the Eastern United States,* ed. Mark Leone and Parker Potter, 183–210. Washington, DC: Smithsonian Institution Press.

Denys, Nicolas. 1908 [1672]. *Description géographique et historique des costes de l'Amérique septentrionale: avec l'histoire naturelle du païs.* Toronto: Champlain Society.

Dillehay, Tom. 2007. *Monuments, Empires, and Resistance: The Araucanian Polity and Ritual Narratives.* Cambridge: Cambridge University Press. https://doi.org/10.1017/CBO9780511499715.

Ehrhardt, Kathleen L. 2005. *European Metals in Native Hands: Rethinking the Dynamics of Technological Change 1640–1683.* Tuscaloosa: University of Alabama Press.

Fitzgerald, William R., Laurier Turgeon, Ruth Holmes Whitehead, and James W. Bradley. 1993. "Late Sixteenth Century Basque Banded Copper Kettles." *Historical Archaeology* 27 (1): 44–57. https://doi.org/10.1007/BF03373558.

Gibson, Susan G. 1980. "Introduction." In *Burr's Hill: A 17th Century Wampanoag Burial Ground in Warren, Rhode Island*, ed. Susan G. Gibson, 9–24. Providence, RI: Haffenreffer Museum of Anthropology, Brown University.

Gosden, Chris. 2004. *Archaeology and Colonialism: Cultural Contact from 5000 BC to the Present*. Cambridge: Cambridge University Press.

Groce, Nina. 1980. "Ornaments of Metal: Rings, Medallions, Combs, Beads, and Pendants." In *Burr's Hill: A 17th Century Wampanoag Burial Ground in Warren, Rhode Island*, ed. Susan G. Gibson, 108–17. Providence, RI: Haffenreffer Museum of Anthropology, Brown University.

Hamell, George R. 1983. "Trading in Metaphors: The Magic of Beads, Another Perspective upon Indian-European Contact in Northeastern North America." In *Proceedings of the 1982 Glass Trade Bead Conference*, ed. Charles Hayes, 5–28. Rochester, NY: Rochester Museum and Science Center.

Harper, J. Russell. 1956. *Portland Point, Crossroads of New Brunswick History*, appendix A. Historical Studies 9. Saint John, NB: New Brunswick Museum.

Harper, J. Russell. 1957. "Two Seventeenth Century Micmac 'Copper-Kettle' Burials." *Anthropologica* 4: 11–36.

Hornborg, Anne-Christine. 2008. *Mi'kmaq Landscapes: From Animism to Sacred Ecology*. Hampshire, UK: Ashgate.

Howey, Meghan C.L. 2011. "Colonial Encounters, European Kettles, and the Magic of Mimesis in the Late Sixteenth and Early Seventeenth Century Indigenous Northeast and Great Lakes." *International Journal of Historical Archaeology* 15 (3): 329–57. https://doi.org/10.1007/s10761-011-0145-y.

Innis, Harold A. 1940. *The Cod Fisheries: The History of an International Economy*. New Haven, CT: Yale University Press.

Joyce, Rosemary A. 2014. "Comments on 'Indigenous People and Foreign Things: Archaeologies of Consumption in the Americas.'" Paper presented at the Society for American Archaeology Annual Meetings, Austin, TX, April.

Kurlansky, Mark. 1997. *Cod: A Biography of the Fish That Changes the World*. New York: Walker and Company.

Le Clercq, Chrestien. 1910 [1691]. *New Relation of Gaspesia: With Customs and Religion of the Gaspesian Indians*. Toronto: Champlain Society.

Loren, Diana. 2013. "Considering Mimicry and Hybridity in Early Colonial New England: Health, Sin and the Body 'Behunc with Beades.'" *Archaeological Review from Cambridge* 28: 151–68.

Martin, Calvin L. 1975. "The Four Lives of a Micmac Copper Pot." *Ethnohistory* 22 (2): 111–33. https://doi.org/10.2307/481641.

Miller, Christopher L., and George R. Hamell. 1986. "A New Perspective on Indian-White Contact: Cultural Symbols and Colonial Trade." *Journal of American History* 73 (2): 311–28. https://doi.org/10.2307/1908224.

Miller, Daniel. 2005. "Consumption Studies as the Transformation of Anthropology." In *Acknowledging Consumption: A Review of New Studies*, ed. Daniel Miller, 263–92. London: Routledge.

Mullins, Paul R. 2011. "The Archaeology of Consumption." *Annual Review of Anthropology* 40 (1): 133–44. https://doi.org/10.1146/annurev-anthro-081309 -145746.

Pauketat, Timothy R. 2013. *An Archaeology of the Cosmos: Rethinking Agency and Religion in Ancient America*. London: Routledge.

Paul, Daniel N. 2000. *We Were Not the Savages: A Mi'kmaq Perspective on the Collision between European and Native American Civilizations: New Twenty First Century Edition*. Nova Scotia: Fernwood.

Petersen, James B., Malinda Blustain, and James W. Bradley. 2004. "'Mawooshen' Revisited: Two Native American Contact Period Sites on the Central Maine Coast." *Archaeology of Eastern North America* 32: 1–71.

Prins, Harald. 2002. *The Mi'Kmaq: Resistance, Accommodation, and Cultural Survival*. Belmont, CA: Wadsworth Group.

Reid, Jennifer. 1995. *Myth, Symbol, and Colonial Encounter: British and Mi'kmaq in Acadia, 1700–1867*. Ottawa: University of Ottawa Press. https://doi.org/10.26530 /OAPEN_578767.

Reid, Jennifer. 2013. *Finding Kluskap: A Journey into Mi'Kmaw Myth*. University Park: Pennsylvania State University Press.

Roberts, Callum. 2007. *The Unnatural History of the Sea*. Washington, DC: Island.

Robinson, Margaret. 2014. "Animal Personhood in Mi'kmaq Perspective." *Societies* 4 (4): 672–88. https://doi.org/10.3390/soc4040672.

Rubertone, Patricia E. 1989. "Archaeology, Colonialism, and 17th Century Native America: Towards an Alternative Interpretation." In *Conflict in the Archaeology of Living Traditions*, ed. Robert H. Layton, 32–45. London: Routledge.

Salisbury, Neal. 1996. "The Indians' Old World: Native Americans and the Coming of Europeans." *William and Mary Quarterly* 53 (3): 435–58. https://doi.org/10 .2307/2947200.

Smith, A. C. 1886. "On Prehistoric Remains and on an Interment of the Early French Period at Tabusintac." *Bulletin of the Natural History Society of New Brunswick* 5: 14–20.

Swenson, Edward R. 2015. "The Materialities of Place-Making in the Ancient Andes: A Critical Appraisal of the Ontological Turn in Archaeological Interpretation." *Journal of Archaeological Method and Theory* 22 (3): 677–712. https://doi.org/10.1007/s10816-014-9202-2.

Taussig, Michael. 1993. *Mimesis and Alterity: A Particular History of the Senses.* London: Routledge.

Trigger, Bruce G. 1987. *The Children of Aataentsic: A History of the Huron People to 1660.* Montreal: McGill-Queen's University Press.

Turgeon, Laurier. 1997. "The Tale of the Kettle: Odyssey of an Intercultural Object." *Ethnohistory* 44 (1): 1–29. https://doi.org/10.2307/482899.

van Dongen, Alexandra. 1996. *One Man's Trash Is Another Man's Treasure: The Metamorphosis of the European Utensil in the New World.* Rotterdam: Museum Boymans-van Beuningen.

Vizenor, Gerald R. 1998. *Fugitive Poses: Native American Indian Scenes of Absence and Presence.* Lincoln: University of Nebraska Press.

Wagner, Mark J. 1998. "Some Think It Impossible to Civilize Them at All: Cultural Change and Continuity among the Early Nineteenth-Century Potawatomi." In *Studies in Culture Contact: Interaction, Culture Change, and Archaeology*, ed. James Cusik, 430–56. Occasional Paper 25. Carbondale: Center for Archaeological Investigations, Southern Illinois University.

White, Bruce M. 1999. "The Woman Who Married a Beaver: Trade Patterns and Gender Roles in the Ojibwa Fur Trade." *Ethnohistory* 46: 109–47.

Whitehead, Ruth H. 1993. *Nova Scotia: The Protohistoric Period 1500–1630.* Curatorial Report 75. Halifax: Nova Scotia Museum.

Zedeño, Maria Nieves. 2008. "Bundled Worlds: The Roles and Interactions of Complex Objects from the North American Plains." *Journal of Archaeological Method and Theory* 15 (4): 362–78. https://doi.org/10.1007/s10816-008-9058-4.

4

Water and Shells in
Bodies and Pots

Mississippian Rhizome,
Cahokian Poiesis

Timothy R. Pauketat
and Susan M. Alt

Never doubt that a small group of thoughtful,
committed citizens can change the world.
Indeed, it is the only thing that ever has.

—Margaret Mead, uncertain source

Humans arose . . . as a fortuitous and
contingent outcome of thousands of linked
events, any one of which could have occurred
differently and sent history on an alternative
pathway.

—Stephen Jay Gould, "The Evolution of
Life on the Earth" *Scientific American*

Understanding human history is about locating the
power to change the world. Before the 2000s, historians, anthropologists, and archaeologists working from
anthropocentric points of view located that power as
human intentionality, much as does Mead, above. She
was not necessarily wrong, but such strict anthropocentrism has faded as considerations of corporeality
and materiality have shown that the human mind
is not a self-contained entity and that agency is not
solely a human attribute (Dobres 2000; Latour 1993;
Malafouris 2013; Meskell 2004; Mills and Walker 2008).

More recently, post-humanist, ontological perspectives have led us to the conclusion that ultimately, the
power to alter webs of relationships derives not *from*
people (or even from other organisms, places, things,
or other relational "nodes") but *from the relations*

DOI: 10.5876/9781607327479.c004

themselves. Relations are those physical properties, experiential qualities, and other flows or movements of substances, materials, and phenomena that become attached to, entangled, or associated with others and, in the process, define not only people but other organisms, things, places, and the like (Ingold 2007). Indeed, entire relational fields—worlds—are always in motion and subject to reconfigurations. Some reconfigurations seem radical, as in small groups of committed citizens changing the world. Others seem less radical, as noted by Gould, above, and appear contingent on thousands of linked events. Should we give precedence to one over the other when seeking to understand human history? We think not.

The two approaches to human history, Mead's and Gould's, are, in fact, compatible using a relational perspective. To show how, we employ Gilles Deleuze and Felix Guattari's concepts of "rhizome" and "territorialization" (Deleuze and Guattari 1987). We apply these paired concepts to the remarkable case of Mississippian culture (figure 4.1), which seemingly appeared and spread across a large portion of continental North America starting a thousand years ago. We focus on regions around greater Cahokia (Pauketat 2004) and begin by returning to the original taxonomic definition of Mississippian as a "way of life" that involved people who made shell-tempered pottery, grew maize crops in the bottomlands of major rivers, and built flat-topped earthen mounds (Griffin 1952, 1967). There was something intuitively right about that definition, though since the 1970s it has been relegated to a historical footnote by researchers seeking the illusory organizations or mental templates that they believe structured "Mississippian societies" (as reviewed by Blitz 2010). As opposed to such reconstructions, our methodology will be genealogical. We will trace the movements and qualities of materials and infer relations (à la Baires 2016; Pauketat and Alt 2005; Weismantel and Meskell 2014), ranging from construction loads in pyramids, to sweating bodies in temples, to maize in pots, to the temper of those pots. We end up immersed in water, with implications for understanding the agency of substances and things and the genesis of Cahokia and other Mississippian places.

The result of our review is a blend of Meade's inspiring dictum on small groups of "committed citizens" and Gould's thoughts on "thousands of linked events." Both are necessary to understand widespread cultural developments and radical historical change. Yes, the historical changes with which we are concerned might be pinned in some ways on the rapid rise of an American Indian city, Cahokia, along the Mississippi River (Pauketat, Alt et al. 2015). However, our current interrogation turns on the deeper undercurrents of such sweeping moves. We conclude that the pervasive changes altering the flow

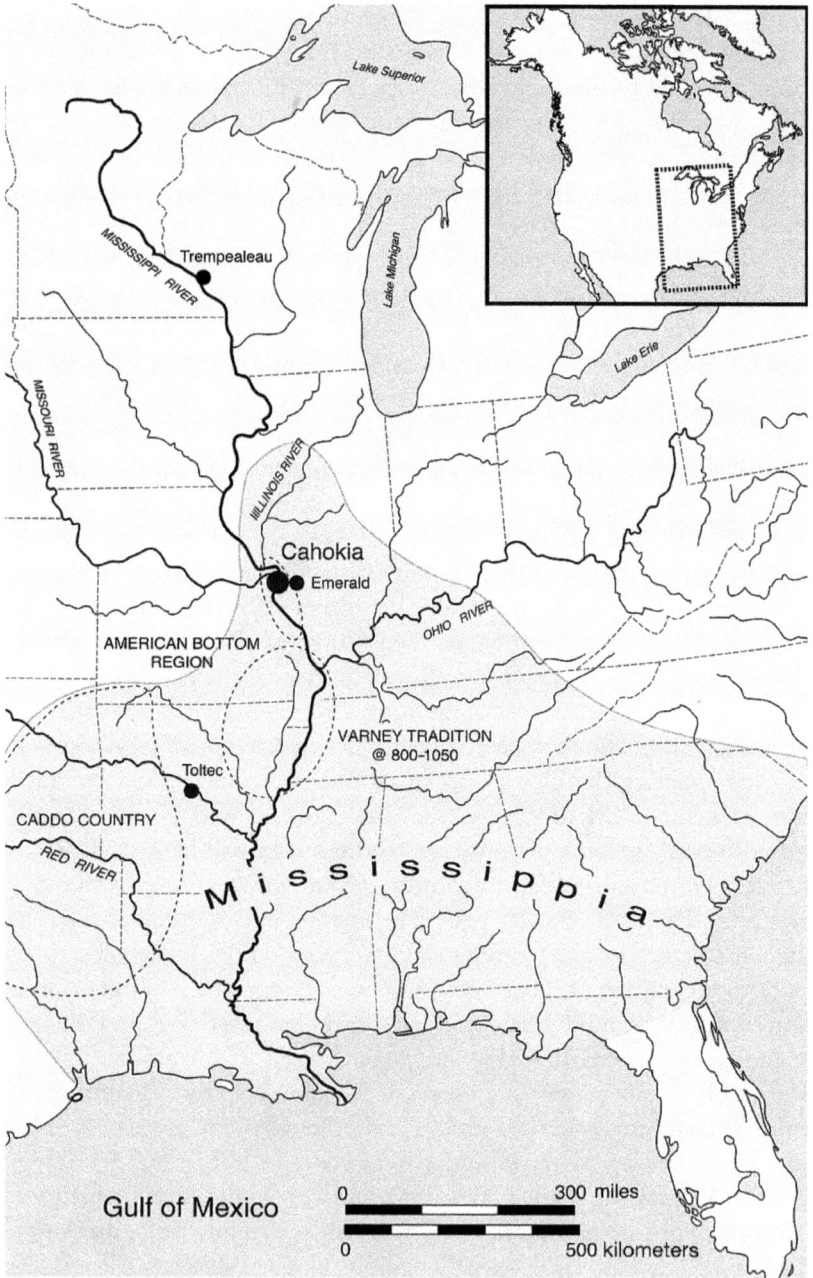

FIGURE 4.1. *Map showing locations of cultural complexes noted in text.*
Original by Timothy R. Pauketat.

of life—the Mississippianization of mid-continental and southeastern North Americans—were rhizomatic and afforded a more dramatic territorialization of relations once coordinated by people and cosmic forces at a higher scale. Whether some or all people intended at the beginning for this to happen seems both unlikely and beside the point.

BEING, BUNDLING, AND BOUNDING

Certainly, as cultural and biological beings, people subsist, make a living, change history, inscribe or incorporate memories, craft meanings, and construct landscapes that constrain their experience (e.g., Costin and Wright 1998; Dobres 2000; Dobres and Robb 2000; Tilley 2004; Van Dyke and Alcock 2003). In addition, people and other sentient beings engage many supposedly inanimate things, substances, materials, places, and phenomena as if they were animate, at least in moments. The reasons would seem to lie in the fact that such things always mediate social relations to some degree or in some moments, contingent on contexts and characteristics (Bennett 2010).

They also mediate nonhuman relations between and among inorganic and organic substances, materials, and phenomena of all kinds. For instance, the minerals in a would-be rock might crystalize to create a distinct entity owing to the reactions between or mediations of elements and chemicals. Similarly, a mountain peak mediates the sky's moist air to produce clouds and, later, rain that then erodes the slope and reshapes the peak. Water, in turn, becomes clouds, lakes, rivers, springs, rain, and snow as it is isolated in relation to other materials and phenomena. Water, of course, also allows a plant to grow and flower, the scent and color of which are bundled together such that they enchant the bee and mediate its flight and ultimately the success of both its colony and the flowering plant. Like the bees, all organisms grow and move because of the substantial and atmospheric affects of their worlds, but in so doing they mediate and reshape the relational configurations of their affective or social fields. In the process, beehives and other places come into existence through physical co-associations and entanglements of beings and matter, which may be replaced or displaced through time.

Foregrounding relations in this way led Timothy Ingold (2000, 2007) to reject Bruno Latour's (1993) notion of network, which for Ingold implied that agents (or actants) exist first. Instead, Ingold adapted a Deleuzian notion of rhizome or, as he calls it, "meshwork." The rhizome is an entangled non-hierarchical mass of relations that cannot be reduced to a singular, static entity since the relations are always in a state of becoming something (aka poiesis).

When the mass is bounded in some way, which is to say "territorialized," the becoming process produces a recognizable entity, a being, place, or thing.

Rhizomes, meshes, and meshworks connote more organic relational connections that emphasize the overall fabric of relations while deemphasizing the entanglements (aka knots, nodes, bundles, assemblages, and so on) that hold the strands of a mesh in place. Indeed, the rhizome—technically a root system that produces nodes (from which, in turn, emerge more roots)—can be more or less bounded or circumscribed across space or through time (see also Pauketat 2013c). Deleuze and Guattari (1987) call this process "territorialization," and it is the opposite of rhizomatization. Each tangle of rhizomatic roots and nodes, for instance, might constitute a relational field that, when territorialized, loses its open edges and potential to grow.

Territorializations can appear, at various points or thresholds, as moments of metamorphosis or poiesis, when one field of relations moves from one state of being or relating into another. The configuration of the resulting mass has properties (shape, density, durability, disposition, directionality, and the like) vis-à-vis the wider field of relations that then mediate the rate and scale of historical changes (Pauketat 2013b). Mediation here is virtually synonymous with agency, or the causal power to create and alter fields of relations. It is that which affords outcomes.

Such mediations are not abstract but affective and experiential. They have power—palpable agentic or affordant qualities. In some sense they might be proactive, confronting people and organisms with their very existence. They do this in part through the senses of the beings affected. For instance, fire transmogrifies that which is burned with obvious sensorial affects and potential historical effects. Features or properties of atmospheres or landscapes induce certain sensorial reactions or relations specifically in or with other materials, phenomena, and substances. These other materials, phenomena, and substances, in turn, along with organisms, have affects of their own. Animals, for instance, have affective qualities that might include odor, appearance, permeability, durability (lifespan), perceptive ability, and biomechanical or habitual modes of movement, among other things. Water from the sky or on the land moves on its own (with the help of gravity) and mixes with earth to produce mud, which, when mixed with temper and molded by human hands, can be hardened by fire to produce ceramic objects that play critical roles for people. Of course, organisms develop, move, reproduce, and mutate during their lifetimes, only then to die and decompose. Consider the mollusk, a locomotive being that lives in the mud and water and produces a durable shell as it develops by consuming microorganisms. Or consider the maize plant, which draws water and nutrients from the earth and grows skyward with the aid of the sun, rain, and human beings to finally produce nourishing grain. The people who would come to be called Mississippians traveled daily between water bodies and agricultural plots, relying intimately on both mollusks and maize for their energy and growth.

Descendants of Mississippians and other variably Mississippianized Woodland and Prairie-Plains people (see DeMallie 2001) actually named and discussed the animating power or life force that could inhabit or imbue people, organisms, places, things, and more, hence affirming the potential vitality of the web of life (Dorsey 1894; Hallowell 1960; Hewitt 1902; Radin 1914). They called it Wakanda, Orenda, Waruksti, or Manitou, depending on their cultural background. Especially revered—full of Wakanda, Orenda, Waruksti, or Manitou—were materials, substances, and phenomena with palpable power, energies, or bioactive properties. These included the sun, moon, stars, wind, water, earth, lightning, fire, smoke, corn, and tobacco. For example, the stars might be understood as ancestral beings that moved across or fell from the night sky (Hall 1997; Lankford 2007). Various objects, buildings, wooden posts, or other spaces might be ensouled or spiritually occupied from time to time. Sacred bundles—wrapped packages of "medicine" (which is to say, potentially animate and powerful things)—were recognized as social persons or even oracles with their own needs and perceptions that required the attentions of and consultations by human keepers and priests (Howard 1981; Murie 1981; Skinner 1913; Wissler 1912; Zedeño 2008).

As elaborated elsewhere, medicine bundles are especially good examples of how the animating life force of Native worlds was fluid, containable, and transferable (Pauketat 2013b). As concentrations, bundles were movements or transferences of the holy forces that in many cases were believed themselves to be living beings or persons. The otherwise dispersed life force(s) they contained or concentrated might be passed from the spirit realm to the human realm, concentrated or dispersed across the cosmos, and passed from human being to human being. Historically, these were carefully curated assemblages of powerful, elemental, and mnemonic objects or substances wrapped in animal skins or textiles, with each item—ranging from bones and stones to sacred tobacco and smoking pipes—articulating a set of larger personal, community, or tribal relations. The act of bundling, often prompted by dreams or visions of holy entities, was a concentration and hence an alteration of any relational field. It changed, rearranged, or reconfigured the potential relationships and mediators of such fields. The act of opening a bundle, especially particularly powerful community or tribal bundles, happened only as part of pre-planned ceremonial occasions—a transference of supernatural power through the bundled objects to the people. Bundle powers could be transferred from a person or people to another person (an apprentice) or people, if care was taken and preparations made to ensure no loss of power in the process.

Of course, medicine bundles are not the only kind of bundles that matter in our present considerations. We might think of any assemblage or entanglement of animate, agentic, or powerful people, places, things, substances, materials, or phenomena as a metaphorical bundle. Indeed, all territorializations of relations—assemblages of things, intersecting movements or entanglements in space, and recollections and embodiments of knowledge, history, or feelings—are bundles in this sense because people, places, things, substances, and phenomena always mediate relations to some degree. This is not to say that bundles were similarly and continuously animate or that they uniformly possessed agency. In fact, animacy, agency, or other mediating powers were clearly *not* fixed attributes of any one type of thing, kind of location, or even sort of human being. Moreover, agency was not the same thing as personhood, the latter a situational characteristic of particular assemblages or bundles of animate or affordant qualities that mediated social identity. The weaker or more elemental the mediation, as in the routine human engagements with earth or water, the more widely dispersed and impersonal (but pervasive) was the agency. The tighter or more densely and thickly entangled the mediations, as in the case of social persons such as a community leader or a medicine bundle, the more bounded and concentrated was the agency.

THE RAW MATERIALS OF MISSISSIPPIANIZATION

The point of such relational thinking is to contextualize the animacy and agency of discrete entities in their wider relational webs. Neither things nor people have agency by themselves. This may seem especially obvious with maize, shell-tempered pots, mounds, and sweat baths, none of which are possible without people. In fact, for some archaeologists, maize agriculture, mound building, sweating, or shell temper were not causal at all but are thought to have been the consequences of dietary, societal, or technological developments. These and other archaeologists assume that such things were the epiphenomenon of Mississippian societal transformations. Earthen pyramids, for instance, were said to passively "correlate" with hierarchical organizations (Peebles and Kus 1977). Likewise, the adoption and spread of maize was said to be a result of Mississippianism (Fritz 1992).

Seemingly, for such archaeologists the specificities of the assemblages of material culture mattered less than the Mississippian societies that assembled and distributed them far and wide (cf. Jennings 2010). However, a closer genealogical consideration of the distribution of maize, shell-tempered pots, and the practices of sweating and mound building suggests a more active and enmeshed role in the Mississippianization of people (see also Baires 2016). Maize, shell, sweat, and mud, mediated by water and fire, are the objects and substances that entangled and territorialized people.

To begin that genealogical consideration, we turn to the pre-Mississippian and early Mississippian world, centered on Cahokia, from about AD 900 to 1100. In particular, we seek to trace the potential relations among water, mollusks, corn, mud, and fire to judge how they mediated and territorialized social relations. Of the organisms (mollusks, corn plants, people), substances (water, mud), and phenomena (fire) to be considered here, all may have been in some sense responsible for the Cahokian poiesis, since all possessed some kind of power to mediate relations. That is, the swirl of affective qualities surrounding *water, mollusks, corn*, and *mud*, transmogrified by *fire*, gathered, reconfigured, and territorialized humanity to produce the Mississippians. To explain, let us work our way backward, beginning with the radical social transformation, also known as Cahokia's "Big Bang" at ca. AD 1050 ± 25, when the city of Cahokia was rebuilt and monumental earthen mounds, maize agriculture, pottery production, and other major developments appeared across the middle of the Mississippi River basin.

EARTH, FIRE, VAPORS, AND SWEAT

By the time the Medieval Warm period (AD 900–1300) had drawn to a close, the majority of the hundreds of thousands of so-called Mississippian people living in the American Midwest and Southeast, from the Carolina Piedmont into the Mississippi valley (see figure 4.1), tended agricultural fields of maize (along with squash, sunflowers, and local grasses). They cooked maize and other foods in homemade pottery jars tempered with crushed mussel shell. Some significant number of these people, in turn, at some point in their lives labored to construct flat-topped earthen pyramids. The highest concentration and largest of these mounds were built at Cahokia starting around AD 1050.

More than just an aggregation of earthen monuments populated by 10,000 or more people, early Cahokia assumes the characteristics of a "cosmic" city (Wheatley 1971). Sometime near AD 1050, workers dismantled, rebuilt, and significantly enlarged what had been a series of village-style habitation areas into an integrated monumental complex featuring three sprawling precincts, each with a monumental core (Pauketat, Alt et al. 2015). The principal precinct was Cahokia proper, which featured a "Grand Plaza" and 120 earthen pyramids, the largest the 30-m-high "Monks Mound," which fronts the great plaza (Fowler 1997). The central pyramids in a series of lesser groups were surrounded by neighborhood houses and public architecture, most of which were aligned to a 5-degree offset grid known to archaeologists as the "Cahokia grid" (Reed 1969; Smith 1969). An earthen causeway ran parallel to this grid alignment for a kilometer south from the plaza through a swampy zone to a mortuary area centered on Rattlesnake Mound (Baires 2014a, 2014b; Pauketat, Emerson et al. 2015). The 5-degree offset and the overall plan of the city reference celestial entities and their motions, especially those connected to the moon and, more than likely, the night, death, and ancestors (Pauketat 2013b; Romain 2015).

For laborers at the time, all earthen construction was a highly ritualized process that probably first entailed cleansing one's body in a ritual vapor, steam, or sweat bath. In fact, some of the circular pyramids at Cahokia, built after AD 1050, seem to have elevated circular rotundas, water temples, or small buildings commonly called "sweat lodges" or "steam baths" (Pauketat 1993; Pauketat et al. 1998:appendix). Excavations into the summit of the Emerald Acropolis, for example, an outlying shrine complex of Cahokia proper, revealed that as much as 10 percent of the late eleventh- and early twelfth-century buildings at that special site was of this circular variety (Alt and Pauketat 2015). These buildings included a small sweat-bath variety built for one to a few people. Near the middle of the sweat-bath floor was a hearth that, similar to historically known examples, would have been filled with red-hot rocks from which steam was produced when water was poured onto them from above. These and other larger rotundas are known at various "nodal" sites in the region as well as at Cahokia (Emerson 1997; Mehrer 1995). Several of the latter are up to 24 m in diameter, with large roof support posts (Pauketat 2005, 2013a). At least one medium-sized building appears to have been covered partially with earth (Pauketat 1993). Another large rotunda at Cahokia appears to have been ritually terminated and buried using a special mixture of yellow and black earth, inferred based on color photos from 1960 (Pauketat 2013a:82).

Across the Midwest and Plains centuries later, such buildings were similar in ways to spirit lodges, medicine lodges, and Midéwiwin "shaking tents." All were spaces where animate forces might engage people (e.g., Bucko 1998; Hallowell 1960; McCleary 2015). In a sweat bath, the spiritual force would include the rocks and the steam themselves (Hallowell 1960:43). The words of the Lakota priest Black Elk, describing a portion of a sweat bath, testify to the animacy of the substances and the building:

> O ancient rocks, *Tunkayatakapaka*, you are now here with us; *Wakan-Tanka* has made the Earth, and has placed you next to Her . . . O Rocks, you have neither eyes, nor mouth, nor limbs; you do not move, but by receiving your sacred breath [the steam], our people will be long-winded as they walk the path of life; your breath is the very breath of life . . . The leader now sprinkles water on the rocks . . . It is now very hot in the lodge, but it is good to feel the purifying qualities of the fire, the air, and the water, and to smell the fragrance of the sacred sage. After these powers have worked well into us, the door of the lodge is thrown open, reminding us of the first age in which we received the Light from *Wakan-Tanka*. (Brown 1953:37–38)

Animation was material, visible, audible, and palpable as water turned to vapors upon contact with hot rock and, filling the hemispherical interior of the building, led to one's skin dripping with sweat. From water-in-pot to steam-from-rocks and water-on-bodies, this was a complete water-cycle experience. One left the bath purified and invigorated (Bucko 1998).

Based on his pan-cultural and diachronic review, Robert Hall (1997) considered circular sweat baths to evoke uterine mythic and practical associations. The history of such lodges is difficult to trace at a continental scale but seems clear in the greater Cahokia region. There, no formal sweat baths were built prior to Cahokia's mid-eleventh-century transformation. Afterward, they were common architectural components of public-religious grounds until about AD 1200, when a series of poorly understood decommissioning events in the region saw the exodus or cessation of circular-building ceremonialism (Pauketat et al. 2013). One of the last circular buildings known in the region was incinerated at a rural nodal site several kilometers north of Cahokia at 809 ± 70 cal BP (Jackson and Millhouse 2003:table 19.1).

Fire was a common mode of de-animating buildings in the region (Baltus and Baires 2012). Burial under a mantle of earth was another common treatment given to special Cahokian buildings. Indeed, the earthen mantle used to bury animate buildings (sometimes following burning) was possibly the first of many in what was eventually recognizable from a distance as a mound (Pauketat 1993). In some of these mounds, as observed recently at a Cahokia-affiliated shrine complex in Trempealeau, Wisconsin, construction fills included loads of earth to which mollusk shells—in this case local bivalves—were added (Pauketat, Boszhardt et al. 2015). Such freshwater shells are known from some pyramids at Cahokia as well, as are Pleistocene-era fossil gastropod shells, which are commonly interpreted by archaeologists to be "incidental" inclusions in löess fills (Moorehead 2000). However, other studies of the Mississippian period into the historic era suggest that earthen construction fills (or "anthroseds") were frequently specially manufactured (e.g., Salzer and Rajnovich 2000).

In addition to the shells, the organically rich, black backswamp (montmorillinitic) muds mined from watery swamp or lake bottoms were commonly used by Cahokians to construct and cap earthen pyramids (Fowler 1997; Pauketat 1993; Reed 2009). Two of the largest of the Cahokia tumuli, Monks Mound and Rattlesnake Mound, for example, included stacked soil blocks and thin-spread mantles of the black silty clay (Baires 2014a; Sherwood and Kidder 2011). Similarly, the single-event construction of the pyramid at the Trempealeau site in Wisconsin contained a black cap that sealed a core construction fill of yellow löess (Pauketat, Boszhardt et al. 2015). Notably, in other Cahokia-related complexes, yellow-plastered pits and temple floors are found capped with black silt or clay plaster, usually after a yellow plaster had first been smeared onto the floors (Pauketat 2013b). It is conceivable that such patterned building and construction styles represent material components of a creation story known to have involved the genesis of earth from water with the aid of water creatures (Hall 1997). As such, mollusk shell inclusions may not have been incidental but, rather, emplaced a living force from this watery world into the earthen monuments of Cahokia beginning about AD 1050 (see also Baires 2016).

Shells, Earth, Maize, and Fire

Far to the south in Mesoamerica, similar sweat baths and circular water shrines were integrated within the trans-regional religious-historical changes of the ninth and tenth centuries AD (Harrison-Buck 2012; McAnany 2012). Shrines in Mesoamerica (and the American Southwest) have been found accompanied by marine shell offerings, most prominently spiral whelk shells. Similar shells are known at Cahokia and across the Mississippian world; and the beginning of the importation of substantial quantities of these shells for the production of beads, gorgets, and cups was coeval with the appearance of circular buildings and platforms, both dating to the beginning of the Lohmann phase (AD 1050–1100). An early reading of this regional diachronic pattern by Hall (1973) led him to infer symbolic connections among water, shells, breath or vapors, and sweating; we may follow his lead and project the characteristic "Ramey scroll"—leitmotif of Cahokia—to have infused the Ramey Incised pot

FIGURE 4.2. *Ramey scroll motifs on a Ramey Incised jar filled with maize. Photo by Timothy R. Pauketat, used with permission of Cahokia Mounds State Historic Site.*

with the power of water and four longitudinally halved conch shells, usually set in a quadri-partitioned design field (figure 4.2; see also Emerson 1989).

More to the present point, almost all ceramic vessels made at and around Cahokia by AD 1100 were manufactured using the same backswamp silty clays Cahokians mined for use in constructing and capping mounds (Porter 1964, 1984). Such muds were less often used prior to the Mississippian era, which is defined based in part on ceramic technology, because of their poor mechanical performance characteristics (Rye 1976; Stimmel et al. 1982). Montmorillinitic muds, that is, have a high shrink-swell ratio when water is added or evaporated, inhibiting their use in constructing pots (Rice 1987). This negative performance characteristic is offset by the addition of calcium and aragonite supplied by burned and crushed mussel shells (Morse and Million 1980; Morse and Morse 1983). In fact, the burned-shell platelets both neutralize the ionic charge of the montmorillinitic clays and impart structure to the vessel wall, improving the durability of the pot and enabling round-bottomed vessel production (Million 1975). The final step of pottery production, of course, was hardening using fire.

Whether they understood it or not, the first potters to have realized the technological benefits of burned-shell and fired backswamp clays and with a genealogical lineage that ties them to Cahokia resided in a restricted locale in southeastern Missouri at least as early as AD 800 (O'Brien and Wood 1998:248–49). Within a couple hundred years, the technology had subsumed the people of the so-called Varney tradition (see figure 4.1). By AD 900 to 1000, certain of these Varney people were migrating to the pre-Mississippian village complex that would become the city of Cahokia (cf. Alt 2002; Kelly 1991; Pauketat 2003). That migration appears to have accelerated through the middle 1000s.

In the greater Cahokia region, the potters of the Terminal Late Woodland era (AD 900–1050) used a locally diverse array of clays and temper types. One southern group, for instance, burned and crushed fossiliferous limestone—locally, often containing traces of mollusk shell–like brachiopods—obtained from vertical exposures of rock in the bluff escarpment that surrounds and demarcates the Mississippi River floodplain (figure 4.3). The Varney potters who made shell-tempered wares and who immigrated to the Cahokia region presumably had a historical impact (Alt 2006). Indeed, most potters in the greater Cahokia region produced shell-tempered wares by AD 1100. Some of the southern potters who made limestone-tempered vessels held out until then, their vessels eventually becoming a specialty ware within the Cahokian realm (Kelly 2002; Pauketat 1998).

In any case, the transfer of shell-tempered technology did not happen abruptly in the Cahokia region or elsewhere in the Mississippian world, unlike other aspects of Mississippianization (e.g., the abrupt reconstruction of Cahokia and the introduction of sweat baths and circular pyramids at ca. AD 1050). The adoption of shell temper was a trans-generational process, as revealed by diachronic plots of shell-tempered sherds in accumulations of refuse (figure 4.4). For such reasons, some have used the diachronic pattern to argue for neo-Darwinian models of Mississippianization (cf. Pauketat 2001).

Similar arguments have been made for the incorporation of maize into the diets of Terminal Late Woodland and Mississippian peoples, though the weight often given corn in explanations has been questioned (Fritz 1992). Like shell temper and montmorillinitic clays, the intensification of maize agriculture occurred as early as AD 700 to the southwest of Cahokia. Maize, which ultimately originated in Mesoamerica, is dated to this time at the Toltec site in central Arkansas and may have been transferred there by way of the American Southwest (Rolingson 1998). By the 800s it had become enmeshed in the lives

FIGURE 4.3. *Brachiopod fossils in Paleozoic (Carboniferous) period limestone from St. Clair County, Illinois. Photo by Timothy R. Pauketat.*

of both Caddoans—who occupied modern-day Arkansas, Louisiana, Texas, and Oklahoma—and Varney-culture people of southeast Missouri and northeast Arkansas. It is now thought to have made a late appearance in the greater Cahokia region, where it was not grown in earnest until AD 900. At that time, the household pottery wares diversified and seem linked in part to maize processing (Kelly et al. 1984). The processing of maize involved first removing the kernels and then either milling them (to produce a batter for baking) or

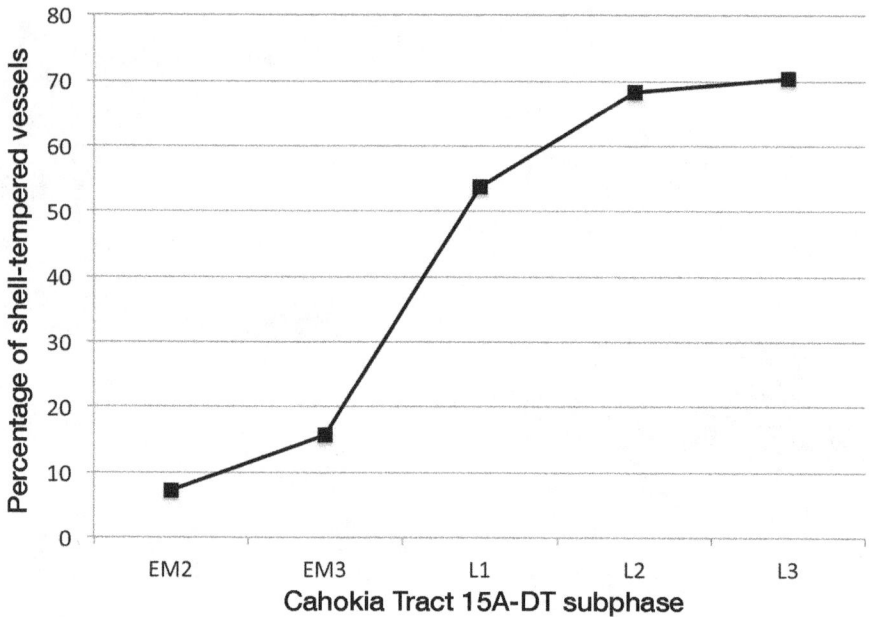

FIGURE 4.4. *Line graph showing increasing amounts of shell temper in vessel assemblages at Cahokia from about AD 900–1100. Image by Timothy R. Pauketat.*

roasting, boiling, and popping them over fire with the aid of ceramic baking pans, jars, and bowls. There is also evidence from the Cahokia region that maize kernels were sometimes processed using lye (ash and water), the latter obtained with the help of special ceramic utensils to filter water through burned limestone powder (Benchley 2003; see limestone-stumpware correlations in Pauketat 2013a).

FROM EMBODIED CONSCIOUSNESS TO CAHOKIAN TERRITORY

The fact that both shell-tempered, backswamp clay pottery technology and maize agriculture were adopted more or less simultaneously (between AD 700 and 900) across the Midsouth and Midwest is striking. So, too, is the fact that maize production preceded Cahokia and other early Mississippian centers in the middle portion of the Mississippi valley by at least a century and a half. The pre-Mississippian era witnessed an influx of Varney-tradition farmers from southeast Missouri who were already farming corn and were predisposed to the floodplain landscapes of bottomland mud and mollusk shell that characterize the Cahokia region. The net effect of locals and non-locals intensively farming maize and producing mollusk shell–tempered ceramics reflects a newly intensified and sustained relationship with the odiferous backwater ecozones of major river bottoms.

Spring flooding of backwater areas and old oxbow lakes by the Mississippi River and its tributaries might have been good or bad for maize cultivation, depending on when and how much the river waters rose. In the early summer, as the river receded and waters in lakes evaporated, mussel shells littered shorelines—many the remains of meals left behind by enterprising raccoons and otters, with any residual remains of the soft creature inside the shells emitting a distinct odor not easily forgotten. People too intensively collected mollusks not only for food but also for use as tools and especially for pottery temper. By AD 1100, almost all potters living around greater Cahokia were producing ceramics using burned mollusk shell temper (Holley 1989; Milner et al. 1984; Pauketat 1998). Moreover, the shell content of the vessel was significant, with estimates indicating that shell temper consisted of as little as 20 percent to as much as 50 percent of the final pot (Steponaitis 1983:20). Depending on the size of the pot and the size and thickness of the shells, many dozens of mussel shells might have been needed for the manufacture of a single ceramic vessel. The densities suggest that potters were producing multiple pots every year (see Pauketat 1989). At this rate and scale, the routine gathering of mussel shells for temper alone would have significantly reconfigured and territorialized the relational fields of people and their associations with the environments—rivers, streams, oxbow lakes, and related swampy waterways—where mollusks thrive.

The fact that this territorialized relational field was developing simultaneous with maize intensification indicates the possibility that the two were intimately entangled. This is not to say, however, that the mode of entanglement was an intentional sort of calorie-maximizing "subsistence strategy" but rather an embodied rhizomatic relationship. Researchers have long noted that maize affords a reshaping of the human "rhythms of everyday life" in part through scheduling; people accustomed to growing other crops throughout the year who incorporate maize have to alter their farming schedule (VanDerwarker et al. 2013:164). The incorporation of maize not only changed how and when people farmed but, more important, how people co-mediated a watery, muddy world of organisms, substances, and phenomena—namely, water, mollusks, mud, and fire.

When it comes to water, for instance, maize is a sensitive plant. It needs the right amount of water at the right moments in its life cycle. Too little water early on and the plant withers. Its ears may be stunted and improperly pollinated. Too much water and the roots rot (Benson et al. 2009). Pre-Mississippian agriculturalists would have certainly understood this delicate balance, scattering their fields into both dry uplands and wetter bottomlands along river ways (Chmurny 1973). Hoeing into the difficult, clayey bottomland soils would have constituted a sensuous reminder not only of their organic richness but also of the muddy soils' utility as clay for pottery manufacture. The advantages of pots fired with the shell inclusions may have taken little time to recognize (Porter 1984). Certainly, contemporary earthenware users in other parts of the world routinely and continually evaluate the functionality of vessels in relation to social identities, gustatory pleasures, and culinary practices (Aronson et al. 1994).

To make a shell-tempered Mississippian pot, both shells and the pot itself would necessarily have been subject to fire. When smothered, the open-air firing process used by Mississippians leads to a reducing atmosphere that embeds black carbon into the pot under production. The black color, common to Cahokia ceramics such as Ramey Incised wares (see figure 4.2), would appear to recapitulate the blackness of the bottomland muds used in earthenware manufacture, even as the shell temper (if not also the Ramey iconography) might mediate the pot much the way it had done earlier in the riverine biotic community from whence it came. Indeed, the vital energy of the mollusk, which is a locomotive creature, would have continued to mediate if not enliven in palpable, perceptible ways the pot or the foods or drinks prepared therein (in the sense of Bennett 2010). Even the fossil shells in limestone afforded a liquid that chemically altered the flavors and digestibility of maize. In this way, the mode of entanglement was a rhizomatic relationship that did not originate in any one place but was an ongoing co-mediation between human and other-than-human organisms, substances, and phenomena.

Such relationships enmeshed people and their agricultural practices, in part because mussel shells also comprised extensions of the human body as tools with which to dig into the earth and with which to consume certain foods from bowls. From the Halliday site, for instance, in the upland hills east of Cahokia, Varney-tradition immigrants from southeast Missouri engaged in intensive maize production using garden hoes with mussel shell blades and, later, cooked maize soups in their earthenware pots (figure 4.5). At Cahokia during its initial Mississippian phase, AD 1050–1100, great feasts were hosted in which delicate mussel shell spoons were employed (Pauketat et al. 2002). At these and similar ceremonial occasions, hosts and performers might manufacture, wear, and gift necklaces of marine shell beads and garments festooned with beads.

Certainly, the honored dead were lavished with marine shell objects. Mortuary remains in the ridge-top mounds of greater Cahokia were showered

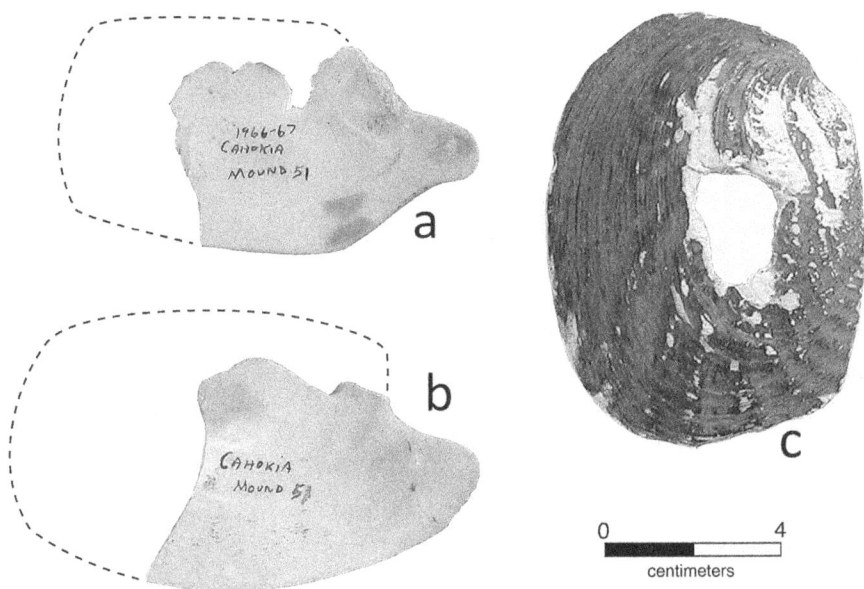

FIGURE 4.5. *Mussel shell tools and utensils from Cahokia's Mound 51 and Sub-Mound 51 pit: a–b, fragmentary spoons; c, mussel shell hoe blade, perforated for the attachment of a handle. Photos by Timothy R. Pauketat, Illinois State Archaeological Survey collections, University of Illinois, Urbana.*

with marine shells, necklaces, beads in various states of production, and beaded costumes (Baires 2016; Fowler et al. 1999). The citizens of Cahokia even built this relationship of living-to-dead into their city's very foundations by way of a causeway that ran from the central Grand Plaza a kilometer south to a mortuary zone. In the process it passed through a watery swamp of black clayey muds and mollusks (Baires 2014b; Baires et al. 2013; Pauketat, Emerson et al. 2015). Hence, from mollusks-in-mud, fossil-shells-in-rocks, mollusk-shells-in-mounds, and shell-hoes-digging-into-earth to shells-in-pots and shells-with-the-dead, shells embodied a complete life-cycle experience. Shell in some sense territorialized the world of the Mississippian farmers; their annual and daily lives were thoroughly mediated by these organisms, as well as the associated substance of water.

Water was itself a (if not *the*) vital ingredient. It was water, after all, that fell from the sky or flowed from the land, that was occupied by mussels, and that was swallowed by animals, people, and the roots of the maize plant. It was water that was added to and then driven by fire from the clay used to make circular pots. It was water that was also driven from the bodies of people who sat in circular baths filled with steam—the perfect vaporous mediation of rock, fire, and water.

Water was, then, agentic (Bennett 2010). As an all-pervasive rhizomatic substance, we could even credit it with the genesis of Mississippian lifeways, much as earlier archaeologists saw Mississippian culture as an outgrowth of riverine environments. But, of course, that greatly oversimplifies the matter, perhaps much as does crediting Cahokia's rise to human agency alone. Thus, rather than isolate water as the singular source or agent, we should point to its thick entanglement with an infinite number of other substances, organisms, and phenomena, including corn, shell, earth, sweat, mussels, people, and fire. It did constrain or territorialize the movements of people, bundling them in a tight web of relations mapped onto specific floodplain-centric landscapes, creating a Mississippian way of life, community, and people. It probably made conceivable or comfortable the rapid transformation of a large village complex into a planned "cosmic" city, Cahokia (Alt 2012; Pauketat, Alt et al. 2015; Pauketat, Emerson et al. 2015).

So what changed around AD 1050? Did the water, mud, shell, and corn entanglements of such a relational field, composed of "thousands of linked events" (Gould 1994), simply gestate Cahokia and the other Mississippian places? Looking back at this place, described earlier, with a relational eye, we should first recognize what Cahokia was: the emplacement of a suite of relations—the physical properties, experiential qualities, and other flows or movements of entangled substances, materials, and phenomena that defined people and all with which they were connected. Cahokia, that is, was the materiality and spatiality of relations that would come to extend and transcend the pre-Mississippian web of corn, shell, earth, sweat, mussels, and fire. This is because the city of Cahokia, at its mid-eleventh-century foundation, folded into the Mississippian rhizome something new: cosmic order. Cahokia at its mid-eleventh-century reinvention connected the ground with the heavens above. That is, Cahokia seems to have bundled water, mud, shell, corn, and more with the cosmos through the cycles of the sun and moon (Pauketat 2013b). The significance of this knotting of a new strand into the fabric of life, this rhizomatic extension of affective experience, was to bind together and hence alter at a larger scale the relational fields of local farmers.

Precisely how this happened exceeds the scope of this chapter, though it is worthy of note that Sarah Baires (2016) emphasizes mortuary rituals and the "release" of human and nonhuman souls as paramount in Cahokia's emergence. Suffice it to say that it need not have been an intentional act by a small group of thoughtful, committed citizens, even if it was contingent on their agency. This is because the Cahokian poiesis was also contingent on the agency of the sun and the moon, if not other seemingly stochastic celestial events, such as a supernova in AD 1054 (Pauketat and Emerson 2008). People, in some sense, were subject to the affects of these luminous bodies.

CONCLUSION

Reconfigured in such a way and at such a scale, the city would have attracted people from far afield, connecting them to cosmic order and, in turn, producing Mississippian culture by realigning human experience in ways that produced something quite unlike the former pre-Mississippian existence (Alt 2006). In essence, Cahokia became what Deleuze and Guattari (1987) would call an "assemblage converter." Perhaps people, especially would-be elites after the fact, took credit for the poiesis. Certainly, some archaeologists would give them full credit. But the real history, considered relationally, is considerably more complicated.

It might even be difficult to evaluate precisely if, when, or how Mississippian culture and the Cahokian poiesis would have been different had the genealogies of just a few of the thousands of co-mediations of people, mollusks, earth, water, and fire been a little different. Then again, it is apparent that reconfigurations of wider relational fields emerged from this greater rhizomatic, Mississippianizing history. This happened through the transfers and concentrations of key mediators—assemblages or bundles of people and technologies—that might be moved. Varney-tradition people, for instance, migrated northward, carrying with them their pottery know-how. This means that Mississippian history was not driven simply by a series of agents, human or otherwise. Rather, history was the result of relations stemming from the particular configurations and dispositions of relational fields.

To understand those configurations and dispositions, emphasis must be placed on the ways in which and the scales at which relations were mediated, which is to say, bundled, assembled, entangled, or territorialized. Those, in turn, are to be understood through the hows: how did the affects of the fields or landscapes and the sensorial engagements, emotional states, and chemical reactions resulting from or attendant to the affective entanglements define the mediators and rearrange the fields of experience? In the case of the Mississippians, little of this could be deduced by starting our investigation with the resulting Mississippian societies. Rather, we have analyzed the qualities and properties of substances and things at the most elemental of experiential levels to appreciate the "ways of life" that undergirded the Cahokian poiesis. After the fact, the rhythms of water, mollusks, corn, mud, and fire, embodied by the people enmeshed therein, would have added meaning and legitimacy to Mississippian life. Without them, there could have been no society.

REFERENCES CITED

Alt, Susan M. 2002. "Identities, Traditions, and Diversity in Cahokia's Uplands." *Midcontinental Journal of Archaeology* 27: 217–36.

Alt, Susan M. 2006. "The Power of Diversity: The Roles of Migration and Hybridity in Culture Change." In *Leadership and Polity in Mississippian Society*, ed. Brian M. Butler and Paul D. Welch, 289–308. Occasional Paper 33. Carbondale: Center for Archaeological Investigations, Southern Illinois University.

Alt, Susan M. 2012. "Making Mississippian at Cahokia." In *The Oxford Handbook of North American Archaeology*, ed. Timothy R. Pauketat, 497–508. Oxford: Oxford University Press.

Alt, Susan M., and Timothy R. Pauketat. 2015. "The Elements of Cahokian Shrine Complexes and the Basis of Mississippian Religion." In *Religion and Politics in the Ancient Americas*, ed. Sarah Barber and Arthur Joyce, 51–74. London: Routledge.

Aronson, Meredith, James M. Skibo, and Miriam T. Stark. 1994. "Production and Use Technologies in Kalinga Pottery." In *Kalinga Ethnoarchaeology: Expanding Archaeological Method and Theory*, ed. William A. Longacre and James M. Skibo, 83–111. Washington, DC: Smithsonian Institution Press.

Baires, Sarah E. 2014a. "Cahokia's Origins: Religion, Complexity, and Ridge-Top Mortuaries in the Mississippi River Valley." PhD dissertation, Department of Anthropology, University of Illinois, Urbana.

Baires, Sarah E. 2014b. "Cahokia's Rattlesnake Causeway." *Midcontinental Journal of Archaeology* 39 (1): 1–19.

Baires, Sarah E. 2016. "A Microhistory of Human and Gastropod Bodies and Souls during Cahokia's Emergence." *Cambridge Archaeological Journal* 27: 245–60. https://doi.org/10.1017/S095977431600055X.

Baires, Sarah E., Amanda J. Butler, B. Jacob Skousen, and Timothy R. Pauketat. 2013. "Fields of Movement in the Ancient Woodlands of North America." In *Archaeology after Interpretation*, ed. Benjamin Alberti, Andrew M. Jones, and Joshua Pollard, 197–218. Walnut Creek, CA: Left Coast.

Baltus, Melissa R., and Sarah E. Baires. 2012. "Elements of Ancient Power in the Cahokian World." *Journal of Social Archaeology* 12 (2): 167–92. https://doi.org/10.1177/1469605311433369.

Benchley, Elizabeth D. 2003. "Mississippian Alkali Processing of Corn." *Wisconsin Archeologist* 84: 127–37.

Bennett, Jane. 2010. *Vibrant Matter: A Political Ecology of Things.* Durham, NC: Duke University Press.

Benson, Larry, Timothy R. Pauketat, and Edward Cook. 2009. "Cahokia's Boom and Bust in the Context of Climate Change." *American Antiquity* 74 (3): 467–83. https://doi.org/10.1017/S000273160004871X.

Blitz, John H. 2010. "New Perspectives in Mississippian Archaeology." *Journal of Archaeological Research* 18 (1): 1–39. https://doi.org/10.1007/s10814-009-9033-y.

Brown, Joseph Epes. 1953. *The Sacred Pipe: Black Elk's Account of the Seven Rites of the Oglala Sioux.* Norman: University of Oklahoma Press.

Bucko, Raymond. 1998. *The Lakota Ritual of the the Sweat Lodge.* Lincoln: University of Nebraska Press.

Chmurny, William W. 1973. "The Ecology of the Middle Mississippian Occupation of the American Bottom." PhD dissertation, Department of Anthropology, University of Illinois, Urbana.

Costin, Cathy, and Rita M. Wright, eds. 1998. *Craft and Cultural Identity.* Archeological Papers of the American Anthropological Association 8. Washington, DC: American Anthropological Association.

Deleuze, Gilles, and Felix Guattari. 1987. *A Thousand Plateaus: Capitalism and Schizophrenia.* Trans. Brian Massumi. Minneapolis: University of Minnesota Press.

DeMallie, Raymond J., ed. 2001. *Handbook of North American Indians,* vol. 13: *Plains.* Washington, DC: Smithsonian Institution.

Dobres, Marcia-Anne. 2000. *Technology and Social Agency.* Oxford: Blackwell.

Dobres, Marcia-Anne, and John Robb, eds. 2000. *Agency in Archaeology.* London: Routledge.

Dorsey, James Owen. 1894. "A Study of Siouan Cults." In *Eleventh Annual Report of the Bureau of Ethnology,* 351–554. Washington, DC: Government Printing Office.

Emerson, Thomas E. 1989. "Water, Serpents, and the Underworld: An Exploration into Cahokia Symbolism." In *The Southeastern Ceremonial Complex: Artifacts and Analysis,* ed. Patricia Galloway, 45–92. Lincoln: University of Nebraska Press.

Emerson, Thomas E. 1997. *Cahokia and the Archaeology of Power.* Tuscaloosa: University of Alabama Press.

Fowler, Melvin L. 1997. *The Cahokia Atlas: A Historical Atlas of Cahokia Archaeology.* Illinois Transportation Archaeological Research Program, Studies in Archaeology 2. Urbana: University of Illinois.

Fowler, Melvin L., Jerome C. Rose, Barbara Vander Leest, and Steven R. Ahler. 1999. *The Mound 72 Area: Dedicated and Sacred Space in Early Cahokia*. Reports of Investigations 54. Springfield: Illinois State Museum.

Fritz, Gayle J. 1992. "'Newer,' 'Better' Maize and the Mississippian Emergence: A Critique of Prime Mover Explanations." In *Late Prehistoric Agriculture: Observations from the Midwest*, ed. William I. Woods, 19–43. Studies in Illinois Archaeology 8. Springfield: Illinois Historic Preservation Agency.

Gould, Stephen Jay. 1994. "The Evolution of Life on the Earth." *Scientific American* 271 (4): 84–91. https://doi.org/10.1038/scientificamerican1094-84.

Griffin, James B. 1952. "Culture Periods in Eastern United States Archeology." In *Archeology of Eastern United States*, ed. James B. Griffin, 352–64. Chicago: University of Chicago Press.

Griffin, James B. 1967. "Eastern North American Archaeology: A Summary." *Science* 156 (3772): 175–91. https://doi.org/10.1126/science.156.3772.175.

Hall, Robert L. 1973. "The Cahokia Presence Outside of the American Bottom." Paper presented at the Central States Anthropological Society, St. Louis, MO.

Hall, Robert L. 1997. *An Archaeology of the Soul: Native American Indian Belief and Ritual*. Urbana: University of Illinois Press.

Hallowell, A. Irving. 1960. "Ojibwa Ontology, Behavior, and World View." In *Culture in History: Essays in Honor of Paul Radin*, ed. Stanley Diamond, 19–52. New York: Columbia University Press.

Harrison-Buck, Eleanor. 2012. "Architecture as Animate Landscape: Circular Shrines in the Ancient Maya Lowlands." *American Anthropologist* 114 (1): 64–80. https://doi.org/10.1111/j.1548-1433.2011.01397.x.

Hewitt, J.N.B. 1902. "Orenda and a Definition of Religion." *American Anthropologist New Series* 4 (1): 33–46. https://doi.org/10.1525/aa.1902.4.1.02a00050.

Holley, George R. 1989. *The Archaeology of the Cahokia Mounds ICT-II: Ceramics*. Illinois Cultural Resources Study 11. Springfield: Illinois Historic Preservation Agency.

Howard, James H. 1981. *Shawnee! The Ceremonialism of a Native Indian Tribe and Its Cultural Background*. Athens: Ohio University Press.

Ingold, Tim. 2000. "Making Culture and Weaving the World." In *Matter, Materiality, and Modern Culture*, ed. Paul Graves-Brown, 50–71. London: Routledge.

Ingold, Tim. 2007. *Lines: A Brief History*. London: Routledge.

Jackson, Douglas K., and Philip G. Millhouse. 2003. *The Vaughn Branch and Old Edwardsville Road Sites*. Research Reports 16. Urbana-Champaign: Illinois Transportation Archaeological Research Program.

Jennings, Justin. 2010. *Globalizations and the Ancient World*. Cambridge: Cambridge University Press. https://doi.org/10.1017/CBO9780511778445.

Kelly, John E. 1991. "The Evidence for Prehistoric Exchange and Its Implications for the Development of Cahokia." In *New Perspectives on Cahokia: Views from the Periphery*, ed. James B. Stoltman, 65–92. Madison, WI: Prehistory.

Kelly, John E. 2002. "The Pulcher Tradition and the Ritualization of Cahokia: A Perspective from Cahokia's Southern Neighbor." *Southeastern Archaeology* 21: 136–48.

Kelly, John E., Steven J. Ozuk, Douglas K. Jackson, Dale L. McElrath, Fred A. Finney, and Duane Esarey. 1984. "Emergent Mississippian Period." In *American Bottom Archaeology*, ed. Charles J. Bareis and James W. Porter, 128–57. Urbana: University of Illinois Press.

Lankford, George E. 2007. *Reachable Stars: Patterns in the Ethnoastronomy of Eastern North America*. Tuscaloosa: University of Alabama Press.

Latour, Bruno. 1993. *We Have Never Been Modern*. Trans. Catherine Porter. Cambridge, MA: Harvard University Press.

Malafouris, Lambros. 2013. *How Things Shape the Mind: A Theory of Material Engagement*. Cambridge, MA: MIT Press.

McAnany, Patricia A. 2012. "Terminal Classic Maya Heterodoxy and Shrine Vernacularism in the Sibun Valley, Belize." *Cambridge Archaeological Journal* 22 (1): 115–34. https://doi.org/10.1017/S0959774312000078.

McCleary, Timothy P. 2015. *Crow Indian Rock Art: Indigenous Perspectives and Interpretations*. Walnut Creek, CA: Left Coast.

Mehrer, Mark W. 1995. *Cahokia's Countryside: Household Archaeology, Settlement Patterns, and Social Power*. DeKalb: Northern Illinois University Press.

Meskell, Lynn M. 2004. *Object Worlds in Ancient Egypt: Material Biographies Past and Present*. London: Berg.

Million, Michael G. 1975. "Research Design for the Aboriginal Ceramic Industries of the Cache River Basin." In *The Cache River Archeological Project: An Experiment in Contract Archeology*, ed. Michael B. Schiffer and John H. House, 217–22. Research Series 8. Fayetteville: Arkansas Archeological Survey, Publications in Archeology.

Mills, Barbara J., and William H. Walker. 2008. *Memory Work: Archaeologies of Material Practices*. Santa Fe, NM: School for Advanced Research Press.

Milner, George R., Thomas E. Emerson, Mark W. Mehrer, Joyce Williams, and Duane Esarey. 1984. "Mississippian and Oneota Period." In *American Bottom Archaeology*, ed. Charles J. Bareis and James W. Porter, 158–86. Urbana: University of Illinois Press.

Moorehead, Warren K. 2000. *The Cahokia Mounds*. Tuscaloosa: University of Alabama Press.

Morse, Dan F., and Michael G. Million. 1980. "Biotic and Nonbiotic Resources." In *Zebree Archeological Project: Excavation, Data Interpretation, and Report on the Zebree Homestead Site, Mississippi County, Arkansas*, ed. Dan F. Morse and Phyllis A. Morse, 11–31. Contract no. DACW 66–76-C-0006. Memphis: Memphis District, US Army Corps of Engineers.

Morse, Dan F., and Phyllis A. Morse. 1983. *The Archaeology of the Central Mississippi Valley*. New York: Academic.

Murie, James R. 1981. *Ceremonies of the Pawnee*, Part I: *The Skiri*. Smithsonian Contributions to Anthropology 27. Washington, DC: Smithsonian Institution Press.

O'Brien, Michael J., and W. Raymond Wood. 1998. *The Prehistory of Missouri*. Columbia: University of Missouri Press.

Pauketat, Timothy R. 1989. "Monitoring Mississippian Homestead Occupation Span and Economy Using Ceramic Refuse." *American Antiquity* 54 (2): 288–310. https://doi.org/10.2307/281708.

Pauketat, Timothy R. 1993. *Temples for Cahokia Lords: Preston Holder's 1955–1956 Excavations of Kunnemann Mound*. Memoirs of the University of Michigan Museum of Anthropology 26. Ann Arbor: University of Michigan.

Pauketat, Timothy R. 1998. *The Archaeology of Downtown Cahokia: The Tract 15A and Dunham Tract Excavations*. Illinois Transportation Archaeological Research Program, Studies in Archaeology 1. Urbana: University of Illinois.

Pauketat, Timothy R. 2001. "Practice and History in Archaeology: An Emerging Paradigm." *Anthropological Theory* 1: 73–98.

Pauketat, Timothy R. 2003. "Resettled Farmers and the Making of a Mississippian Polity." *American Antiquity* 68 (1): 39–66. https://doi.org/10.2307/3557032.

Pauketat, Timothy R. 2004. *Ancient Cahokia and the Mississippians*. Cambridge: Cambridge University Press.

Pauketat, Timothy R. 2005. "Mounds, Buildings, Posts, Palisades, and Compounds." In *The Archaeology of the East St. Louis Mound Center*, Part I: *The Southside Excavations*, ed. Timothy R. Pauketat, 113–92. Transportation Archaeological Research Reports 21. Urbana: Illinois Transportation Archaeological Research Program, University of Illinois.

Pauketat, Timothy R. 2013a. *The Archaeology of Downtown Cahokia II: The 1960 Excavation of Tract 15B*. Studies in Illinois Archaeology 8. Urbana: Illinois State Archaeological Survey.

Pauketat, Timothy R. 2013b. *An Archaeology of the Cosmos: Rethinking Agency and Religion in Ancient America*. London: Routledge.

Pauketat, Timothy R. 2013c. "Bundles of/in/as Time." In *Big Histories, Human Lives: Tackling Problems of Scale in Archaeology*, ed. John Robb and Timothy R. Pauketat, 35–56. Santa Fe, NM: School for Advanced Research Press.

Pauketat, Timothy R., and Susan M. Alt. 2005. "Agency in a Postmold? Physicality and the Archaeology of Culture-Making." *Journal of Archaeological Method and Theory* 12 (3): 213–37. https://doi.org/10.1007/s10816-005-6929-9.

Pauketat, Timothy R., Susan M. Alt, and Jeffery D. Kruchten. 2015. "City of Earth and Wood: Cahokia and Its Material-Historical Implications." In *A World of Cities*, ed. Norman Yoffee, 437–54. Cambridge: Cambridge University Press. https://doi.org/10.1017/CHO9781139035606.027.

Pauketat, Timothy R., Robert F. Boszhardt, and Danielle M. Benden. 2015. "Trempealeau Entanglements: An Ancient Colony's Causes and Effects." *American Antiquity* 80 (2): 260–89. https://doi.org/10.7183/0002-7316.80.2.260.

Pauketat, Timothy R., and Thomas E. Emerson. 2008. "Star Performances and Cosmic Clutter." *Cambridge Archaeological Journal* 18 (1): 78–85. https://doi.org/10.1017/S0959774308000085.

Pauketat, Timothy R., Thomas E. Emerson, Michael G. Farkas, and Sarah E. Baires. 2015. "An American Indian City." In *Medieval Mississippians: The Cahokian World*, ed. Timothy R. Pauketat and Susan M. Alt, 20–31. Santa Fe, NM: School for Advanced Research Press.

Pauketat, Timothy R., Andrew C. Fortier, Thomas E. Emerson, and Susan M. Alt. 2013. "A Mississippian Conflagration at East St. Louis and Its Political-Historical Implications." *Journal of Field Archaeology* 38 (3): 210–26. https://doi.org/10.1179/0093469013Z.00000000054.

Pauketat, Timothy R., Lucretia S. Kelly, Gayle J. Fritz, Neal H. Lopinot, Scott Elias, and Eve Hargrave. 2002. "The Residues of Feasting and Public Ritual at Early Cahokia." *American Antiquity* 67 (2): 257–79. https://doi.org/10.2307/2694566.

Pauketat, Timothy R., Mark A. Rees, and Stephanie L. Pauketat. 1998. *An Archaeological Survey of Horseshoe Lake State Park, Madison County, Illinois*. Report of Investigations 55. Springfield: Illinois State Museum.

Peebles, Christopher S., and Susan M. Kus. 1977. "Some Archaeological Correlates of Ranked Societies." *American Antiquity* 42 (3): 421–48. https://doi.org/10.2307/279066.

Porter, James W. 1964. *Thin Section Descriptions of Some Shell Tempered Prehistoric Ceramics from the American Bottoms*. Research Report 7. Carbondale: Lithic Laboratory, Southern Illinois University Museum.

Porter, James W. 1984. "Thin Section Analysis of Ceramics." In *The Robinson's Lake Site (11-Ms-582)*, ed. George R. Milner, 133–216. FAI-270 Site Reports, vol. 10. Urbana, IL: American Bottom Archaeology.

Radin, Paul. 1914. "Religion of the North American Indians." *Journal of American Folklore* 27 (106): 335–73. https://doi.org/10.2307/534739.

Reed, Nelson A. 1969. "Monks and Other Mississippian Mounds." In *Explorations in Cahokia Archaeology*, ed. Melvin L. Fowler, 31–42. Bulletin 7. Urbana: Illinois Archaeological Survey.

Reed, Nelson A. 2009. "Excavations on the Third Terrace and Front Ramp of Monks Mound, Cahokia: A Personal Narrative." *Illinois Archaeology* 21: 1–89.

Rice, Prudence M. 1987. *Pottery Analysis: A Sourcebook*. Chicago: University of Chicago Press.

Rolingson, Martha Ann. 1998. *Toltec Mounds and Plum Bayou Culture: Mound D Excavations*. Arkansas Archeological Survey Research Series 54. Fayetteville: Arkansas Archeological Survey.

Romain, William F. 2015. "Moonwatchers of Cahokia." In *Medieval Mississippians: The Cahokian World*, ed. Timothy R. Pauketat and Susan M. Alt, 33–42. Santa Fe, NM: School for Advanced Research Press.

Rye, Owen S. 1976. "Keeping Your Temper under Control: Materials and the Manufacture of Papuan Pottery." *Archaeology and Physical Anthropology in Oceania* 11 (2): 106–37.

Salzer, Robert J., and Grace Rajnovich. 2000. *The Gottschall Rockshelter: An Archaeological Mystery*. St. Paul: Prairie Smoke.

Sherwood, Sarah C., and Tristram R. Kidder. 2011. "The DaVincis of Dirt: Geoarchaeological Perspectives on Native American Mound Building in the Mississippi River Basin." *Journal of Anthropological Archaeology* 30 (1): 69–87. https://doi.org/10.1016/j.jaa.2010.11.001.

Skinner, Alanson. 1913. *Social Life and Ceremonial Bundles of the Menomini Indians*. Anthropological Papers of the American Museum of Natural History 13, part 1. New York: American Museum of Natural History.

Smith, Harriet. 1969. "The Murdock Mound, Cahokia Site." In *Explorations into Cahokia Archaeology*, ed. Melvin L. Fowler, 49–88. Bulletin 7. Urbana: Illinois Archaeological Survey.

Steponaitis, Vincas P. 1983. *Ceramics, Chronology, and Community Patterns: An Archaeological Study at Moundville*. New York: Academic.

Stimmel, Carole, Robert B. Heiman, and R.G.V. Hancock. 1982. "Indian Pottery from the Mississippi Valley: Coping with Bad Raw Materials." In *Archaeological Ceramics*, ed. Jacqueline S. Olin and Alan D. Franklin, 219–28. Washington, DC: Smithsonian Institution Press.

Tilley, Christopher. 2004. *The Materiality of Stone: Explorations in Landscape Phenomenology*. Oxford: Berg.

Van Dyke, Ruth M., and Susan E. Alcock, eds. 2003. *Archaeologies of Memory.* Oxford: Basil Blackwell. https://doi.org/10.1002/9780470774304.

VanDerwarker, Amber M., Gregory D. Wilson, and Dana N. Bardolph. 2013. "Maize Adoption and Intensification in the Central Illinois River Valley: An Analysis of Archaeobotanical Data from the Late Woodland through Early Mississippian Periods (AD 600–1200)." *Southeastern Archaeology* 32 (2): 147–68. https://doi.org/10.1179/sea.2013.32.2.001.

Weismantel, Mary, and Lynn Meskell. 2014. "Substances: 'Following the Material' through Two Prehistoric Cases." *Journal of Material Culture* 19 (3): 233–51. https://doi.org/10.1177/1359183514546803.

Wheatley, Paul. 1971. *The Pivot of the Four Quarters.* Chicago: Aldine.

Wissler, Clark. 1912. *Ceremonial Bundles of the Blackfoot Indians.* Anthropological Papers of the American Museum of Natural History 7, part 2. New York: American Museum of Natural History.

Zedeño, María Nieves. 2008. "Bundled Worlds: The Roles and Interactions of Complex Objects from the North American Plains." *Journal of Archaeological Method and Theory* 15 (4): 362–78. https://doi.org/10.1007/s10816-008-9058-4.

5

The Inalienable-Commodity Continuum in the Circulation of Birds on the North American Plains

María Nieves Zedeño,
Wendi Field Murray,
and Kaitlyn Chandler

From early accounts of indigenous trade centers, where exotic goods moved through myriad hands, to classical and contemporary studies of market economies, people around the world regard trade and exchange as the glue that binds society together (Kovacevich and Callaghan 2013). Archaeological modeling of trade and exchange has generally approached goods as passive and external to social relations wherein goods function as gifts or commodities. Yet the specific roles goods play in traditional modes of circulation are profoundly connected to their condition of personhood. Personhood implies that sociality, that is, a transaction involving other than human persons—whether these constitute tangible or intangible goods—is a social act between the giver and the good and between it and the receiver inasmuch as it is a social act between people engaged in the transaction.

In this chapter we deploy a contextual and relational approach to native value systems and illustrate, through examples of the acquisition and exchange of bird goods among northern Plains tribes of the Missouri River basin, the effect of personhood on the various social roles birds, bird objects, bird knowledge, and bird-related services played in native economies. We argue alongside Kopytoff (1986) and Godelier (1999) that the commoditization of inalienable goods or the inalienable qualities goods may acquire during their life histories is a process deeply embedded in the

DOI: 10.5876/9781607327479.c005

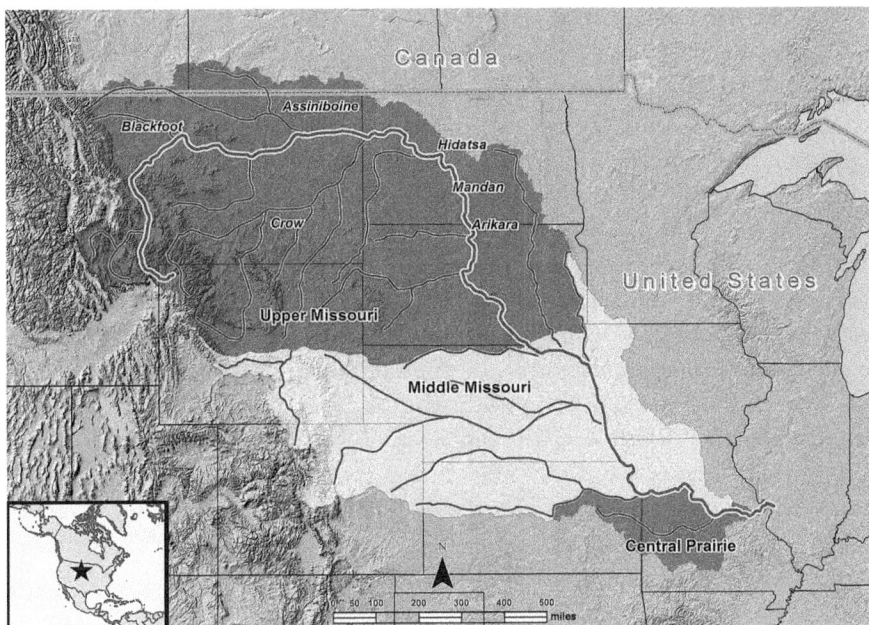

FIGURE 5.1. *Missouri River basin and tribal locations. From Chandler et al. 2017:fig. 2.1.*

specific social and historically contingent contexts in which they circulate. We further suggest that goods can circulate simultaneously in different but interconnected systems of value, not only providing people with the opportunity for accumulating prestige and authority but also opening the possibility for sizable economic gain. Finally, we examine the effect of culture contact in the valuation of native goods.

The chapter begins with a working definition of "good" and a brief overview of contemporary approaches to gifts, commodities, and inalienable possessions to show how these are not categories of goods that neatly correspond to distinctive modes of circulation; rather, they are *roles* goods may assume in complex value systems, and certain roles are dependent upon conditions of personhood. Next, we discuss the dynamics of bird personhood in the northern Plains (specifically the Missouri River basin, figure 5.1); last, we discuss the influence of value systems involving the circulation of birds and bird parts on political authority, wealth accumulation, and the reproduction of social institutions.

WHEN IS A GOOD A PERSON?

Good is defined here as an inclusive term for natural resources, objects of human manufacture, knowledge, and services. We cast this definition broadly to emphasize the importance of considering both the tangible and intangible character of exchangeable and inalienable goods. Just as goods are diverse, so are the contexts in which they circulate. Early twentieth-century anthropologists, notably Durkheim (1965) Malinowski (1922), Mauss (1925), and Lévi-Strauss (1964), differentiated goods according to two general modes of circulation—gift and commodity—emphasizing the predominance of the former as a means of reciprocity in primitive society. Gifts are those goods that typically circulate in social networks. In these networks, the social capital of gifting is more valuable than the good itself, the latter acting as a bond between those engaged in reciprocity. The centrality of the Potlatch in the constitution and reproduction of social and political bonds in the Pacific Northwest (Roth 2002) and of shell objects in the rise of political inequality among societies in the Pacific Islands (Aswani and Sheppard 2003; Malinowski 1922; Mosko 2000; Weiner 1992) represents long-standing anthropological examples of the intricacy of gift exchange.

Commodities, in contrast, are meant to circulate in a market economy where the main goal is not to attain prestige or fulfill a social obligation but to incur economic gain. Commodity exchange has generally been discussed in twentieth-century anthropological literature in the context of complex (non-capitalist) societies where conflict and inequality are inherent in each interaction (e.g., Durkheim 1965; Sahlins 1972). Critiques of the classic models of trade and exchange (e.g., Appadurai 1986; Aswani and Sheppard 2003; Godelier 1999; Gregory 1982; Thomas 1991; Weiner 1992) argue that gift and commodity have been treated as two essentialized categories that mask the range of variation in modes and contexts of circulation; as Ferry (2002:335) notes, this categorization ignores the multiplicity of roles certain goods may play in producing and trading communities. In addition, treatments of gift and commodity exchange seldom consider the condition of personhood in valuation systems underlying the circulation of goods (but see Gell 1998; Godelier 1999).

In her revision of reciprocal exchange in the Trobriand Islands, Weiner (1992) calls attention to the existence of a third kind of good, which she names "inalienable possession" and models after Mauss's (1925) conundrum embodied in "the gift." Inalienable possessions are goods that circulate in a paradoxical context, where the owner of the goods simultaneously keeps the goods and gives them away or does not circulate them at all. There are fundamental differences between gifts and commodities, on the one hand, and inalienable possessions, on the other. The most significant difference is that gifts and commodities are consumed as they change hands (in other words, they are lost to the giver), whereas inalienable possessions are conserved or even multiplied in the act of exchange (kept by the giver). Weiner indicates that inalienable possessions generally can only be circulated under special circumstances in which the giver's identity remains embedded in that which he or she gives. Godelier (1999:123) elaborates this idea further when he includes sacra—those goods that embody gods and spirits on earth and thus are essentially inalienable—into the enigma of the gift. Moving forward, Ferry's (2002) study of silver production and trade as a cooperative industry in modern Guanajuato, Mexico, clearly illustrates that there are contexts in which goods can be both movable (ore-commodity) and immovable (vein-place/possession). She provocatively introduces the term "inalienable commodity" to illuminate a seemingly paradoxical context in which silver ore, while circulating in the global commodity market, is never truly lost to the miners but eventually returns as social patrimony.

From these works we are left pondering whether and under what circumstances a given good can be gift, commodity, inalienable possession, social patrimony, or a permutation of the above. If we assume that goods may be persons and thus capable of sociality, then the answer to this question may be found by, first, scrutinizing those realms in which goods display interactive, performative, transformative, and fluid dispositions of personhood and, second, by ascertaining how such dispositions are associated with valuation and circulation. By valuation we do not simply mean the worth of goods; we also refer to the ontological and epistemological principles goods embody, their place in the social order, and their relative importance for bestowing economic wealth and political authority as well as sustaining society and culture.

Interactive dispositions of personhood are common to all things, as goods have the basic ability to affect and be affected by those (humans, other things) with whom they engage as they create and define places, paths, and positions— this much is broadly accepted by contemporary students of behavior, agency, and materiality (e.g., Dobres and Robb 2000; Meskell 2004; Miller 2005; Mills and Walker 2008; Scheiber 2015; Schiffer and Miller 1999). Performative dispositions bring goods into the realm of the sign and the symbol (Keane 2003; Fogelin 2012). Things have the ability to communicate information about their worth and to denote abstract concepts and realities. The display of material icons (say, the Christian cross, a Kachina mask, or a Kula necklace) or the utterance of a prayer conveys meanings that are explicit to the viewers and listeners in the particular context of display, that may be carried to other contexts, and that can lend structure to future social practices.

Transformative dispositions, in contrast, reflect the power of goods to transmute into something altogether different under certain circumstances or to change the tangible and intangible qualities of those (humans, things) with whom they engage. Kachina masks, for example, are made to represent ancestral Pueblo spirits, and thus they are iconic objects; yet those who wear masks in a public ritual are not simply conveying this meaning to the participants—they *become* the spirits of the masks (Mills 2004; Fowles 2013). A Kachina mask is therefore a person whose transformative disposition fundamentally alters the substance of the wearer during the performance of the rite and even in his or her afterlife. Performative and transformative dispositions are fluid as they, too, are subject to social mores and historical contingencies. Among the Great Lakes Ojibwa, for example, a story involving supernatural beings is a living, multidimensional thing that when put into the written word, "flattens out" or loses its life and dimensionality because the characters in the story are no longer able to perform their roles as they would in storytelling. Ojibwa social mores apply to objects' behavior just as they apply to people; personhood may be lost as a result of infringements of the social order incurred by things during their life histories. By the same token, inert things may become persons by virtue of their conduct (Zedeño et al. 2011:21).

Clearly, the dispositions and conditions of personhood that goods possess and the value(s) people bestow upon them are best displayed when different kinds of goods come together in interactive contexts. Among Plains tribes, for example, ceremonial bundles constitute a kind of complex object composed of two or more tangible and intangible goods. Bundles are literally small "universes" made of deliberate and historically contextualized landscapes, objects, songs, stories, rights, and more (Lokensgard 2010; Zedeño 2008, 2009). Each bundle and each good it contains have inalienable properties that both complement one another and speak to political and cultural authority, historical events, moral rules and obligations, the sociality of the supernatural, and the well-being of the owner's community. This does not preclude bundles and their contents from also bringing the potential for gainful exchange: the possession and circulation of bundles plays an important role in the accumulation of economic and social capital. Yet the broader social significance of the bundle and its power to work toward the greater good and to enable cultural reproduction remains with the people as social patrimony (Pard 2015). Our research on the cultural significance of birds (alone and as bundle components) for several Missouri River tribes (see figure 5.1) suggests not only that bird goods can exhibit various dispositions of personhood but also that they play complementary roles in multiple value systems, depending on the contextual and historical circumstances that influence their circulations within and between tribes.

BIRDS AND THE MISSOURI RIVER TRIBES

Birds are a category of goods that, with a few notable exceptions (e.g., Falk 2002; Parmalee 1977), tends to fall into the background of discussions of material culture, probably because they make up a small portion of the zooarchaeological record. Yet birds are among the most ubiquitous and interactive resources. Hundreds of species of birds frequent the Missouri River basin, some passing through seasonally on the Central Flyway that runs along the river from Canada to the Gulf Coast and some inhabiting the region year-round. A "flyway" is a general flight path used by birds during periods of migration, providing access to sources of food, water, and habitats with relatively few major geographic barriers, such as mountains. The Central Flyway narrows into an hourglass shape near the Platte and Missouri River valleys, offering one of the most diverse concentrations of bird species in North America (Johnsgard 2012).

This astonishing world of birds has captured the attention of visitors to the northern Plains since European arrival in the region in the eighteenth century (e.g., Audubon 1960; Jenkinson 2003; Witte and Gallagher 2008). Written and oral accounts of the northern Plains trade during the protohistoric and historic periods (Mitchell 2012; Wood and Thiessen 1985), combined with archaeological remains of a variety of birds, provide ample evidence of how birds and bird goods participate in multiple contexts of interaction. They may be complicit in the creation or maintenance of social relations and political alliances and be ascribed differential value based on the context of transfer or their intended versus actual use. Long-term research in national parks, forests, and Indian reservations, along with conversations with Blackfoot, Assiniboine, Hidatsa, Crow, Mandan, and Arikara people, has revealed (sometimes in startling detail) that birds are central to group and individual identity, which is reified through enduring and continuing cultural practices. This fundamental relationship, which dates as early as the Paleoindian period (e.g., Hill and Rapson 2008; Krech 2009), is expressed in myriad ways, as discussed below.

The attribution of value to birds derives both from their unique status as gods (Thunderbird) or as people of the air, or "wingeds," and from the complexity of their relationship to human beings (Chandler et al. 2017). In the Native American world, birds are consummate communicators, capable of engaging people, animals, and things in conversation and of influencing behaviors and decisions. Birds are members of a spiritual community, barometers of a community's well-being, and a tangible connection to the spiritual world that sustains them: birds bridge the spiritual and corporeal worlds (Murray 2009). The spiritual power intrinsic in some birds may be acquired by humans through dreams or visions, transferred from one person to another, or tapped through the incorporation of a bird or bird part—feather, claw, or bone—into objects such as pipes, flutes, drums, headdresses, necklaces, or bundles. As Chandler and colleagues (2017:2) note, this agency transcends human-bird reciprocation, extending to human interaction with bird parts, bird habitats, and features associated with human-bird interaction as, for example, eagle-trapping pits and lodges and avian reincarnations of human souls.

Birds are also agents of social prestige and political power. The best-known representations of "the Indian" in North America generally include a Native American in a large feathered headdress or perhaps with a single feather or the body of an entire bird affixed on the back of his or her head. While these styles are by no means ubiquitous to all North American Indians, they demonstrate the widespread importance of bird parts in material culture. Catlin's (1989) and Bodmer's (Wood et al. 2007) portraits of native people they encountered on their journey through America's interior in the 1830s rarely show a subject without some kind of avian adornment, whether feathered headgear, a feathered fan, a staff, a shield, jewelry, or another object (figure 5.2). Bird parts, too, are used for utilitarian purposes, as well as to decorate pieces of regalia or ceremonial objects and to denote personal identity and belonging. Finally, birds (gallinaceous birds and waterfowl) also provide a subsistence complement to bison, corn, and fish for some tribes. As they participate in multifarious social interactions, birds thus provide unparalleled opportunities to illustrate systems of valuation within the various contexts in which goods with inalienable properties in one context may be commoditized or deployed for the accumulation of wealth, power, and prestige in another and yet remain social patrimony.

BIRD GODS AND SPIRITS

Birds figure prominently in origin stories across the Plains, but there is one bird without an emergence story: the god Thunderbird. It is thought that this legendary creature was present in the cosmos before the creation of the earth. Thunderbird has homes in the Rocky Mountains and in certain buttes that dot the Missouri River Trench. Origin stories indicate that this god was not always benevolent. Yet it gifted humans with their most powerful objects, such as

FIGURE 5.2. *Mandan war chief with his favorite wife. George Catlin, 1861–69. Courtesy, National Gallery of Art, Washington, DC.*

the Blackfoot Thunder Pipe. According to the pipe origin story, Thunderbird was known for stealing women and blinding their husbands with lightning. Men engaged the help of Raven to confront Thunderbird, and Raven won the battle. In restitution, Thunderbird gave his pipe to the Blackfoot (McClintock 1999:251). Humans, too, helped Thunderbird in times of need, as when the Hidatsa culture hero Pack's Antelope rescued Thunderbird's eaglets from being eaten by evil snakes (water gods). In return, Thunderbird transformed the great hunter into a bird and, after giving him his sacred songs, sent him to the prairie to kill and eat evil snakes. After a time, Pack's Antelope took on a male human form and brought all his sacred songs and powers back to his people (Beckwith 1930:92–95). These origin stories illustrate the fundamentally reciprocal relationship between humans and gods; each interaction involves the gifting of objects, knowledge, and services and both parties enter into an alliance where mutual rights and obligations exist. In this alliance, only the pure form of a god's power is inalienable; his gifts of hunting and song are not, in the sense that they can be transferred from one individual to another along with sizable amounts of property.

Although humans may obtain power from many elements of the natural and supernatural worlds, the communicative nature of birds gives them an uncanny ability to transfer knowledge and power to people, animals, and other things. Certain birds (eagle, loon, owl, meadowlark, duck) are considered to be very ancient and thus wiser than others, but any bird, even the tiny chickadee, has the potential to transfer something to others (Chandler et al. 2017). Birds may engage individuals who seek their help through fasting and vision quests and transfer to them a song, a piece of magical knowledge, or a particular object along with rules and rights of use. The seeker, in return, agrees to use his or her transfer to exert good deeds among the people (Wissler and Duvall 1912). The newly acquired gift binds the individual and the bird in a reciprocal, inalienable relationship (in Weiner's 1992 strict sense of the term) that lasts as long as the rules of engagement (including liturgical order, specific votive offerings, and behavioral taboos) are observed. In general, this kind of gift has a singularized life history in that it does not transfer but stays with an individual throughout the person's life, although on occasion a part of this personal "medicine" or magical knowledge may be passed on to another. Also inalienable are the offerings made to the bird spirit in acknowledgment of its help.

Birds also contribute pure power to sacred bundles, and they do so in body and spirit (Bowers 1992, 2004; McClintock 1999; Wissler and Duvall 1912). These inalienable contributions generate complementary and reciprocal relationships among things inside the bundle, magnifying its power and the ability of the bundle holder to achieve a lofty goal. While ceremonial bundles are social patrimony, they, too, circulate among initiated individuals, often accompanied by sizable property exchange. Some bundle items can also circulate in a restricted context. In the past, this exchange involved items with the capacity for personhood, such as beaver pelts, buffalo hides, and horses, as well other valuables including blankets, star quilts, and foodstuffs; today, transfers are paid in cash. In the transfer from one bundle holder to another, the giver accrues social and ritual prestige (as well as property commensurate with the importance of that being transferred) while the receiver gets the rights and duties of the bundle. Bundles have the ability to give visions that the receiver may use to his or her own ends or to help people, thus opening another door for accumulation of goods; in time, he or she will transfer the bundle yet again (Lowie 1919). Among the Blackfoot, the more social patrimony an individual transfers to others, the more knowledgeable and powerful he or she becomes, until all possible transfers available in society have been received and subsequently passed on to another person: that is the highest status an individual can achieve in society.

PRECIOUS BIRDS

Missouri River tribes traditionally kept closed systems of knowledge that were vital to the reproduction of society. These closed systems not only applied to the transfer of supernatural powers and social patrimony, but in some societies they also extended to the manufacture of everyday objects such as arrows and pottery (Hollenback 2012). Knowledge was held individually, as part of corporate institutions such as secret societies and bundle groups, and in farming tribes (e.g., Mandan, Arikara), clans, and moieties (Bowers 1992, 2004; Wissler 1916). In some cases it continues to be so. As a result, the mere act of wanting to know something others have mastered requires a formal transfer in which the receiver of knowledge brings "gifts" in payment for the rights to know and to act on that knowledge. While many of these exchanges are nominal, those associated with precious goods are expensive and complex. Control mechanisms may be instituted to strictly limit access to valuables, and they can differ from one society to another. One context of exchange that involves the strictly controlled formal transfer of practices and rights relating to birds from a master to an apprentice is eagle knowledge.

As representatives of the god Thunderbird, eagle persons are supremely powerful and thus occupy the highest place in the order of birds; according to Mandan tradition, they lived in sky villages with the Sun and the Moon while the world below was just being created (Bowers 2004:117). Eagles also have the ability to impersonate human culture heroes and to transform everything they touch—their power is distributive (Beckwith 1930; Murray 2009, 2011; Wilson 1928). A complex of bird stories explains how eagles came from the sky and brought many gifts to the people. Eagle-thunderbirds are central characters in the Mandan Okipa Ceremony (Warren 2007:12); in the Assiniboine, Crow, and Hidatsa Sun Dance; and in the Blackfoot Okan, or Medicine Lodge, as well as many other rites and bundles associated with thunder rituals and eagle trapping (Chandler et al. 2017; Murray 2009, 2011). Not surprisingly, eagles and their parts are precious and much coveted for a variety of practices; thus, their transfer value was once very high. Feathers of the golden eagle and less so of the bald eagle were indispensable in ceremonial paraphernalia as well as in war. They were worn by men as insignias of leadership and bravery; they also signified personal wealth. Eagle bones were fashioned into ceremonial and medicinal whistles believed to be more powerful than any other whistle. Talons were kept as personal amulets or affixed to regalia (Murray 2009). Those who possessed the rights to eagles were highly regarded in society.

The possession of eagle rights meant the catcher had the knowledge and ability to attract a specific type of eagle (golden or bald, depending on the intended use) at a specific point in its biological life (immaturity). In this sense, the eagle presented itself to the catcher. The act of catching was in itself the receipt of a gift from the captured to the capturer. Among the Mandan and Hidatsa, eagle trapping was a gift of black bear spirits. Bear-trapping pits dotted the Missouri River bluffs, and so do those used by the people. The bears gifted eagle-trapping rights and duties to the people in exchange for plant medicine. These rights included songs, rituals such as the sweat lodge, fasting, self-torture, trapping techniques, and eagle power. All this knowledge was aided by the power of the eagle-trapping bundle, which generally included the foot of a black bear, an ash digging stick wrapped in bear hide and buffalo hair, a buffalo skull, eagle tail feathers and plumes, and a sacred snare (Wilson 1928:145). The transfer of eagle rights was a long-term process of exchange between master and apprentice—over a period of many years, the apprentice provided gifts and commodities to the master in exchange for portions of the eagle rights until the transfer was complete. Cultural protocols dictated that eagle-trapping rights could only be transferred four times over the course of a lifetime, after which the owner lost the authority to make such transfers. These protocols remain in place for the transfer of eagle medicine today, even though trapping was severely restricted in the early twentieth century and later forbidden under the Endangered Species Act (1973) and the Eagle Protection Act (1962) (Murray 2009, 2011).

The origin and transfer protocols of eagle trapping among the Blackfoot are less known, even though they trapped extensively in the richest golden eagle habitat at the foothills of the Rocky Mountain front and adjacent prairie. Stories told to McClintock (1999:428) suggest that it may have been an individual right passed on from father to son. Eagle trapping was a highly prestigious and holy activity imbued with taboo and ceremony. It had associations with coyote and coyote medicine songs as well as ghosts. Trapping pits are found in great numbers on the northern portion of Blackfoot territory in southern Saskatchewan (Kennedy and Reeves 2013) and the Porcupine Hills in southern Alberta. Several pit locations are known in Montana in what is now the Blackfeet Indian Reservation (McClintock 1999).

Trapping techniques, including the construction of a large pit where the trapper would lie in wait for an eagle to eat the bait placed on the brush disguising the pit, were fairly similar among the Missouri River tribes. Other protocols varied. For example, the Mandan and Hidatsa organized winter eagle-trapping expeditions led by a bundle holder; they built conical wooden lodges near eagle-trapping sites to perform their ceremonies and place eagle offerings (Wilson 1928). Among the Blackfoot, eagle trapping was carried out by an individual with rights, perhaps accompanied by an apprentice. The night before the expedition, the trapper and his wife consumed berry soup and sang ghost songs and eagle songs; the trapper then rubbed his body with the smoke of sweetgrass to mask his body odor. Sexual intercourse and sewing with awls were not permitted. In the morning the trapper headed for the pit carrying a human skull whose ghost would protect him and a six-foot-long stick to keep other birds and animals away. An expedition could fetch up to forty eagles, but one to eight eagles were brought back on average. Eagles were trapped and killed and then brought back home for a thanking feast. An eagle tipi lodge was erected just outside the camp. Eagles were placed on upright forked sticks inside the tipi and left to rot until the feathers could be plucked without damaging them. While on the poles, the eagles were fed by stuffing pemmican inside their beaks as a thanking offering and gesture of generosity to incur the beneficence of future eagles (Grinnell 1920:237–40).

THE MULTIVALENT TAIL FEATHER

The gift of eagle feathers originates in Mandan creation stories (Bowers 2004) and continues to be a highly regarded and honorable gift. Eagle feathers have diverse trajectories; their widespread value and popularity rests on the fact that feathers carry the inalienable power of the eagle and the thunderbird, as described by Murray (2009:42), and thus are considered persons. Feather fans are often used ceremonially to direct the incense smoke. Among the Mandan and Hidatsa, bald eagle feathers were used on the sacred child's pipe and in the associated ceremony (Wilson 1928:141). Eagle feathers were required in naming and adoption ceremonies and to cleanse or repair bundles. The calumet pipe was adorned with the feathers of mature and immature eagles (Allen 1983:4; Jenkinson 2003:57). They were also used in the Grass Dance that was bought from the Santee Sioux during the 1780s; society members wore feather bustles while dancing and carried small wooden guns decorated with eagle feathers to signify their wartime accomplishments (Gilman and Schneider 1987:159). Eagle feathers were in huge demand during ceremonial giveaways, when victorious warriors danced with and distributed several war bonnets to the participants (Zedeño et al. 2006). A war bonnet required thirty-six black-tipped tail feathers of a golden eagle and each eagle only has twelve such feathers, so eagle-trapping rights could fetch material wealth for those who held them (Murray 2009).

The Blackfoot used golden "war" eagle feathers to make their upright war bonnets (figure 5.3) and dancing bustles for the men and for distinguished

FIGURE 5.3. *Blackfoot straight-up bonnet with double feather trailer. From Scriver 1990:49.*

horses, as well as for healing implements and other ceremonial items. Scriver (1990) cataloged the contents of a number of Blackfoot bundles, many of which contain eagle feathers and bone artifacts. Tail feathers were only associated with men, except for the feathers found in the Natoas (Okan, or

Medicine Lodge) Bundle and the headdress worn by the Holy Woman of the Okan. Eagle wing feathers were found in the Crow-Has-Water Society Bundle and eagle wing bone whistles in the Iniskim Bundle. Personal and healing bundles also had eagle bone whistles and sucking tubes for extracting poison. Women's bundles usually only had ocher-dyed plumes, which were also found in the Ghost Bundle. The Holy Feather hand game included game pieces ornamented with dyed plumes. The Beaver Bundle, which explains the mysteries of the Blackfoot cosmos, contained mummified bodies of several water and sky birds and animals as well as an eagle feather fan. Its Water Pipe was sometimes adorned with underwing eagle feathers.

BIRD COMMODITIES

The widespread value and popularity of eagle feathers coupled with unequal distribution of eagles and eagle rights within and across the Missouri River tribes created a huge demand for them. Long-distance trade networks had been in place probably since the tenth century, but they flourished and expanded shortly before Europeans arrived in the region (Mitchell 2012). Archaeological excavations in ancestral Mandan lodges attest to the diversity of birds (more than 20 species) found in certain households that presumably specialized in processing birds and feathers for ceremonies and trade (Falk 2002). In the earliest contact account, La Vérendrye visited the Mandan in 1738 and commented that "these people dress leather better than do any other tribes, and do very fine work on furs and feathers" (quoted in Thwaites 1904:221; see also, Burpee 1927). He also noted the importance of trading bird parts within and between tribes, explaining that the Mandan "knew well how to profit thereby in trading their grain, tobacco, peltries, and *painted feathers*, which they know the Assiliboille [Assiniboine] highly value" and that the latter "had purchased everything which their means permitted, such as painted buffalo-robes; skins of deer and antelope well dressed and ornamented with fur; *bunches of painted feathers*; peltries; wrought garters, *headdresses*, and girdles" from the Mandan (quoted in Thwaites 1904:221, emphasis added). The trade of feathers for agricultural products and other goods fostered an intricate social and economic network among the Mandan, Hidatsa, Arikara, Crow, Assiniboine, and Blackfoot tribes, based on the strengths and wants of each tribe (Chandler et al. 2017). Such wants and needs ranged from basic subsistence to esoteric knowledge and power objects or persons.

Hudson Bay Company records dating to the turn of the nineteenth century note that European traders relied on waterfowl and other non-migratory bird species as a food source, as well as for trade (Hudson Bay Company Archives n.d.). Goose and partridge feathers; crane, eagle, goose, and swan quills; and swans skins were also frequent trade items across the northern Plains. The Assiniboine served as middlemen between the Europeans and other tribes during early inland trade by the Hudson Bay Company's York Factory (Ray 1974:68–69). Having adopted certain notions of trade from their European partners, they acquired European trade goods and passed them on to other Plains tribes at a significant markup, exchanging their "used and deteriorated kettles, axes, knives, guns, and other trade goods" for corn, leather, feathers, and other material less abundant in their territory (Ray 1974:88; Rodnick 1938). In this way they obtained valued eagle feathers for use in dress, regalia, and ceremonial items (Denig 2000:195; Will and Hyde 1964:179–80). In time of need, such precious goods could also be exchanged for staples and medicine without loss of personhood on the part of the precious good. The same type of eagle tail feathers formally transferred to an eagle-trapping apprentice within strictly ritualized parameters could also be traded to an Assiniboine partner for the price of a horse, a gun, or a number of bison robes (Chandler et al. 2017). Accounts of the Columbia Dalles trade center compiled by Griswold (1954) further indicate that golden eagle feathers were traded to the northwestern tribes.

The Blackfoot's most prized possession was a good buffalo runner that could partner with the hunter in a successful bison kill. Trade in these horses provides a clear picture of just how valuable eagle feathers were in the commodity market. Grinnell (1920:240) noted that in the north, where golden eagles abounded, the Blackfoot could purchase a good horse with five golden eagles, compared to further south where only two eagles could purchase the same. A Blackfoot (North Peigan) consultant explained that his male ancestors were eagle trappers by occupation and that the golden eagle feathers were prized so highly for their godly power and the prestige they imparted to their owners that only one eagle feather might be traded for a horse in certain contexts. Matthews (1877:28) also reported that the Mandan could trade a single tail feather from a golden eagle to another tribe for a "buffalo-horse, i.e., a horse swift enough to outrun a young adult buffalo in the fall."

Clearly, individuals with eagle-trapping rights could amass large fortunes as a corollary of their profession (Hungry-Wolf 2006:136). For example, Brings-down-the-Sun, "a celebrated medicine man of the north," according to McClintock (1999:312), supported his family through eagle trapping by trading the feathers he acquired to the Piikani (Blackfeet) in the south. The Piikani used them for regalia and ceremonial objects (McClintock 1999:428, 432), as well as to fund other important projects such as the horse trade. His descendant told the authors that through the eagle feather trade, Brings-down-the-Sun was able to support seventeen wives, each of whom gave him children for ten straight years. Indisputably, as Grinnell (1920:236) states, "before the Whites came to Blackfoot country, the Indian standard of value was the eagle tail-feathers."

Other precious birds also circulated in economic and social networks. Red birds (mostly woodpeckers), for example, are associated with the origin of rainbows (Thwaites 1906:374), and they also appear in the Mandan story of "Brown Old Man" as the leader of the birds a long time ago when black bears trapped eagles (Bowers 2004:382). Red Bird was captured by Old Black Bear but explained to the bear that if he was killed, no more birds would be left. Old Black Bear released him, but birds like Red Bird were never seen again. Red Bird's son, Brown Old Man, could turn himself into a spotted eagle and brought buffalo and rain to the people (Bowers 2004:376). This story reveals both the importance of red birds in Mandan culture and their value as exotic trade items in native networks. Maximilian recorded the trade of pileated woodpecker heads to be used on the pipe in the Mandan Adoption Ceremony (cited in Bowers 2004:329; Thwaites 1906:319). The pileated wood-pecker's historical range did not reach far above the mouth of the Missouri River, although its range has expanded over the past forty years. The scarcity of this type of woodpecker added "a considerable expense" to the acquisition of such a pipe, which required the bird's upper bill and distinctive red crown (Thwaites 1906:319). The birds' heads are associated with Old-Woman-Who-Never-Dies and corn, perhaps because they live far to the south where Old-Woman resides. The head of a pileated woodpecker had to be brought from St. Louis, and it was traded for a large buffalo robe, horses, and corn (Bowers 2004:330; Thwaites 1906:320). The Blackfoot valued the exotic Carolina para-keet, also from the south, which was occasionally found inside personal bun-dles or affixed to the stem of a ceremonial pipe (figure 5.4) (Scriver 1990).

Stories also tell that the ancient Mandan traded the yellow crescent of mead-owlarks for shell bowls from a (mythological?) tribe they called the Maniga, which lived on the opposite side of the Mississippi at the point where it flows into the ocean (Bowers 2004:132, 156). Meadowlarks were sometimes dropped into the river as people crossed it to calm rough waters. The meadowlark was also valued because it warned war parties of nearby enemies, and it was a pre-dominant character in the Okipa Ceremony. In the past, when white buffalo robes were very scarce, they were a highly valued trade item. When a visiting tribe came to a village offering one of these robes, the Mandan would bring the most prized items in their possession; among them were "*skins of red birds,*

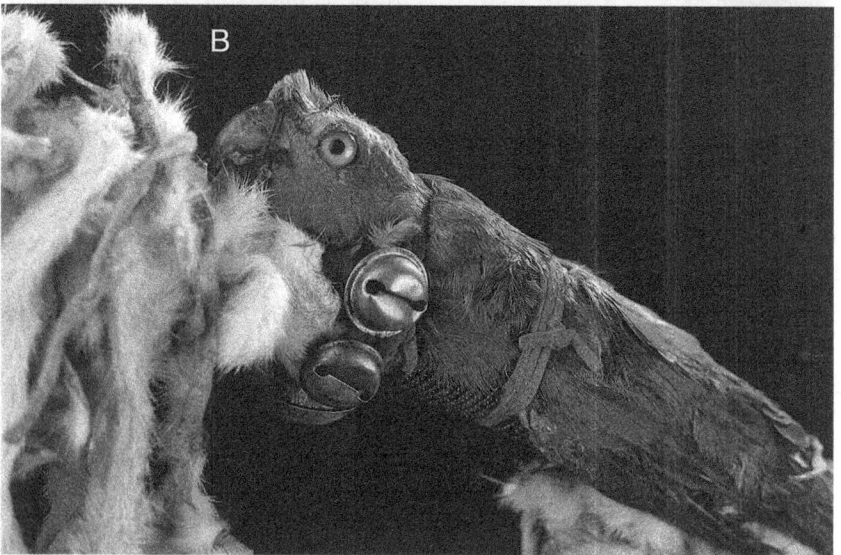

FIGURE 5.4. *Little Dog Thunder Medicine Pipe (a) decorated with a Carolina parakeet (b) (Blackfoot). From Scriver 1990:262–63.*

buffalo robes tanned, *heads of meadow larks* and dried bears' intestines which they used as ribbons" (Beckwith 1938:107, emphasis added).

Waterfowl furnish yet another example of the complexity of aboriginal value systems. Waterfowl figure prominently in stories of emergence across the Plains. Geese, loons, trumpeter swans, and various ducks are ubiquitous elements in bundles; their heads were affixed to calumets, and their likeness was carved in bone and stone (Chandler et al. 2017). The late Blackfoot linguist Darrell Kipp observed that in ancient Blackfoot society, loons were even more valuable than eagles (Kipp, personal communication, 2004). Among the Blackfoot, loons and ducks were an intrinsic component of the Beaver Bundle. Duck eggs were sacred food consumed during ceremonies. For the Mandan, waterfowl are the children of Old-Woman-Who-Never-Dies because female souls reincarnate in waterfowl after death. They, too, belong in various Mandan, Hidatsa, Arikara, and Crow bundles and ceremonial paraphernalia (Bowers 1992, 2004; Lowie 1919).

And yet, Hudson Bay Company records indicate that European traders relied on waterfowl as a food source obtained through trade with native hunters. Europeans also procured goose and partridge feathers; crane, eagle, goose, and swan quills; beaks, talons, and swan skins from natives and traded them for furs, with the Assiniboine serving as middlemen between the Europeans and other tribes (Chandler et al. 2017). Painted feathers of various birds were ubiquitously dyed for inclusion in bundles as well as in regalia. European traders introduced Old World natural and chemical dyes to the tribes, which became very popular over time. Magenta, indigo, violet, yellow, and bright green were the most common colors found in historical bundle contents. Packets of European dyes, which were highly regarded for the brilliant colors they lent to bird feathers and quills, also became a part of the bundles just as the holiest and most transformative native paints were, thus completing the inalienable-commodity–inalienable continuum.

CONCLUSION

Birds are foremost of the many resources encompassed by native Missouri River cosmologies. Collectively, birds and complementary resources, including animals, plants, minerals, and landforms, are all engaged in cultural and social reproduction. Some of these complementary resources are persons by birthright (e.g., bears), while others have the potential to become persons at some point in their trajectory. Some resources are valued as subsistence staples, while others are not. Together they sustain crucial links between the natural and spiritual worlds, shape or influence the life histories of people and other objects, and occupy a central position in the matrix of cultural belief and practice—all of which come to bear in the economic, social, and political web created in the process of trade or exchange.

Just as classic anthropological models of trade and exchange essentialize the inalienable-commodity continuum and attach the resulting categories to certain types of social organization, archaeologies of material culture tend to fix objects into systems of meaning and value that do not consider the malleable disposition of goods, their capacity for personhood either as intrinsically powerful objects or as objects that may become alive through ritual protocols, and the impact historical events and cultural contexts have on their value. The ultimate and perhaps the only inalienable possession is the pure power the gods imbue in people and goods; not even the dispositions of personhood are fully inalienable, as they are for the most part historically and contextually contingent. Among the Missouri River tribes, gifts, commodities, and inalienable possessions may be best understood as situational roles in a fluid, dynamic social world not unlike that found in Highland New Guinea (Godelier 1999) or New Georgia (Thomas 1991), while social patrimony lends those roles an inalienable quality in the order of things.

Whereas there are goods (notably, feathers from powerful birds such as the eagle) generally recognized as always precious or valuable gifts and earned honors, others can accumulate value in the course of their historical trajectories. The exotic Carolina parakeet, for example, is a bird not found in Blackfoot mythology or ritual, yet it could be "adopted" into the life history of a bundle or a sacred object; by the same token, certain gifts from the gods may enter the commodity exchange by virtue of their place in the order of things. Weiner (1992) concludes that object inalienability is an exclusive and cumulative identity associated with its owners' life histories and authenticated by myth and genealogy. In contrast, following Inomata (2013) and Aswani and Sheppard (2003), we suggest that strict inalienability is an extremely difficult status for any object to permanently achieve. The alternative Ferry (2002) provides to this conundrum is to realize that inalienability may be found not in the object itself but in the social patrimony (the greater good) gift exchange and commodity trade create and return, sometimes multiplied, to those who procured and circulated the goods in the first place.

In our case study, "keeping while giving" (*sensu* Weiner 1992) is manifested in the act of *transfer*, where unevenly distributed power and knowledge may be tapped by potentially anyone who has the fortitude and the means to enter the gift exchange that it requires. Through transfer, the pure power of the gods spreads from person to person, from group to group, and from people to thing and vice versa, but it is not lost to the giver unless the rules that accompany that which is powerful are broken. The Blackfoot, for one, are convinced that the power of sacred objects is not intrinsic to them: it is the god-given knowledge about things obtained through the transfer that imbues them with life force. Anyone could possess anything, but without the transfer the possession is inert. Transgressing the rules of the transfer would thus kill an object's power and potential for personhood. The very nature of the transfer implies that the circulation of powerful and precious goods, not simply as gifts but as commodities, may bring economic gain to the giver while allowing the receiver to participate in social and religious activities that require the possession of such goods. However, if the goods were procured by the giver outside the rules of the transfer, then the receiver may end up with something that has no power and thus no value.

Transfer is also a means to attain economic wealth, prestige, and political authority through the possession of ritual knowledge and corresponding bundles and objects by certain individuals and corporate institutions with expensive and exclusive membership. Participation in formal transfers, in theory, opens the possibility for upward mobility; in practice, the cost of the transfer, in particular the transfer of sacred bundles and eagle rights, can be prohibitive. The transfer thus serves an important role in social organization and reproduction because it is used to institute control mechanisms in the circulation of goods; consequently, it helps preserve the value system and the hierarchical position between those who hold powerful knowledge and those who cannot acquire such knowledge. Before the spread of the fur trade, corporate institutions held individual aggrandizement in check by keeping certain knowledge and rights within the institution and regulating the transfer. In the historic period, however, trading partnerships spread and concepts of the exchange value of goods evolved as a result of European influence, thus providing opportunities to aggrandize through wealth accumulation. Acquisitive power could, in turn, allow individuals to enter into expensive and exclusive transfers that would otherwise have been beyond their reach (Zedeño 2017). This case challenges Weiner's (1992) position that relinquishing inalienable possessions somehow results in either the loss or the temporary shift of hierarchical position; to the contrary, as Mosko (2000:381) observes in the Trobriand Islands case, the fluid disposition of supposedly inalienable goods in the context of exchange does not always defeat hierarchy.

Eagle feathers provide the clearest example of a valuation system centered in the situational and historical roles feathers play in the transfer. Eagles come from the gods and are thus inalienable; feathers carry the communicative, performative, and transformative power of the gods. People obtain rights to eagle trapping and feather handling through transfers from the gods or from those who hold those rights; through these rights, they are able to obtain and circulate feathers in the commodity exchange for economic gain. Those who acquire the feathers can continue trading them for other valuables and goods (e.g., horses) or can reincorporate them into insignias of identity and prestige, ceremonial objects, and sacred bundles, the latter of which are social patrimony. Unless they are desecrated, eagle feathers conserve their dispositions of personhood (as alive and possessors of pure power) and their value to society. Within the contextual and relational approach to trade and exchange we presented here, a given good may shift roles along a continuum of value that oscillates between two extremes—the commodity and the inalienable possession—or that can simultaneously become an inalienable commodity.

REFERENCES CITED

Allen, Walter E. 1983. "Eagle Trapping along the Little Missouri River." *North Dakota History* 50 (1): 4–22.

Appadurai, Arjun. 1986. "Introduction: Commodities and the Politics of Value." In *The Social Life of Things: Commodities in a Cultural Perspective*, ed. Arjun Appadurai, 3–63. Cambridge: Cambridge University Press. https://doi.org/10.1017/CBO9780511819582.003.

Aswani, Shankar, and Peter Sheppard. 2003. "The Archaeology and Ethnohistory of Exchange in Precolonial and Colonial Roviana: Gifts, Commodities, and Inalienable Possessions." *Current Anthropology* 44 (S5 supp.): S51–S78. https://doi.org/10.1086/377667.

Audubon, Maria R. 1960. *Audubon and His Journals*, vols. 1 and 2. New York: Charles Scribner's Sons.

Beckwith, Martha Warren. 1930. *Myths and Hunting Stories of the Mandan and Hidatsa Sioux*. New York: Abraham's Magazine Service Press.

Beckwith, Martha Warren. 1938. *Mandan-Hidatsa Myths and Ceremonies*. Memoirs of the American Folklore Society 32. New York: G. E. Stetchard.

Bowers, Alfred W. 1992 [1965]. *Hidatsa Social and Ceremonial Organization*. Lincoln: University of Nebraska Press.

Bowers, Alfred W. 2004 [1950]. *Mandan Social and Ceremonial Organization*. Chicago: University of Chicago Press.

Burpee, Lawrence J., ed. 1927. *Journals and Letters of Pierre Gaultier de Varennes de la Vérendrye and His Sons*. Toronto: Champlain Society.

Catlin, George. 1989. *North American Indians*. Ed. Peter Matthiessen. New York: Penguin Group.

Chandler, Kaytlin, Wendi Murray, Maria Nieves Zedeño, Samrat Clements, and Robert Jones. 2017. *The Winged: A Missouri River Ethno-ornithology*. Anthropological Papers of the University of Arizona 78. Tucson: University of Arizona Press.

Denig, Edwin T. 2000. *The Assiniboine*. Ed. J.N.B. Hewitt. Norman: University of Oklahoma Press.

Dobres, Marcia Anne, and John Robb, eds. 2000. *Agency in Archaeology*. New York: Routledge.

Durkheim, Emile. 1965 [1912]. *The Elementary Forms of Religious Life*. New York: Free Press.

Falk, Carl. 2002. "Fish, Amphibian, Reptile, and Bird Remains." In *Prehistory on First Street NE: The Archaeology of Scattered Village, Mandan, North Dakota*, ed. Stanley Ahler, 7.1–7.25. Submitted to the City of Mandan and North Dakota Department of Transportation. Flagstaff, AZ: Paleo Cultural Research Group.

Ferry, Emma E. 2002. "Inalienable Commodities: The Production and Circulation of Silver and Patrimony in a Mexican Mining Cooperative." *Cultural Anthropology* 17 (3): 331–58. https://doi.org/10.1525/can.2002.17.3.331.

Fogelin, Lars. 2012. "Material Practice and the Metamorphosis of a Sign: Early Buddhist *Stupas* and the Origin of Mahayana Buddhism." *Asian Perspective* 51 (2): 278–310.

Fowles, Severin. 2013. *An Archaeology of Doings: Secularism and the Study of Pueblo Religion*. Santa Fe, NM: School for Advanced Research Press.

Gell, Alfred. 1998. *Art and Agency: An Anthropological Theory*. New York: Clarendon.

Gilman, Carolyn, and Mary Jane Schneider. 1987. *The Way to Independence: Memories of a Hidatsa Indian Family, 1840–1920*. St. Paul: Minnesota Historical Society Press.

Godelier, Maurice. 1999. *The Enigma of the Gift*. Chicago: University of Chicago Press.

Gregory, Chris A. 1982. *Gifts and Commodities*. London: Academic.

Grinnell, George Bird. 1920. *Blackfoot Lodge Tales: The Story of a Prairie People*. New York: Charles Scribner's Sons.

Griswold, Gillet. 1954. "Aboriginal Patterns of Trade between the Columbia Basin and the Northern Plains." Master's thesis, Department of Anthropology, University of Montana, Missoula.

Hill, M. G., and D. J. Rapson. 2008. "Unresolved Taphonomic Histories, Interpretive Equivalence, and Paleoindian Faunal Exploitation." Paper presented at the Annual Meetings for the Society of American Archaeology, March 26–30, Vancouver, BC.

Hollenback, Kacy L. 2012. "Disaster, Technology, and Community: Measuring Responses to Smallpox Epidemics in Historic Hidatsa Villages, North Dakota." PhD dissertation, School of Anthropology, University of Arizona, Tucson.

Hudson Bay Company Archives. n.d. "York Factory Fur Returns, B239/1." *Manitoba Provincial Archives, Winnipeg.*

Hungry-Wolf, Adolf. 2006. *Blackfoot Papers*, vol. 1: *Piikani History and Culture.* Skookumchuck, BC: Good Medicine Cultural Foundation.

Inomata, Takeshi. 2013. "Negotiation of Inalienability and Meanings at the Classic Maya Center of Aguateca, Guatemala." *Archaeological Papers of the American Anthropological Association* 23 (1): 128–41. https://doi.org/10.1111/apaa.12020.

Jenkinson, Clay. 2003. *A Vast and Open Plain: The Writings of the Lewis and Clark Expedition in North Dakota 1806–1808.* Bismarck: State Historical Society of North Dakota.

Johnsgard, Paul A. 2012. *Wings over the Great Plains: Bird Migrations over the Central Flyway.* Zea E-Books Book 13. https://digitalcommons.unl.edu/cgi/view content.cgi?referer=https://www.bing.com/&httpsredir=1&article=1012&contex t=zeabook.

Keane, Webb. 2003. "Semiotics and the Social Analysis of Material Things." *Language and Communication* 23 (3–4): 409–25. https://doi.org/10.1016/S0271-5309(03)00010-7.

Kennedy, Margaret, and Brian O.K. Reeves. 2013. "Plain-Rocks in a Row: Some Ideas about Rock Alignments in the Northern Plains." Paper presented at the 71st Annual Plains Anthropological Conference, Loveland, CO, October 2–6.

Krech, I.I.I. Shepard. 2009. *Spirits of the Air: Birds and American Indians in the South.* Athens: University of Georgia Press.

Kopytoff, Igor. 1986. "The Cultural Biography of Things: Commoditization as Process." In *The Social Life of Things: Commodities in Cultural Perspective*, ed. Arjun Appadurai, 64–92. Cambridge: Cambridge University Press. https://doi.org/10 .1017/CBO9780511819582.004.

Kovacevich, Brigitte, and Michael Callaghan. 2013. "Introduction: Inalienability, Value, and the Construction of Social Difference." *Archaeological Papers of the American Anthropological Association* 23 (1): 1–13. https://doi.org/10.1111/apaa.12012.

Lévi-Strauss, Claude. 1964. *The Elementary Structures of Kinship.* Boston: Beacon.

Lokensgard, Kenneth Hayes. 2010. *Blackfoot Religion and the Consequences of Cultural Commoditization.* Burlington, VT: Ashgate.

Lowie, Robert H. 1919. *The Tobacco Society of the Crow Indians.* Anthropological Papers No. 21(2):101–200. New York: American Museum of Natural History.

Matthews, Washington. 1877. *Ethnography and Philology of the Hidatsa Indians.* Washington, DC: US Government Printing Office.

Mauss, Marcel. 1925. *The Gift: Forms and Functions of Exchange in Archaic Societies.* New York: W. W. Norton.

McClintock, Walter. 1999. *The Old North Trail: Or, the Life, Legends, and Religion of the Blackfeet Indians.* Lincoln: University of Nebraska Press.

Meskell, Lynn. 2004. *Object Worlds in Ancient Egypt: Material Biographies Past and Present.* New York: Berg.

Miller, Daniel, ed. 2005. *Materiality.* Durham, NC: Duke University Press. https://doi.org/10.1215/9780822386711.

Mills, Barbara. 2004. "The Establishment and Defeat of Hierarchy: Inalienable Possessions and the History of Collective Prestige Structures in the Pueblo Southwest." *American Anthropologist* 106 (2): 238–51. https://doi.org/10.1525/aa.2004 .106.2.238.

Mills, Barbara, and H. William Walker, eds. 2008. *Memory Work: Archaeologies of Material Practice.* Santa Fe, NM: School for Advanced Research Press.

Mitchell, Mark. 2012. *Crafting History in the Northern Plains: A Political Economy of the Heart River Region 1400–1750.* Tucson: University of Arizona Press.

Mosko, Mark S. 2000. "Inalienable Ethnography: Keeping-While-Giving and the Trobriand Case." *Journal of the Royal Anthropological Institute* 6 (3): 377–96. https://doi.org/10.1111/1467-9655.00022.

Murray, Wendi Field. 2009. "'The Gods Above Have Come': A Contemporary Analysis of the Eagle as a Cultural Resource in the Northern Plains." Master's thesis, School of Anthropology, University of Arizona, Tucson.

Murray, Wendi Field. 2011. "Feathers, Fasting, and the Eagle Complex: A Contemporary Analysis of the Eagle as a Cultural Resource in the Northern Plains." *Plains Anthropologist* 56 (218): 143–53. https://doi.org/10.1179/pan.2011.013.

Pard, Allan. 2015. "Repatriation among the Piikani." In *We Are Coming Home*, ed. Gerry Conaty, 119–34. Edmonton: Athabaska University Press.

Parmalee, Paul W. 1977. "Avifauna from Prehistoric Arikara Sites in South Dakota." *Plains Anthropologist* 22 (77): 189–222. https://doi.org/10.1080/2052546.1977.11908808.

Ray, Arthur J. 1974. *Indians in the Fur Trade: Their Role as Trappers, Hunters, and Middlemen in the Lands Southwest of Hudson Bay, 1660–1870.* Toronto: University of Toronto Press.

Rodnick, David. 1938. "Fort Belknap Assiniboine of Montana." PhD dissertation, Department of Anthropology, University of Pennsylvania, Philadelphia.

Roth, Christopher F. 2002. "Goods, Names, and Selves: Rethinking the Tsimshian Potlatch." *American Ethnologist* 29 (1): 123–50. https://doi.org/10.1525/ae.2002 .29.1.123.

Sahlins, Marshall D. 1972. *Stone Age Economics.* Chicago: Aldine.

Scheiber, Laura. 2015. "Paths, Places, and Positions: Exploring Rocky Mountain Landscapes as Resource, Symbol, Wilderness, and Refuge." In *Engineering Mountain Landscapes: An Anthropology of Social Investment*, ed. Laura Scheiber and Maria Nieves Zedeño, 23–48. Salt Lake City: University of Utah Press.

Schiffer, Michael Brian, and Andrea R. Miller. 1999. *The Material Life of Human Beings: Artifacts, Behavior, and Communication*. London: Routledge.

Scriver, Bob. 1990. *Blackfeet Artists of the Northern Plains*. Kansas City: Lowell.

Thomas, Nicholas. 1991. *Entangled Objects*. Cambridge, MA: Harvard University Press.

Thwaites, Reuben Gold, ed. 1904. *Original Journals of the Lewis and Clark Expedition: 1804–1806*, vol. 1. New York: Dodd, Mead.

Thwaites, Reuben Gold, ed. 1906. *Early Western Travels 1748–1846*, vol. 23. Cleveland: Arthur H. Clark.

Warren, Robert E. 2007. "Thunderbird Effigies from Plains Village Sites in the Northern Great Plains." In *Plains Village Archaeology: Bison-Hunting Farmers in the Central and Northern Plains*, ed. Stanley A. Ahler and Marvin Kay, 3–14. Salt Lake City: University of Utah Press.

Weiner, Annette. 1992. *Inalienable Possessions: The Paradox of Keeping While Giving*. Berkeley: University of California Press. https://doi.org/10.1525/california /9780520076037.001.0001.

Will, George F., and George E. Hyde. 1964. *Corn among the Indians of the Upper Missouri*. Lincoln: University of Nebraska Press.

Wilson, Gilbert L. 1928. "Hidatsa Eagle Trapping." *Anthropological Papers of the American Museum of Natural History* 30 (4): 99–245.

Wissler, Clark, ed. 1916. "Societies and Dance Associations of the Blackfoot Indians." In *Societies of the Plains Indians*, ed. Clark Wissler, 359–460. Anthropological Papers of the American Museum of Natural History, vol. 11. New York: American Museum of Natural History.

Wissler, Clark, and David Duvall. 1912. *Social Organization and Ritualistic Ceremonies of the Blackfoot Indians*. Anthropological Papers of the American Museum of Natural History 7. New York: American Museum of Natural History.

Witte, Stephen S., and Marsha V. Gallagher, eds. 2008. *April–September 1833: The North American Journals of Prince Maximilian of Wied*. Norman: University of Oklahoma Press.

Wood, W. Raymond, Joseph C. Potter, and David Hunt. 2007. *Karl Bodmer's Studio Art: The Newberry Library Bodmer Collection*. Chicago: University of Illinois Press.

Wood, W. Raymond, and Thomas D. Thiessen, eds. 1985. *Early Fur Trade on the Northern Plains: Canadian Traders among the Mandan and Hidatsa Indians, 1738–1818*. Norman: University of Oklahoma Press.

Zedeño, Maria Nieves. 2008. "Bundled Worlds: The Roles and Interactions of Complex Objects from the North American Plains." *Journal of Archaeological Method and Theory* 15 (4): 362–78. https://doi.org/10.1007/s10816-008-9058-4.

Zedeño, Maria Nieves. 2009. "Animating by Association: Index Objects and Relational Taxonomies." *Cambridge Archaeological Journal* 19 (3): 407–17. https://doi.org/10.1017/S0959774309000596.

Zedeño, Maria Nieves. 2017. "Rethinking the Impact of Abundance on the Rhythm of Bison Hunter Societies." In *Abundance: An Archaeological Analysis of Plenitude*, ed. Monica Smith, 23–44. Boulder: University Press of Colorado. https://doi.org/10.5876/9781607325949.c002.

Zedeño, Maria Nieves, Kacy Hollenback, Christopher Balsadú, Vania Fletcher, and Samrat Miller. 2006. *Cultural Affiliation Statement and Ethnographic Resource Assessment Study for Knife River Indian Villages National Historic Site, Fort Union Trading Post National Historic Site, and Theodore Roosevelt National Park, North Dakota*. Final Report Submitted to the National Park Service, Midwest Regional Office, DSCESU Cooperative Agreement CA-1248-00-002. Tucson: Bureau of Applied Research in Anthropology, University of Arizona.

Zedeño, Maria Nieves, Samrat Miller, and Kacy Hollenback. 2011. *Sleeping Bear Dunes National Lakeshore and the Inland Consent Decree of 2007—Ethnographic Resource Management and Tribal Access Considerations*. Final Report Prepared for the National Park Service, Midwest Regional Office, Contract Agreement H1200050003J6068080030 (DSCESU). Tucson: Bureau of Applied Research in Anthropology, University of Arizona.

6

Objects with Voices among the Ancient Maya

Matthew Looper

People in many societies consider objects (in addition to gods, spirits, and other nonhuman entities) to be alive and to accomplish concrete social action. In ancient Greece, for example, early cult statues as well as non-iconic images were thought to move and see and could cause a range of effects on humans and nature, including terror, death, and sterility (Freedberg 1989:33). The animacy of these objects is directly addressed in inscriptions; for example, a phallic stone from Antibes bears the cheeky first-person inscription "I am Terpon, servant of the noble Aphrodite" (Freedberg 1989:67). The notion that texts speak through inscribed objects is also common in ancient Egypt, Mesopotamia, and Anatolia, such as the Hittite "speaking buildings" (Meriggi 1962).

The concept of "objects" as expressing agency is also widely attested in the Maya ethnographic record. Highland Maya images of saints placed on home altars are said to eat and drink the offerings left to them; dance costumes may rattle swords as they are venerated; crafted objects see, hear, and move (Hinojosa 2011:87; see also Vogt 1993:17–20). Devotees may examine the cigarettes placed in the mouths of Maximon figures for signs of slow burning, indicating that the saint is smoking satisfactorily (Cook 2000:155). The Zinacanteco Tzotzil Maya of Mexico consider a wide range of phenomena in addition to saintly images to possess innate souls (c'ulel), including domesticated animals and plants such as maize,

DOI: 10.5876/9781607327479.c006

salt, houses, hearth fires, crosses, musical instruments, and other deities (Vogt 1993:19). Perhaps the most famous examples of animate "objects" among the Maya are the Talking Crosses that appeared during the nineteenth-century "Caste War" in the eastern Yucatan, Mexico, which persist to the present (Reed 2001:150–51). Although they were recognized as "manmade," the crosses were seen as containers for the divine essence of Christ and therefore as agents endowed with the power of speech and prophecy. In contemporary Yucatan, these crosses are understood to be growing from within earth; and the nonhuman persons associated with them must be fed, clothed, housed, and otherwise cared for (Astor-Aguilera 2010:103, 162). These examples reflect general Maya perspectives on nonhuman persons as "cultural composites of multiple invisible beings, some named and some not, that communicate through various objects" (Houston 2014:100).

The processes by which objects are related to agency are complex, involving a number of material transformations and performative acts. Among the Kaqchikel Maya, binding, beating, dousing, heating, and speaking words of invocation may be performed to prepare nonhuman agents for participation in rites of a religious or medical nature (Hinojosa 2011; see also Stross 1998:35). In the Yucatan, communicating objects or structures, such as bundles, crosses, and stones, mediate the ancestral relationships between nonhuman and human persons (Astor-Aguilera 2010:120). Because the Yucatec Maya define personhood as the attachment of a sentient being to an object, the concept of binding (*piix* 'sheath') or tethering is fundamental to their concept of agency (Astor-Aguilera 2010:103, 161–62). From this perspective, the activation of an object does not bring it to life but rather summons beings to a particular locale where they may be addressed and controlled (Astor-Aguilera 2010:171). Analogously, the breaking of the object does not kill the spirits residing within but merely severs the communication link between the human and nonhuman persons (see Astor-Aguilera 2010:206).

Despite these ethnographic considerations, in the academic fields of history, art history, anthropology, and archaeology, agency has traditionally been seen as the purview of humans, residing in either individuals (the traditional liberal humanist view) or society (Marxism; see Dobres and Robb 2000; Knappett and Malafouris 2008). In recent years, both archaeologists and art historians have addressed the notion of nonhuman agency, frequently within the context of a revaluation of the cultural significance of materiality versus discourse (e.g., Freedberg 1989; Gosden 2005; Mitchell 1996; Olsen 2003; Shanks 1998; Sillar 2009). The shift from signified (equated with idea/mind) to signifier (corresponding to material object/body) places emphasis on what objects do and are rather than on what they say or represent (see Daston 2004:20). Nevertheless, such an approach perpetuates an ingrained ontology based on the opposition between the spiritual and material (see MacGaffey 1993, 1994). Power, which is required by agents to bring about certain effects (see Karp 1986:137), is displaced to one pole or the other when spirit and matter are bifurcated. Thus, scholars often fall back on the traditional concepts of fetishism (the power of material) or animism (the power of spirit in matter) to explain the supposed agency of things (Ingold 2007:12).

In one widely cited theory of the agency of things, formulated by anthropologist Alfred Gell (1998), created objects are not merely signifiers but may substitute for social agents (see Tanner and Osborne 2007). However, Gell (1998:6) is careful to explain that objects do not actually "speak." He theorizes that objects are in fact secondary distributors of agency, which must reside primarily in (animate) humans (see also Gardner 2007:103). Indeed, the process whereby agency is inferred ("abduction": e.g., the smile suggesting a friendly person) is explicitly semiotic: objects still stand for something else, though they "point" to it rather than stand apart from it like a symbol. By casting things as metaphors for social relations, Gell's theory seems similar to several other recent conceptualizations of agency (Latour 1999; Law 1999:4; see also Bynum 2011:281).

Art historians have also explored the agency of images; however, until recently, these studies have been limited to representational art. Thus, unlike Gell's indexical theory of agency, art historians tend to view agency in terms of iconicity. An important example is David Freedberg's art historical study of response to art, which asserts that objects achieve agency by a fusion of image with prototype (conflation of signified and signifier; Freedberg 1989:77). He states, "What joins all such writers in their views of the effectiveness (good and bad) of images is the tacit belief that the bodies represented on or in them somehow have the status of living bodies" (Freedberg 1989:12). Another art historian, W.J.T. Mitchell, draws the opposite conclusion, suggesting that it is precisely the artistic representation of the human form that guarantees powerlessness. Drawing on the concept of commodity fetishism, in which commodities occlude the true relationships of production, he concludes that the agency and animacy of images is a "constitutive fiction" wherein images are construed, through the process of interpretation, as "scapegoats in the social field of human visuality" (Mitchell 1996:81). To Mitchell, representations are unable to actually do work because they are not actually bodies; they only look like bodies and are therefore mirror images that surrogate desires. In the final analysis, artworks from this perspective are little more than vacuous, powerless shells that apparently desire "nothing at all" (Mitchell 1996:82).

Mitchell (1996:71) is typical of other scholars intent on creating generalizing theories, who explicitly acknowledge their reticence to place "things" in the driver's seat, even raising the specters of fetishism, idolatry, animism, or other "dangerous forms of reductionist essentialism" (Jones and Cloke 2008:81; see also Gosden 2005; Ingold 2008). Others redefine agency of things essentially in terms of causality—as the capacity of physical entities (like Tupperware) or events (like an earthquake) to "shape" culture or society (see Clarke 1997; Passoth et al. 2012:1–4; Pauketat 2013:29). Ingold (2007:12) reduces agency of things to processual networks: "Things are alive or active not because they are possessed of spirit—whether in or of matter—but because the substances which they comprise continue to be swept up in circulations of the surrounding media that alternately portend their dissolution or—characteristically with animate beings—ensure their regeneration" (see also Pauketat 2013:28–34). Ingold (2013:96–97) argues that the very concept of agency is flawed—even in the human context—since humans, as well as other living beings and "things," are caught up in action. He cites Jones and Boivin's observation that "causality does not lie with human agents . . . Instead it is the reiterative quality of performance that produces agency and causality" (Jones and Boivin 2010:351). Ingold concludes by recasting agency in terms of life, which generates action by virtue of its materials. While this critique of the concepts of animism and agency is warranted, the generalized reframing of agency as vitality does little to explain why in a certain cultural context, people might consider some non-human entities to be alive while others are not. We might also argue that this approach to agency basically employs a language of social relations and material "realities" expressive of a worldview specific to the social sciences of post-Enlightenment Europe that may have little to do with native ontologies and, thus, with conceptions of agency (see discussion in MacGaffey 1994:130). Indeed, as noted above, the Maya pay a great deal of attention to the desires and actions of nonhuman entities that may or may not be tethered to materials or bodies. As Vogt famously states with reference to the contemporary Tzotzil Maya: "The most important interaction in the universe is not between persons, nor between persons and objects, but among the innate souls of persons and material objects" (Vogt 1993:19).

In this chapter, then, I would like to discuss the agency of objects—their capacity to express power and do "lively" things—within a specific sociocultural context. In doing so, I shift away from universalizing theories of agency, which tend to ignore native precepts. As Bynum suggests, these native theories "are evidence about the attitudes and assumptions of those who shaped and were shaped by the objects themselves, and they offer a sort of evidence modern theories cannot provide" (Bynum 2011:280–81). In addition, the fact that we are studying "non-human living entities that act" necessitates a specific cultural viewpoint, as there is no a priori definition of "human," of "thing," or of "life." As observed by Pickering, "Within different cultures human beings and the material world might exhibit capacities for action quite different from those we customarily attribute to them" (Pickering 1995:245). Because of varying attitudes toward the agency of objects even within a culture, it seems of little use to categorically state that certain objects are alive and others are not. Rather, it is essential to delineate the way "beings of all kinds, more or less person-like or thing-like, continually and reciprocally bring one another into existence" (Ingold 2006:10).

Gell (1998) suggests that the proper domain for the analysis of art is not the "abstraction" of iconography, symbolism, or culture but rather the dynamic context of social interaction, which unfolds in time. While not denying the importance of social interaction in understanding artistic artifacts, cultural systems such as glyphic inscriptions and iconography still provide us with essential tools for understanding Maya art and society; in fact, they occasionally refer directly to local notions of agency. The evidence from Maya iconography and hieroglyphic inscriptions provides a unique perspective for theorizing agency—one that complements modern theory and implies a diversity of views concerning the relationship of human and nonhuman persons. I cite select case studies—focusing on one in particular—that demonstrate the Maya conception of agency as activated within and encompassing both materials and meanings. Houston (2014) highlights the fact that Maya notions of matter imply the storage of energies and latent powers. The ancient Maya associated various specific sculptural materials, particularly wood and stone and especially jade, with divine essences and gods. Through human manipulation, the animate potencies inherent in these materials could be manifested and controlled. In this chapter I suggest adding shell to the list of spiritually powerful media, but in addition I argue that the ancient Maya considered language an essential medium for the expression of vital power. By cutting and inscribing shells (and other media) with hieroglyphic texts, the ancient Maya allowed these materials to "speak," which was understood to be a manifestation of agency and liveliness. From this perspective, the agency of "things" is not a belief that is projected onto the material world. Instead, it is anchored in material but is dependent upon practice and discourse for realization.

BREATHING AND SPEAKING OBJECTS

In ancient Maya art and texts, a variety of persons are attributed the power of speech. Most commonly, hieroglyphic inscriptions refer to speech using the quotative particle *che/che'en/chehen* "so they say" (Grube 1998).[1] In some instances *che* appears at the end of the dedicatory phrase on ceramics, where it seems to serve as a general discourse marker. On two monuments at Copán (Papagayo step and Stela 34), *che'en* appears between a phrase and the name of the ruler, attributing speech in a specific way to a royal (human) person. The particle *che/che'en/chehen* also reports the speech of certain objects, such as an inscribed bone from Tikal that ends with "so his bone says." Similarly, Ceibal Hieroglyphic Stairway Tablet 9 utilizes the particle in the phrase "so his sculpture says" (Grube 1998:548). A different usage of *che* occurs in three inscriptions from the northern Yucatan that seem to suggest time periods as speakers. On a Chochola-style vessel (K8017), this expression appears in the sentence *uwojol chanlajuun tuun ta huxlajuun ajaw tubaah* . . . "his glyphs are made on the fourteenth year of k'atun 13 Ajaw, it says on the day and the year for him . . ." A similar expression appears on the Xcombec Glyphic Panel (Stela) as well as the Hieroglyphic Doorway at Sisilha (see Graña-Behrens 2002:365; Taf. 142). Grube (1998:553) interprets these passages as evidence that the time periods, as gods, were in fact speaking. As indications of speech that is both narrated and written, these particles were an important expression of the recitative aspect of ancient Maya literacy, in which oral performance of texts was the norm (see Houston 2000:155).

Another quotative marker in Maya inscriptions is based on the verb *a'al*, meaning "say" (Grube 1998:544–45). The verb appears twice on Tikal Miscellaneous Text 176 (the "Hummingbird Vase" from Burial 196), in a context of reported speech . . . *ya'aljiiy tz'unuun ti itzamkokaaj* ". . . said the hummingbird to Itzamnah" (figure 6.1).[2] The mythical context of this text and its associated image may relate to Maya concepts of birds and other animals as messengers (see Houston et al. 2001:5, fig. 2; Houston et al. 2006:227–51). Additional speakers in Maya art may be identified by the appearance of "speech scrolls": wavy lines, often terminating in hieroglyphic texts. These are particularly common during the Late Classic period (ca. AD 600–800), and they emerge from the mouths of human beings and gods alike (Houston et al. 2006:154, figs. 4.14e, 4.22a, 7.1, 7.2). A speech scroll decorated with beads is used to represent song (Houston et al. 2006:156, fig. 4.19). In other cases, texts are positioned within effigy mouths. A particularly vivid example appears at the site of Copán in Honduras on the riser of the step leading to the inner chamber of Temple 22, the facade of which is rendered as a monster mouth. This inscription contains numerous first-person markers as well as a quotative

FIGURE 6.1. *Tikal Miscellaneous Text 176, the "Hummingbird Vase" (Kerr 8008). Rollout photograph by Justin Kerr.*

marker (*ya'aljiiy*) assigning the speech to a god (Stuart 1992:175). Thus, when it was recited in ritual performance, the temple acted as a ventriloquist, saying "On 5 Lamat, my k'atun is completed."

Another important type of speaking (or singing) object is the musical instrument. An example appears on the Postclassic Santa Rita Murals in Belize, in which a divine musician on the left side plays a stationary drum (figure 6.2; Gann 1900:pl. 31). The drum is meticulously rendered with a bound hide head, a globular body, and stepped legs. Multicolored sound scrolls stream out of the drum's head, as well as out of the mouth of the skull that adorns its body. The scrolls arc toward a dancer who performs in front of the drum, branching toward his head and feet and essentially enveloping him in sound. Although other musical instruments in Postclassic Maya paintings are depicted with emerging sound scrolls (e.g., Dresden Codex 1880:34a), the explicit rendering of scrolls emerging from the drum's mouth at Santa Rita suggests a comparison of the sound of a drum to a voice (Houston et al. 2006:262). An earlier, Terminal Classic period hand drum recovered from the Structure E-51 midden at Altun Ha (Belize) is personified, like that depicted at Santa Rita (figure 6.3; Pendergast 1990:fig. 108). Its gaping mouth suggests an analogy between the sound produced by the instrument and the song/voice of the depicted being. Other musical instruments, such as a three-chambered whistle (K6095), have sound holes in the position of a deity's mouth, possibly suggesting a merging of instrumental sound with divine voice. Finally, the spire of the trumpet known as the Pearlman conch was worked with an image of a hunting deity, implying that the sound of the trumpet is equivalent to the voice of the god

FIGURE 6.2. *Mural from Santa Rita, detail. After Gann 1900:pl. 31.*

(figure 6.4; see Coe 1982:120–23; Coe and Kerr 1997:115; Houston, Stuart, and Taube 2006:264; Schele and Miller 1986:308–9; Zender 1999:77–82).

A SPEAKING SHELL

The above examples of speaking or singing bones, sculptures, temples, and drums highlight the agency of objects among the ancient Maya; but because

FIGURE 6.3. *Altun Ha hand drum from Str. E-51 midden. Author drawing after Pendergast 1990:fig. 108.*

most of these examples are manipulated or performed by other beings (humans or gods), from the Gellian perspective they might be characterized as secondary agents. They act, but did the drum require the activation by human/divine performers to make it speak or sing? While these examples imply that objects do things in the world, there is no indication of exactly how this agency was affected.

Another example from Maya art and writing allows for a more nuanced reading of how agency was activated in the context of certain objects. Specifically, it illustrates how agency was intimately connected to the acts of writing/reading, as well as to the associations of vital breath with speech. This object is the Cleveland shell plaque, an unperforated piece of queen conch (*Strombus gigas*) shell measuring 16.5 cm long (figure 6.5; Schele and Miller 1986:155, pl. 59a). The finely incised image from this plaque depicts a male lord wearing a deer headdress and smoking a thin cigar. He bends forward, gesturing gracefully to a large conch shell placed before him with the aperture pointed upward. The inscription of this plaque begins "great tribute ... for you, said the trumpet to the deer" (*chak patan ? ta hat ya'aljiiy huub ti chij*) (see Zender 2010:85). The identity of the depicted man as mythical or historical is uncertain as he is only referred to as a "deer," though hunters are sometimes depicted wearing similar deer headdresses elsewhere in Maya art (e.g., K1373). The remainder of the text is a series of names and titles that identifies the owner of the plaque as the lord "Jewel Jaguar," a priest or "guardian" from an unknown locale in the western Maya region (Doyle 2010:114).[3]

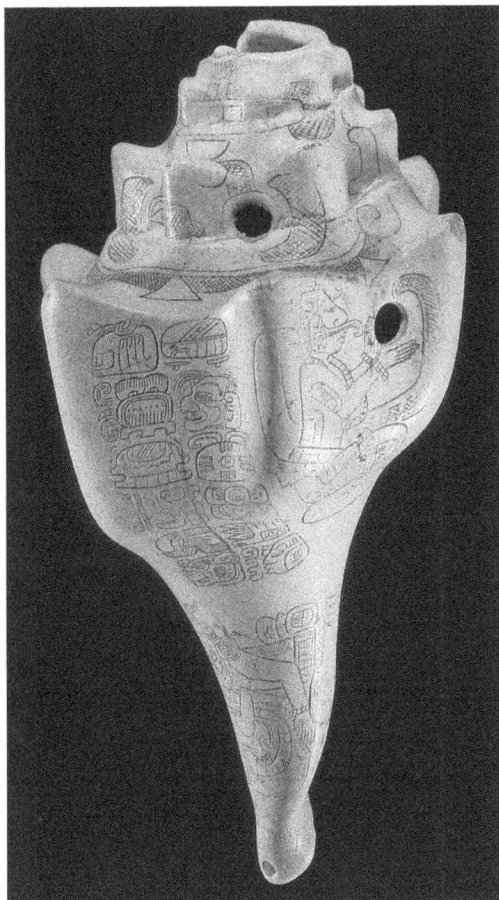

Figure 6.4. *Incised conch shell trumpet, Chrysler Museum, Norfolk, VA 86.457 (Kerr 0519). Photograph by Justin Kerr.*

In the image, the serpent that emerges from the aperture of the conch shell embodies the shell's "breath" or voice conveying the message of tribute (Houston et al. 2006:264). The content of this inscription complements the high-status textiles worn by the deer-man, as well as the elegantly thin cigar he smokes, which relates to Maya concepts of consumption and leisurely life at court (see Houston et al. 2006:116). The shell material of which the plaque was made may also have conveyed a message of wealth, given that such works of art were the products of trained, full-time specialists, likely associated with royal courts (see Emery and Aoyama 2007; Velázquez Castro 2012:439). Shells are part of the suite of materials and craft items—along with jewelry, feathers, and fine cloth—the Maya used as the conventional representation of tribute

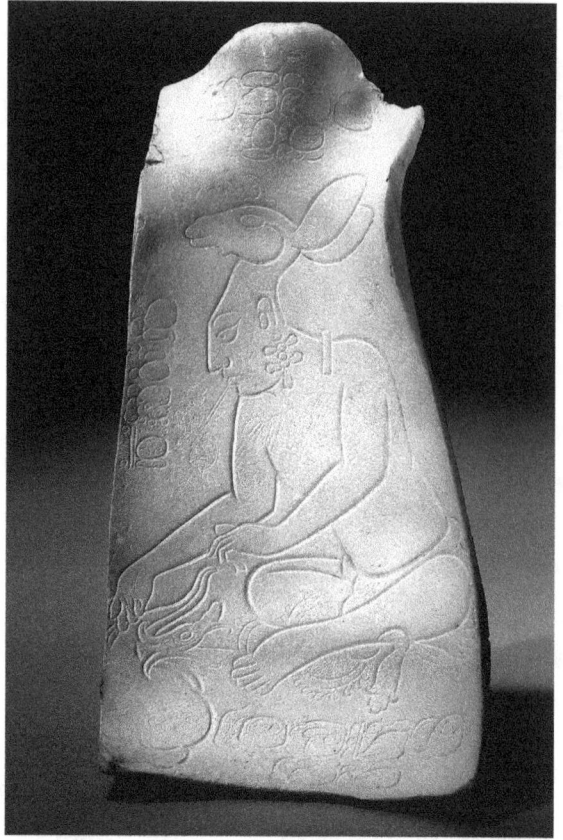

FIGURE 6.5. *Incised conch shell plaque, Cleveland Museum of Art, Norweb Collection 1965.550 (Kerr 2880). Photograph by Justin Kerr.*

(e.g., K1204, 1366, 1392, 1489, 1491, see Stuart 1995:363; Houston 2014:81). Maya inscriptions identify tribute offerings as *patan*, literally "something that is worked or made" but referring more broadly to office, cargo, work, or service rendered (Stuart 1995:354, 370–73).[4] This very term appears on the Cleveland plaque with reference to the tribute promised to the deer-man. The text and image on the plaque reflexively signify the economic value of this luxury object carved from shell.

The Cleveland plaque is particularly important because it clearly embodies the modality of agency of objects. Indeed, the combination of text, image, and medium of the plaque allows us to identify a number of participants involved in a complex "text act," analogous to the "speech act," an utterance that serves a function in communication (see Grube 1998:555). These include (1) the text inscribed on the surface of the shell plaque, (2) the depicted conch shell, and

(3) the material qualities of the conch shell piece from which the plaque was fashioned. Text act 1 involves the use of a quotative verbal expression in the text, which serves to conflate a spoken text with a written representation. It is thus the inscription itself that is speaking. However, the spatial interaction of text and image implies a simultaneous text act (2) in which the depicted conch shell trumpet speaks. In addition, the inscription interacts with (3) the materiality of the conch shell surface, merging the object with the speaker. In Maya art, conch shells were commonly employed as a symbol for breath as well as ancestors (Taube 2010:236; Houston 2014:81). The words inscribed on a shell fragment were therefore closely analogous to ancestral speech, and the shell plaque itself continuously speaks the message conveyed in the text.

The materiality of the plaque implies yet another way in which the shell "speaks," through the medium of tinkling of the shell plaque against other items of stone or shell, the resonant sounds of a conch shell held to the ear, or the sounds produced using a conch shell as a trumpet. Although the conch depicted on the Cleveland plaque is not clearly rendered in the form of a trumpet, this association is implied by the presence of an anthropomorphic deer as well as the caption, which attributes speech specifically to a "trumpet." In ancient Maya art, conch shell trumpets were intimately associated with the deer hunt and its related gods (see Houston et al. 2006:264). One extant Maya conch shell trumpet (the Pearlman conch) is carved in the form of a hunting god (see figure 6.4; Zender 1999:77). Zender (1999:80) asserts that conch shell trumpets were associated with ritual deer calling, and indeed, on K2578 and K4336, deities blow conch shell trumpets in the company of caped deer. The ritualized use of a shell to lure deer possibly relates to hunting tactics. In modern deer hunting, various mouth-blown or pneumatic devices fitted with reeds can be blown to make sounds that imitate the vocalizations of deer and are believed to attract them. Although the extant ancient Maya trumpets simply have a hole for blowing, some detailed representations show a mouthpiece inserted into this orifice (e.g., K1646). One wonders if these mouthpieces may have included a reed or other vibrating element that would have produced grunting or wheezing tones similar to modern deer callers.

The breath of the conch shell as a medium of speech in the Cleveland plaque is related to a discrete set of objects that exhibit similar behavior. In Maya art, jadeite ornaments are the most important category of objects that exhale breath, though in this context it is typically a particular type of "ensouled" breath called "white maize flower? breath" (*sak ? ik'*; Houston and Taube 2000:267; see also Houston 2014:125–33). In Maya art, this breath emanates from the noses and mouths of living or dead beings as a long curling strand, similar to a speech scroll but terminating in the "white 'flower' breath" glyphic collocation (Houston and Taube 2000:fig. 4). It also appears in the form of a serpent or as floral emblems with bifurcated "fragrance" scrolls. The "white 'flower' breath" is particularly associated with jade ear spools and bell-shaped disks placed at the end of ceremonial bars held by rulers (Houston et al. 2006:156). As these ornaments exhale breath serpents, they give birth to gods (Taube 2005:39). Ear spools also served as portals for the solar apotheosis of rulers (Taube 2005:39–42). The ear spools thus enabled the transformation and interaction of ruler, ancestors, and gods. Wearing objects of jade such as ear spools afforded Maya elites a direct physical link to the ancestors and gods, since these objects embodied vital forces and opened the pathway to the realm of the afterlife.

There is yet another dimension to the way agency seems to be activated through the Cleveland plaque. Houston (2014:105) comments on the persistent pictorial qualities of the ancient Maya script, the blurring of the boundary between image and text, and the discreteness and irreducibility of its signs—all of which seem to suggest the status of glyphs as "objects and beings in the world." Moreover, the Maya propensity to "animate" graphemes by adding faces or even complete bodies could have been a way of conveying the living character of writing itself (Houston 2014:118). In conclusion, it seems likely that the Maya would have conceived of the inscriptions on jade ornaments or shells such as the Cleveland plaque as materializations of the ancestors' living speech. The understanding that an inscribed object was something that "speaks" (rather than something that was "read") motivates a reconsideration of the potential agency of any ritually sanctified stone, paper, ceramic, or other inscribed surface. The Maya may have believed such inscribed objects to be specially enabled to speak the words of the ancestors.

In summary, it is the interaction of the writer/viewer/reader with the shell material that enables the agency of the plaque. The physical process of writing (i.e., engraving lines in segments of cut shell) and the act of reading/reciting bring the words of the ancestors into existence and activate the latent power of the shell. In addition, the shell plaque was owned by an elite person (a priest or "guardian") who, when holding it in his hand, would have perceived the image as if it were a reflection in a mirror. The voices of the shell (depicted and "actual") converge in communicating their portent of tribute. The reciprocity of user and object inherent in the creation and use of this artwork denies the culture/matter dichotomy that typifies much of the discussion of the animacy of "things" (see Graves-Brown 2000:1).

AGENCY AND LIVING WORDS IN MAYA ART

As noted, some modern theorists equate anthropomorphism or naturalism (verisimilitude) with agency (e.g., Daston 2004; Freedberg 1989). This idea has deep roots in European culture, as exemplified by Giambattista Alberti's discussion of the power of painting in his treatise *De pictura* (1435): "Painting possesses a truly divine power in that not only does it make the absent present (as they say of friendship), but it also represents the dead to the living many centuries later, so that they are recognized by spectators with pleasure and deep admiration for the artist . . . Through painting, the faces of the dead go on living for a very long time" (trans. Freedberg 1989:44). Later in the text, Alberti affirms the role of painting in inspiring religious devotion and awe. In short, it is the illusionistic power of painting that makes it suitable as an animating medium. These notions of the power of illusionism are also reflected in the writings of certain photographic theorists, who found their gazes returned by the subjects (see Barthes 1981; Benjamin 1999:512). The capacity of photographs to become agents has been widely observed both in Europe, where the technique originated, and in its applications abroad (Behrend 2003).

These perspectives, however, should not be assumed to be universal. Bynum (2011:282), for example, concludes that in late Medieval Europe, agency did not relate to visual similarities but was inherent in the materiality of objects, manifested in miraculous transformations, incorruptibility, and unusual behavior. Similar conclusions are reached by Dean (2010) in her consideration of the vitality of rock in Inca worldview. For the Bakongo peoples of Central Africa, a non-representational appearance does not detract from the effectiveness or animacy of a *nkisi*, which may be either a figural sculpture (the familiar so-called nail fetish) or an assemblage formed around bottles, gourds, or other objects (see MacGaffey and Harris 1993:75–77). Likewise, for the contemporary Kaqchikel Maya of Comalapa, visual cues are of little importance in the creation and use of effigies for surrogate healing ceremonies, called *k'al k'u'x* (Hinojosa 2011). Loosely translated as "bound essences," these objects are little more than crossed sticks or brooms to which are tied the unwashed clothes of the afflicted person. The clothing is a surrogate for the sick person because it is imbued with his or her spiritual imprint, signaled by a distinctive odor. As Hinojosa (2011:92) asserts, "If the k'al k'u'x treatment works, it is not because the surrogate effigy looks like the sufferer, but because the sufferer is physically built into the effigy." In other words, the effigy achieves its healing function by serving as a vital physical nexus among the ceremony, the patient, and his or her soul. Although the contemporary Maya do sometimes use portrait-like images such as photographs as surrogates during certain rituals, especially witchcraft, verisimilitude is generally of little importance to the ritual animation of things.

Analogously, I argue that for the Maya, agency was not necessarily tied to naturalism. In only a few of the examples discussed above—the musical instruments—agential or vital objects are more or less anthropomorphic in the sense that they have a visage. However, the conch shell depicted in the Cleveland plaque doing the speaking represents a nonhuman entity, as do numerous other epigraphic contexts that employ quotative particles to record speech (i.e., the Ceibal Hieroglyphic Stairway and the incised bone from Tikal MT 167). This suggests that as in many other cultures, a nonhuman appearance does not disqualify objects from being agents.

Instead, the Maya seem to have considered certain materials such as shell and jade to possess qualities of speaking through breathing akin to people, gods, birds, animals, and musical instruments. For Freedberg (1989:51), speaking is only one of the common "low-level" criteria used to gauge the agential effectiveness of representational art. However, for the Maya, speaking is not merely a symptom but a primary expression of the agential roles of certain objects. In ancient contexts, painting implied writing (both are *tz'ihb*), which enabled the dialogues through which intelligent thought (wisdom and knowledge) was propagated. Among the Maya of the past and today, agency is not the exclusive capacity of humans; nor is it a quality bestowed upon or inferred to be present in various entities. It is instead inherent in discourse through the interrelated media of writing/text and speech/breath.

An analogy may be drawn between the Maya procedures for activating certain materials and those used by the Bakongo peoples to enable their *minkisi*. Far from the mystified material objects early Europeans thought them to be, *minkisi* are conceived as vehicles through which the powers of the dead (*bakisi*) are controlled by a healer/diviner/priest, called a *nganga* (MacGaffey 1977, 1993, 1994). To activate these "portable graves," the diviner uses a variety of substances, including minerals from the land of the dead, items chosen for their names, and various attacking objects, such as the heads of venomous snakes (MacGaffey 1993:37, 62–63). Noteworthy in their formulation of agency is the power of language, expressed not only in incantations of activation but also in the extensive use of punning and metaphor, which binds meaning to materials and enables the diviner to interact with the *bakisi* through the object (MacGaffey 1994:125). In conclusion, like the ancient Maya shell and jade objects, the animacy and hence agency of the *minkisi* is not primarily focused on images but rather is enabled by speech acts and power materials. In the ancient Maya case, these acts are constituted through the processes of writing and reading. Both Bakongo and Maya agencies refuse to be thrust toward either pole of the Saussurean sign but instead depend upon the interaction of both discourse and materiality to achieve social effects.

The examples discussed in this chapter cast doubt on conventional theories that associate the agency of things with either fetishism or animism. The "commonsense" logic is that a sophisticated, educated person cannot accept images as other than things; therefore, any person who does so is naive, childish, primitive, or perverse (Mitchell 1996:71). Freedberg's account of how the animacy of objects happens is equally simplistic. It asserts that people lack mystical abilities; hence they create objects to contemplate the divine and eventually mistake the object for the divine (Freedberg 1989:65). It is therefore a lack of spiritual awareness that results in the concept of agential images. This sounds suspiciously similar to Hegel's belief that Africans lacked adequate notions of universality and were thus prone to worship any material "junk" that appeared before them (see MacGaffey 1994:125). In contrast, the Cleveland shell plaque reveals the sophisticated way the Maya perceived the artist, viewer, and ancestors communicating through the medium of cut conch shell. The ancient Maya summoned the forces inherent in materials through breath and speech, especially within the context of reading (aloud) and writing. It is not merely the materiality of the shell or a simple belief in spiritual powers that expressed agency but its intimate connection and genesis within social discourses of empowerment.

NOTES

1. For an alternative interpretation of the form "*che'en*," see Hull et al. (2009:36–37n9). See also discussion in Law et al. (2013:E39–E40n2).

2. I would like to acknowledge the input of Yuriy Polyukhovych, who helped me refine several of the epigraphic readings and interpretations used in this chapter.

3. For various interpretations of the *ajk'uhuun* title borne by Jewel Jaguar, see Zender (2004); Jackson and Stuart (2001).

4. See also translations in Stuart (2006); Tokovinine and Beliaev (2013); Speal (2014).

REFERENCES CITED

Astor-Aguilera, Miguel Angel. 2010. *The Maya World of Communicating Objects: Quadripartite Crosses, Trees, and Stones*. Albuquerque: University of New Mexico Press.

Barthes, Roland. 1981. *Camera Lucida: Reflections on Photography*. New York: Hill and Wang.

Behrend, Heike. 2003. "Photo Magic: Photographs in Practices of Healing and Harming in East Africa." *Journal of Religion in Africa; Religion en Afrique* 33 (2): 129–45. https://doi.org/10.1163/15700660360703114.

Benjamin, Walter. 1999. "Little History of Photography." In *Selected Writings*, vol. 2: *1927–1934*, trans. Rodney Livingstone et al., ed. Michael W. Jennings, Howard Eiland, and Gary Smith, 507–30. Cambridge, MA: Belknap Press of Harvard University Press.

Bynum, Caroline Walker. 2011. *Christian Materiality: An Essay on Religion in Late Medieval Europe*. New York: Zone Books.

Clarke, Alison J. 1997. "Tupperware: Product as Social Relation." In *American Visual Culture: The Shape of the Field*, ed. Ann Smart Martin and J. Ritchie Garrison, 225–51. Winterthur, DE: Henry Francis DuPont Winterthur Museum.

Coe, Michael D. 1982. *Old Gods and Young Heroes: The Pearlman Collection of Maya Ceramics*. Jerusalem: Israel Museum.

Coe, Michael D., and Justin Kerr. 1997. *The Art of the Maya Scribe*. New York: Harry N. Abrams.

Cook, Garrett W. 2000. *Renewing the Maya World: Expressive Culture in a Highland Town*. Austin: University of Texas Press.

Daston, Lorraine. 2004. "Speechless." In *Things That Talk*, ed. Lorraine Daston, 9–26. Brooklyn: Zone Books.

Dean, Carolyn. 2010. *A Culture of Stone: Inka Perspectives on Rock*. Durham, NC: Duke University Press. https://doi.org/10.1215/9780822393177.

Dobres, Marcia-Anne, and John E. Robb. 2000. "Agency in Archaeology: Paradigm or Platitude?" In *Agency in Archaeology*, ed. Marcia-Anne Dobres and John E. Robb, 1–17. London: Routledge.

Doyle, James. 2010. "Catalog Entry 35." In *Fiery Pool: The Maya and the Mythic Sea*, ed. Daniel Finamore and Stephen D. Houston, 114–15. New Haven, CT: Peabody Essex Museum.

Dresden Codex. 1880. *Codex Dresdensis Maya*. Introductory material by Ernst Förstemann. Leipzig: A. Naumann.

Emery, Kitty F., and Kazuo Aoyama. 2007. "Bone, Shell, and Lithic Evidence for Crafting in Elite Maya Households at Aguateca, Guatemala." *Ancient Mesoamerica* 18 (1): 69–89. https://doi.org/10.1017/S0956536107000089.

Freedberg, David. 1989. *The Power of Images: Studies in the History and Theory of Response*. Chicago: University of Chicago Press.

Gann, Thomas W.F. 1900. *Mounds in Northern Honduras*. Bureau of American Ethnology Nineteenth Annual Report to the Secretary of the Smithsonian Institution, 1897–98. Washington, DC: Government Printing Office.

Gardner, Andrew. 2007. "Agency." In *Handbook of Archaeological Theories*, ed. R. Alexander Bentley, Herbert D.G. Maschner, and Christopher Chippindale, 95–108. Lanham, MD: Altamira.

Gell, Alfred. 1998. *Art and Agency: An Anthropological Theory*. Oxford: Clarendon.

Gosden, Chris. 2005. "What Do Objects Want?" *Journal of Archaeological Method and Theory* 12 (3): 193–211. https://doi.org/10.1007/s10816-005-6928-x.

Graña-Behrens, Daniel. 2002. "Die Maya-Inschriften aus Nordwestyukatan, Mexiko." PhD dissertation, Pre-Columbian Studies and Cultural Anthropology, Rheinischen Friedrich-Wilhelms-Universität, Bonn.

Graves-Brown, Paul M. 2000. "Introduction." In *Matter, Materiality, and Modern Culture*, ed. Paul M. Graves-Brown, 1–9. London: Routledge.

Grube, Nikolai. 1998. "Speaking through Stones: A Quotative Particle in Maya Hieroglyphic Inscriptions." In *50 Years of Americanist Studies at the University of Bonn: New Contributions to the Archaeology, Ethnohistory, Ethnolinguistics, and Ethnography of the Americas*, ed. Sabine-Salazar Sáenz, Carmen Arellano Hoffmann, Eva König, and Heiko Prümers, 543–58. Markt Schwaben, Germany: Verlag Anton Saurwein.

Hinojosa, Servando Z. 2011. "Ritual Effigies and Corporeality in Kaqchikel Maya Soul Healing." *Ethnology* 50 (1): 79–94.

Houston, Stephen D. 2000. "Into the Minds of the Ancients: Advances in Maya Glyph Studies." *Journal of World Prehistory* 14 (2): 121–201. https://doi.org/10.1023/A:1007883024875.

Houston, Stephen D. 2014. *The Life Within: Classic Maya and the Matter of Permanence*. New Haven, CT: Yale University Press.

Houston, Stephen D., John S. Robertson, and David Stuart. 2001. *Quality and Quantity in Glyphic Nouns and Adjectives*. Research Reports on Ancient Maya Writing 47. Washington, DC: Center for Maya Research.

Houston, Stephen D., David Stuart, and Karl Taube. 2006. *The Memory of Bones: Body, Being, and Experience among the Classic Maya*. Austin: University of Texas Press.

Houston, Stephen D., and Karl Taube. 2000. "An Archaeology of the Senses: Perception and Cultural Expression in Ancient Mesoamerica." *Cambridge Archaeological Journal* 10 (2): 261–94. https://doi.org/10.1017/S095977430000010X.

Hull, Kerry, Michael D. Carrasco, and Robert Wald. 2009. "The First-Person Singular Independent Pronoun in Classic Ch'olan." *Mexicon* 31 (2): 36–43.

Ingold, Tim. 2006. "Rethinking the Animate, Re-Animating Thought." *Ethnos* 71 (1): 9–20. https://doi.org/10.1080/00141840600603111.

Ingold, Tim. 2007. "Materials against Materiality." *Archaeological Dialogues* 14 (1): 1–16. https://doi.org/10.1017/S1380203807002127.

Ingold, Tim. 2008. "When ANT meets SPIDER: Social Theory for Arthropods." In *Material Agency: Toward a Non-Anthropocentric Approach*, ed. Carl Knappett and Lambros Malafouris, 209–15. New York: Springer. https://doi.org/10.1007/978-0-387-74711-8_11.

Ingold, Tim. 2013. *Making: Anthropology, Archaeology, Art, and Architecture*. London: Routledge.

Jackson, Sarah, and David Stuart. 2001. "The Aj K'uhun Title: Deciphering a Classic Maya Term of Rank." *Ancient Mesoamerica* 12 (2): 217–28. https://doi.org/10.1017/S0956536101122030.

Jones, Andrew M., and Nicole Boivin. 2010. "The Malice of Inanimate Objects: Material Agency." In *The Oxford Handbook of Material Culture Studies*, ed. Dan Hicks and Mary Carolyn Beaudry, 333–51. Oxford: Oxford University Press.

Jones, Owain, and Paul Cloke. 2008. "Non-Human Agencies: Trees in Place and Time." In *Material Agency: Toward a Non-Anthropocentric Approach*, ed. Carl Knappett and Lambros Malafouris, 79–96. New York: Springer. https://doi.org/10.1007/978-0-387-74711-8_5.

Karp, Ivan. 1986. "Agency and Social Theory: A Review of Anthony Giddens." *American Ethnologist* 13 (1): 131–37. https://doi.org/10.1525/ae.1986.13.1.02a00090.

Knappett, Carl, and Lambros Malafouris. 2008. "Material and Nonhuman Agency: An Introduction." In *Material Agency: Toward a Non-Anthropocentric Approach*, ed. Carl Knappett and Lambros Malafouris, ix–xix. New York: Springer. https://doi.org/10.1007/978-0-387-74711-8.

Latour, Bruno. 1999. "On Recalling ANT." In *Actor Network Theory and After*, ed. John Law and John Hassard, 15–25. Oxford: Blackwell.

Law, Danny, Stephen Houston, Nicholas Carter, Marc Zender, and David Stuart. 2013. "Reading in Context: The Interpretation of Personal Reference in Ancient Maya Hieroglyphic Texts." *Journal of Linguistic Anthropology* 23 (2): E23–E47. https://doi.org/10.1111/jola.12008.

Law, John. 1999. "After ANT: Complexity, Naming, and Topology." In *Actor Network Theory and After*, ed. John Law and John Hassard, 1–14. Oxford: Blackwell.

MacGaffey, Wyatt. 1977. "Fetishism Revisited: Kongo Nkisi in Sociological Perspective." *Africa: Journal of the International Africa Institute* 47 (2): 172–84. https://doi.org/10.2307/1158736.

MacGaffey, Wyatt. 1993. "The Eyes of Understanding: Kongo Minkisi." In *Astonishment and Power*, ed. Wyatt MacGaffey and Michael D. Harris, 21–103. Washington, DC: Smithsonian Institution Press.

MacGaffey, Wyatt. 1994. "African Objects and the Idea of Fetish." *Res* 25: 123–31.

MacGaffey, Wyatt, and Michael D. Harris. 1993. *Astonishment and Power*. Washington, DC: Smithsonian Institution.

Meriggi, Piero. 1962. *Hieroglyphisch-hethitisches Glossar*. Wiesbaden: Harassowitz.

Mitchell, W.J.T. 1996. "What Do Pictures *Really* Want?" *October* 77: 71–82. https://doi.org/10.2307/778960.

Olsen, Bjørnar. 2003. "Material Culture after Text: Re-Membering Things." *Norwegian Archaeological Review* 36 (2): 87–104. https://doi.org/10.1080/0029365 0310000650.

Passoth, Jan-Hendrik, Birgit Peuker, and Michael Schillmeier. 2012. "Introduction." In *Agency without Actors? New Approaches to Collective Action*, ed. Jan-Hendrik Passoth, Birgit Peuker, and Michael Schillmeier, 1–11. London: Routledge.

Pauketat, Timothy R. 2013. *An Archaeology of the Cosmos: Rethinking Agency and Religion in Ancient America*. New York: Routledge.

Pendergast, David M. 1990. *Excavations at Altun Ha, Belize, 1964–1970*, vol. 3. Toronto: Royal Ontario Museum.

Pickering, Andrew. 1995. *The Mangle of Practice: Time, Agency, and Science*. Chicago: University of Chicago Press. https://doi.org/10.7208/chicago/9780226668253 .001.0001.

Reed, Nelson A. 2001. *The Caste War of Yucatan*, rev. ed. Palo Alto, CA: Stanford University Press.

Schele, Linda, and Mary Ellen Miller. 1986. *The Blood of Kings: Dynasty and Ritual in Maya Art*. Fort Worth: Kimbell Art Museum.

Shanks, Michael. 1998. "The Life of an Artifact." *Fennoscandia Archaeologica* 15: 15–42.

Sillar, Bill. 2009. "The Social Agency of Things? Animism and Materiality in the Andes." *Cambridge Archaeological Journal* 19 (3): 367–77. https://doi.org/10.1017 /S0959774309000559.

Speal, C. Scott. 2014. "The Evolution of Ancient Maya Exchange Systems: An Etymological Study of Economic Vocabulary in the Mayan Language Family." *Ancient Mesoamerica* 25 (1): 69–113. https://doi.org/10.1017/S0956536114000078.

Stross, Brian. 1998. "Seven Ingredients in Mesoamerican Ensoulment: Dedication and Termination in Tenejapa." In *The Sowing and the Dawning: Termination, Dedication, and Transformation in the Archaeological and Ethnographic Record of Mesoamerica*, ed. Shirley B. Mock, 31–39. Albuquerque: University of New Mexico Press.

Stuart, David. 1992. "Hieroglyphs and Archaeology at Copan." *Ancient Mesoamerica* 3 (1): 169–84. https://doi.org/10.1017/S0956536100002388.

Stuart, David. 1995. "A Study of Maya Inscriptions." PhD dissertation, Department of Anthropology, Vanderbilt University, Nashville, TN.

Stuart, David. 2006. "Jade and Chocolate: Bundles of Wealth in Classic Maya Economies and Ritual." In *Sacred Bundles: Ritual Acts of Wrapping and Binding in Mesoamerica*, ed. Julia Guernsey and F. Kent Reilly, 127–44. Barnardsville, NC: Boundary End Archaeology Research Center.

Tanner, Jeremy, and Robin Osborne. 2007. "Introduction: 'Art and Agency' and Art History." In *Art's Agency and Art History*, ed. Robin Osborne and Jeremy Tanner, 1–27. Malden, MA: Blackwell. https://doi.org/10.1002/9780470776629.ch.

Taube, Karl. 2005. "The Symbolism of Jade in Classic Maya Religion." *Ancient Mesoamerica* 16 (1): 23–50. https://doi.org/10.1017/S0956536105050017.

Taube, Karl. 2010. "Catalog Entry 75." In *Fiery Pool: The Maya and the Mythic Sea*, ed. Daniel Finamore and Stephen D. Houston, 236–37. New Haven, CT: Peabody Essex Museum.

Tokovinine, Alexandre, and Dmitri Beliaev. 2013. "People of the Road: Traders and Travelers in Ancient Maya Words and Images." In *Merchants, Markets, and Exchange in the Pre-Columbian World*, ed. Kenneth Hirth and Joanne Pillsbury, 169–200. Washington, DC: Dumbarton Oaks Research Library and Collection.

Velázquez Castro, Adrián. 2012. "Pre-Columbian Maya Shell Objects: An Analysis of Manufacturing Techniques." In *Ancient Maya Art at Dumbarton Oaks*, ed. Joanne Pillsbury, Miriam Doutriaux, Reiko Ishihara-Brito, and Alexandre Tokovinine, 433–39. Washington, DC: Dumbarton Oaks Research Library and Collection.

Vogt, Evon Z. 1993. *Tortillas for the Gods: A Symbolic Analysis of Zinacanteco Rituals*, 2nd ed. Norman: University of Oklahoma Press.

Zender, Marc Uwe. 1999. "Diacritical Marks and Underspelling in the Classic Maya Script: Implications for Decipherment." MA thesis, Department of Anthropology, University of Calgary, Alberta.

Zender, Marc Uwe. 2004. "A Study of the Classic Maya Priesthood." PhD dissertation, Department of Archaeology, University of Calgary, Alberta.

Zender, Marc Uwe. 2010. "The Music of Shells." In *Fiery Pool: The Maya and the Mythic Sea*, ed. Daniel Finamore and Stephen D. Houston, 83–85. New Haven, CT: Peabody Essex Museum.

7

Can Tools Have Souls?

Maya Views on the Relations between Human and Other-than-Human Persons

Julia A. Hendon

When my co-editor and I began talking about the ideas that led to this book, we found ourselves returning to A. Irving Hallowell's foundational work on personhood: "While in all cultures 'persons' comprise one of the major classes of objects to which the self must become oriented, this category of being is by no means limited to *human* beings . . . But in the social sciences and psychology, 'persons' and human beings are categorically identified" (Hallowell 2002 [1960]:20, original emphasis).

As discussed in the introduction to this volume, Hallowell's insights form one beginning point for the anthropological interest in the self, personhood, and identity. Theoretical approaches that focus on material or relational ontologies, animism, the social life of things, symmetrical relationships, and related topics have turned this interest into a prominent focus in recent decades. My chapter is a way for me to bring together two interests—object-based agency and crafting—that have dominated my research in recent years. I accept the applicability of personhood beyond the conflation with human beings that Hallowell rightly decries. This perspective also requires me to move beyond the common assumption in the social sciences that objects are "mere receptacles for human categories" (Latour 1993:52). The idea of objects as agents has become an important theoretical strand in anthropology. My interest in object-based agency has led me to the broader concept of objects as persons, not just

DOI: 10.5876/9781607327479.c007

person-like entities. I have emphasized the relational and intersubjective nature of personhood for both humans and objects, taking object to mean primarily manufactured items—things made by human beings—in the cultural and historical setting of the Mesoamerican societies of Mexico and Central America before and after European colonization (Hendon 2010, 2012; Hendon et al. 2014). The Mesoamerican world is replete with other-than-human persons. This approach to personhood is based on a philosophical framework that does not restrict personhood to the living, the human, and the corporeal. My other research interest centers on crafting as a social process. Using such types of crafting as weaving and making clay figurines, I have argued that the making of things contributes to an embodied sense of self and plays a key role in the creation of a relational and intersubjective personhood for both humans and objects. Objects exercise agency as part of this kind of relational personhood (Hendon 2006, 2010; Joyce et al. 2014).

This chapter gives me the opportunity to shift focus somewhat. Rather than consider the end result of crafting, I concentrate on items used to make something or to carry out some task—in other words, the tools or implements or equipment required for the task.[1] A crafter's sense of self develops in part through enskillment, the process of becoming proficient in the manipulation of materials and the use of tools resulting in an enhanced understanding and ability to create things recognized as well made (or not so well made). A large part of being skilled and expert at one's craft is being adept at understanding the interplay among raw material, end result, and those tools of the trade in use in a particular cultural or historical context (Bleed 2008; Hendon 2006; Ingold 2001, 2013; Keller 2001; Mauss 2006; Portisch 2010).

I expand on these issues by first discussing some of the culturally embedded perspectives on personhood and agency in Mesoamerica. The second part of the chapter examines a range of sources that include indigenous literature, ethnographic studies, documentary sources, visual imagery, and archaeological finds. I deliberately keep my focus narrow. My goal for this chapter is to see how rich and detailed an understanding I can develop for Mesoamerica. If we are serious about the idea that multiple ontologies exist within and across cultures or as a consequence of particular historical trajectories or forms of identity, then I argue that such an in-depth approach has as much value as efforts to compare cross-culturally in search of universally "non-Western" perspectives.

I then turn to what these sources tell us about implements in particular, with special emphasis on those that are important to crafting. I demonstrate that the equipment vital to the technologies of crafting has or has the potential to have the same qualities of personhood—including agency, animacy, possession of a soul, the ability to form relations with others, and intersubjectivity—that Mesoamerican ontologies consider human beings have the potential to possess. Such potential is not always realized for humans or for other kinds of objects (Hill, this volume). I consider, therefore, when and how personhood does emerge in humans and tools. Finally, I discuss the broader implications of a focus on tools for the understanding of questions of both personhood and crafting in Mesoamerica.

By considering information from a diverse range of Mesoamerican groups, I hope to discern common cultural threads that represent distinct understandings of ways of being and ways of acting in the world. Before the Spanish conquest, these understandings reflected the long-term processes of cultural, political, and economic contact among societies in the region, processes that allow modern scholars to refer to the area as Mesoamerica (Clark and Pye 2000; Joyce 2004). As part of the colonization process, these understandings came into dialogue with the beliefs and perspectives of the invaders, a dialogue that has continued ever since and been marked by extreme differences in power and control.

My willingness to take such a long-term perspective does not mean I consider indigenous peoples to be "timeless" or "outside of history" and thus living exactly as their ancestors did. My perspective is quite the contrary (see Hendon 2010). Engaging with a diversity of sources and historical moments reflects my conviction that it is possible to identify a set of philosophical and ontological beliefs about the nature of the world that have informed Mesoamerican cultural understandings and which are reflected in their interactions with one another, the post-conquest dominant society, and the natural and human-built world in which they live (Hendon 2010, 2012).

Ways of doing things and ways of being in the world intersect in interesting ways with the materiality of traditional technologies. Central to the perspective adopted in this chapter is the recognition that it is practices as much as or even more so than abstract structures that provide the means by which people in Mesoamerica developed an understanding of self and society (see Alberti 2012). John Monaghan (1995:13) calls such understandings "theories of social action." In a discussion of John Watanabe's work on the Mam-speaking Maya of Santiago Chimaltenango, also known as Chimbal, Monaghan credits Watanabe with highlighting "the open-ended, emergent, and creative dimensions of communication as opposed to the constraints it places on actors. Thus we can see that although the institutional forms traditionally associated with the Maya have disappeared from Chimaltenango . . . the people of Chimbal remain Maya and continue to be a community even though they are not the Maya of the past" (Monaghan 1995:13; see also Watanabe 1992).

MESOAMERICAN UNDERSTANDINGS OF PERSONHOOD AND AGENCY

People in Mesoamerica have found many ways to express their understanding of how the world came to be, how it works, why "volitional beings" (Astor-Aguilera 2010:71) exist, and how they should live. This understanding is often identified by outsiders as religious in nature, but the separation between religion and other aspects of society is artificial: "It is not at all clear that a discrete category of ritual action ever existed" in Mesoamerica (Monaghan 1998a:48). That is to say, the desire to bracket off some set of activities as religious and others as economic, political, quotidian, or social does not allow us to appreciate fully the perspectives of the people we are studying. Miguel Angel Astor-Aguilera (2010:3) has discussed the same issue, writing that "Mesoamerican cosmologies are more about a daily social way of life revolving around conceptions of self, personhood, and a sense of place relating to what is both visible and invisible" than they are about "what one could term codified religion founded on classifications based on binaries of the sacred and the profane."

Personhood and the self in Mesoamerica before and after European colonization are not limited to the individual human being/body. Further, there is not just one self per person, however that person is materialized. One's identity or being is not predicated on assumptions of a bounded, autonomous individuality that is restricted to the living, human beings, or tangible entities (see, e.g., Astor-Aguilera 2010; Gossen 1996; Houston and Stuart 1989; Monaghan 1995; Pitarch Ramón 1996; Vogt 1969, 1976; Watanabe 1992). Since these elements of the self can be separated from the physical being to form connections and relations with other individuals, groups, natural forces, and the dead, they exist across time and space beyond the boundaries of a particular body or lifespan. Indeed, these essences must be fixed or tethered through ritualized practices involving objects and places (Astor-Aguilera 2010). Tethering can be undone as well, so that the essence of personhood becomes disconnected from a human being, an object, a place, or an animal.

Important aspects of the definition of personhood in Mesoamerica are the passage of time, one's relationship with the landscape one inhabits, the kinds of actions one engages in, the relationships one is part of, and the way those actions contribute to social memory (Hendon 2012). Concepts that have been translated as "destiny," "co-essence," or "soul" connect to Mesoamerican views on the spatial and temporal ordering of existence. These concepts thus lie at the heart of a Mesoamerican understanding of personhood. A person's destiny is tied to the temporal system because it is shaped by day of birth, as determined by the indigenous calendar systems that were the basis of measuring time before the Spanish conquest (Monaghan 1998b; Tedlock 1992).

Although day of birth is important, it is not determinative. Persons must also work to achieve or mitigate their destiny through appropriate behavior. This shared understanding of the consequences of temporal positioning forms part of how Mesoamerican peoples define themselves in both space and time. The daily movement of the sun makes visible the passage of time and provides a way of orienting the body. The sun becomes responsible for and linked to the destinies associated with the diurnal periods defined through its movements. The interaction between temporality and human action means that destiny is both "part of the body *and* subject to an outside power—the internal and external complexly intersecting" (Monaghan 1998b:139, original emphasis).

Co-essences/souls are the multiple parts or elements of selfhood that from a Mesoamerican perspective are not necessarily circumscribed by the physical body (Astor-Aguilera 2010; Gossen 1996, 1999; Guiteras-Holmes 1961; Monaghan 1998b; Pitarch Ramón 2011; Vogt 1965, 1969, 1976; Watanabe 1992). As something that is independent of the body, souls may be shared, linking an individual with other beings, not all of which are human, animate, or alive (by Western standards). The concept of co-essences or souls connects entities that seem to be completely separate because they belong to different phenomenal categories or states of existence. These entities can be linked together through a shared temporal position determined by when they were born or came into existence. It might be assumed that personhood defined in this way necessarily restricts itself to biological beings that come into existence through a literal birthing process. As discussed below, giving birth and being born are not restricted to biological entities or to a particular set of physical processes. Co-essences can also be material objects. Mesoamerican concepts of personhood are not "based on an absolute assumption of human uniqueness" (Monaghan 1998b:144).

One of the trickiest parts of understanding and describing other-than-one's-own ontologies is the need to de-anthropocentrize the discussion. Or, as Rosemary Joyce and Susan Gillespie put it, to no longer "perpetuate the separation of humans and objects" (Joyce and Gillespie 2015:8). Among those who have addressed this issue for Mesoamerica, Astor-Aguilera has provided the most explicit analysis that is worth quoting at length. Astor-Aguilera defines nonhuman persons as "indigenous cultural composites of multiple invisible beings, some named and some not, that communicate through various objects" (Astor-Aguilera 2010:100). He goes on to write that "the human body . . . is no different from other sorts of material objects. A person within my Maya consultants' world view is simply an object that has sentient agency tethered to it. Persons can be and are attached to things other than humans" (Astor-Aguilera 2010:103). Jill Furst (1995:64–70), in her exploration of Aztec concepts of the soul, notes that one of the primary animating forces (*tonnalli*) is implanted in infants by deities through breathing and drilling into the child before birth, processes that would seem to be ways of tethering features that create agency and personhood.

In his collection of Tzotzil Maya dreams and stories from the *municipio* of Zinacantán (Chiapas, Mexico), Robert Laughlin found that "it is believed that an individual's possessions are representative of himself, have acquired his soul. Corn, too, shares its soul with the farmer, his family, and his farm tools" (Laughlin and Karasik 1988:9; see also Laughlin 1976). Evon Vogt (1969:370–71), writing about the same *municipio* in Chiapas, elaborates further on this point: "The phenomenon of the soul is by no means restricted to the domain of human beings. Virtually everything that is important and valuable to Zinacantecos possesses a soul: domesticated plants ... houses and household fires; wooden crosses erected on sacred mountains, inside caves, and beside waterholes; saints whose 'homes' are inside the Catholic churches; musical instruments used in their ceremonies; all the various deities in the Zinacanteco pantheon."

Thus, objects can do more than acquire a trace of a person's co-essence. They have souls in their own right and enter into relations with other souls. As Vogt (1969:371) observes, "The most important interaction going on in the universe is not between persons nor between persons and material objects, but rather between souls inside these persons and material objects." This analysis is supported by other discussions of souls, who possesses them, and how they relate to personhood (e.g., Gossen 1999; Pitarch Ramón 2011; Watanabe 1992).

Personhood develops through participation in social interactions and relations that make up a local theory of production (Monaghan 1998a) and sustain a "shared 'way of being'" (Watanabe 1992:90). Participation provides evidence of one's moral status and social identity. Attempts by Spanish religious authorities in the sixteenth and seventeenth centuries to define personhood as a property of individuals possessed of an integral body, mind, and soul continually run up against indigenous willingness to use the same words for all these supposedly separate phenomenal classes, indicating a philosophical perspective that conceptualizes them as similar. Brian Stross (1998:31) states that "Native Mesoamericans ... attributed a soul to all living things and considered all of nature to be alive." This is a good starting point, as it places us firmly in an alternative ontology. The next step is to consider how, given this ontological starting point, animate entities become persons. In other words, is being animate enough to make a human being or an object or an animal or a natural force a person? Personhood is not restricted to human beings but it is not extended to all, either. This raises the question I now turn to: When and how do objects become persons?

"Being alive . . . or being human, for that matter, is not enough to be considered a person" (Astor-Aguilera 2010:207). Participation in appropriate actions and socially recognized relations creates persons (Astor-Aguilera 2010; Gillespie 2001, 2008; Monaghan 1998a; Nash 2015; Watanabe 1992). Objects, animals and plants, and other nonhuman entities may become persons in their own right not only by being infused with a human being's essence. Like people, they are part of the ordered existence created by beliefs about time and space (Monaghan 1998b). They are born/made (in effect, crafted), exist for a period of time in one form, and then come to an end or transform into something else. This sequence is analogous to the human life cycle, and such an analogy can be discerned in how people in Mesoamerica interact with their material possessions. People and objects, the living and the dead, the animate and the inanimate, the corporeal and the non-corporeal are transformed into persons through their connection to systems of measuring time and making landscapes that exist above and beyond any individual lifespan or period of existence. As noted earlier, social relations are also integral to the transformation of an entity, whether human or not, into a person.

Aztec visual imagery and written documents produced after the conquest by, among others, the Franciscan friar Bernardino de Sahagún illustrate the ways infants and children could become persons (Eberl 2013; Furst 1995; Joyce 2000b). Examples of rhetoric recorded in the Florentine Codex,[2] for example, refer to a newborn as raw material. The midwife repeatedly refers to the newborn in this way: "O precious necklace, O quetzal feather, O jade, O armlet, O turquoise" (Sullivan 1994:141).

As discussed by Rosemary Joyce (2000b), these speeches emphasize the importance of transformative processes that apply equally to the human body as to the piece of turquoise or lump of jade or bird feathers. Children's bodies are pierced, cut, smoothed, molded, and polished. Furst (1995) has discussed the way Aztec deities help imbue a person with *tonalli* through use of a fire drill applied to the human body. Markus Eberl (2013) demonstrates further the transformation and manipulation of children's bodies through an analysis of images of codices in the Borgia Group, a set of pictorial texts created before the conquest in the Mixteca-Puebla-Tlaxcala area of Mexico (Boone 2006; Jansen 2006a, 2006b; Nicholson 2006). They contain sections on the rituals children were subjected to, often at the hands of deities. It is tempting to read these written and visual texts as metaphors, but to do so misunderstands the Mesoamerican ontologies they reflect. Children are transformed into persons by their parents, midwives, priests, other adults, and deities through actions that require certain tools.

Descriptions of rituals associated with the birth of a child or with later moments in a child's life cycle emphasize the presentation of gender-specific tools to babies or older children. The Florentine Codex and the Codex Mendoza[3] depict in words and images how the Aztec midwife would give a miniature set of weapons to an infant boy and a miniature set of spinning and weaving tools to an infant girl (Berdan and Anawalt 1992 3:57v–60r, 70r). Bishop Diego de Landa's sixteenth-century account of Yucatec Maya life includes a description of the presentation of tools to children that represented the crafts they would practice as they grew older. This presentation took place in a particular month in a highly ritualized context, thus connecting social identity and time (Tozzer 1941:159; see also Joyce 2000a).

Like the human body, objects in Mesoamerica are not merely a means to an end. As social persons or potential social persons, they have the capacity for agency. They are nonhuman actors that help shape the relationships of which they are a part through their properties, their purpose, and their connections to social institutions, projects, or relations above and beyond the individual interactions in which they participate. Agency, from this perspective, is not about intentionality or a particular state of being, such as being human or even alive. Objects, like people, function as agents because their properties cause things to happen and induce people to relate to them in certain ways and based on the outcome of what they do, in some context and in relation to some other (human or not) (Miller 2010).

Part of the process of becoming a person for humans and nonhumans occurs through shared participation in the productive actions that bring the objects into being—that is to say, crafting. The Maya of the Guatemalan town of Santiago Atitlan, for example, believe that "weavings are not just woven but in fact born" (Prechtel and Carlsen 1988:123) through the movements of the woman's body and the loom to which she is attached. Childbirth and weaving become part of a series of linked actions describing the ordering of space and time: "As is true with the weaving of cloth (and the birthing of humans), the rising of the sun allows for the world to be regenerated" (Prechtel and Carlsen 1988:126). I have argued previously that figurines made out of clay during the ninth to eleventh centuries in the lower Ulúa River valley and Copán River valley of Honduras became persons through the conditions of their production, their involvement in ritualized activities tied to the celebration of life-cycle or seasonal events in the life of the household, and their burial—sometimes intact and sometimes broken—in association with domestic spaces (Hendon 2010, 2012). These objects are relatively easy for us to accept as person-like because they look like people (and were clearly designed to do so). But equally important are the ways they enter into relationships with people, other objects, and places—ways that are central to the social reproduction of the self and for the creation of social memory. When these characteristics are taken into account, it becomes possible to see how personhood extends beyond the person-like in terms of appearance to other kinds of materials such as textiles.

THE PERSONHOOD AND AGENCY OF TOOLS

The discussion presented so far makes a strong argument that the Meso-american perspective on personhood encompasses a wide range of beings and states of being. My efforts to think about how and when tools might become persons has been made more difficult by the fact that I have found far more discussion of souls or co-essences in terms of human beings and animals than other kinds of material objects (e.g., Gossen 1974, 1996, 1999; Guiteras-Holmes 1961; Vogt 1965, 1969, 1976; Wagley 1949). Vogt mentions houses, musical instruments, and such religious objects as crosses and saints' statues (Vogt 1976:19, 1998). In discussing funerary rituals, Vogt (1976) and Stross (1998) note that items associated with the deceased may be broken or marred in some way to make it possible for the souls of these objects to go with the soul of the human person with whom they were associated. Stross connects this ontological perspective to archaeological finds of smashed objects or objects with holes drilled in them in locations that would render the object difficult or impossible to use for practical purposes.

Because of my focus on crafting, however, I am interested in developing a more precise understanding of implements and equipment as persons and agents. Tools are fundamental aspects of the material world in which people live. Discussions of technologies of crafting, farming, and others have tended to privilege the functional aspects of these implements, but a robust literature exists that reframes technology as a set of relationships between people and between people and the materials with which they work; as transformative processes that change both people and materials; as bodies of knowledge that must be transmitted from experts to novices; as the result of choices affected by the combination of cultural values, resource availability, and the physical properties of those resources; and as embodiments of values and beliefs (see Franklin 1999; Hendon 2006; Ingold 2001; Killick 2004).

Tools, or at least certain kinds of implements, appear in some examples of Mesoamerican visual imagery in association with figures usually referred to as gods or deities, which are often personifications of natural, creative, and ancestral forces. In addition to the Borgia Group codices already mentioned, several Maya codices can be cited. The Madrid Codex, generally believed to date from the end of the Late Postclassic period in the fifteenth century (Vail and Aveni 2004), contains almanacs in which deities are shown engaging in a variety of actions, including weaving, carving, painting, and planting over the course of some defined period of time connected to the Maya timekeeping systems (Anders 1967; Hernández and Bricker 2004; Vail 2004; Vail and Bricker 2004). Productive, creative, and destructive actions are featured also in the Dresden Codex (Hendon 2006; Thompson 1972), another surviving manuscript created before the Spanish conquest. Thunderstorm/Ch'a Chaak, for example, fishes with a net, hunts, rows, and drums in the almanacs devoted to him (Tedlock 2010:213–28). Action is implied through the Ch'a Chaak's holding of an ax. Female deities in the Madrid and Dresden codices, as in other visual imagery, often wear spindles in their headdress (Hendon 1999, 2006; Tedlock 2010:161–64).

These sources establish the importance of creative action or crafting. To get a better sense of tool agency and personhood, however, I turn to written and oral sources that flesh out the ways tools become persons through their actions, interactions, and associations. Let me start with the third creation attempt in the Popol Vuh, a K'iche' Maya text that has survived in an eighteenth-century transcription (Tedlock 1993). The creator deities have failed twice in their efforts to make creatures that can speak and thus pray to them. The third time, they make people out of wood, but these manikins lack the necessary spirit and soul to be persons that can engage in the efficacious actions necessary to a way of being in the world. Animals and objects rise up and attack the wood people, voicing their dissatisfaction with their treatment.

> Then came the small animals and the large animals, and sticks and stones struck their faces. And all began to speak: their earthen jars, their griddles, their plates, their pots, their grinding stones, all rose up and struck their faces . . . And the grinding stones said: "We were tormented by you; every day, every day, at night, at dawn, all the time our faces went *holi, holi, huqui, huqui*, because of you . . .
> But now that you are no longer men, you shall feel our strength. We shall grind and tear your flesh to pieces," said their grinding stones. (Recinos 1950:91)

The griddles and pots add their voices to the complaints before turning the tables on the wooden people: "Pain and suffering you have caused us.

Our mouths and faces were blackened with soot; we were always put on the fire and you burned us as though we felt no pain" (Recinos 1950:92). Finally, the three hearthstones that supported the cooking pots "hurled themselves straight from the fire against their heads causing them pain" (Recinos 1950:92).

Potters in Amatenango del Valle, Chiapas, related a variant of this story to June Nash (2015) in which the unresponsive and inanimate humans were made of clay instead of wood. Here the story has a gentler, more positive ending. Once given a heart, an organ central to Maya concepts of animacy and identity (Pitarch Ramón 2011), the clay humans become able to act and interact like true persons.

In other stories, a hoe can work on its own but is reluctant to do so. It must be whipped to convince it to do what it can (Gossen 2002:81–83). A rope bleeds when cut (Burns 1983:74–78). Ritual healers have a sacred *mesa*, or table, that communicates and a chain that hears (Oakes 1951:150–52). A clay pot that can turn stones into *tamalitos* only does so when it chooses to. It provides food for a poor woman who engages in appropriate actions through prayers and offerings. But the pot withholds its transformative abilities when stolen, turns itself to stone when threatened with violence, and verbally dresses down its abusers. Afterward, it disappears (Sexton and Rodríguez-Mejía 2010:105–7). In other tales, a pot talks and fills itself with beans and tortillas, a bell talks and moves, flutes have souls, or a magic wand talks (Laughlin and Karasik 1988:85, 186, 191, 207–8, 214). More widely discussed in the anthropological literature are the communicating crosses that emerged at various points in Chiapas and Yucatan (Astor-Aguilera 2010; Burns 1983; Reed 1964).

Studying how people in Highland Guatemala used *manos* and *metates*, Michael Searcy talked to Q'eqchi', K'iche', and Poqomam Maya women and men. Although he was interested in these grinding implements as functional items, he discovered that they were agents capable of causing things to happen and harming those who mistreated them. Although these grinding stones do not physically assault transgressors as in the Popol Vuh, they can affect human fertility and reproduction, cause sickness, or break, rendering them unusable by others. He concludes that they have the ability to "control their own destiny" (Searcy 2011:95).

I noted earlier that the Maya living in Santiago Atitlan told Martin Prechtel and Robert Carlsen (1988) that textiles are born, not made. Terms used to describe looms further support their personhood and suggest that looms are also born rather than made. Looms have a mouth, a head, ribs, a heart/umbilicus, and a butt. Warping boards, used to set the warp threads in order before they are threaded on the loom, also possess a heart, a head, a foot. The loom sticks are described as embodiments of female deities associated with midwifery and childbirth. Although Prechtel and Carlsen do not describe it this way, the association they note seems to match the process Astor-Aguilera calls tethering—aspects of the Ixoc Ahaua deities are tethered to the loom sticks, giving the sticks a soul and making them persons. Warping boards, the loom, and weaving itself have features that are person-like (e.g., head, heart).

PAST PERSPECTIVES

Depositional practices provide one way for archaeologists to infer the personhood of objects and people (Joyce and Pollard 2010; Mills and Walker 2008). Items related to crafting or making have been found in caches, which are contexts in which objects and sometimes incomplete human skeletal remains come to rest. These contexts are not trash or production sites but settings that bring together objects and other materials in patterned, structured ways that give insight into their life cycle, biography, and itineraries (Hendon 2000; Joyce and Gillespie 2015).

Household settings provide a rich source of examples, perhaps because crafting is so intertwined with daily life in Mesoamerica and because domestic settings were important places for the kinds of actions described earlier that create ways of being and doing. One can find many examples in the published literature that I will not attempt to summarize here to keep this chapter to a reasonable length. I use my own research and that of colleagues working in the Lower Ulúa River valley in north-central Honduras and in the Copán valley in the western mountains of the country near the border with Guatemala during the sixth to eleventh centuries AD. Jeanne Lopiparo's work at farming settlements along the Ulúa riverbank revealed an ongoing process of rebuilding houses, burials of humans, and deposition of a wide range of crafted objects and tools used to create those objects. Molds for creating figurines and other items of clay were one prominent element of these deposits (Lopiparo 2003; Lopiparo and Hendon 2008; Hendon et al. 2014). At the hilltop site of Cerro Palenque in the same valley, I found a deposit designed to mark the termination of one building and the initiation of a new building placed over the old one. This deposit contained obsidian tools, a small *hacha* (a woodworking tool), broken pots, and human bone (Hendon 2010). Earlier excavations at the same settlement by Rosemary Joyce (1991) uncovered obsidian or chert bifaces and *manos* placed in the fill of buildings. Moving further west into the mountain valley of Copán, home to a Maya kingdom, we see similar practices, including the placement of tools such as obsidian blades, polishing stones, and grinding stones in caches in association with domestic and public spaces (Aoyama 1995; Diamanti 2000; Gerstle and Webster 1990; Gonlin 1993; Hendon 2000, 2010, 2012; Hendon et al. 1990; Willey and Leventhal 1979; Willey et al. 1994).

CONCLUDING THOUGHTS

The personhood of tools comes through despite the greater focus on humans and animals in the ethnographic literature. Rather than follow the approach that claims that the whole world is animate or that objects become persons through their association with people, I would argue that personhood is assigned to or conferred on a range of entities. Making the effort to avoid anthropocentrism, I would argue that what we are seeing here is a process of intersubjectivity in which personhood develops for all actors through the associations and relationships they enter into. To use Astor-Aguilera's analysis, souls are tethered to human bodies and to implements through practice, particularly practices connected to crafting and other forms of production. As persons, they are part of actions and interactions that make their personhood manifest.

NOTES

1. These terms are essentially synonymous in common English-language usage. There is a tendency to consider "equipment" as referring to the whole suite of physical resources needed, including tools or implements. Here, I use them interchangeably.

2. The Florentine Codex was compiled in the late sixteenth century by Bernardino de Sahagún and his students (Dibble 1982).

3. The Codex Mendoza was produced in the sixteenth century by Aztec scribes/ artists at the request of the Spanish viceroy (Berdan and Anawalt 1992).

REFERENCES CITED

Alberti, Benjamin. 2012. "Cut, Pinch, and Pierce: Image as Practice among the Early Formative La Candelaria, First Millennium AD, Northwest Argentina." In *Encountering Imagery: Materialities, Perceptions, Relations*, ed. Ing-Marie Back Danielsson, Fredrik Fahlander, and Ylva Sjöstrand, 13–28. Stockholm Studies in Archaeology. Stockholm: Department of Archaeology and Classical Studies, University of Stockholm.

Anders, Ferdinand. 1967. *Codex Tro-Cortesianus (Codex Madrid)*. Graz, Austria: Akademische Druck-u. Verlagsanstalt.

Aoyama, Kazuo. 1995. "Microwear Analysis in the Southeast Maya Lowlands: Two Case Studies at Copan, Honduras." *Latin American Antiquity* 6 (2): 129–44. https://doi.org/10.2307/972148.

Astor-Aguilera, Miguel Angel. 2010. *The Maya World of Communicating Objects: Quadripartite Crosses, Trees, and Stones.* Albuquerque: University of New Mexico Press.

Berdan, Frances F., and Patricia R. Anawalt, eds. 1992. *The Codex Mendoza.* Berkeley: University of California Press.

Bleed, Peter. 2008. "Skill Matters." *Journal of Archaeological Method and Theory* 15 (1): 154–66. https://doi.org/10.1007/s10816-007-9046-0.

Boone, Elizabeth. 2006. "Fejérváry-Mayer, Codex." In *The Oxford Encyclopedia of Mesoamerican Cultures*, ed. Davíd Carrasco. Oxford: Oxford University Press. Accessed February 5, 2018. http://www.oxfordreference.com/view/10.1093/acref/9780195108156.001.0001/acref-9780195108156-e-230.

Burns, Allan F. 1983. *Epoch of Miracles: Oral Literature of the Yucatec Maya.* Austin: University of Texas Press.

Clark, John E., and Mary E. Pye. 2000. "The Pacific Coast and the Olmec Question." In *Olmec Art and Archaeology in Mesoamerica*, vol. 58, ed. John E. Clark and Mary E. Pye, 217–51. Studies in the History of Art. Washington, DC: National Gallery of Art.

Diamanti, Melissa. 2000. "Excavaciones en el conjunto de los Patios E, F, y M, Grupo 9N-8 (Operación XV)." In *Proyecto Arqueológico Copán Segunda Fase: excavaciones en el área urbana de Copán, Tomo IV*, ed. William T. Sanders, 21–341. Tegucigalpa, Honduras: Secretaría de Cultura, Artes y Deportes, Instituto Hondureño de Antropología e Historia.

Dibble, Charles. 1982. "Sahagún's *Historia*." In *Florentine Codex: General History of the Things of New Spain, Introduction and Indices*, trans. Arthur J.O. Anderson and Charles E. Dibble, 9–23. Santa Fe, NM, and Salt Lake City: School of American Research and University of Utah.

Eberl, Markus. 2013. "Nourishing Gods: Birth and Personhood in Highland Mexican Codices." *Cambridge Archaeological Journal* 23 (3): 453–76. https://doi.org/10.1017/S0959774313000437.

Franklin, Ursula M. 1999. *The Real World of Technology*, rev. ed. Toronto: House of Anansi Press.

Furst, Jill L.M. 1995. *The Natural History of the Soul in Ancient Mexico.* New Haven, CT: Yale University Press.

Gerstle, Andrea D., and David Webster. 1990. "Excavaciones en 9N-8, conjunto del patio D." In *Proyecto Arqueológico Copán Segunda Fase: excavaciones en el área urbana de Copán, Tomo III*, ed. William T. Sanders, 25–368. Tegucigalpa, Honduras: Secretaría de Estado en el Despacho de Cultura y Turismo, Instituto Hondureño de Antropología e Historia.

Gillespie, Susan D. 2001. "Personhood, Agency, and Mortuary Ritual: A Case Study from the Ancient Maya." *Journal of Anthropological Archaeology* 20 (1): 73–112. https://doi.org/10.1006/jaar.2000.0369.

Gillespie, Susan D. 2008. "Aspectos corporativos de la persona (personhood) y la encarnación (embodiment) entre los Mayas del Periodo Clásico." *Estudios de Cultura Maya* 31: 65–89.

Gonlin, Nancy. 1993. "Rural Household Archaeology at Copan, Honduras." PhD dissertation, Department of Anthropology, Pennsylvania State University, State College.

Gossen, Gary H. 1974. *Chamulas in the World of the Sun: Time and Space in a Maya Oral Tradition*. Cambridge, MA: Harvard University Press.

Gossen, Gary H. 1996. "Animal Souls, Co-essences, and Human Destiny in Mesoamerica." In *Monsters, Tricksters, and Sacred Cows: Animal Tales and American Identities*, ed. A. James Arnold, 80–107. Charlottesville: University Press of Virginia.

Gossen, Gary H. 1999. *Telling Maya Tales: Tzotzil Identities in Modern Mexico*. New York: Routledge.

Gossen, Gary H. 2002. *Four Creations: An Epic Story of the Chiapas Mayas*. Norman: University of Oklahoma Press.

Guiteras-Holmes, Calixta. 1961. *Perils of the Soul: The World View of a Tzotzil Indian*. New York: Free Press of Glencoe.

Hallowell, A. Irving. 2002 [1960]. "Ojibwa Ontology, Behavior, and World View." In *Readings in Indigenous Religion*, ed. Graham Harvey, 18–49. London: Continuum.

Hendon, Julia A. 1999. "Spinning and Weaving in Pre-Hispanic Mesoamerica: The Technology and Social Relations of Textile Production." In *Mayan Clothing and Weaving through the Ages*, ed. Barbara Knoke de Arathoon, Nancie L. González, and J. M. Willemsen Devlin, 7–16. Guatemala City: Museo Ixchel del Traje Indígena.

Hendon, Julia A. 2000. "Having and Holding: Storage, Memory, Knowledge, and Social Relations." *American Anthropologist* 102 (1): 42–53. https://doi.org/10.1525/aa.2000.102.1.42.

Hendon, Julia A. 2006. "Textile Production as Craft in Mesoamerica: Time, Labor, and Knowledge." *Journal of Social Archaeology* 6 (3): 354–78. https://doi.org/10.1177/1469605306067841.

Hendon, Julia A. 2010. *Houses in a Landscape: Memory and Everyday Life in Mesoamerica*. Durham, NC: Duke University Press.

Hendon, Julia A. 2012. "Objects as Persons: Integrating Maya Beliefs and Anthropological Theory." In *Power and Identity in Archaeological Theory and Practice: Case Studies from Ancient Mesoamerica*, ed. Eleanor Harrison-Buck, 82–89. Salt Lake City: University of Utah Press.

Hendon, Julia A., William T. Fash, and Eloísa Aguilar Palma. 1990. "Excavaciones en 9N-8, Conjunto del Patio B." In *Proyecto Arqueológico Copán Segunda Fase: Excavaciones en el área urbana de Copán Tomo II*, ed. William T. Sanders, 110–293. Tegucigalpa, Honduras: Secretaría de Estado en el Despacho de Cultura y Turismo, Instituto Hondureño de Antropología e Historia.

Hendon, Julia A., Rosemary A. Joyce, and Jeanne Lopiparo. 2014. *Material Relations: The Marriage Figurines of Prehispanic Honduras*. Boulder: University Press of Colorado.

Hernández, Christine, and Victoria R. Bricker. 2004. "The Inauguration of Planting in the Borgia and Madrid Codices." In *The Madrid Codex: New Approaches to Understanding an Ancient Maya Manuscript*, ed. Gabrielle Vail and Anthony Aveni, 277–320. Boulder: University Press of Colorado.

Houston, Stephen, and David Stuart. 1989. *The Way Glyph: Evidence for "Co-essences" among the Classic Maya*. Washington, DC: Center for Maya Research.

Ingold, Tim. 2001. "Beyond Art and Technology: The Anthropology of Skill." In *Anthropological Perspectives on Technology*, ed. Michael B. Schiffer, 17–31. Albuquerque: University of New Mexico Press.

Ingold, Tim. 2013. *Making: Anthropology, Archaeology, Art, and Architecture*. London: Routledge.

Jansen, Maarten E.R.G. 2006a. "Borgia, Codex." In *The Oxford Encyclopedia of Mesoamerican Cultures: The Civilizations of Mexico and Central America*, ed. Davíd Carrasco. Oxford: Oxford University Press. 10.1093/acref/9780195108156.001.0001.

Jansen, Maarten E.R.G. 2006b. "Vaticanus B, Codex." In *The Oxford Encyclopedia of Mesoamerican Cultures: The Civilizations of Mexico and Central America*, ed. Davíd Carrasco. Oxford: Oxford University Press. 10.1093/acref/9780195108156.001.0001.

Joyce, Rosemary A. 1991. *Cerro Palenque: Power and Identity on the Maya Periphery*. Austin: University of Texas Press.

Joyce, Rosemary A. 2000a. *Gender and Power in Prehispanic Mesoamerica*. Austin: University of Texas Press.

Joyce, Rosemary A. 2000b. "Girling the Girl and Boying the Boy: The Production of Adulthood in Ancient Mesoamerica." *World Archaeology* 31 (3): 473–83. https://doi.org/10.1080/00438240009696933.

Joyce, Rosemary A. 2004. "Mesoamerica: A Working Model for Archaeology."
In *Mesoamerican Archaeology: Theory and Practice*, ed. Julia A. Hendon and
Rosemary A. Joyce, 1–42. Malden, MA: Blackwell.

Joyce, Rosemary A., and Susan D. Gillespie. 2015. "Making Things out of Objects
That Move." In *Things in Motion: Object Itineraries in Anthropological Practice*,
ed. Rosemary A. Joyce and Susan D. Gillespie, 3–19. Santa Fe, NM: School for
Advanced Research Press.

Joyce, Rosemary A., Julia A. Hendon, and Jeanne Lopiparo. 2014. "Working with
Clay." *Ancient Mesoamerica* 25 (2): 411–20. https://doi.org/10.1017/S0956536114
000303.

Joyce, Rosemary A., and Joshua Pollard. 2010. "Archaeological Assemblages and
Practices of Deposition." In *The Oxford Handbook of Material Culture Studies*, ed.
Dan Hicks and Mary C. Beaudry, 291–309. Oxford: Oxford University Press.

Keller, Charles M. 2001. "Thought and Production: Insights of the Practitioner."
In *Anthropological Perspectives on Technology*, ed. Michael Brian Schiffer, 33–45.
Albuquerque: University of New Mexico Press.

Killick, David. 2004. "Social Constructionist Approaches to the Study of Technology."
World Archaeology 36 (4): 571–78. https://doi.org/10.1080/0043824042000303746.

Latour, Bruno. 1993. *We Have Never Been Modern*. Trans. Catherine Porter.
Cambridge, MA: Harvard University Press.

Laughlin, Robert M. 1976. *Of Wonders Wild and New: Dreams from Zinacantán*.
Smithsonian Contributions to Anthropology 22. Washington, DC: Smithsonian
Institution Press.

Laughlin, Robert M., trans., and Carol Karasik, ed. 1988. *The People of the Bat: Mayan
Tales and Dreams from Zinacantán*. Washington, DC: Smithsonian Institution
Press.

Lopiparo, Jeanne. 2003. "Household Ceramic Production and the Crafting of Society
in the Terminal Classic Ulua Valley, Honduras." PhD dissertation, Department of
Anthropology, University of California, Berkeley.

Lopiparo, Jeanne, and Julia A. Hendon. 2008. "Honduran Figurines and
Whistles in Context: Production, Use, and Meaning in the Ulua Valley." In
Mesoamerican Figurines: Small-Scale Indices of Large-Scale Social Phenomena, ed.
Christina T. Halperin, Katherine A. Faust, Rhonda Taube, and Aurore Giguet,
51–74. Gainesville: University of Florida Press.

Mauss, Marcel. 2006 [1947]. "Technology." In *Techniques, Technology, and Civilisation*,
ed. Nathan Schlanger, trans. Dominique Lussier, 97–140. New York: Durkheim
Press/Berghan Books.

Miller, Daniel. 2010. *Stuff*. Cambridge, MA: Polity.

Mills, Barbara, and William H. Walker, eds. 2008. *Memory Work: Archaeologies of Material Practice*. Santa Fe, NM: School of Advanced Research Press.

Monaghan, John. 1995. *The Covenants with Earth and Rain: Exchange, Sacrifice, and Revelation in Mixtec Sociality*. Norman: University of Oklahoma Press.

Monaghan, John. 1998a. "Dedication: Ritual or Production?" In *The Sowing and the Dawning: Termination, Dedication, and Transformation in the Archaeological and Ethnographic Record of Mesoamerica*, ed. Shirley B. Mock, 47–52. Albuquerque: University of New Mexico Press.

Monaghan, John. 1998b. "The Person, Destiny, and the Construction of Difference in Mesoamerica." *Res* 33: 137–46.

Nash, June. 2015. "Mayan Artisan Production: Creation of the World and Re-Creation of Another World." In *Artisans and Advocacy in the Global Market: Walking the Heart Path*, ed. Jeanne Simonelli, Katherine O'Donnell, and June Nash, 19–41. Santa Fe, NM: School for Advanced Research Press.

Nicholson, H. B. 2006. "Borgia Group of Pictorial Manuscripts." In *The Oxford Encyclopedia of Mesoamerican Cultures: The Civilizations of Mexico and Central America*, ed. Davíd Carrasco, 1:98–101. Oxford: Oxford University Press. 10.1093 /acref/9780195108156.001.0001.

Oakes, Maud. 1951. *The Two Crosses of Todos Santos: Survivals of Mayan Religious Ritual*. Bollingen Series 27. Princeton, NJ: Princeton University Press.

Pitarch Ramón, Pedro. 1996. "Animismo, colonialism y la memoria histórica Tzeltal." *Revista Espanola de Antropologia Americana* 26: 183–203.

Pitarch Ramón, Pedro. 2011. "Los dos cuerpos mayas: Esbozo de una antropología elemental indígena." *Estudios de Cultura Maya* 37: 149–78.

Portisch, Anna Odland. 2010. "The Craft of Skillful Learning: Kazakh Women's Everyday Craft Practices in Western Mongolia." In *Making Knowledge: Explorations of the Indissoluble Relation between Mind, Body, and Environment*, ed. Trevor H. J. Marchand, 59–75. Malden, MA: Wiley-Blackwell.

Prechtel, Martin, and Robert S. Carlsen. 1988. "Weaving and Cosmos among the Tzutujil Maya of Guatemala." *Res* 15: 123–32.

Recinos, Adrián. 1950. *Popol Vuh: The Sacred Book of the Ancient Quiché Maya*. Trans. Delia Goetz and Sylvanus Morley. Norman: University of Oklahoma Press.

Reed, Nelson. 1964. *The Caste War of Yucatan*. Stanford, CA: Stanford University Press.

Searcy, Michael T. 2011. *The Life-Giving Stone: Ethnoarchaeology of Maya Metates*. Tucson: University of Arizona Press.

Sexton, James D., and Fredy Rodríguez-Mejía. 2010. *The Dog Who Spoke and More Mayan Folktales/El Perro que habló y más cuentos mayas*. Norman: University of Oklahoma Press.

Stross, Brian. 1998. "Seven Ingredients in Mesoamerican Ensoulment: Dedication and Termination in Tenejapa." In *The Sowing and the Dawning: Termination, Dedication, and Transformation in the Archaeological and Ethnographic Record of Mesoamerica*, ed. Shirley Boteler Mock, 31–39. Albuquerque: University of New Mexico Press.

Sullivan, Thelma. 1994. *A Scattering of Jades: Stories, Poems, and Prayer*. Ed. T. J. Knab. New York: Touchstone.

Tedlock, Barbara. 1992. *Time and the Highland Maya*, rev. ed. Albuquerque: University of New Mexico Press.

Tedlock, Dennis. 1993. *Breath on the Mirror: Mythic Voices and Visions of the Living Maya*. San Francisco: HarperSanFrancisco.

Tedlock, Dennis. 2010. *2000 Years of Mayan Literature*. Berkeley: University of California Press.

Thompson, J. Eric S. 1972. *A Commentary on the Dresden Codex, a Maya Hieroglyphic Book*. Philadelphia: American Philosophical Society.

Tozzer, Alfred M. 1941. *Landa's Relación de las cosas de Yucatán*. Papers of the Peabody Museum of American Archaeology and Ethnology, vol. 18. Cambridge, MA: Peabody Museum of American Archaeology and Ethnology.

Vail, Gabrielle. 2004. "A Reinterpretation of *Tzolk'in* Almanacs in the Madrid Codex." In *The Madrid Codex: New Approaches to Understanding an Ancient Maya Manuscript*, ed. Gabrielle Vail and Anthony Aveni, 215–52. Boulder: University Press of Colorado.

Vail, Gabrielle, and Anthony Aveni. 2004. "Research Methodologies and New Approaches to Interpreting the Madrid Codex." In *The Madrid Codex: New Approaches to Understanding an Ancient Maya Manuscript*, ed. Gabrielle Vail and Anthony Aveni, 1–30. Boulder: University Press of Colorado.

Vail, Gabrielle, and Victoria R. Bricker. 2004. "*Haab* Dates in the Madrid Codex." In *The Madrid Codex: New Approaches to Understanding an Ancient Maya Manuscript*, ed. Gabrielle Vail and Anthony Aveni, 171–214. Boulder: University Press of Colorado.

Vogt, Evon Z. 1965. "Zinacanteco 'Souls.'" *Man* 65: 33–35. https://doi.org/10.2307/2797520.

Vogt, Evon Z. 1969. *Zinacantan: A Maya Community in the Highlands of Chiapas*. Cambridge, MA: Belknap Press, Harvard University Press. https://doi.org/10.4159/harvard.9780674436886.

Vogt, Evon Z. 1976. *Tortillas for the Gods: A Symbolic Analysis of Zinacanteco Rituals*. Cambridge, MA: Harvard University Press.

Vogt, Evon Z. 1998. "Zinacanteco Dedication and Termination Rituals." In *The Sowing and the Dawning: Termination, Dedication, and Transformation in the*

Archaeological and Ethnographic Record of Mesoamerica, ed. Shirley Boteler Mock, 21–30. Albuquerque: University of New Mexico Press.

Wagley, Charles. 1949. *The Social and Religious Life of a Guatemalan Village*. Memoir 71. Menasha, WI: American Anthropological Association.

Watanabe, John M. 1992. *Maya Saints and Souls in a Changing World*. Austin: University of Texas Press.

Willey, Gordon R., and Richard M. Leventhal. 1979. "Prehistoric Settlement at Copan." In *Maya Archaeology and Ethnohistory*, ed. Norman Hammond and Gordon R. Willey, 75–102. Austin: University of Texas Press.

Willey, Gordon R., Richard M. Leventhal, Arthur A. Demarest, and William L. Fash. 1994. *Ceramics and Artifacts from Excavations in the Copan Residential Zone*. Cambridge, MA: Harvard University Press.

8

Torres Strait Islanders of northeast Australia (figure 8.1) are marine subsistence specialists whose identity and social world are intimately connected with the sea. Social actors in this maritime world extend well beyond people—they include the human dead, the sea and the land, live and dead animals, and a broad array of objects. These people, animals, and objects all interact socially, emotionally, and physically on a broad range of epistemological and ontological levels that confound Western dichotomies such as physical and spiritual, culture and nature, object and subject, and mind and body (cf. Latour 1993). In a previous study I explored the relational and recursive fields of engagement among Torres Strait Islander hunters, their marine mammal prey, the bones of those prey, and hunting charms (McNiven 2010). More recently, I have focused on what I termed the "dialogical matrix" between humans (alive and dead) and prey (alive and dead), again using anthropological and archaeological information (McNiven 2013). The present chapter extends these discussions of relationality and agency to the largest movable object used by Torres Strait Islanders—double-outrigger sailing canoes.

Anthropologist Alfred Haddon (1890:381) rightly observed that the "large canoes of the Torres Straits Islanders of former times must have been very imposing objects when painted with red, white, and black, and decorated with white shells, black feathers, and flying streamers." Yet Torres Strait Islander canoes were far

Torres Strait Canoes as Social and Predatory Object-Beings

Ian J. McNiven

DOI: 10.5876/9781607327479.c008

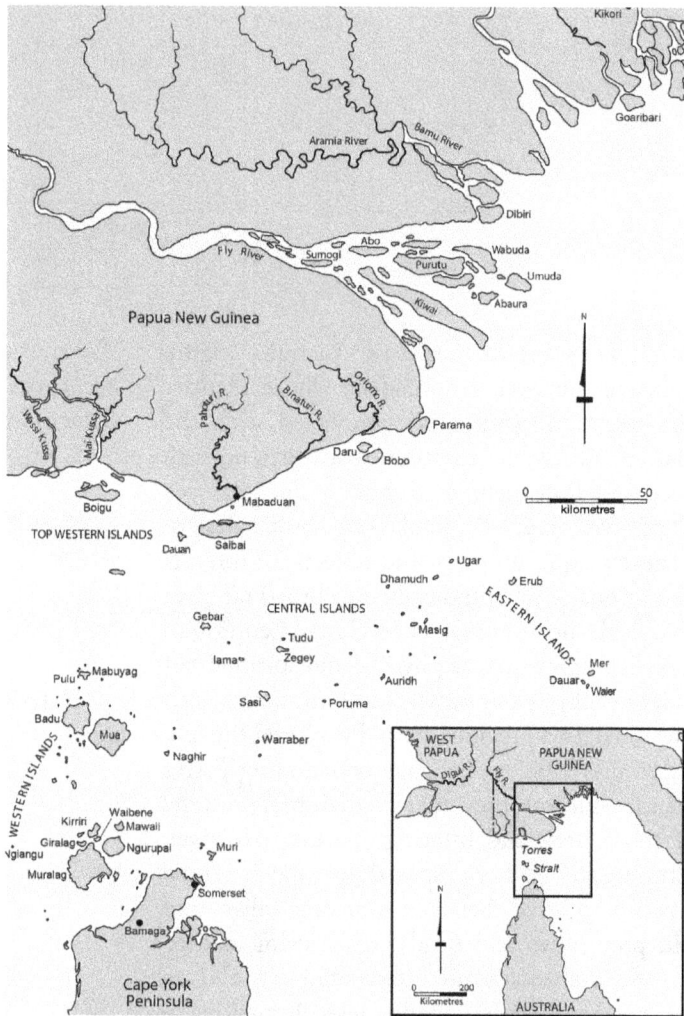

FIGURE 8.1. *Map of Torres Strait and adjacent region of south-central New Guinea*

more complex and dimensional than inert and highly decorated marine transport vessels—they were *object-beings* from the beginning to the end of their lives. The biographical life cycle of Torres Strait canoe object-beings commenced with the felling of trees that bleed in the swamps of lowland New Guinea, from which huge canoe hulls were laboriously carved with stone adzes. Transferred into Torres Strait through exchange networks, in the hands of Islanders the object-being status of canoes was modified and elaborated materially and conceptually through a series of what I identify as four non–mutually exclusive and interdependent socialization processes of animic elaboration—anthropomorphism, zoomorphism, intentionalization, and predatorization. These processes of animation and transformation raise the question of the extent to which formation of Torres Strait canoe object-beings also involved recognition of sentience and the capacity for autonomous action. This chapter elaborates on these processes and issues of animancy and sentience within the broader contexts of theoretical conceptualizations of object agency and object-beings and anthropological understandings of Melanesian canoes as object-beings and other-than-human persons.

OBJECT-BEINGS AND AGENCY

The concept of agency has taken front stage in much archaeological theorizing over the past couple of decades (e.g., Dobres and Robb 2000; Robb 2010). A key development is the notion that "agency is not a characteristic of individuals but of relationships" (Robb 2010:494). The idea that agency is seen to operate as forms of social relationships has also been extended to objects and material agency. As Gell (1998:123) notes, "It does not matter, in ascribing 'social agent' status, what a thing (or a person) 'is' in itself; what matters is where it stands in a network of social relations." In short, "Agency is the ability to act in particular ways, where more than one course of action is possible" (Layton 2003:451). In common with the material structuration of Giddens and Bourdieu, Gell (1998:36) proposed that objects mediate social relationships and operate as "secondary agents" with ascribed agency by people ("primary agents"). In this guise, objects are not agents but act as extensions/expressions (indices) of the social agency of, and imputed by, their maker or user (Layton 2003:451; see also Lindstrøm 2015). Furthermore, "Material objects do not have intentionality themselves, but they do have causal efficacy" (Droogan 2013:154).

The notion of ascribed agency or the projection, imbuement, or imputation of (secondary) agentive qualities onto an object does not necessarily create a social relationship but presupposes an existing relational ontology between the object and people. It is not so much a projection or an ascription as a pre-understanding of the co-determining qualities of and relationship between the object and people. In non-Western cultural settings, the phenomenal world is rarely engaged objectively, given that nonhuman objects are rarely positioned as ontologically external to culture within the separate domains of matter and nature and subject and object (Alberti and Marshall 2009:347–48; Barad 2007; Ingold 2007). People comprehend and understand the world through the cultural lens of their own ontological and epistemological internal subjectivities. Humans dwell in uniquely relational ecologies of entities (objects and beings), materialities (tangible and intangible), and temporalities (past, present, and future).

In contrast to the ontologically problematic notion of projected or ascribed (secondary) agency is the inherent agency of objects. Gell (1998:114) hints at the existence of inherent agency in objects of human manufacture using the example of religious structures. Such structures, Droogan (2013:160) notes, are "the material manifestations of a superhuman agency and potency, even though they are the remains of human labour." Furthermore, "These buildings, ruined or still functioning, are ultimately examples of the agency of human beings. Yet, the narratives and actions of individuals and groups that are played out in their vicinity are in response to a perceived non-human agency, perhaps that of a deity, ancestor or other powerful non-human source" (Droogan 2013:160).

Perhaps the least understood area of agency theorization is the extent to which humanly made object-beings involved not only the materialization of inherent agency but also animacy and the autonomous capacity for intentional and purposeful action and perhaps even sentience (Brown and Walker 2008; Sillar 2009). In an important paper, Alberti and Marshall (2009:350–51) point out that the epistemological notion of inscription follows a "representationalist logic" whereby the form, meaning, and agency of objects is "read off" as the manifest "embodiment" of "beliefs" and "worldviews." Alternatively, they advocate a "literalist (i.e., non-representationalist)" approach, informed by the "radically essentialist" ontology of Henare and colleagues (2007), whereby objects are beings in their own right. The extent to which animate object-beings possess intentionalized agency because of possession or the embodiment of an animating vital force or even soul, spirit, or spirit life force in a Tylorian sense is an issue for ongoing discussion (Gell 1998:96–154; Harvey 2005; Ingold 2007; Zedeño 2009). What does seem clear is that the expression of object-being agency and intentionality is invariably within an active and participatory social context with humans (Gell 1998; Zedeño 2009). As Jones and Boivin (2010:346) note, "Intentionality is a property of the relationship between people and things." Object-beings, as other-than-human beings/persons, should not be seen as "accessories" but as social partners, actors, and participants in human action and broader social arenas.

MELANESIAN CANOE OBJECT-BEINGS

Melanesian canoes provide considerable scope to explore notions of object-beings, agency, animism, and personhood. Best known are *kula* canoes of the Trobriand Islanders of eastern Papua New Guinea, made famous by Malinowski (1922), with Gell (1998) showcasing ornately carved *kula* canoe prows as an example of agency and enchantment par excellence. Bell and Geismar (2009:12) posit that Malinowski saw *kula* canoes in a strict functionalist/instrumentalist sense, citing "the canoe is made for a certain use, and with a definitive purpose; it is a means to an end, and we, who study native life, must not reverse this relation, and make a fetish of the object itself" (Malinowski 1922:105). They argue that "Malinowski's point was an important part of this nascent anthropological rationality: artifacts are fabricated by people to be used and, despite the claims of their makers, anthropologists should not impute agency to them. This approach helped to refocus anthropology away from the seductive charms of objects themselves onto issues of exchange, kinship, and theories of social function and structure" (Bell and Geismar 2009:12). Yet in ensuing sentences Malinowski (1922:105, emphasis added) immediately qualified his functionalist/instrumentalist statement:

> In the study of the economic purposes for which a canoe is made, of the various uses to which it is submitted, we find the first approach to a deeper ethnographic treatment. Further sociological data, referring to its ownership, accounts of who sails in it, and how it is done; information regarding the ceremonies and customs of its construction, a sort of typical life history of a native craft—all that brings us nearer still to the understanding of what his canoe truly means to the native . . . Even this, however, does not touch the most vital reality of a native canoe. For a craft, whether of bark or wood, iron or steel, lives in the life of its sailors, and it is more to a sailor than a mere bit of shaped matter. To the native, not less than to the white seaman, a craft is surrounded by an atmosphere of romance, built up of tradition and of personal experience. It is an object of cult and admiration, *a living thing*, possessing its own individuality.

Based principally on fieldwork on Kiriwina Island, Malinowski (1922) elaborates on a wide range of rituals and magical "spells" associated with the construction and launch of large *waga* (seagoing canoes). Yet surprisingly, little more was said about canoes as a "living thing." However, Malinowski (1922:421) notes that "the effects of magic are something superadded to all the other effects produced by human effort and by natural qualities." Such magical spells are also considered to possess a degree of intentionality and even autonomy, such that "the beating of a canoe with two bunches of grass, one after the other, in order first to extract its heaviness and then impart to it lightness, has a meaning parallel to the spell but independent of it" (Malinowski 1922:407). Instructively, another "magical rite" is aimed at a "change of mind" such that "the canoe makes up its mind to run quickly" (Malinowski 1922:133). In this sense, through particular ritual performances, Trobriand Islanders strategically manipulated and animated the agency of canoes.

Munn (1977, 1986:138–40) provides more detailed and nuanced insights into the embodied dimensions of *kula* canoes in relation to Gawa Island society. Critical is the notion of "spatiotemporal transformations" whereby a canoe's "life" or "fabrication cycle" entails development through a series of "conversion planes" from the intra-island (Gawa) world of canoe production and exchange to the inter-island (Massim) world of *kula* exchange (Munn 1977:39–40). The red wood of the hull is "metaphorically identified with internal bodily fluids" and blood (gendered female and from which a "fetus is formed") (Munn 1986:138). White wood used to make outriggers is gendered male and smeared with "seminal fluid and female discharge . . . suggesting the male element mingling with the female in sexual intercourse" (Munn 1986:140; see also Tambiah 1983). The two types of gendered wood intimately link the fabric of canoes to the land, clan territories, and "corporeal property"—a link reinforced by the naming of some canoes after plots of clan land (Munn 1977:41–42). Ongoing production entails ritual transformation of a canoe's symbolic "inanimate" properties of "heaviness" associated with land to the symbolic "animate" properties of "lightness," "slipperiness," and "speed" associated with the sea (Munn 1977:41). In addition, the heavily carved and decorated prowboard is "heavily anthropomorphized" such that the canoe "projects the image of the ceremonially decorated person, especially a youthful man" (Munn 1986:138). Such elaborate "beautification" adornments (e.g., carved prowboards, shells, and streamers) not only form part of the animic transformation of canoes but also help enchant *kula* exchange partners (Munn 1977:50). Anthropomorphism extended to intentionalizing the "canoe's own desires," such as "want to drink" (when caulking goes dry), "hungry" (when obtaining *kula* shell valuables), and "smell" (when near land) (Munn 1986:145). Thus, a *kula* canoe "encodes its producers in itself" such that "potency" is "embodied" as an extension of personhood (Munn 1986:147).

Drawing on her research on Vakuta Island in the Trobriand Islands, Campbell (2002) similarly records the spiritual and ritual dimensions of large ocean-going *kula* canoe (*masawa*) manufacture. Central is transformation of a tree (associated with land, anchoring, and heaviness) into a canoe hull (associated with the sea, mobility, and lightness). Important in this process is ritual removal of spirits and witches who inhabit the bottom and tops of trees, respectively. Campbell (2002:153) qualifies this act as "the first opportunity to secure the canoe as an artifact of men." This process is associated with transformation of an "undomesticated" tree (associated with "anti-social and uncontrollable beings") into a "controllable," domesticated, and "social entity" (Campbell 2002:156). Newly constructed *kula* canoes are ritually bathed in shallow waters off the village beach, which is seen as analogous to similar ritual bathing of women pregnant with their first child (Campbell 2002:157).

Campbell (2002:91, 108, original emphasis) documents that zoomorphized *kula* canoe carvings and attachments add extra qualities to canoes that "encodes attributes . . . [and] certain *features* of animals . . . that convey qualities of motion, aesthetics and behaviours considered successful to kula" voyaging expeditions and the intentionalized "desire to secure" prized shell valuables. Examples include a prow attachment of a double row of shells (*Ovula ovum*), which forms the "mouth of the canoe" (Campbell 2002:159). The spot where the two rows of shell meet is painted red, which gives the appearance of teeth reddened from chewing betelnut. As betelnut chewing in "company" is often associated with "love and beauty magic," the reddened shells (teeth) are associated with "attracting and seducing" *kula* exchange partners (Campbell 2002:159). Similarly, depiction of certain animal body parts is linked metaphorically to desired outcomes of *kula* exchanges: teeth, beak, and mouth (gripping prey = holding onto shell valuables), eye (a focus of sexual desire = attracting shell valuables), and throat (taste = desire for large and famous shell valuables) (Campbell 2002:93–94). Stylized depictions of butterflies on canoe splashboards reference how a "butterfly moves effortlessly upon the currents of the wind and it is this ability that they [Vakutans] hope will be emulated by the outrigger canoe" (Campbell 2002:95). The "principal 'animal' of the prowboard" is the osprey, which is central to procurement of large quantities of *kula* shell valuables because of the bird's wisdom and highly successful predatory behavior (Campbell 2002:99, 129–35, 140). The fact that a treetop becomes the prow end of a canoe and is the place where ospreys sit to look out for fish is not unrelated (Campbell 2002:163–64, 177). In short, the "design units on the kula prow and splashboards are fundamentally about the representation of desired characteristics seen in the natural world to be 'successful.' The 'animals' used for representation on the boards are enlisted for the success of a kula expedition" (Campbell 2002:149). To what extent Vakutan seagoing canoes could be considered object-beings in their own right is not discussed explicitly by Campbell (2002).

Further anthropomorphic understanding of the ontological status of Melanesian canoes comes from the work of Lipset and Barlow with estuarine

Murik fisherfolk near the mouth of the Sepik River, Papua New Guinea (Barlow and Lipset 1997; Lipset 2005, 2014). The Murik not only "vehicularize" their bodies as "canoe-bodies" but also travel in humanly constructed canoes that are "personified" as bodies. This dual notion of "bodies as canoes" and "canoes as bodies" is seen by Lipset (2014) to be part of a broader cultural tradition of canoe identity, personhood, and habitus in the Austronesian world (see also Ballard et al. 2004). Embodiment of canoes began with the felling of a tree and a log that was a "being" whose gender required ritual transformation from female to male (Barlow and Lipset 1997:10–11). From a gendered perspective, canoe launching rites were analogous to initiation of boys into warriors (male) and birth (female). Central was anointing the canoe with powerful substances such as red ochre, penile blood, and blood from a sacrificed dog and possibly a captured woman (Barlow and Lipset 1997:15). Launching rites saw transformation of the canoe from "an inert, man-made object into a cosmic agent of productivity on behalf of the descent group and, ultimately, of the community" (Barlow and Lipset 1997:14). The result was a new (nonhuman) "person" and "citizen" in the community (Barlow and Lipset 1997:28, 30).

A Murik seagoing trade canoe featured various carved "images" that "animated the vessel and imbued it with the fortifying presence of its ally, the male cult" (Barlow and Lipset 1997:23). The images included carved birds (e.g., sea eagles) and bird motifs to "impart both lightness and speed to the canoe" and to express "the desire that the canoe would 'fly' directly to its destination" (Barlow and Lipset 1997:22). As personified beings, Murik canoes also possessed stomachs, hands, and prow heads (Lipset 2014:32–33). Prows in particular reveal that "canoes are not inert, value-neutral objects but they possess embodiments and capabilities that make them no less moral than sentient human spirits. No less than human beings, they are canoe-bodies" (Lipset 2014:33). Complex anthropomorphic and zoomorphic spirit prow carvings all look forward with "a multiplicity of eyes deciphering the moral character of space, reckoning whether it harbors, or will harbor, friend or foe" (Lipset 2014:34). This intentionalized and subjective "task of surveillance" also "evokes a human subject, sentient, generative, moving through space, transgressing its boundaries," and expressing a "desire for mastery" of social domains (Lipset 2014:34–35). Thus, while Murik seagoing canoes are independent object-beings, the expression of agency and animacy is within the context of human social endeavors such as raiding and exchange expeditions.

Tilley (1999) documents the "heavily anthropomorphized form" of Wala Island outrigger canoes, northwest Malekula, Vanuatu. The canoes embody a "big man," complete with individual names and metaphorical mouth and eyes (prow bird figurehead), ears (prow tassels), penis sheath (stern tassels), arms and legs (outrigger booms), fingers and toes (outrigger float attachment sticks), palm of hand and sole of foot (outrigger float), and belt (attachment to rim of canoe) (Layard 1942:462; Tilley 1999:115). In addition to being overtly masculine, Wala canoes also possess female dimensions, such as use of female-gendered woods for ("vulva-shaped") hulls and outriggers (Tilley 1999:117–18). The elaborate and highly ritualized processes of making and consecrating large seagoing canoes in northwest Malekula converted "inanimate materials into an embodied subject" (Tilley 1999:124; see also Layard 1942). Through construction and consecration rituals involving pig sacrifices, a Wala canoe "acquired a high rank, like a big man and a 'soul,' and was gendered as male" (Tilley 1999:124). Following Layard (1942:470–72), Tilley (1999:124, original emphasis) notes that "these vessels were considered not only to live like human beings of high rank (in a large house), but also to die, and mortuary rites appropriate to the status of a high-ranking big man were performed for *wrecked* vessels. Those which were not wrecked during their lifetime were allowed to die a 'natural' death, i.e., to slowly rot away in their tabooed boat house. Timber was never taken away for firewood or any other use."

TORRES STRAIT CANOES AS OBJECT-BEINGS

Do ocean-going canoes of Torres Strait Islanders, a Melanesian people of northeast Australia, fit within the broader context of socialized and intentionalized Melanesian canoe object-beings? Torres Strait Islander double-outrigger sailing canoes measured up to 21 m in length and were the largest marine vessels used by any group of Indigenous Australians (figure 8.2) (for detailed overviews of Torres Strait canoes, see Haddon 1937; Lawrence 1994; McNiven 2015a). They were capable of holding twenty–thirty people and tons of produce and objects, including hunted dugongs (marine mammals) weighing over 300 kg. Their life at sea ranged from hunting trips for turtles and dugongs (an exclusively male activity) to fishing, seasonal settlement relocation, and trading trips between islands and between the adjacent mainlands of New Guinea to the north and Australia to the south (by men, women, and children) across 700 km of sea space (McNiven 2015b). Although use of canoes across Torres Strait largely ceased at the end of the nineteenth century, detailed ethnohistorical and anthropological recordings from that century provide tantalizing glimpses of the complex lives and biographical life histories of these vessels (see Kopytoff 1986; Van de Noort 2011). While the behavioral life of Torres Strait canoes involved manufacture, use, maintenance, and discard (see Skibo and Schiffer

FIGURE 8.2. *Hand-colored lithograph of a canoe at Erub, eastern Torres Strait, drawn by Harden Sidney Melville in 1844–45 and published in Melville ([1849]:pl. XIX). Melville was an artist on the HMS Fly expedition (Jukes 1847). Courtesy, State Library of New South Wales, Q84/126.*

2008), below I focus on the ontological dimensions of canoe lives. Ironically, this complex and multidimensional maritime life began not in Torres Strait but in the adjacent swampy coastal lowlands of southern New Guinea.

TRANSFORMATION

All large Torres Strait outrigger canoes started their lives as tree object-beings in the lowland forests of the Fly River delta of the adjacent coast of Papua New Guinea (see figure 8.1). During fieldwork in 1888, Haddon (1890:341) recorded:

> The large canoes in the Straits all come from Daudai [New Guinea coast opposite Torres Strait], about the neighbourhood of the Fly River. I was told the logs were cut and hollowed at Wabad (Wabuda?) [Island] and fitted with a single small outrigger. Thence they passed through the hands of the Kiwai and Mowat [Mowatta] people on the mainland of New Guinea, and across to the island of

Saibai. Here they are re-rigged with two outriggers, and a gunwale is fitted and the canoe decorated with a figure-head, bow ornament, and otherwise ornamented with feathers and shells. From Saibai the canoes found their way to the other islands of the western division of the Straits.

After follow-up fieldwork in 1898, Haddon (1904:296) added: "The large canoes all come from the delta of the Fly River. I was told in 1888 that the logs were cut and hollowed out at Wabad and fitted with a single outrigger. In 1898 we were informed they came from Wabad and Dibi, the former is evidently Wabuda [Island] and the latter Dibiri [Island]. The late Rev. James Chalmers (*Journ. Anth. Inst.* XXXIII. 1903[a, b], pp. 111, 117) refers to canoes being made at and exported from Dibiri and other villages near the mouth of the Fly River, on its left bank."

Chalmers (1903b:123) also commented on the scale of canoe output: "The large and best canoes are dug out at the villages near the mouth of the [Fly] river on the left [east] bank. Once I called there, and all along the bank, in front of the village, were quite a hundred large canoes, covered with coconut leaves. My boat's crew were natives of Ipisia and Saguane [villages on Kiwai Island], and, as soon as those ashore saw them, the coconut leaves were thrown aside and the canoes exposed for sale."

Early twentieth-century records provide glimpses of the elaborate secular and ritual processes associated with transformation of tree object-beings into canoe object-beings with production of canoe hulls at the mouth of the Fly River (Landtman 1927; Lawrence 1994, 2010; Riley 1925). Riley (1925:110) observed that before the carefully selected tree was chopped down, these words were spoken: "You now stand up a tree; we are going to cut you down; you will presently walk about on the top of the water; by and by we shall decorate you." The root end of the tree was always the bow end of the canoe, and it would take forty–sixty men to drag a canoe to the riverbank (Riley 1925:113). Riley (1925:109) noted that construction was staggered because of other commitments; thus "to complete one may take from six to twelve months, after which finishing touches are given to it." Landtman (1927:209) made these observations: "While the work [hollowing out the tree trunk] was in progress the workers were not allowed to swim in the sea, for this would not only harm the canoe, but themselves as well. There existed an association between the tree and the canoe-builder: the sap flowing from the cuts in the tree was its blood, and by way of a sympathetic connection between the two, the builder's skin was thought to have been pierced in a magical sense, so that if he got into the sea, the water would penetrate his body and drag him down."

After decoration, the final act of transformation was as follows: "The old couple also 'wake up' the canoe by swinging a bullroarer close to the bow of it, first in reference to the harpooning of a dugong or turtle, and then a second time for the capturing of the animal, these two actions being looked upon as distinct" (Landtman 1927:211).

ANTHROPOMORPHISM AND ZOOMORPHISM

Torres Strait canoes were anthropomorphized and zoomorphized by the addition and attribution of a range of anatomical features. The bow of the canoe served as a head, the stern of the canoe was a tail, and the main body of the canoe hull seems to have functioned as a torso. The overall anthropomorphic/zoomorphic form of Torres Strait canoes is revealed in a series of three sketches of canoes from Mabuyag in western Torres Strait by local senior cultural expert Gizu (figure 8.3:top).

Bow (HEAD)

In 1844–45 Sweatman noted that "the bow is highly ornamented with carving, paint, shells and emu [cassowary] feathers, being often fashioned into a rude resemblance of a human head" (cited in Allen and Corris 1977:35). These features included separate eye, mouth, and beard elements across the bow plus the attachment of prow figureheads.

An "eye" element is located on the triangular-shaped weatherboard behind the prow washboard at the front of the canoe (e.g., figures 8.2, 8.3:top, 8.4:top). Raven (1990:140) reports that on Boigu in the northern strait an eye "was painted on canoes to assist them in locating prey." Similarly, on Kiwai Island at the mouth of the Fly River immediately northeast of Torres Strait, Landtman (1927:211) recorded that "the man provides the bow of the canoe with painted eyes, also gluing on real eyes of a *rúburúbu* or *warío* (two large hawks)." As a result, the canoe was seen to have the same capacity as men to see dugongs and turtles while out on hunting trips (Landtman 1927:211).

A "mouth" element is located on the canoe prow and often took the form of a woven framework that extended beyond the tip of the canoe hull (figures 8.2–8.4). The framework essentially represented an open mouth with upper and lower jaws, usually lined with shell attachments that possibly represented teeth. Haddon (1912:215) stated explicitly that this attachment was referred to as *gud* (mouth) in Kala Lagaw Ya (western Torres Strait language).

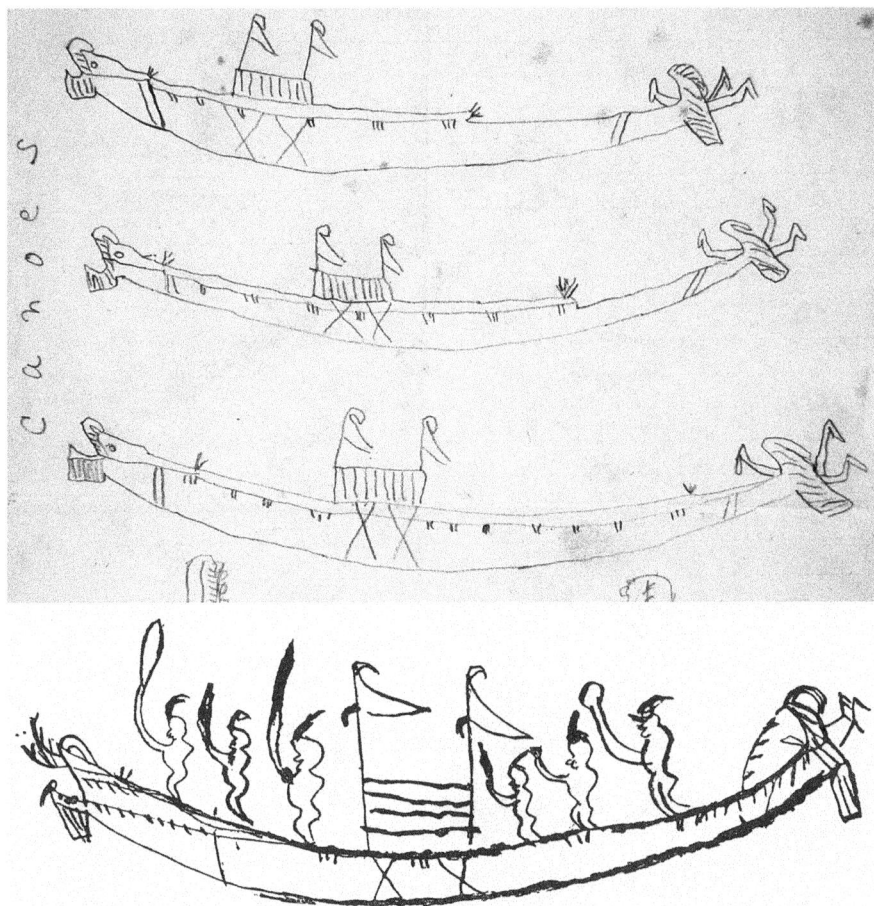

FIGURE 8.3. *Top: Detail of a drawing of three canoes, probably by Gizu, Mabuyag. Courtesy, Cambridge University Museum of Archaeology and Anthropology, 2010.624. Note head with eye, mouth, and beard elements at bow on the left. Bottom: Drawing by Sunday of Mabuyag showing men performing "the turtle ceremony" with bullroarers in a canoe at Goemu village (Haddon 1904:fig. 51). Both drawings obtained by Alfred Haddon in 1898.*

A "beard" element is usually located directly below the mouth element and consists of tassels of plant fibers hanging down such that they usually drag through the water during voyaging (figures 8.2–8.4). In 1840 d'Urville observed that prows of canoes at Tudu in the central strait have an attachment that "represented an old man with a long beard of seaweed" (1846, cited in Rosenman 1987 2:550). Haddon (1912:215) recorded that Torres Strait canoe

FIGURE 8.4. *Torres Strait canoe prows. Top left: Detail of a canoe bow taken from a village scene, Treacherous Bay, Erub. Watercolor by Edwin Porcher, April 1845, HMS Fly expedition. Courtesy, National Library of Australia, nla.pic-an 4101896. Top right: Detail of canoe bow off Mer. Watercolor by Edwin Porcher, 1845, HMS Fly expedition. Courtesy, National Library of Australia, nla.pic-an4101817. Middle left: Detail of the bow of Adi, a canoe on Mabuyag. Photograph by Alfred Haddon, 1898. Courtesy, Cambridge University Museum of Archaeology and Anthropology, N.37892.ACH2. Middle right: Detail of the bow of Ausun, a canoe on Mabuyag. Drawing by Alfred Haddon (Haddon 1937:fig. 115). Lower left: Detail of canoe on beach, Tudu. Lithograph by Louis Le Breton. Excerpt from original published in d'Urville (1846:pl. 190). Lower right: Detail of the bow of Bruwan, a Kaurareg canoe from Muralag. Pencil sketch and watercolor by Oswald Brierly, 1850. Courtesy, State Library of New South Wales, PXC 281.*

prows feature "a fringe of shredded young coco-nut leaves" that "represents a beard, *imus*," according to the Meriam of the eastern strait. Furthermore, "Tufts of cassowary feathers may also be inserted along the sides of the end-board [washboard], along part of the junction of the weather-board and gunwale, and at the end of the former; these feathers are called 'whiskers' by the Miriam [*sic*]" (Haddon 1912:215).

Some canoe prows featured figureheads in the form of either a single anthropomorphic head or twin zoomorphic bird heads. In terms of anthropomorphic figureheads, King (1837:754) observed that some Torres Strait canoes "have the head carved with the figure of a man, ornamented with strings of cowries." Haddon (1904:353) recorded that anthropomorphic figureheads represented *dogai*, who in western Torres Strait were a "class of powerful beings, or bogeys . . . who generally were on the look out to do mischief . . . some however were good . . . [and] they could assume a seductive appearance" (figure 8.5). As all *dogai* were female (Haddon 1904:353), the addition of *dogai* figureheads suggests attribution of female gender for at least part of the canoe. In addition, *dogai* figureheads likely imbued canoes with some form of spiritual protection or spiritual agency in terms of voyaging success (McNiven 2015a:177). In terms of zoomorphic bird figureheads, Haddon (1912:215) documented two such examples on Mabuyag—one where "the heads, *ngagalau kwik*, represent the sea-eagle, *ngagalaig*," the other carving "*kisu kwik* . . . portraying a hawk-like bird, *kisulaig*" (figure 8.5).

STERN (TAIL)

Haddon (1904:338) observed that on top of a canoe stern post "a wooden fish's tail was sometimes present which, from its shape, was almost certainly intended to represent the tail of a king-fish or one of the allied predaceous gigantic mackerel. All these creatures are voracious fishers" (see also Haddon 1912:216).

HULL (TORSO)

Few details are available on the major central section of the canoe hull between the "head" and the "tail" and whether it was modified to visually enhance association with a body or torso. Haddon (1912:209) remarked that in western Torres Strait language the phrase for removing bilge water from a canoe was *usi depaupli*, where *usi* is "urine or bilge water." Ray (1907:163) added that *usi* also meant "bladder." This association among urine, bladder, and bilge water is remarkable as it suggests strongly that the accumulation of bilge water

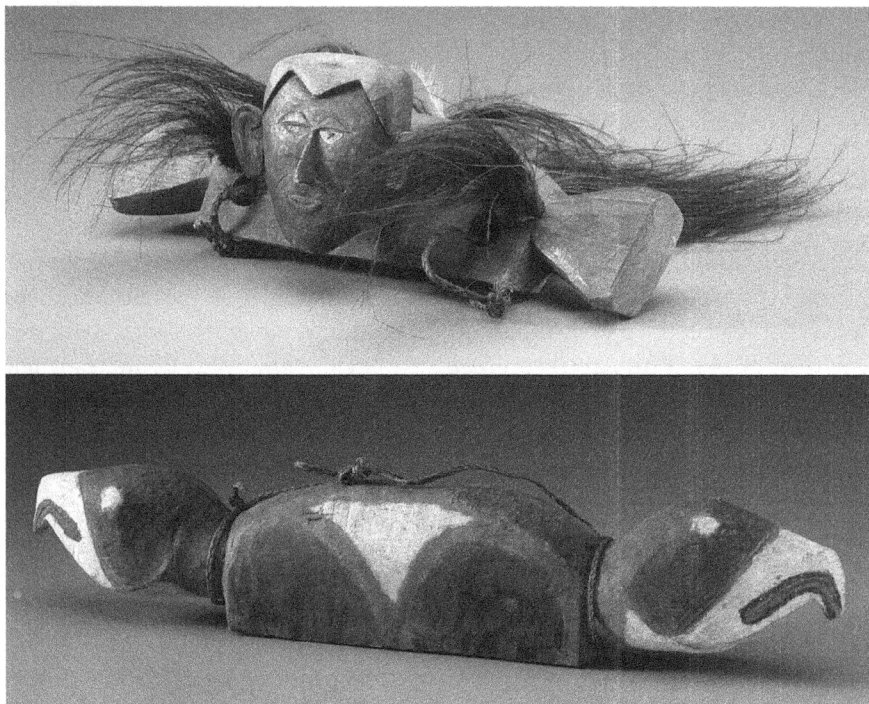

FIGURE 8.5. *Western Torres Strait canoe figureheads. Top: Figurehead with a female (anthropomorphic) dogai head with characteristic large ears, Saibai. Collected by Alfred Haddon 1898. Courtesy, Cambridge University Museum of Archaeology and Anthropology, Z.9697. Length: 43 cm (Moore 1984:59). Bottom: Figurehead with two heads representing the sea-eagle (ngagalaig), Mabuyag. Collected by Alfred Haddon 1898. Courtesy, Cambridge University Museum of Archaeology and Anthropology, Z.9698. Length: 48 cm (Moore 1984:50).*

is linked to the process of urination, implying that a canoe is considered an animate being with bodily functions.[1]

INTENTIONALIZATION AND PREDATORIZATION

Torres Strait canoes were intentionalized and predatorized to seek out the two key hunted food items: turtle and dugongs. Both dugongs and especially turtles were hunted by men with harpoons and canoes. Success in hunting turtles and dugongs was assisted by hunters undertaking a range of tangible and intangible activities to help ensure that canoes expressed an intentionalized desire to seek out these key prey animals. These activities included inscribing representations of predatory fish onto canoes, attaching carved representations of the tails of predatory fish to canoe sterns, attaching hunting magic charms to the bows and sterns of canoes, and giving specific names to canoes (discussed below).

FISH IMAGES

In 1840 d'Urville recorded a large representation of a fish (which he identified as a "porpoise") on the bow weatherboard of a canoe on the beach at Tudu (figure 8.4). Brierly's 1850 illustration of the canoe *Bruwan* features a zoomorphic creature on the starboard side of the bow, while Haddon's 1888 watercolor painting of a canoe bow from Mabuyag reveals what he describes as a stylized representation of a fish, possibly a remora (*gapu*) (Haddon 1912:214) (figure 8.4). In the 1840s Brierly (cited in Moore 1979:104) also observed representations of remora on the gunwale at the stern of Kaurareg canoes in southwest Torres Strait (figure 8.6): "I observed a bit of carving near the stern, on one side, and from the strong resemblance it bore to the sucker fish's head, looking down upon it from above, the outline of the sucker on the head, the projecting lower jaw which would be seen beyond the upper one, and the position of the eyes, placed near the mouth at the side, had all been observed and were characteristics of the fish which could not be mistaken. Upon my pointing to it and asking what it was, Cheakow immediately answered *gapoo queekoo*— '*gapu's* head.'"

HUNTING MAGIC CHARMS

A broad range of portable hunting magic charms was either carried onboard canoes or attached to canoe hulls. These charms were intended to help hunters obtain turtles and dugongs by attracting prey to hunters, and vice versa. Small wooden carvings of turtles and dugongs were placed in the bow of canoes as hunting charms (Haddon 1904:333–38, 1912:390, 1935:86). In addition, parts of special plants and "the head, oesophagus and probably trachea of a turtle stuffed" with special plants were "fastened" to the bow, the stern, or both of canoes to magically aid the capture of turtles (Haddon 1904:330). Small carvings of fish were taken onboard canoes, and resin chewed with plant "medicine" and "spat on the bow of a canoe" would magically assist with success in obtaining fish and large cone shells used as valuables (Haddon 1908:218).

FIGURE 8.6. *Detail of the stern of Bruwan, a Kaurareg canoe from Muralag, southwest Torres Strait. Note engraved representation of a remora's head at the stern end of the gunwale (enlarged view shown in top left). Pencil sketch and watercolor by Oswald Brierly, November 6, 1849. Courtesy, Mitchell Library, State Library of New South Wales, PXA 510.*

In 1849 Brierly recorded that the stern staves were similar to staves forming part of a turtle-hunting magic shrine on Turtle Island and suggested that the canoe staves were associated with attracting turtles for hunting (cited in Moore 1979:105, 122, 198, 210). Haddon (1904:338; see also Ray 1907:129) adds that on Mabuyag he recorded stern staves with serrated edges and terminations carved to "represent" the head of either a "frigate-bird" (*womer/waumer*) or, more occasionally, a "sea-eagle" (*ngagalaig*), which he thought indicated "a magical significance" and use as turtle/dugong "charms" (figure 8.7). Both the frigate-bird and sea-eagle staves, along with the frigate-bird and sea-eagle figureheads and kingfish tail carvings (described above), are animals that according to Haddon (1912:216) "are voracious catchers of fish, and the representation of them would therefore be obvious to the native mind. Their use would therefore

FIGURE 8.7. *Canoe stern staves (gozed), Mabuyag. Collected by Alfred Haddon, 1898. Courtesy, Cambridge University Museum of Anthropology and Archaeology, Z.9693a and Z.9693b.*

be analogous to that of the canoe [hunting] charms." This view is consistent with a pair of White-breasted Sea Eagle (*Haliaeetus leucogaster*) claws with palm-leaf ties collected from Mabuyag in 1933 that were "used in canoes on fishing and fighting expeditions" and "held in the middle of the canoe in both hands in order to draw near, by magic, the enemy's canoe" (Florek 2005:77).

NAMES

It is possible that the names given to canoes (often painted on the gunwale after European contact) in some cases contributed to the expression of intentionalized and predatory agency. For example, in 1849 Brierly (cited in Moore 1979:150–51) recorded the names and meanings of a number of Kaurareg canoes from the southwest strait, including "*Uzanna*, which means a large net," "*Bidthem*—a poisonous snake" (both possible references to the hunting of turtles), and "*Maleel*, meaning iron bar" (a possible reference to the desire for much-coveted iron). As Brierly (1849, cited in Moore 1979:150) notes, the Kaurareg "are great wreckers and pull the ships [European wrecks] to pieces as much as they can to get the iron bars which they call *maleel*." On the island of Mabuyag in west-central Torres Strait, Haddon (1904:308) recorded a large canoe named *Waumeran* that most likely is a reference to *waumer*, the predatory frigate-bird (Rod Mitchell, personal communication, 2014).

WAKING UP

An important insight into the possibility of the intentionality of canoes extending into sentience is provided by rituals of "waking up" canoes prior to voyaging. Landtman (1927:211) observed at Mawatta village on the New Guinea coast opposite Torres Strait that people "wake up" a canoe by swinging a bull-roarer close to the bow, not only during the construction of canoes (discussed above) but also prior to hunting expeditions. In what may be a related reference to Torres Strait Islanders, Haddon (1904:331) recorded that on Mabuyag, "preparatory to starting out to catch the floating turtles the men took a bull-roarer from the *agu* [turtle shrine] and swung it over the canoe" (figure 8.3:bottom).

DISMEMBERMENT AND DISPERSAL

While Torres Strait canoes were "owned" by men of high status, in reality, payments to canoe hull makers in New Guinea using shell valuables were made in installments that extended for the life of the canoe. Full payment and final ownership, ironically, was complete once a canoe's voyaging life was over. Following the situation with Gawa *kula* canoes described by Munn (1977:45), it is possible that Torres Strait canoes were inalienably linked to their New Guinea producers. Landtman (1927:214) reported that "when at last the canoe broke up, the owner sent the seller an armshell or string of dogs' teeth (which highly valued ornaments seem to have been conventionally regarded as the last installment in paying for a canoe), and, to emphasize the significance of this gift, he attached a small piece of the broken craft to it." Furthermore, "If a canoe got wrecked or was destroyed in some other way shortly after its purchase, the owner sent in the ordinary final payment, together with a piece of the ruined vessel, as mentioned above, but no further installment after that" (Landtman 1927:215).

A number of small canoes in Torres Strait were observed to have been manufactured from sections of large canoes (Barham and Harris 1987:94; Haddon 1904:75, 104, 1908:25, 1912:158, 207; MacGillivray 1852 2:40). In addition to the recycling of large canoes into smaller canoes and the use of hull fragments in the final canoe payment, fragments of old canoe hulls were known to have been re-carved into canoe washboards on Dauan (Moresby 1875:4), house doors on Mer (Haddon 1912:105, 1935:300), and receptacles for carrying freshly caught fish on Dauar (Haddon 1908:16), while the centerboard was used as a standing platform on dugong-hunting platforms (Haddon 1912:167; Riley 1925:133). However, fragments of old canoes were also transformed into new objects used in a range of spiritually charged and ritual contexts. Examples include hull fragments used as house taboo markers on Mabuyag (Haddon 1904:270), corpse stretchers on Mer (Haddon 1935:323), and grave goods on Mabuyag (Haddon 1904:286). Similarly, sections of gunwale were carved and used in turtle-hunting ceremonies on Pulu by the people of Mabuyag (Haddon 1935:353; Moore 1984:148), central canoe platform and crates were used as a support for the Waiat spirit-being figure on Dauar (Haddon 1908:277, 1935:fig. 47), and a stern post was carved into a tobacco charm on Dauan (Haddon 1904:346, 1908:207).

Fragmentation and ritualization may help contextualize a curious 33-cm-long fragment of a canoe stern post with evidence of a carved human face collected by Haddon from Tudu in 1888 (Moore 1984). The highly weathered condition of the carving indicates curation for some time and strongly suggests that the object held special significance that extended beyond its time as part of a canoe.

In a related sense, the complex mortuary practices of Torres Strait Islanders involved body fragmentation such that skulls were kept by families for divination, while skulls, jaws, and limb bones could be incorporated into various ritual objects and selected bones were often interred in rock niches or buried (e.g., Haddon 1904:248–61, 362, 364, 1908:266–69, 1935:321). Similarly, bodies taken in raids were usually decapitated, with skulls and jaws used in a range of ritual and spiritually charged contexts, while eyes and cheek flesh could be eaten to gain strength (e.g., Haddon 1904:369, 1908:275, 1935:387). As with dead people, the inalienable bodies and personhood of dead canoes were similarly fragmented, distributed, and used in a wide range of new social and ritual contexts that acknowledged a dead canoe's ongoing sociality, agency, enchainment, and entanglement (see Chapman 2000; Hodder 2012).

DISCUSSION

Torres Strait canoes were complex object-beings whose inherent capacities for animacy and intentionalized agency were given expression by people through a wide range of anthropomorphic and zoomorphic processes. These processes were central to how canoe object-beings were socialized to become active and useful members of Torres Strait Islander communities. Culturally relevant animacy and agency were achieved through a range of strategies of predatorization such that canoes desired and helped facilitate access to both food items (e.g., turtles and dugongs) and objects (e.g., iron from shipwrecks). The expression of intentionalized desire by Torres Strait canoe object-beings has direct parallels with other parts of Melanesia where canoes were similarly described as expressing "desires" during voyages for fast speed and prized shell exchange valuables (e.g., Barlow and Lipset 1997; Campbell 2002; Munn 1977, 1986).

Critically, the animacy and agency of Torres Strait canoe object-beings were not the result of projection, imbuement, or ascription by people. Animacy and agency were inherent vital qualities traceable back to the trees on the New Guinea mainland from which canoe hulls were shaped. As Ingold (2006:10) reminds us: "Animacy, then, is not a property of persons imaginatively projected onto the things with which they perceive themselves to be surrounded. Rather—and this is my second point—it is the dynamic, transformative potential of the entire field of relations within which beings of all kinds, more or less person-like or thing-like, continually and reciprocally bring one another into existence. The animacy of the lifeworld, in short, is not the result of an infusion of spirit into substance, or of agency into materiality, but is rather ontologically prior to their differentiation." Thus, the addition of painted eyes to prows helped express the inherent capacity of canoes to see prey, the attachment of wooden carvings of carnivorous fish tails to sterns helped express the inherent capacity of canoes for predatory desires, and so on.

The degree to which Torres Strait canoe object-beings were considered sentient and autonomous object-beings is more difficult to determine using existing anthropological and historical sources. No explicit records were found to match notions of Torres Strait canoe object-beings generally possessing a life force and sentience, as documented in other parts of Melanesia by Lipset (2014) and Tilley (1999). However, Haddon's anthropological writings and Lawrie's (1970) detailed compendium of legendary stories provide a number of examples to support the view that Torres Strait canoes operated as autonomous, sentient object-beings in certain ontological contexts. First, the "waking up" of canoes prior to hunting trips implies some notion of an object-being with a life force and perhaps with sentience. Second, the castaway concept of *sarup* (see below) reveals that the sea and canoe could conspire against and reject mariners, which was tantamount to a death sentence. Third, Sigai, an important anthropomorphic culture hero and ceremonial cult founder of the Kulkalgal people of central Torres Strait, "took on the form of a canoe" and "moved of its own volition" (Lawrie 1970:253–54), which suggests that canoes could be sentient and autonomous object-beings in specific spiritual contexts. This inference is corroborated by Bomai, an anthropomorphic culture hero and ceremonial cult founder of the Meriam of eastern Torres Strait, who similarly had the capacity to change into a canoe and various marine animals (Haddon 1908:33–36, 1935:71).

A little understood dimension of the sociality of canoes is their relationship with the sea. Previously, I have discussed seascapes as anthropomorphized spiritscapes that can be engaged socially by people (McNiven 2004, 2008). The concept of Torres Strait canoes as object-beings raises the question of to what extent canoes engaged with the sentient qualities of the sea, and vice versa, independent of human agency. Apart from hunting magic (described above), it is known that Torres Strait Islanders could alter the nature of engagements between canoes and marine elements through ritual practices. Examples include special magic to ensure that whales either avoid "destroying" canoes or destroy the canoes of enemies (Hunt 1899:8; see also Haddon 1935:106, 169), to bring up winds for favorable and unfavorable sailing conditions (Haddon 1890:402, 1904:351), and to ensure a favorable voyaging pathway through rough seas (Haddon 1904:352).

Perhaps the clearest indication that canoes and the sea could interact socially independent of humans is revealed by the concept of *sarup* (castaways). Those unfortunate mariners who became shipwrecked through a canoe mishap at sea but managed to make it ashore alive as castaways were known as *sarup* and were invariably killed (irrespective of whether they came ashore on their home island or the island of another community) (Haddon 1935:196, 349–50). Indeed, "If a canoe overturned more than about thirty yards from the shore, all who had been onboard it became *sarup*" (Lawrie 1970:74). Thus, a "*sarup* was a man without hope from the moment that his canoe sank" (Lawrie 1970:74). In a sense, people became *sarup* because they had been rejected by both the sea and its agent, the canoe. *Sarup* executions were considered necessary, as castaways were deemed physically and mentally unstable and hence metaphysically dangerous to communities. Scott's (2004:263) ethnographic work on Erub in the eastern strait describes this human-sea relationship and the fate of *sarup*: "The proper relationship of mind to physical reality is mastery through conformity to powers that transcend human agency. Navigation at sea, an omnipresent reminder of such power, has long symbolised this relationship. According to tradition, to lose harmony with the sea was tantamount to a loss of mind and human status. Individuals were frequently rendered insane by such an ordeal and survivors might be considered as good as dead. Shipwrecked individuals, *sarup*, were regarded with fear, as no longer fit for society."

Westerdahl (2005:3) refers to a boat as a potent "liminal agent," and Torres Strait canoes expressed such liminality in a broad range of contexts. Apart from association with the concept of *sarup*, canoe liminality was realized through the mix of male and female gender attributes mirrored behaviorally in the almost daily alternations between fishing trips on reefs where both men and women were involved and turtle- and dugong-hunting trips, which were undertaken only by men. Furthermore, all trips involved transitioning between the onto-logical domains of the beach/village (inactive/resting) and the sea (active/hunt-ing/voyaging) (see Munn 1977). For Torres Strait Islanders, the sea itself was a liminal domain, as mariners shared the waters with the voyaging dead. That is, ghosts of the dead (known as *markai* in the western strait and *lamar* in the east-ern strait), traveling in their spirit canoes, could also be seen by mariners (e.g., Lawrie 1970:29–30, 40, 276–77). Among the Kaurareg of the southwest strait in the 1840s, Brierly recorded that "when the wind blows and the clouds break open, they will point to them and say, *Markieli warroo-ya ypoo*—'The *markai* (spirits) are looking at the turtle in the water,' and say that the spirits come down and take the turtle up into the clouds and eat them" (cited in Moore 1979:151). Haddon (1904:358) similarly recorded that "on ordinary occasions the *markai* paddle the canoe in the open sea on calm nights to catch turtle, dugong or fish."

The liminality of spiritual canoes of the dead illustrates the multidimensional ontological status of Torres Strait canoe object-beings (see also Brady 2010). A further dimension to canoe liminality is revealed by their transformational ontological status whereby canoes changed into other entities. In addition to culture heroes such as Bomai, who had the capacity to transform into a canoe, turtle, dugong, porpoise, crayfish, and whale (see above), legendary stories men-tion the magical transformation of feathers and coconut shells into canoes and the transformation of canoes into star constellations and stones that can still be seen today (Haddon 1904:51, 1908:3–4, 315, 1935:132; Lawrie 1970:19, 97, 132, 153). Examples of the latter include the canoes of Tagai, Abob, and Malo on the reef edge on Mer, Kuyam's canoe on Gebar, and the Seven Blind Brothers' canoe on Mua (Haddon 1904:75, 1908:26; Lawrie 1970:3–4, 33, 97, 305, 332).

CONCLUSION

Torres Strait canoes and many Melanesian canoes more generally were object-beings that were intentionalized and predatorized through a range of ritualized strategies to facilitate socially and culturally desirable engage-ments with the marine realm (prey and elements). This animate ontological status alerts archaeologists to the potential agentive dimensions of marine vessels as socialized actors in maritime contexts. While the extent to which Torres Strait canoes possessed sentience and autonomy outside of very specific spiritual and ontologically fluid transformational contexts remains uncertain, they clearly were anthropomorphized and zoomorphized as specific forms of animate object-beings. In this sense, Torres Strait canoes fit within a broader Melanesian cultural context in which canoes were similarly materialized and socialized as object-beings through human formulation and intervention. Bell and Geismar (2009:4, 6, original emphasis) encapsulate these views well with their notion of "materialization," seen as "an ongoing lived *process* whereby concepts, beliefs and desires are given *form* that are [*sic*] then *transformed* and *transforming* in their social deployment." Informed by Appadurai (1986), they add that "by taking a processual view of objects, their concreteness emerges as a momentary point in a spectrum of making, use and dissembling that constitutes their biographies, their social lives" (Bell and Geismar 2009:5). In this sense, the agentive lives of Torres Strait canoes materialized and unfolded while participating within complex and dynamic relational matrices and co-constitutive social arenas involving people (alive and dead), animals (alive and dead), spirit-beings (tangible and intangible), other object-beings (animate and inanimate), and the sentient realm of the sea.

ACKNOWLEDGMENTS

The core of this chapter was presented as a paper in the Towards Social Maritime Archaeologies session at the 2006 Theoretical Archaeology Group conference in Exeter. I thank session organizer Robert van de Noort, as well as John Chapman, for helpful feedback. Cambridge University Museum of Archaeology and Anthropology kindly provided access to the Haddon photographic and material culture collection. Thanks also to volume editors Eleanor Harrison-Buck and Julia Hendon for the kind invitation to contribute to this volume and for helpful comments on earlier drafts. This paper was written during a visiting fellowship at Oxford University. Special thanks to St. Cross and All Souls Colleges for logistical support. Helpful comments on an earlier draft of this chapter were kindly made by Lynette Russell.

NOTE

1. Here Haddon mistakenly identified "western" for "eastern." In the Western-Central Torres Strait language (WCTS), 'bilge water' is *sal* (masculine); "bail" is (*sal*) *anara-* (*anara-* 'dig, hoe, bail, rake, sweep, scrape, clear throat), (*sal*) *pama-* (*pama-* dig,

scoop out, bail), *sal adha-* (*adha-* take/put out). There is no link to *mimi* 'urine.' However, the Meriam Mìr (eastern Torres Strait language) word *usi* ('bladder, urine, bilge water'; the verb *depaup-* means 'bale') may be related to WCTS *wœsai~usai* 'stink, stench, rot, putrefaction' (Rod Mitchell, linguist, pers. comm. July 9, 2020).

REFERENCES

Alberti, Benjamin, and Yvonne Marshall. 2009. "Animating Archaeology: Local Theories and Conceptually Open-Ended Methodologies." *Cambridge Archaeological Journal* 19 (3): 344–56. https://doi.org/10.1017/S0959774309000535.

Allen, Jim, and Peter Corris, eds. 1977. *The Journal of John Sweatman: A Nineteenth Century Surveying Voyage in North Australia and Torres Strait*. St. Lucia: University of Queensland Press.

Appadurai, Arjun. 1986. "Introduction: Commodities and the Politics of Value." In *The Social Life of Things: Commodities in Cultural Perspective*, ed. Arjun Appadurai, 3–63. Cambridge: Cambridge University Press. https://doi.org/10.1017/CBO9780511819582.003.

Ballard, Chris, Richard Bradley, Lise Nordenborg Myhre, and Meredith Wilson. 2004. "The Ship as Symbol in the Prehistory of Scandinavia and Southeast Asia." *World Archaeology* 35 (3): 385–403. https://doi.org/10.1080/0043824042000185784.

Barad, Karen. 2007. *Meeting the Universe Halfway: Quantum Physics and the Entanglement of Matter and Meaning*. Durham, NC: Duke University Press. https://doi.org/10.1215/9780822388128.

Barham, Anthony J., and David R. Harris. 1987. "Archaeological and Palaeoenvironmental Investigations in Western Torres Strait, Northern Australia." Final Report to the Research and Exploration Committee of the National Geographic Society on "the Torres Strait Research Project."

Barlow, Kathleen, and David Lipset. 1997. "Dialogics of Material Culture: Male and Female in Murik Outrigger Canoes." *American Ethnologist* 24 (1): 4–36. https://doi.org/10.1525/ae.1997.24.1.4.

Bell, Joshua A., and Haidy Geismar. 2009. "Materialising Oceania: New Ethnographies of Things in Melanesia and Polynesia." *Australian Journal of Anthropology* 20 (1): 3–27. https://doi.org/10.1111/j.1757-6547.2009.00001.x.

Brady, Liam M. 2010. *Pictures, Patterns, and Objects: Rock Art of the Torres Strait Islands, Northeastern Australia*. North Melbourne: Australian Scholarly Publishing.

Brown, Linda A., and William H. Walker. 2008. "Prologue: Archaeology, Animism, and Non-Human Agents." *Journal of Archaeological Method and Theory* 15 (4): 297–99. https://doi.org/10.1007/s10816-008-9056-6.

Campbell, Shirley F. 2002. *The Art of Kula*. Oxford: Berg.

Chalmers, James. 1903a. "A Vocabulary of the Bugi Language, British New Guinea." *Journal of the Anthropological Institute of Great Britain and Ireland* 33: 111–16.

Chalmers, James. 1903b. "Notes on the Natives of Kiwai Island, Fly River, British New Guinea." *Journal of the Anthropological Institute of Great Britain and Ireland* 33: 117–24. https://doi.org/10.2307/2842999.

Chapman, John. 2000. *Fragmentation in Archaeology: People, Places, and Broken Objects in the Prehistory of South Eastern Europe*. London: Routledge.

Dobres, Marcia-Anne, and John E. Robb, eds. 2000. *Agency in Archaeology*. London: Routledge.

Droogan, Julian. 2013. *Religion, Material Culture, and Archaeology*. London: Bloomsbury.

d'Urville, Jules Dumont. 1846. *Voyage au Pole Sud et dans l'Oceanie: Atlas pittoresque*, vol. 2. Paris: Gide et J. Baudry.

Florek, Stan. 2005. *The Torres Strait Islands Collections at the Australian Museum*. Technical Reports of the Australian Museum 19. Sydney: Australian Museum.

Gell, Alfred. 1998. *Art and Agency: An Anthropological Theory*. New York: Oxford University Press.

Haddon, Alfred C. 1890. "The Ethnography of the Western Tribe of Torres Straits." *Journal of the Anthropological Institute of Great Britain and Ireland* 19: 297–446. https://doi.org/10.2307/2842024.

Haddon, Alfred C. 1935. *General Ethnography*, vol. 1. *Reports of the Cambridge Anthropological Expedition to Torres Straits*. Cambridge: Cambridge University Press.

Haddon, Alfred C. 1937. *Canoes of Oceania*, vol. 2: *The Canoes of Melanesia, Queensland, and New Guinea*. Bernice P. Bishop Museum Special Publication 28. Honolulu, HI: The Museum.

Haddon, Alfred C., ed. 1904. *Sociology, Magic, and Religion of the Western Islanders*, vol. 5. *Reports of the Cambridge Anthropological Expedition to Torres Straits*. Cambridge: Cambridge University Press.

Haddon, Alfred C., ed. 1908. *Sociology, Magic, and Religion of the Eastern Islanders*, vol. 6. *Reports of the Cambridge Anthropological Expedition to Torres Straits*. Cambridge: Cambridge University Press.

Haddon, Alfred C., ed. 1912. *Arts and Crafts*, vol. 4. *Reports of the Cambridge Anthropological Expedition to Torres Straits*. Cambridge: Cambridge University Press.

Harvey, Graham. 2005. *Animism: Respecting the Living World*. New York: Columbia University Press.

Henare, Amiria, Martin Holbraad, and Sari Wastell. 2007. "Introduction: Thinking through Things." In *Thinking through Things: Theorising Artefacts Ethnographically*, ed. Amiria Henare, Martin Holbraad, and Sari Wastell, 1–31. London: Routledge.

Hodder, Ian. 2012. *Entangled: An Archaeology of the Relationships between Humans and Things*. Oxford: Wiley-Blackwell. https://doi.org/10.1002/9781118241912.

Hunt, Archibald E. 1899. "Ethnographical Notes on the Murray Islands, Torres Straits." *Journal of the Anthropological Institute of Great Britain and Ireland* 28 (1–2): 5–19. https://doi.org/10.2307/2842924.

Ingold, Tim. 2006. "Rethinking the Animate, Re-Animating Thought." *Ethnos* 71 (1): 9–20. https://doi.org/10.1080/00141840600603111.

Ingold, Tim. 2007. "Materials against Materiality." *Archaeological Dialogues* 14 (1): 1–16. https://doi.org/10.1017/S1380203807002127.

Jones, Andy M., and Nicole Boivin. 2010. "The Malice of Inanimate Objects: Material Agency." In *The Oxford Handbook of Material Culture Studies*, ed. Dan Hicks and Mary C. Beaudry, 333–51. Oxford: Oxford University Press.

Jukes, Joseph B. 1847. *Narrative of the Surveying Voyage of HMS Fly*. 2 vols. London: T. & W. Boone.

King, Phillip P. 1837. "Voyage of the Colonial Schooner *Isabella*, in Search of the Survivors of the Charles Eaton." *Nautical Magazine* 6: 654–63, 753–60, 799–806.

Kopytoff, Igor. 1986. "The Cultural Biography of Things: Commoditization as Process." In *The Social Life of Things: Commodities in Cultural Perspective*, ed. Arjun Appadurai, 64–92. Cambridge: Cambridge University Press. https://doi.org/10.1017/CBO9780511819582.004.

Landtman, Gunnar. 1927. *The Kiwai Papuans of British New Guinea*. London: Macmillan.

Latour, Bruno. 1993. *We Have Never Been Modern*. Cambridge, MA: Harvard University Press.

Lawrence, David. 1994. "Customary Exchange across Torres Strait." *Memoirs of the Queensland Museum* 34 (2): 241–446.

Lawrence, David. 2010. *Gunnar Landtman in Papua: 1910 to 1912*. Canberra: Australian National University Press. https://doi.org/10.26530/OAPEN_459258.

Lawrie, Margaret. 1970. *Myths and Legends of Torres Strait*. St. Lucia: University of Queensland Press.

Layard, John. 1942. *Stone Men of Malekula*. London: Chatto and Windus.

Layton, Robert. 2003. "Art and Agency: A Reassessment." *Journal of the Royal Anthropological Institute* 9 (3): 447–64. https://doi.org/10.1111/1467-9655.00158.

Lindstrøm, Torill C. 2015. "Agency 'in Itself': A Discussion of Inanimate, Animal, and Human Agency." *Archaeological Dialogues* 22 (2): 207–38. https://doi.org/10.1017/S1380203815000264.

Lipset, David. 2005. "Dead Canoes: The Fate of Agency in Twentieth-Century Murik Art." *Social Analysis* 49 (1): 109–40. https://doi.org/10.3167/015597705780996309.

Lipset, David. 2014. "Living Canoes: Vehicles of Moral Imagination among the Murik of Papua New Guinea." In *Vehicles: Cars, Canoes, and Other Metaphors of Moral Ambivalence*, ed. David Lipset and Richard Handler, 21–47. New York: Berghahm.

MacGillivray, John. 1852. *Narrative of the Voyage of HMS* Rattlesnake. 2 vols. London: T. & W. Boone.

Malinowski, Bronislaw. 1922. *Argonauts of the Western Pacific: An Account of Native Enterprise and Adventure in the Archipelagoes of Melanesian New Guinea*. London: Routledge and Kegan Paul.

McNiven, Ian J. 2004. "Saltwater People: Spiritscapes, Maritime Rituals, and the Archaeology of Australian Indigenous Seascapes." *World Archaeology* 35 (3): 329–49. https://doi.org/10.1080/0043824042000185757.

McNiven, Ian J. 2008. "Sentient Sea: Seascapes as Spiritscapes." In *Handbook of Landscape Archaeology*, ed. Bruno David and Julian Thomas, 149–57. Walnut Creek, CA: Left Coast.

McNiven, Ian J. 2010. "Navigating the Human-Animal Divide: Marine Mammal Hunters and Rituals of Sensory Allurement." *World Archaeology* 42 (2): 215–30. https://doi.org/10.1080/00438241003672849.

McNiven, Ian J. 2013. "Between the Living and the Dead: Relational Ontologies and the Ritual Dimensions of Dugong Hunting across Torres Strait." In *Archaeologies of Relationality: Humans, Animals, Things*, ed. Christopher Watts, 97–116. London: Routledge.

McNiven, Ian J. 2015a. "Canoes of Mabuyag and Torres Strait." *Memoirs of the Queensland Museum—Culture* 8 (1): 127–207.

McNiven, Ian J. 2015b. "Precarious Islands: Kulkalgal Reef Island Settlement and High Mobility across 700 km of Seascape, Central Torres Strait and Northern Great Barrier Reef." *Quaternary International* 385: 39–55. https://doi.org/10.1016/j.quaint.2014.09.015.

Melville, Harden Sidney. [1849]. *Sketches in Australia and the Adjacent Islands, Selected from a Number Taken during the Surveying Voyage of HMS "Fly" and "Bramble" under the Command of Capt. F. P. Blackwood, R.N., during the Years 1842–46*. London. Dickinson.

Moore, David R. 1979. *Islanders and Aborigines at Cape York*. Canberra: Australian Institute of Aboriginal Studies.

Moore, David R. 1984. *The Torres Strait Collections of A. C. Haddon*. London: British Museum Publications.

Moresby, John. 1875. "Recent Discoveries at the Eastern End of New Guinea." *Journal of the Royal Geographical Society* 44: 1–14. https://doi.org/10.2307/1798775.

Munn, Nancy D. 1977. "The Spatiotemporal Transformations of Gawa Canoes." *Journal de la Société des Oceanistes* 33 (54–55): 39–53. https://doi.org/10.3406/jso.1977.2942.

Munn, Nancy D. 1986. *The Fame of Gawa: A Symbolic Study of Value Transformation in a Massim (Papua New Guinea) Society.* Cambridge: Cambridge University Press.

Raven, Michelle M. 1990. "The Point of No Diminishing Returns." PhD dissertation, Department of Anthropology, University of California, Davis.

Ray, Sidney H. 1907. *Linguistics*, vol. 3. *Reports of the Cambridge Anthropological Expedition to Torres Straits.* Cambridge: Cambridge University Press.

Riley, E. Baxter. 1925. *Among Papuan Headhunters.* London: Seeley, Service.

Robb, John. 2010. "Beyond Agency." *World Archaeology* 42 (4): 493–520. https://doi.org/10.1080/00438243.2010.520856.

Rosenman, Helen. 1987. *An Account in Two Volumes of the Two Voyages to the South Seas by Captain (Later Rear-Admiral) Jules S-C Dumont D'Urville.* Honolulu: University of Hawaii Press.

Scott, Colin H. 2004. "'Our Feet Are on the Land, but Our Hands Are in the Sea': Knowing and Caring for Marine Territory at Erub, Torres Strait." In *Woven Histories Dancing Lives: Torres Strait Islander Identity, Culture, and History,* ed. Richard Davis, 259–70. Canberra: Aboriginal Studies Press.

Sillar, Bill. 2009. "The Social Agency of Things? Animism and Materiality in the Andes." *Cambridge Archaeological Journal* 19 (3): 367–77. https://doi.org/10.1017/S0959774309000559.

Skibo, James M., and Michael B. Schiffer. 2008. *People and Things: A Behavioral Approach to Material Culture.* New York: Springer. https://doi.org/10.1007/978-0-387-76527-3.

Tambiah, Stanley J. 1983. "On Flying Witches and Flying Canoes: The Coding of Male and Female Values." In *The Kula: New Perspectives on Massim Exchange,* ed. Jerry W. Leach and Edmund Leach, 171–200. Cambridge: Cambridge University Press.

Tilley, Chris. 1999. "The Metaphorical Transformation of Wala Canoes." In *Metaphor and Material Culture,* ed. Chris Tilley, 102–32. Oxford: Blackwell.

Van de Noort, Robert. 2011. *North Sea Archaeologies: A Maritime Biography, 10,000 BC to AD 1500.* Oxford: Oxford University Press.

Westerdahl, Christer. 2005. "Seal on Land, Elk at Sea: Notes on and Applications of the Ritual Landscape at the Seaboard." *International Journal of Nautical Archaeology* 34 (1): 2–23. https://doi.org/10.1111/j.1095-9270.2005.00039.x.

Zedeño, María N. 2009. "Animating by Association: Index Objects and Relational Taxonomies." *Cambridge Archaeological Journal* 19 (3): 407–17. https://doi.org/10.1017/S0959774309000596.

9

The performative actions through which West Africans ensure their well-being are often subsumed by analysts under the rubric of ritual and religion, but in practice a wide range of actions and media is involved. My central argument is that archaeological exploration of these practices requires contextualized analysis of things as diverse as "ornaments" and animal bones, as I illustrate through a case study centered on the Banda area of west-central Ghana. I proceed from the premise that we should consider practices of well-being as a condition of personhood. Whether engaging individuals, families, or broader collectives, actions centered on well-being relationally engage bodies of varying form (humans, animals, non-corporeal spirit beings) through diverse media (words, prepared food, drink, plant substances, objects). Practices may focus on individual bodies, as, for example, the wearing of amulets endowed with protective power. Others, like the pouring of libations accompanied by invocations, connect the living to their ancestral forbears, while those centered on shrines secure outcomes through the medium of things and offerings that attract spirit beings who possess the power to intercede in human affairs. While diverse in form, all these actions have a relational dimension and lived effects (Meyer and Houtman 2012).

Early descriptions of these practices by European merchants on the so-called Guinea coast were shaped by an emerging ontology that bifurcated first souls (Pietz 1987:28) and later minds from bodies and bodies from

Efficacious Objects and Techniques of the Subject

"Ornaments" and Their Depositional Contexts in Banda, Ghana

Ann B. Stahl

DOI: 10.5876/9781607327479.c009

world (Espirito Santo and Tassi 2013). As explored in detail by Pietz (1985, 1987, 1988), these early perceptions laid the foundation for theories of "fetishism" (see also Meyer and Houtman 2012:14–15). Perceived as standing apart from "rational" activity (Taves and Bender 2012), they were long portrayed as the domain of "belief"—or, more condemningly, "superstition"—rather than efficacious practice. The cultural relativism that informed early twentieth-century ethnography produced less judgmental descriptions (e.g., Rattray 1927:1–24) that were continuous nonetheless, with the premise that these practices belonged to a religious domain and were part of enduring "tradition." This elided the processes through which "the notion of traditional religion itself developed in the context of the encounter between Christian missionaries and indigenous priests" (Meyer 2012:91; also Meyer and Houtman 2012; Pietz 1985, 1987, 1988). It equally elided the ways West Africans responded to changing circumstances through improvisational practice (Barber 2007a; Ingold and Hallam 2007), a process archaeologists have recently begun to explore (Norman 2014; Ogundiran 2002, 2014; Richard 2010; Stahl 2002, 2008, 2015b). Mid-twentieth-century scholarship further solidified a dichotomous view of belief and practical action in its privileging of mind and language as sites of meaning making coupled with a view of religion as symbolic activity that "stands apart from the truly useful" (Keane 2010:190; see also Espirito Santo and Tassi 2013).

Recent scholarship has challenged these perspectives on diverse fronts. As richly exemplified in this volume, contemporary archaeologists take seriously relational ontological perspectives, directing analytical attention to the practices through which personhood and a state of well-being was secured vis-à-vis a broader landscape of nonhuman spirit beings (Harrison-Buck and Hendon, this volume). Yet we have paid less attention to how Western understandings of these "alternative" ontologies emerged. Scholars like Meyer (2012) and Pietz (1985, 1987, 1988, 1995) remind us that European understandings of non-European practice were shaped by historically specific intercultural interaction (also Bernault 2006). Vocabularies and concepts forged in processes of interaction were subsequently wrested from those contexts and taken to stand "in general" for non-Western societies. They were deployed in turn by missionaries, colonial officials, scholars, and colonized subjects as they negotiated practice and value in the colonial contexts from which ethnographers extrapolated "tradition." Used comparatively (Stahl 1993, 2001:19–40; Wylie 2002), archaeology's material evidence holds potential to illuminate these negotiations of personhood and well-being in genealogically connected (Gosden 2005:203–6) but dynamic ways (e.g., Keane 2010). But in doing so we need to be mindful of how these entangled conceptual and practical histories may be carried forward in our analytical vocabularies and frameworks (Bernault 2006; Espirito Santo and Tassi 2013; Meyer and Houtman 2012), a point no less pertinent to the concepts of relationality and personhood that are gaining purchase in contemporary scholarship (Fowler 2004:34).

In this chapter I build on recent literatures in African ethnography, history, and art history to explore how villagers of the western Volta River basin in Ghana negotiated well-being over several centuries of shifting interregional and intercontinental entanglements. Inspired by recent literature that explores how personhood emerges through bodily techniques and things in motion (e.g., Warnier 2007, 2011, 2012, 2013), I focus attention on bangles, rings, beads, and other objects typically classified as "ornaments," a category that masks their agency in negotiations of well-being (see Glaze 1978). I use their itineraries or biographies as a pathway for discerning how these objects or things configured subjects and well-being through their actions on bodies (Loren 2010) but also through their circulations apart from them (see also Ogundiran 2002, 2014).[1] I briefly situate the study in relation to literature that approaches personhood as a relational process in which things participate. A telescoped case study follows in which I explore how we can use the visual properties and depositional contexts of ornaments to illuminate their operations as efficacious objects in dynamic processes of well-being and personhood (Harrison-Buck and Hendon, this volume).

THE DYNAMICS OF WELL-BEING AND TECHNIQUES OF THE SUBJECT

A growing literature highlights the incorporative ethos and openness to new affordances (Knappett 2004) demonstrated by Africans as they improvised their practice in relation to shifting topologies of power, opportunity, and constraint, particularly those related to interregional and intercontinental entanglements over recent centuries (Allman and Parker 2005; Barber 2007a; Drewal 1996; Kodesh 2008; Meyer 1999; Norman 2014; Ogundiran 2014; Ogundiran and Saunders 2014; Schildkrout and Keim 1990:190–93; Trapido 2013). Objects newly available through emerging global connections were readily incorporated through what Guyer and Belinga (1995; also Doris 2011) characterize as "compositional" practice. Combined with attention to what Warnier (2007, 2009, 2012:331–32), following Mauss (1979), termed "techniques of the subject," these literatures underscore the need to surmount an earlier preoccupation with verbalized meaning and knowledge to more fully understand how personhood is produced through a subject's relations with things (Warnier 2007:8–9).

Warnier and others of the Matière à Penser (M à P) working group (Warnier 2007:22) have argued that objects, materials, and the actions through which relations are produced are part and parcel of techniques of the subject (Warnier 2007, 2009, 2012:331–32). Their approach builds on an earlier anthropology of techniques (e.g., Lemonnier 1992). However, M à P scholars are critical of the narrow focus on technique as "efficacious action on *matter*" that characterizes the "anthropology of techniques" approach (Warnier 2009:460, original emphasis), as they are of the tendency to treat ritual and symbolism as epiphenomenal and ideational (see also Keane 2003:410, 2008). M à P scholars argue that this narrowness undermined Mauss's earlier intuition that techniques, as "efficacious action," shape subjectivity (Warnier 2009:461) or, alternatively, personhood (Fowler 2004, 2010:364–74). Warnier's project reclaims Mauss's insight through a "unified anthropology of techniques" (Warnier 2009:469) that includes traditional and efficacious action on bodies (Warnier 2009:460, 465). Consistent with a broader project of surmounting the obdurate and artificial division between "'spirit' and 'matter'" (Keane 2003:409), Warnier's (2007) *The Pot-King* illuminates the "sensori-motor culture" through which persons are socially formed in relationship with things. In its phenomenological underpinnings, this focus bears resemblance to Munn's analysis of Gawan *kula* exchange as an "action system" that coordinately produces "objective structures of the social world, and the specific forms of subjective experience" (Munn 1983:279). Persons are formed through gestures and sensory engagements with materials and objects, with ontological implications in that "men and women of different groups and in different walks of life are not made of the same stuff" (Warnier 2012:328, also 2011; Ingold 2011; Hendon, this volume). Here, we might extend this insight to take account of the principle of symmetry discussed by Harrison-Buck and Hendon (this volume), with the implication that not all objects or animals are "made of the same stuff."

Among techniques of the subject, Mauss included practices of ritual, magic, and religion. Long viewed as the domain of symbol and meaning, logocentrically conceived, scholars increasingly recognize ritual as a realm of performative engagement with substances, nonhuman persons, and objects and thus as part of a broader "dialectic of people and things" (Meskell 2005:4) that is productive of embodied subjectivities and social relations (Bell 1992; Houtman and Meyer 2012). Within an African context, scholars further emphasize compositional practices—what in other contexts has been termed "bundling" (Keane 2003; Pauketat 2013; Zedeño 2008). For Keane (2003:414), bundling is about co-presence of qualities in an object that shifts its "relative value, utility, and relevance across contexts"; however, archaeologists and other scholars have used the concept to refer to compositions or assemblages of objects with distinct origins and qualities that in their combination possess affective power, as, for example, African shrines, which can range from single objects to complex compositions of diverse things and materials that are typically a site of offertory activity (see Doris 2011; Insoll 2013:167–68; Stahl 2008).

Warnier's emphasis on subject making resonates with Wells's (2012) recent exploration of the visual ecology of Bronze and Iron Age Europe as gleaned through its materiality. Building on Gibson's ecological psychology, Wells describes visual perception as a relational process grounded in materiality, such that seeing "involves a person's bodily experience of the world" (Wells 2012:21). He acknowledges shared properties of seeing: the role of lines in "framing," the way curved lines create an illusion of movement, the role of texture in drawing attention to surfaces, and features that create "eye-catching" objects (Wells 2012:26–32). However, he argues the need to contextualize "seeing" and explore how visual ecology was reconfigured as people were exposed to new materials, objects, styles, and what Gibson termed "affordances" (Wells 2012:32), a relational quality of objects vis-à-vis their surroundings that offers possibilities for action. By examining commonalities, distinctions, and specificities in the visual aspects of different kinds of late prehistoric European artifacts (pottery, metal objects) and contexts (burials, settlements), Wells identifies changes in the visual world involving color, standardization of form, and the framing of visual fields as Europeans participated in broader networks of commercial activity and wider spheres of object circulations. His study thus reminds us that visuality is among the techniques of the subject to whose temporality we should be attuned.

Wells's attention to the visual ecology of objects can in turn be enriched by Robb's (2015:166) discussion of what he terms "object design as a middle range theory of material culture." Robb highlights the ways elements of an object's design can cue users into responses; for instance, the fly motif painted on the men's urinal in Amsterdam's Schipol Airport that compels action as a target or Gell's (1992) oft-cited reference to the Trobriand Islanders' boat prow that exemplifies what Gell terms a technology of enchantment. Focusing analysis on design features, seen through the lens of emplaced convention rather than "universal" logic, "locates efficacy in material things themselves and how they incorporate and guide anticipated responses . . . pinning down exactly how material actants are active" (Robb 2015:169). Robb encourages us to study the flows of action in which people and things are enmeshed, as I endeavor to do below in considering how ornaments operate in relation to both bodies and the shrine bundles into which they were sometimes incorporated.

Urging us to augment theory with analytical method, Robb focuses on how an object's design cues prompt efficacious social action. He highlights five among a range of processes that can be cued: enchantment, irresistibility, disruption, standard setting, and objects that, through their exceptional qualities, act as a "cognitive trap" or magical entity. The first evokes effects through its qualities—the canoe prow of Gell's Trobriand example; the second operates as definitive "key symbols" (Robb 2015:172) understood through foundational values, often objects that operate as prestige goods; the third ritually disrupts, for example, through inversions of the "normal"; standard setters "assert standards" as part of "low-key normality" or habitus (Robb 2015:170); and the last, through their exceptional qualities, provoke fascination, sometimes by contradiction, as, for example, the use of fossils or ancient stone tools in ritual (see Brück and Jones, this volume) or the incorporation of "anomalous bodies" of twins or dwarfs, among other possibilities (Robb 2015:173). Such design elements and their cues provide, along with insights into the affordances of their composite materials and their use contexts, a methodological "way in" to better understand how material things achieve effects—in short, to how they become efficacious objects, whether in isolation or combinations, as I explore below.

Finally, Keane's (2003, 2010) perspectives on "marking" and "bundling" as material semiotic processes (see Crossland 2015 for a discussion) usefully augment these perspectives on how objects cue action with ontological effects, whether by shaping visual ecology (Wells 2012) or through their role in sensori-motor culture (Warnier 2012). Building on Peircean realism, Keane underscores the role of objects as mediators of social processes, not as mere signs to be read but rather as "an *instigation* to certain sorts of action" that are "subject to historical dynamics" (Keane 2003:418–19, original emphasis). As such, he offers tools that help us appreciate semiotic ideology as a social and historical process and objects as "part of the shared experiences and actions that mediate sociality" (Keane 2010:194). Marking is one such process. Marking trains attention by setting off an object, a context, or an action as unusual in relation to what is received as "normal." Marking makes these a focus for special attention and therefore makes them available for debate, action, and potentially new purposes without necessarily compelling these purposes. As such, marking can provide a source of creative action and innovation (Keane 2008:S113; e.g., Schoenbrun 2016). Bundling, too, builds on both the history and potential of semiotic forms, yielding combinations or "assemblages" that are the "outcome of contingent factors of historical context" (Keane 2008:S115), which in turn are available as affordances for future action.

As these and other literatures (Harrison-Buck and Hendon, this volume) demonstrate, we have seen growing awareness of objects' subject-forming power and their role in producing and shaping relations between humans and nonhumans, alongside methodological innovations in how to study these processes. But these insights sit in uneasy relationship with conventions of archaeological reporting in which objects are often reduced to lists in tables, augmented by a few illustrations from which to gauge their visual form. Parsed on the basis of their constituent materials (ceramic, glass, iron, copper alloy), presumed "function," or both, reporting conventions typically reduce complex object itineraries to a singular dimension of the multiplex performative contexts in which they operated. Suspended as tabular entries in site reports, objects rest several analytical steps removed from their contextual associations and the depositional practices that configured their animate relations (cf. Loren 2010; Ogundiran 2014). As such, our reporting conventions elide what might be learned about their participation in forming personhood through techniques of the subject, including those configured by the "visual ecology of the everyday" (Wells 2012:72).

My focus here is on objects typically classed in archaeological reporting as "ornaments." This term implies a particular use value as captured by the Oxford English Dictionary's definition as "a thing used to make something look more attractive but usually having no practical purpose." This definition builds on a view that adornment is representational rather than an ontologically significant practice that, through intimate bodily engagements, produced subjects (infants, children, emerging adults, women, men).[2] The latter is a process captured, for example, in the Senufo term *yawiige*, defined as a "thing worn as protective medicine or [a] charm" (Glaze 1981:76; see also Schildkrout and Keim 1990:123–41). Taking a cue from Wells (2012), I explore the sensorial qualities of bangles, beads, and rings and, based on aspects of their form and analogical insight, consider how ornaments participated in techniques of the subject at a time when the western Volta River basin of present-day Ghana was being drawn into first Saharan and later Atlantic trade networks of recent centuries. I discuss how ornaments may have marked local bodies with effect (Keane 2003; Loren 2010). Focusing on archaeological contexts from about the fourteenth through the nineteenth centuries, I glean insight into the shifting topology of person-making techniques by following the itineraries, associations, and depositional contexts of beads, bangles, and rings. I argue that following their itineraries using cues from their depositional contexts of recovery can help us glean a wider set of human and nonhuman relations—particularly with dogs and pythons—produced through ornaments and their interactions. This study yields insight into the compositional practices that involved a movement of ornaments from bodies, to which they likely lent protective power, to their depositional contexts of recovery in which some participated as elements of shrine bundles. Through their itineraries and affordances and as relational elements within bundles, ornaments participated in a dynamic repertoire of practices of well-being and personhood.

COMPOSITIONAL PRACTICE

Among the key technologies of personhood documented for regions of tropical and subtropical West Africa are practices of bodily modification, dress, and ornamentation. Some, like scarification and other bodily modification, leave little archaeological trace, aside from rare sculptural evidence (e.g., Ife terracottas and bronzes [Garlake 1990:112–13]). Other practices, like ornamentation, can be gleaned from the archaeological evidence of adornments including the bangles, rings, and beads described below. Bound up in the intimate sphere of "traditional" body work, these practices are nonetheless dynamic and enmeshed in broader political economic landscapes, as we are reminded by Goody and Goody's (1996:83) suggestion that labrets were adopted by groups subject to slaving to discourage raiders from abducting their women by making them unattractive. So, too, did labrets later become a particular focus of mid-twentieth-century government officials who aimed to eradicate the practice of lip piercing in an effort to bring "civilized" behavior to Ghana's northern regions (Goody and Goody 1996:85). As such, technologies of personhood are an arena through which we should anticipate scope for dynamic compositional practice as West Africans navigated the shifting topology of intercontinental connections.

Akin to what Gosden (2005:208) characterized as the "general excitation of the object world" associated with an expanding Roman horizon, the centuries of Saharan and Atlantic trade were characterized by flows of materials, objects, commodities, and associated technologies that provided resources for compositional practice and, through them, effects on people. As Wells has argued for Bronze and Iron Age Europe, these were centuries during which newly accessible materials and objects likely affected the "visual ecology of the everyday" (Wells 2012:72). Expanding Saharan networks provided growing access to imported copper alloys, which were widely valued as prestige metals in pre-colonial Africa. As detailed by Herbert (1984), copper and its alloys were distinct in their malleability, color, luminosity, texture, and sound by comparison to clay and iron (see also Howey, this volume). Valued for their redness, copper alloys were often used to fashion ornaments and objects that extended the visual ecology of West African peoples as these alloys became more readily accessed through Saharan exchange. So, too, did glass. Setting aside spectacular exceptions like the first millennium AD Kissi sites in northeastern Burkina Faso, where glass beads were abundant in mortuary contexts (Magnavita 2003), imported glass beads were generally rare prior to the intensification of European trade. As visually "eye-catching" objects (Wells 2012:18–19), imported glass beads expanded the colors, textures, and shapes of objects used to adorn bodies. Though at times perhaps secreted beneath clothing, the addition of glass beads to the repertoire of adornment in a context in which cloth was likely a rarity would have disrupted the "low-key normality" (Robb 2015:173) of beads fashioned from locally or regionally available materials, like the occasional fired clay, shell, or bone beads recovered from sites in the area.

Glass beads from sites earlier than the eighteenth century in the Banda sequence are monochromatic and small. The polychromatic beads of complex design that became available through eighteenth-century and later European trade further extended the value register (Stahl 2002). The latter were incorporated into the sacred bead assemblages of Banda's "founding families" (Stahl 2001:55–56) and became central to rites of passage and to the performative distinction of chieftaincy (Caton 1997; Stahl 2002). Together with the elaboration and proliferation of textile design that accompanied Atlantic trade (e.g., Steiner 1985), the effects of new things acquired through first Sahara and later Atlantic exchange on the visual ecology and compositional practices of Volta basin peoples after about AD 1200 bear closer investigation (cf. Wells 2012:68–69).

Beads were historically and are today valued in Banda and Ghana more generally for their protective as well as ornamental capacity (Caton 1997). Worn on the wrists, ankles, and waist, strings of beads are considered efficacious in forming the bodies of children—particularly girls—as they grow and mature. They play a visually prominent role in certain life transitions, as, for example, the sacred heirloom beads worn during puberty and marriage rites or the sacred strands that require careful ceremonial treatment before being used in the annual yam festival or at the funeral of a chief. Others are worn more routinely and intimately. The rattling of women's waist beads, secreted beneath their cloth, is considered an attractant and holds power of sexual arousal. Elder women stress the medicinal qualities of beads, particularly those used to protect children, the properties of which are enhanced by a solution of roots soaked in water in which the beads are rinsed. Specific beads are associated with particular maladies, and the power to invoke a bead's curative potential is the province of specific knowledgeable women. As made clear by the elders who spoke with Caton (1997:41–43), contemporary assemblages of sacred beads must be treated appropriately before being exposed to view through the pouring of libations, the singing of songs accompanied by dance and rhythmic gong playing, and the offering of food. These actions relationally connect the living to an ancestral presence that is fundamentally bound up in personal and social well-being. Thus, beads in Banda and in Ghana more generally are not merely ornamental but are imbued with the power to heal, protect, and form bodies; enhance beauty and sexuality, and facilitate life transitions. They are part and parcel of traditional technologies of self that are nonetheless dynamic and compositional, as implicated in the recontextualization of imported beads into the area's sacred bead assemblages (Stahl 2002).

Amulets known as *suman* among the Asante of present-day Ghana provide another example of compositional practice as documented by a remarkable collection of nineteenth-century documents found in the Danish archives and studied by Owusu-Ansah (1991). *Suman* are "man-made objects inhabited by special forces deemed efficacious in satisfying . . . [specific] needs" (Owusu-Ansah 1991:118). A particular form was in high demand among elites and non-elites alike in nineteenth-century Asante (Dupuis 1966 [1824], part 2:xi; Owusu-Ansah 1991:10). Produced by Muslims, these amulets were created by writing select passages from the Koran on paper, which was carefully folded into small packets, bound in cotton, and sewn into leather packets worn as a necklace or bracelet or sewn onto war smocks (Owusu-Ansah 1991:12, fig. 1:107). Sometimes their efficacy depended on imbibing water in which the object with the text had been washed (Owusu-Ansah 1991:108–10). The documents in the Danish archives include instructions for making amulets that were in demand during the nineteenth century, including charms for protection in battle, everyday protection, causing ill to an enemy, bringing wealth and peace, securing marriage and ensuring fecundity, and general purposes (Owusu-Ansah 1991:43). Made by skilled practitioners possessed of esoteric knowledge, these charms were accorded considerable power, as described by the British trade emissary T. Edward Bowdich who reported that the Asante "believ[e] firmly that they make them invulnerable and invincible in war, paralyse the hand of the enemy, shiver their weapons, divert the course of balls, render both sexes prolific, and avert all evils but sickness (which they can only assuage) and natural death" (Bowdich 1966:271). As an example of compositional practice and dynamic techniques of the subject, non-Muslim Asante and others throughout the forest and wooded savanna regions of present-day Ghana embraced these objects produced by Muslim practitioners, valuing them for their power of protection.

As I detail below, ornaments, as objects with the power to form bodies, also participated as components of shrines, illustrating Robb's (2015:177) point that "things' design features form affordances that extend beyond their original projects." Shrines are well recognized in the literature on West Africa as a compositional technology open to improvisation and franchising that creates ritual networks when powerful shrines are acquired and transferred to new settings (Allman and Parker 2005; Dawson 2009; Insoll 2006; Parish 1999; Parker 2004). Diverse in their form and scalar power, shrines figure prominently in contemporary and historical West African ritual practice. They typically comprise bundles of materials and things that are focal points for performative, efficacious actions that include offerings of various forms (cooked foods, the blood of sacrificed animals, invocations and powerful words). Despite their diversity, African shrines are unified by the ability to affect relations between human and nonhuman persons. As loci of efficacious action, their configurations and the practices focused on them produce what Keane (2010:188) terms "markedness" and "absence" in relation to the "habitual and repetitive activities that surround them." Refusing the "invidious dichotomy" (Keane 2010:190) that distinguishes the utilitarian and the symbolic, Keane encourages instead a focus on how archaeological patterns can help us discern what was singled out for "attentiveness and interest" (2010:191) vis-à-vis an unmarked flow of daily action. Shrines, as socially produced focal points for action, cannot be reduced to "representations" of nonhuman spirit agents (Keane 2010:192)—whether ancestors or gods—but rather as loci and what Keane (2010:194) terms "indexical entailments" through which those nonhuman agents can be enticed into efficacious action through appropriate performative action.

But not as traditions frozen in amber, for both gods and religious repertoires have histories (Allman and Parker 2005; Trapido 2013). These histories are shaped by what Barber (2007b:111), following Guyer (2004), terms the "productivity" of the Atlantic African interface, a feature that can be extended to earlier periods when woodland savanna-dwelling West Africans participated in Sudanic and Saharan networks that ultimately connected peoples of subtropical latitudes to the Mediterranean world, a time to which we now turn in west-central Ghana's Banda area.

BANGLES, RINGS, AND BEADS IN CONTEXTS OF SOCIAL ACTION

The Banda Research Project (BRP) has focused investigation on how daily life in a rural setting in west-central Ghana was configured in relation to broader social, political, and economic entanglements. These include involvement in the Niger River trade from the early second millennium AD, the Atlantic trade from the sixteenth century, and the imposition of British colonial rule in the late nineteenth century (Stahl 2001). Our excavations have centered on village sites characterized by low mounds, some formed through the collapse of earthen-walled structures, others built up through metal-working activities, and others created through refuse disposal. Here I focus on the modest quantities of bangles, rings, and beads, augmented by small numbers of cowrie shells and drilled teeth (table 9.1), we have recovered from three village sites that provide the foundation of a phase-based sequence for the area (Stahl 2007): Ngre Kataa (NK), type site for the Ngre phase, encompassing the thirteenth to about the second half of the fifteenth centuries; Kuulo Kataa (KK), type site for the Kuulo phase, which extends from the early fifteenth through mid-seventeenth centuries; and Makala Kataa (MK), type site for the Makala phase, which encompasses most of the eighteenth and nineteenth centuries. While these sites overlap somewhat in their occupations—some mound deposits at Ngre Kataa are contemporary with those at Kuulo Kataa, and both sites were occupied in Makala phase times—the sites provide a time-transgressive sequence that lends insight into continuities and changes in daily practice across centuries when Banda was connected first to north-facing Niger trade networks and later to emergent Atlantic trade networks. These shifting networks brought new affordances (materials, objects, foods, possibilities for social action), as well as new challenges (of slaving and political economic demands of expansionist polities, including colonizing powers; for details, see Stahl 2001:82–106, 2015c).

The objects summarized in table 9.1 are recognizable as "ornaments" by archaeologists and Banda community members alike. We can readily imagine their intimate association with bodies and their connection to well-being, as suggested by historical and ethnographic insights on beads and amulets summarized above. So, too, were iron bangles (figures 9.1 and 9.2) and rings (figure 9.3) recognized as objects that confer protection and power (Hahn 1996:111–12; Kröger 2001:468–78; Rattray 1927:fig. 7, no. 6 and caption), as local members of our archaeological team often observed when we encountered these objects during the course of excavation. Iron bangles, reportedly worn on the upper arm, protected warriors from harm during battle. Iron rings are associated with individuals who possess the knowledge and skills to mediate with spirits—so-called fetish priests. While some of these objects may have entered depositional contexts unintentionally (a valued bead lost when its ligature broke) or through discard (a broken bangle tossed away), a subset was recovered from object clusters that can, with some confidence, be interpreted as shrines, as

TABLE 9.1. Summary of ornaments (rings, bangles, and beads) by raw material and by site. NK = Ngre Kataa; KK = Kuulo Kataa; EM = Early Makala; LM = Late Makala; Cu = copper alloy; Fe = iron.

	Object	NK	KK	EM	LM	Total
Rings	Cu earring	5	3	1	0	9
	Cu finger ring	10	10	2	0	22
	Fe finger ring	9	22	0	0	31
	Total	**24**	**35**	**3**	**0**	**62**
Bangles	Cu	0	2	0	0	2
	Fe	28 (16)[a]	13(3)[a]	2 (1)[a]	0	43
	Ivory	5	47	0	0	52
	Total	**33**	**62**	**2**	**0**	**97**
Beads	Glass	15	15	40	56	126
	Stone unidentified	1	0	1	4	6
	Stone carnelian	5	4	4	0	13
	Stone quartz	1	5	0	0	6
	Fired clay	5	17	6	1	29
	Bone	1	1	0	0	2
	Shell	2	4	6	44	56
	Cu	4	0	7	0	11
	Total	**34**	**46**	**64**	**105**	**249**
Drilled Teeth		1	12	0	0	13
Cowries		10	10	9	22	51
	Iron point	15	11	6	3	35
	Total excavated m³	143	168	132	90	

[a] n including fragments (n that are complete)

I describe below. Their varied depositional histories push us to consider the objects' itineraries and the varying contexts in which "ornaments" operated. But first I offer some observations on their visual ecology, particularly as they relate to Keane's concepts of bundling and marking discussed above.

SERPENTINE MIMESIS IN BANGLES AND RING

Most of the bangles recovered from Banda sites are made from iron. As a valued material, iron was commonly re-forged rather than discarded. When

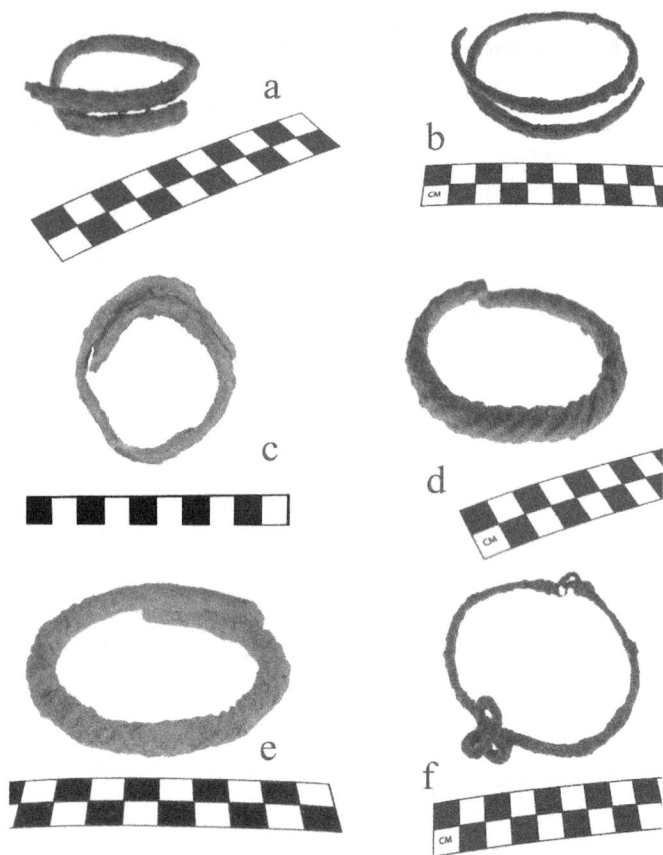

FIGURE 9.1. *Iron bangles from Ngre Kataa. a, b, c: semi-spiral overlapping coil; d: spiral-twisted closed form; e: spiral-twisted overlapping closed form; f: closed looped form. a, b, d–f are from Ngre Kataa, Mound 6 shrine cluster; c is from Ngre Kataa Mound 7. Scale in centimeters. Photo by the author.*

discarded, it was subject to corrosive weathering, so that most archaeologically recovered iron occurs as friable amorphous fragments. We cannot, therefore, take the number of archaeologically recovered iron bangles and rings as a guide to how common they were in the past. More than half of the iron specimens listed in table 9.1 and detailed in table 9.2 were corroded fragments, some possibly originating from a single bangle. However, details of form and style can be gleaned for a subset of well-preserved bangles (n = 20). Some are,

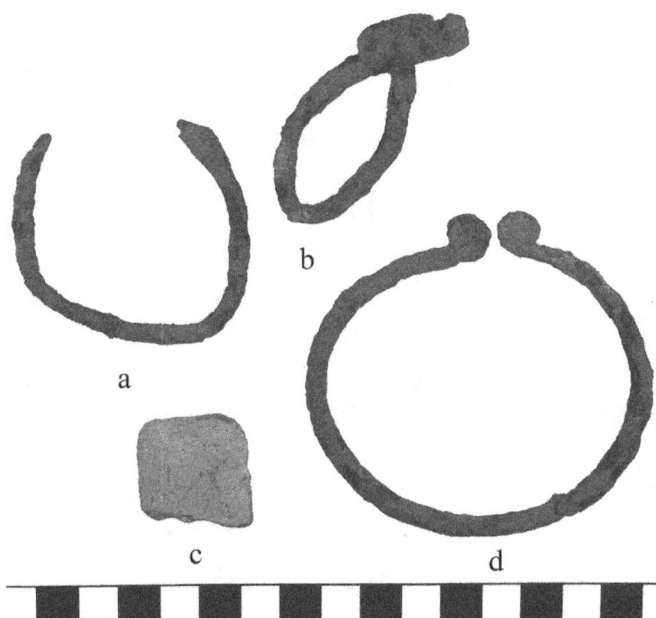

FIGURE 9.2. *Iron bangles and a gunflint from the Kuulo Kataa Mound 131 shrine. a: semicircular open bangle; b: bent semicircular open bangle with coiled end; c: gunflint; d: semicircular open bangle with coiled ends. All three bangles fashioned from spiral-twisted iron. Scale in centimeters. Photo by the author.*

in their lines and form, suggestive of snakes and, as I will argue below based on faunal remains, a mimetic expression of pythons (e.g., Glaze 1975:29, fig. 14, 1978:65, fig. 6).

Nine complete iron bangles were semi-spiral in form (table 9.2: "O" for overlapping, count in parentheses; figure 9.1a–c, e). Formed from a flattened or rounded iron bar, their ends overlapped to varying degrees. The spiral effect expands their vertical dimension in a fashion reminiscent of a coiled snake. Three other complete bangles and two fragments were fashioned from spiral-twisted iron rods (figure 9.1b, e, 9.2a–c). Two (one whole, one fragmentary) were semicircular open bangle forms (Kröger 2001:468n2) whose ends culminated in a tight coil (figure 9.2b, d). Finger rings were similarly made. A subset of finger rings made from iron (n = 9) and copper alloy (n = 4) were, like the bangles, formed with overlapping ends (figure 9.3a–e, i), with one example in the form of a double ring (figure 9.3k). One copper alloy ring was

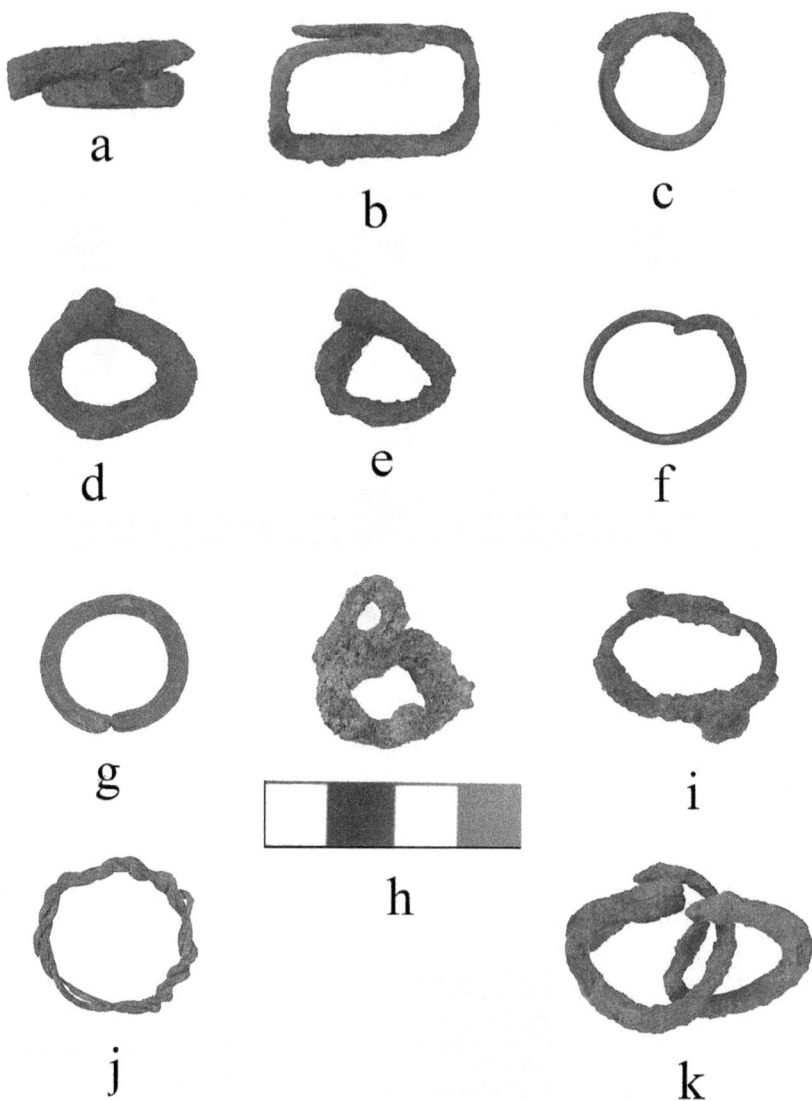

FIGURE 9.3. *Iron and copper alloy rings from Ngre and Kuulo Kataas. a–e: iron, overlapping coil; f: copper alloy overlapping coil; g: copper alloy closed form; h: iron closed form with loop; i: iron overlapping coil form, spiral-twisted metal with a loop; j: copper alloy, twisted wire; k: double iron ring, overlapping coil form. a–b: Kuulo Kataa Mound 131; c: Makala Kataa Mound 6; d: Kuulo Kataa Mound 138; e–g: Kuulo Kataa Mound 118; h: Kuulo Kataa Mound 129; i–k: Ngre Kataa Mound 6. Scale in centimeters. Photo by the author.*

TABLE 9.2. Summary of bangles and rings by site context and raw material. Fe = iron; Cu = copper alloy. Shaded context is an identifiable shrine. Bolded mounds are those where python vertebrae were found.

| | | Bangles[a] | | | | | Rings[a] | | | | |
| | | Fe | | Cu | | | Finger Ring | | Earring | "Gong ring" | |
Site	Mound	Whole	Frag.	Whole	Frag.	Subtotal	Fe	Cu	Cu	Fe	Subtotal
NK	**4**					0		2 (1O)			2
KK	138					0	1 (1O)			1	2
NK	3					0		1			1
NK	6	14 (7O; 1S)	8			22	7 (3O)	3	2		12
NK	7	2 (1O)	2 (1S)			4	2	3	2	1	8
NK	**8**		2			2			1	1	2
KK	**148**					0	3	1 (1S)			4
KK	101		2			2	1	2 (1O)			3
KK	118	1 (1O)	1		1	3	4 (1O)	3 (1O)	2		9
KK	119					0	2				2
KK	129		2	1		3	6 (1O)		1		7
KK	**130**		3			3	1	2			3
KK	102		1			1		1			1
KK	**131**	2 (2S)	1 (1S)			3	4 (3O)	1			5
KK	125					0		1			1
MK	**5**					0		1	1		2
MK	6	1	1			2		1 (1O)			1
	Total	20 (9O; 3S)	23 (2S)	1	1	**45**	31 (9O)	22 (4O; 1S)	9	3	65

[a] total N (O: subset of N with overlapping ends; S: subset of N with spiral twist)

fashioned from a thin spiral-twisted rod and another from two copper alloy wires, twisted together and formed into a closed ring (figure 9.3j). In another variant, two distinctive bangles were fashioned from a continuous rounded iron rod that was looped three times to form a topknot-like embellishment on the closed-form bangle (figure 9.1f). A ring evocative of this same form was made from a thin spiral-twisted iron rod, formed into a single top loop. The ring was closed with a twist of its overlapping ends (figure 9.3i; see also 9.3h).

In their lines, all of these forms are arguably serpentine. Their coiled and spiraled morphology evokes movement (Wells 2012:28–29), none more so than the ring made from a thin rounded copper alloy rod worked into a series of eight undulating back-to-back S-shaped loops, the ring closed with a thin sheet of metal (figure 9.4a). A final serpentine object—one that less obviously falls into the category of "ornament"—appears to be a modified version of a long-shafted triangular-headed projectile point that we occasionally recover from Banda sites. The projectile's shaft was deliberately looped into a series of back-to-back S-curves that culminated in a "tail" extending perpendicularly from the body, its head rising above its undulating body (figure 9.4b). In both its anomalous form that bundled (sensu Keane 2003) characteristics of a projectile point with serpentine qualities and its depositional association with a distinctive lost wax-cast twinned figurine (see Stahl 2013:62), it likely operated in Robb's (2015:172) terms as a magical object. In relation to the bodies on which they were worn and the contexts into which they were deposited, these objects invoked qualities of snakes in relational practices of well-being and personhood, whether through use as bodily ornaments or as constituents of shrine clusters, as described below.

As widely documented ethnographically, serpentine forms have associations of power for many African groups. Pythons in particular are understood as spiritually potent animals. Their remarkable qualities, including the ability to morph into humans (Glaze 1978:68), are linked to rain, gods, and the control of witchcraft. Images of pythons are often depicted on objects and buildings (Bognolo 2010:42–59, 64–67; Glaze 1975:29, 64, 1978:66–67; Werness 2006:335–36) or inscribed on landscapes (Norman and Kelly 2004). Bracelets mimetic of pythons are central to the work of Senufo diviners in Côte d'Ivoire, given the python's role as a messenger and medium capable of connecting humans with the nonhuman spirits whose actions determine human well-being (Glaze 1975:66, 1978:66–67, 1981:76–78). So, too, do python bracelets possess curative power, facilitating what Glaze (1978:67) characterizes as a "life-sustaining communication channel with spirits." In a richly insightful paper on "python work" around Lake Victoria in eastern Africa, Schoenbrun (2016) combines

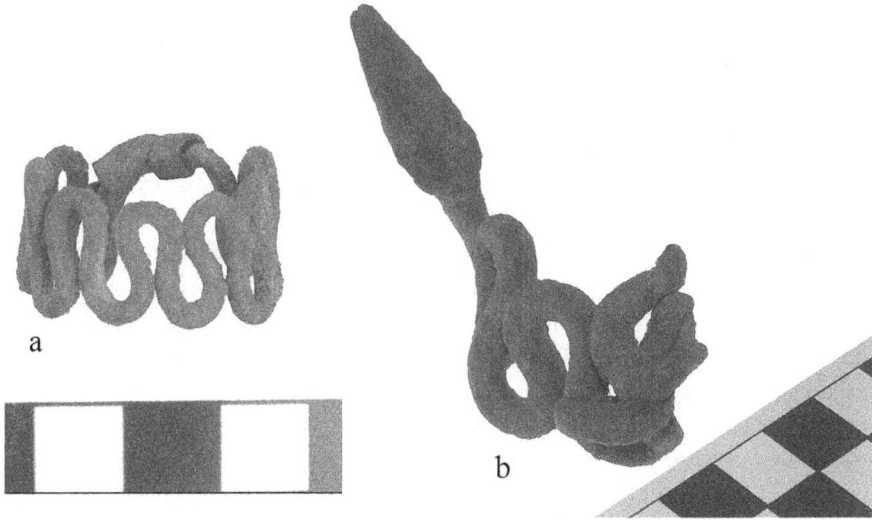

FIGURE 9.4. *Serpentine objects from Kuulo Kataa. a: copper alloy serpentine ring; b: serpentine iron "point." Scale in centimeters. Photo by the author.*

historical, linguistic, and archaeological sources to document the role pythons played as a material conceptual metaphor in a "constellating" process (Wenger 1998:126–27) that forged new political and economic relations among groups in a period of changing rain regimes and reconfigured agricultural systems. Their distinctive "bodies, life-course, and behavior separated pythons from other kinds of snakes and other kinds of predators," making them good to think and act with (Schoenbrun 2016:218). Schoenbrun explores how, through conceptual metaphor and marking (Keane 2003, 2010) by mediums or public healers, python work was a means by which people navigated a spiritually dangerous terrain in a period of change. While not arguing a direct parallel with the role pythons played in these settings, I explore below intriguing evidence from Banda-area sites that depositional practice brought parts of python bodies into relation with ornaments of serpentine form. This evidence suggests that pythons—as well as dogs (Stahl 2008 and below)—were animals differentially bound up in techniques of the subject and practices of well-being over the centuries discussed here.

This chapter builds on an earlier study (Stahl 2008) in which I traced the biographies (here itineraries) of dogs, pythons, pots, and beads to explore the dynamics of ritualization (Bell 1992) in Atlantic-era Kuulo and Makala phase contexts. There, I adduced evidence that dogs were likely used as sacrificial animals in Kuulo phase contexts, their butchery and dispersal participating "in ritualized production of social relations" (Stahl 2008:180) and, more broadly, in the well-being and personhood that is my focus here. Dog sacrifice fell into abeyance (albeit unevenly) in eighteenth- and nineteenth-century Makala phase contexts. That study also explored the contemporary and recent historical practice of secreting shrine bundles—often including glass beads—in pots, a practice also documented in Makala but not in earlier Kuulo phase contexts. The Makala phase was a time, too, when beads, particularly those acquired through international exchange, were recontextualized as components of ritual practice through their incorporation into the sacred bead assemblages described in Caton's (1997) study (and above). These data suggested "a dynamism surrounding shrines and sacrificial practices that can only be discerned through close attention to depositional practice" (Stahl 2008:184), a point I pursue below with reference to the ornaments that are my focus here.

Our more recent work at Ngre Kataa allows me to extend insight into the fourteenth and fifteenth centuries when Banda villagers' broader networks were north-facing ones that connected them to the Niger River and the Saharan trade. Evidence from Ngre Kataa provides additional insight into the use of dogs in ritual practice (below), but I begin by outlining the evidence for pythons as ritually charged agents in the negotiation of human well-being and the dynamism of this practice over the centuries covered by this study. I probe the depositional contexts from which serpentine bangles and rings were recovered as a way to explore their potential role as "magical objects" (Robb 2015:172) whose efficacy likely emerged from their mimetic relations with the power of pythons. My aim is to explore how, by following these ornaments, we may discern practices of marking and bundling (Keane 2003, 2010) in relation to other ritually salient objects and depositional contexts that emerged through practices by which people negotiated their well-being.

PYTHONS IN RITUALIZED PRACTICE

Eleven mounds contexts across the three sites considered here yielded a total sixty-five constrictor (Boidae) vertebrae, many identifiable as *Python sebae* (African Rock Python).[3] With one exception, they were recovered as single or sometimes several skeletal elements from "generalized" deposits that were neither obvious "midden" nor living surfaces. The exception was a cluster of thirty vertebrae—many burned—concentrated in upper levels of a late Kuulo phase mound (Mound 131; hereafter KK M131) at Kuulo Kataa (highlighted in gray in tables 9.2 and 9.3) that was occupied late in the sixteenth or early in the seventeenth century when the effects of emerging Atlantic networks were beginning to be felt. These vertebrae were part of a tightly clustered composition that included an iron hoe blade, three imported hexagonal blue glass beads, part of a large ceramic bowl, an imported gunflint, and several iron bangles and rings (table 9.3; figures 9.2a–d, 9.3a–b). As detailed in table 9.2, two bangles and one bangle fragment were fashioned from spiral-twisted iron, the complete examples culminating in coiled ends. Four objects resembling finger rings—though one was large and rectangular in form (figure 9.3b)—had overlapping ends, as described above. This context thus brought into direct association spiral-twisted and coil-form bangles and rings with constrictor vertebrae in what appears to be a shrine cluster that bundled locally produced iron and ceramic objects with imports (glass beads and a gunflint) acquired through Atlantic trade networks in what was arguably a python shrine.[4]

Deposited late in the Kuulo phase, this composition provides a basis for "following" python vertebrae (e.g., Stahl 2008, 2010, 2015a) to other contexts where they appear as single elements or several vertebrae spread across related excavation levels. Unlike the KK M131 context described above, these were not part of obvious (to an archaeological eye) bundles that we would call shrines. But what is their relationship, if any, to the iron bangles and rings argued above are visually mimetic of snakes? While not all bangles and rings were recovered from contexts that yielded constrictor vertebrae, many mound contexts yielded both, as indicated by those bolded in table 9.2. Moreover, a listing of ornaments and other "special" small finds (e.g., the gunflint mentioned above) hints at a pattern in which constrictor vertebrae are often loosely associated with specific kinds of ornaments, as indicated in table 9.3. Included are iron and copper alloy rings and bangles, ivory bangles, beads fashioned from various raw materials, cowries, as well as other more singular objects with ritualized connotations, as discussed below. In some cases these objects were distributed across a range of levels, for example, Mound 130 at Kuulo Kataa (KK M130). In other mounds (KK M118 and M148) they occurred within a narrow vertical range but not in the clustered fashion described above for KK M131.

As indicated by totals at the bottom of table 9.3, none of these objects occurred in large numbers at the sites considered here. Patterns of co-occurrence are therefore more suggestive than definitive. Nonetheless, a simple measure like the percentage of each recovered in general association with constrictor vertebrae (table 9.3, bottom) hints at recurrent, though dynamic (see below) depositional practices that brought some ornaments into conjunction with skeletal elements of these spiritually powerful animals. Constrictor vertebrae occurred more often in general association with iron (65%) and copper alloy (36%) rings

TABLE 9.3. Contexts with python vertebrae and associated "ornaments"; numbers indicate counts. Shaded context is an identifiable shrine.

Site	Mound	Unit	Levels	Python NISP	Rings Fe[a]	Rings Cu	Bangles Fe[b]	Bangles Cu	Bangles Ivory[c]
NK	3	42N 30W	9	1					
		40N 36W	6	1					
	4	Unit 1	3–7	8					
	7	14N 24E	2–4	1		1			
		14N 28E	3–5	1	1	1			
	8	8N 127E	1–4	2					1
			9–14	2	1	1			
KK	148	68E 50N	1–6	2		1			1
		68E 52N	2–6	1					1
		70E 50N	3–6	1	1				3
		70E 52N	5	2					
	101	2W 2S	2–7		1(1)	1			
			9–14	1		1	1		4
	118	62W 4N	3–5			1	1		
		66W 6N	6–8	1	3(1)		1(1)		
		68W 6N	1		1(1)				
	129	68E 4N	2–8		2(1)				1
			10–19	3	4(1)		2	1	3
	130	93E 110N	12	1					
		95E 110N	5–8			1			
			10–15	1			1(1)		2
		95E 108N	2–4						
			9–16	1		1			2
		95E 106N	6–13	1			1		3
	131	126E 140N	1–2	30	4 (3)		3		
MK	5	4E 0S	10	2					
		4E 2S	4–5	2					
total				65	19	8	10	1	21
total all sites				65	31	43	52	2	52
Percent of total (excluding Late Makala)					61	36	23	50	40

[a] total N (subset with overlapping ends)
[b] total N (subset of complete)
[c] minimum number; may be more fragments
[d] C = carnelian; Q = quartz

| | Beads[d] | | Shell | Cowries | Other (N) |
Stone	Glass	Clay			
1 (C)					[Cu ring: twisted]
					Ceramic handle: twisted coils (1)
				1	Jar w/ pedestal base in interior KK95–143; Brass 'bell' (1)
				1	Ivory 'hair pin' (4); Polished greenstone (1)
					Brass twinned figurine (1); Serpentine projectile (1); Inverted pot KK95–451
		1			Canid femur; Broken grinding stones, glassy slag
					Copper 'ear ring,' level 8 (1)
					1 iron ring with additional loop
		1			Clay bead with cross-hatch
				1	
		1	1		Drilled Canis mandible (1)
					Brass figurines (2); drilled Canis canine (1)
1(C)				1	Drilled teeth: bovid incisor (1); Canis canine (1); carnivore (1)
1(Q)					Drilled teeth: bovid incisor (1); Canis canine (1)
	3 (blue)				Gunflint (1); Hoe blade (1); vessel KK00–176
				1	
3	3	3	1	5	
21	70	28	12	29	
14	4	11	8	17	

and ivory bangles (40%) than with iron bangles (18%). Glass and shell beads, though never numerous in contexts older than the nineteenth century (table 9.1), were seldom recovered in association with constrictor vertebrae (4% and 8%, respectively), the exception being the three glass beads included in the KK M131 shrine bundle described above. Though percentages are small, stone or clay beads more commonly occurred in general association with python skeletal elements than did beads of glass or shell. A unique fired clay bead recovered from the same level as a python vertebra in KK M130 (Unit 93E 110N) was banana-shaped, its outer curve decorated with fine cross-hatched incision, perhaps mimicking a snake's reticulate patterning given the serpentine resonances of other objects described above. In another Kuulo phase mound (KK M148), a unique strap handle fragment, broken from a ceramic vessel, was fashioned from two clay coils twisted around one another (figure 9.5b) while another was untwisted (KK M130; figure 9.5a). Considered among the wider array of objects, these, too, have serpentine resonances. Also notable was the association of constrictor vertebrae with a group of drilled dog (*Canis*) canines and a drilled dog mandible in KK M130 (table 9.3 "other"), all in general association with two lost wax-cast copper alloy human-like figurines with a squatting posture, elbows back, hands on knees, that likely functioned as aids in divination (see discussion in Stahl 2013:56–58).

What might we glean from these patterns despite the admittedly small samples? First, some objects that operated on bodies as ornaments, particularly iron rings with overlapping ends but also copper rings and ivory bangles, were more likely to be deposited in general association with constrictor vertebrae than were others (e.g., iron bangles). Second, Kuulo phase contexts yielded higher frequencies and more co-occurrence among ornaments in depositional contexts than did earlier Ngre phase or later Makala phase contexts. This suggests a waxing and waning of ritualized practice that brought ornaments into conjunction with one another in depositional contexts and with skeletal elements of spiritually potent animals (pythons and dogs). But what is revealed if we follow the pathways of iron bangles for which python vertebrae were not an "attractant"? Where were they deposited, and are there indications that they, too, were incorporated into ritual practice? Pursuing iron bangles, including those of serpentine form, suggests that practices emergent in Ngre phase contexts intensified in the Kuulo phase contexts. Particularly revealing here is evidence from Ngre Kataa Mound 6 (NK M6), to which I now turn.

NK M6 formed through recurrent practices of metal working and ritual practice over decades and perhaps as long as two centuries (for details, see Stahl 2013, 2015b). Metallurgy is well recognized as a spiritually challenging craft that is often

FIGURE 9.5. *Ceramic handles from Kuulo Kataa and beads from Ngre Kataa Mound 6. Scale in centimeters. Photo by the author.*

ritualized and personified in African contexts (Herbert 1993; McNaughton 1988; Schmidt 1997, 2009). NK M6 is no exception. As I have developed elsewhere (Stahl 2013, 2015b), several shrine clusters positioned within the mound formed part of a relational meshwork (sensu Ingold 2000) or scaffolding (Knappett 2011:106) that attracted protective forces and ensured efficacious outcomes in this dangerous craftwork. Though space precludes full description, suffice to say that iron bangles were a notable and unequivocally associated element of the mound's shrine bundles. Fourteen whole and seven iron bangle fragments were recovered from NK M6 contexts, along with seven iron and three copper alloy rings (figure 9.1a–b, d–f; figure 9.3i–k). Though this was a metallurgical workshop at which iron and copper alloys were forged and fashioned into finished objects (see Haaland et al. 2002 on the trajectories and "stations" involved in metal working), these bangles and rings were not simply lost or deposited here; rather, they were deliberately incorporated into shrines, positioned so as to frame (Wells 2012:52–69) or mark ritualized object compositions.[5]

Upper levels of NK M6 yielded a particularly complex shrine composed of multiple object clusters covering several square meters (see Stahl 2015b for details). Each cluster included whole bangles of varying form, all seemingly deliberately positioned in relation to the partial ceramic vessels and other objects amid these compositions. One cluster centered on a large ceramic vessel, its perimeter marked by (minimally) four iron bangles positioned at intervals. All were either semi-coiled or spiral-twisted, as described above (Stahl 2013:figs. 8–9). In another cluster, a continuous circular iron bangle with no evidence for spiral twist—and therefore lacking in serpentine valences—was positioned below a vertically oriented pot lid, atop which was a dog cranium and below which were two carefully placed dog mandibles (right and left sides; Stahl 2013:figs. 10b, 10d). Placed amid the largest composition was another iron bangle—spiral-twisted and of semi-coil form and therefore serpentine—positioned adjacent to a set of miniature iron manacles similar to those ethnographically documented in neighboring areas to have been part of divination paraphernalia (Förster 1987:50, illus. 24; Glaze 1978:fig. 12; Stahl 2013).[6] Close by were the two distinctive bangles with the tri-loop "topknot" (figure 9.1f) described above. Though iron and copper alloy rings were found elsewhere in NK M6—including the ring with a top loop that echoes the form of the tri-looped bangles—none appeared as a component of these shrine bundles.

A smaller ritualized bundle in lower NK M6 levels comprised a bangle associated with a single twinned lost wax-cast copper alloy figurine, similar to those described above from KK M130, alongside a water-rounded quartz pebble and two iron blade fragments. Twins are widely considered in West Africa to possess supernatural powers, and twinned figures were commonly mimetically invoked in divination processes, as, for example, among Senufo groups (Glaze 1975:65, 1981:72–74).

Notably, whether part of a shrine bundle or not, these serpentine ornaments were concentrated in upper levels of NK M6 and other mounds at Ngre Kataa, hinting that the ritualized practice into which body ornaments were incorporated was an emergent practice that did not characterize Ngre Kataa's earliest occupation. The inclusion of bangles as a recurrent element of upper-level NK M6 shrine contexts suggests a connection between their power vis-à-vis bodies and their operations as part of shrine assemblages. Extrapolating from ethnographic contexts where iron bangles confer protection from bodily harm and mediate with the world of nonhuman beings (Glaze 1975:66, 1978:66; Hahn 1996:111–12), we might imagine that the bangles found at Ngre Kataa conferred similar protection and power as they circulated into shrine contexts. But while more than half of the complete iron bangles recovered from NK M6—which account for 70 percent of all the whole bangles recovered from the three sites under discussion (table 9.2)—were either semi-coiled or spiral-twisted, NK M6 deposits yielded no constrictor vertebrae. Isolated python bones occurred in three other mounds at Ngre Kataa (NK M3, M4, and M8), but only in NK M7 did a constrictor vertebra occur in conjunction with serpentine bangles (table 9.2). As a site of craftwork rather than routine domestic occupation, it is understandable that NK M6 yielded relatively modest quantities of faunal remains. Yet notable in this respect are the carefully positioned *Canis* remains included in the large shrine that capped NK M6 (above and described more fully in Stahl 2015b).

Turning to dogs, our recent excavations extend insight to earlier Ngre phase contexts where, as seen in table 9.4, dogs were present—at times, as described for NK M6 above, in ritualized contexts. However, dogs were not as prominent in the Ngre phase faunal assemblage as in later Kuulo phase contexts, barely registering in the percentage of faunal composition at Ngre Kataa. In later Makala phase contexts, ritualized use of dogs waned, though, as noted above (also Stahl 2008), available evidence suggests differential practice across the region in this period. Drilled *Canis* canines, presumably used as ornaments and deposited in association with constrictor vertebrae and iron rings and bangles at KK M130 (table 9.3), have been recovered only from Kuulo phase contexts. The emerging pattern is thus one in which we see dogs deployed in ritualized practice in Ngre (thirteenth to fifteenth century) phase contexts but not with the intensity seen in Kuulo (fifteenth to seventeenth century) phase contexts, after which the practice waned, albeit unevenly, in Makala (eighteenth to nineteenth century) Makala phase contexts—further underscoring the dynamic improvisation of ritual practice and negotiations of personhood in this period of shifting global entanglements. In sum, a pattern that emerges from available data is that pythons were deployed in mimetic but not bodily form in the context of the NK M6 metallurgical workshop, while the carefully placed dog skull and mandible hints that the practice of dog sacrifice documented more fully for the Kuulo phase was in place during these earlier centuries.

TABLE 9.4. Canid remains from Makala, Kuulo, and Ngre Kataas. NISP = number of identified specimens; MNI = minimum number of individuals; total NISP = all vertebrate fauna.

Context	Canid NISP	MNI	Volume (m³)	NISP/m³	MNI/m³	Total NISP	% Canid
Late Makala	11	2	90	0.12	0.02	3,028	0.40
Early Makala	9	2	132	0.07	0.02	2,441	0.40
Kuulo Kataa MP	19	5	9	2.11	0.56	1,802	1.05
Kuulo Kataa KP	574	36	159	3.60	0.23	27,778	2.07
Ngre Kataa	72	6	143	0.50	0.04	7,070	0.01

Turning briefly to beads and their associations, python vertebrae appear to have "attracted" beads made of clay and stone, as outlined above. NK M6 also yielded a small number of glass beads, including three of diverse origins (based on preliminary assessment of their chemical composition)[7] among the capping shrine. A blue-green tubular drawn glass bead fragment was made from a silica-based mineral soda lime (m-Na-Ca) glass generally associated with Mediterranean sources. Another blue-green opaque tubular wound bead was characterized as high PbSn (figure 9.5h). A third bead was a tubular European millefiori type, characterized by a beige core and black outer glass with complex swirled designs appearing in the lighter color (figure 9.5g). Two stone carnelian beads (figure 9.5c–d) were associated with the capping shrine as well, the source of which may be western India (Insoll et al. 2004). Two fired clay beads recovered from NK M6 but not associated with an identifiable shrine feature were fired to a red color and showed remnant red slip (figure 9.5e). Given that Banda pottery is seldom fired red, the bead's red-fired color enhanced by red slip raises the intriguing possibility that a subset of the ceramic beads mimicked carnelian beads, some of which were of a similar tubular form. A fourth glass bead (figure 9.5f) from NK M6 was an opaque yellow barrel-shaped drawn glass bead similar in composition to mineral soda-alumina (m-Na-Al) glass known to have been produced in India (James Lankton, personal communication, August 18, 2011).

Though few in number, these finds indicate that glass and carnelian beads—bodily ornaments deriving from exchange networks that linked Banda villagers to broader Mediterranean and Indian Ocean worlds—were brought together with serpentine bangles (but not snake vertebrae) through compositional practice in this shrine assemblage. The result was arguably a new semiotic form

(Keane 2008:S114) that bundled the power of pythons with qualities associated with these imported beads. At the same time, the beads stretched local visual ecology through their novel colors and forms. The specific semantics of that semiotic bundle remain elusive; however, the fact that it was repeated and elaborated upon in the later KK M131 shrine bundle (above) speaks to its saliency and resonance—its power as an association that was good to act with (Schoenbrun 2016)—in a period of transforming external relations. At the same time, available evidence suggests a diminished role for bangles and rings in later Makala phase contexts of the nineteenth century (tables 9.2 and 9.3) at a time when imported glass beads came to play increasingly prominent roles in local body techniques and practices of well-being (Stahl 2002).

CONCLUSION

The evidence summarized above supports both general and contextually specific insights regarding "techniques of the subject" and the production of well-being as a dimension of personhood. First and foremost, these techniques are dynamic. Archaeological sources lend insight into how people, through interactions with objects and animals, engaged in efficacious practice aimed at enhancing their well-being. The contours of how they did so through dynamic and creative engagement with nonhuman objects and beings can be gleaned by tracing the itineraries of "ornaments," from their interactions with the bodies they helped form through the depositional contexts that brought them into meaningful associations with other objects and substances and nonhuman beings. These associations, along with those bundled in their visual form (Wells 2012) and design cues (Robb 2015:177), provide a "way in" to illuminate the techniques of subject that were ontologically productive of past peoples. In the contexts considered here, we see that serpents—and probably more specifically, pythons—were an agentic nonhuman "semiotic form" (Keane 2008:S114) that appears emergent in Ngre phase contexts and intensified in Kuulo phase contexts before waning during the Makala phase, underscoring Keane's point (2008:S115) that "semiotic forms accumulate new features over time, contributed by different people, with different projects, in different contexts." Objects mimetic of snakes first appear in Ngre phase contexts, though not in levels associated with the site's earliest occupation. Both python vertebrae and serpentine ornaments occur at Ngre Kataa, but their depositional co-occurrence intensifies during the Kuulo phase, at the same time we see hints of mimesis in new objects and media (the serpentine projectile and the twisted-coil handle and incised bead fashioned from clay). Throughout these phases serpentine elements—whether the vertebrae of once powerful living creatures or through their mimetic counterparts—marked contexts and bodies and bundled qualities in ways that proved less compelling or efficacious for later Makala phase villagers as they negotiated changes associated with the expansion of the Asante empire into which Banda was forcibly incorporated in the last quarter of the eighteenth century.

Dogs, too, waxed and waned as participants in the praxis of well-being. They appear as elements of shrine bundles in metal-working contexts at Ngre Kataa, though they are less common in the faunal assemblage there compared to later Kuulo phase contexts where evidence for butchery and dispersal of their body parts suggests their more routine use as animal sacrifices (Stahl 2008)—a practice that diminishes, albeit unevenly, during Makala phase times.

As "ornaments" mimetic of pythons, I argue that bangles and rings were efficacious objects with dynamic ontological significance for Banda villagers. In early contexts, iron bangles and rings, likely of local manufacture and made from locally available raw materials, operated in relation to both bodies and shrine bundles. Copper alloys imported through northern trade networks reshaped the local visual ecology and were used to fashion both familiar (rings) and novel (earrings) ornaments in Ngre phase contexts. Beads fashioned from locally available materials were augmented from Ngre phase times with small numbers of glass beads, diverse in origin. Some locally produced fired-clay beads mimicked in color and form the carnelian beads now circulating through Saharan networks (figure 9.5e). Through time, imported glass beads circulated more widely and became an affordance increasingly central to technologies of the subject, playing the intimate and central role they came to play in rites of passage and demonstrations of power in the late twentieth century as documented by Caton (1997; see also Ogundiran 2002). While there is scope to more fully investigate how these diverse objects enchanted, disrupted, or set standards (Robb 2015), a contextual analysis underscores that they were actively involved in techniques of the subject, inclusive of practices of well-being, in diverse and dynamic ways.

By following the itineraries of bangles, beads, rings, and the bodies of spiritually salient nonhuman beings, we can begin to discern how things can "become sources of new intuitions, habits, and concepts" (Keane 2008:S123), remaking context and providing new affordances for future action. Through these we can glean something of the relational processes through which Banda villagers dynamically negotiated well-being across centuries of changing interregional and intercontinental connections in genealogically connected ways, even if aspects of their semantic bundling and its operations remain opaque.

ACKNOWLEDGMENTS

Thanks to Eleanor Harrison-Buck and Julia Hendon for their invitation to contribute to this volume despite my inability to participate in the session that launched it and for their patience as I've developed this chapter. Banda Research Project (BRP) excavations at the sites discussed here have been supported by the National Science Foundation (SBR-9410726, SBR-9911590, and BCS-0751350), the Wenner Gren Foundation for Anthropological Research (Grant 5133), and the National Geographic Society (Grant 4313–90). Research was conducted under license of the Ghana Museum and Monuments Board, and I gratefully acknowledge their support and that of the Ghana National Museum and colleagues at the Department of Archaeology and Heritage Studies at the University of Ghana. I am grateful to Peter Stahl, who undertook the faunal identifications referenced here, and to James Lankton for his elemental analysis of a subset of Banda beads. The greatest debt is owed to Banda people, including the past and current Paramount Chief and Traditional Council, for their continued support of BRP activities and the many men and women of Banda who have contributed to the project over the last three decades.

NOTES

1. In previous work (Stahl 2008, 2010, 2015a) I have drawn on Kopytoff's (1986) notion of object biography in exploring the history and circulations of objects in and out of the Banda area. A more recent literature challenges the biography metaphor for its life history implications of a birth, maturation, senescence, and ultimately "death," as well as its inability to account for the transformations of things through time and space (Hahn and Weiss 2013:7). This has led some to adopt an "itinerary" metaphor, which is argued to better capture the capacity of things "to be present in different contexts, to appear differently in each of these moments and particular modes" (Hahn and Weiss 2013:9; see also Joyce and Gillespie 2015). I use the term *itineraries* here, though I still see value in the biographies metaphor for conjuring the sedimented histories of objects accrued through their circulations and contextual relations. So, too, do I acknowledge debates over the connotations of "objects," "things," and "materials" (e.g., Hicks 2010:81–94; Ingold 2007; Meyer and Houtman 2012). I use each of these terms, though with the implication that they reference dynamic rather than fixed entities.

2. I consider gendered aspects of crafting elsewhere (Stahl 2016). Here I do not take up questions of gendered practice, in part for limitations of space but equally because ethnographic sources suggest that the gendered uses of ornaments are complex and overlapping. When combined with the dynamism of practice that is apparent in the Banda sequence, this is a topic well beyond the scope of this chapter.

3. Our excavation strategies centered on mounds, some sampled through a single 1 meter × 2 meter test unit and others through contiguous 2 meter × 2 meter units. Excavation units are designated by the coordinates of their north and east corners in a grid system based on a 0N/0W zero point.

4. Space constraints preclude a detailed discussion of shrines and their varied forms in Africa. For a discussion, see Dawson (2009) and Insoll (2006). More information on the forms and associations of contemporary and historic shrines and their archaeological manifestation in Banda can be found in Stahl (2008, 2013, 2015b).

5. Of note is an image in Glaze (1978:69, fig. 17) showing a circular earthen-walled Senufo shrine house associated with healing. The building is encircled—marked—by a painted image of a python. These resonances between practices of well-being documented ethnographically among Senufo and other groups in contemporary Côte d'Ivoire, Burkina Faso, and Mali cited throughout this chapter and the archaeological contexts discussed here suggest that Banda villagers formerly participated in a broader constellation of practice (Roddick and Stahl 2016; Stahl 2013) for which we have frustratingly few comparative archaeological data sets. At the same time, we should exercise caution in imagining these as practices associated with a specific ethnic-linguistic group.

6. The miniature manacles and their context are described more fully elsewhere (Stahl 2013:61, fig. 11, 2015b:65, fig. 5.9). They remind us that conditions of well-being and personhood were not only produced relationally but could equally be challenged or denied through relational material processes (Stahl 2015c).

7. James Lankton conducted laser-ablation inductively coupled plasma mass spectrometry (LA-ICP-MS) analysis of a sample of Banda beads. The characterizations reported here are based on his preliminary assessment of their chemical profiles as determined by LA-ICP-MS.

REFERENCES CITED

Allman, Jean, and John Parker. 2005. *Tongnaab: The History of a West African God.* Bloomington: University of Indiana Press.

Barber, Karin. 2007a. "Improvisation and the Art of Making Things Stick." In *Creativity and Cultural Improvisation*, ed. Elizabeth Hallam and Tim Ingold, 25–41. Oxford: Berg.

Barber, Karin. 2007b. "When People Cross Thresholds." *African Studies Review* 50 (2): 111–23. https://doi.org/10.1353/arw.2007.0079.

Bell, Catherine. 1992. *Ritual Theory, Ritual Practice.* Oxford: Oxford University Press.

Bernault, Florence. 2006. "Body, Power, and Sacrifice in Equatorial Africa." *Journal of African History* 47 (2): 207–39. https://doi.org/10.1017/S0021853706001836.

Bognolo, Daniela. 2010. *The Gan of Burkina Faso: Reconstitution of the History and Symbolics of a Little-Known Kingdom*. Genève: Bacheron Constantin.

Bowdich, T. Edward. 1966 [1819]. *Mission from Cape Coast Castle to Ashante*, 3rd ed. Ed. W.E.F. Ward. London: Frank Cass.

Caton, Alex Suzanne. 1997. "Beads and Bodies: Embodying Change in Bead Practices in Banda, Ghana." MA thesis, Department of Anthropology, State University of New York, Binghamton.

Crossland, Zoe. 2015. "The Signs of Mission: Rethinking Archaeologies of Representation." In *Materializing Colonial Encounters: Archaeologies of African Experience*, ed. François G. Richard, 129–51. New York: Springer. https://doi.org /10.1007/978-1-4939-2633-6_5.

Dawson, Allan Charles, ed. 2009. *Shrines in Africa: History, Politics, and Society*. Calgary: University of Calgary Press.

Doris, David T. 2011. *Vigilant Things: On Thieves, Yoruba Anti-Aesthetics, and the Strange Fates of Ordinary Objects in Nigeria*. Seattle: University of Washington Press.

Drewal, Henry John. 1996. "Mami Wata Shrines: Exotica and the Construction of Self." In *African Material Culture*, ed. Mary Jo Arnoldi, Christraud M. Geary, and Kris L. Hardin, 308–33. Bloomington: Indiana University Press.

Dupuis, Joseph. 1966 [1824]. *Journal of a Residence in Ashantee*, 2nd ed. London: Frank Cass.

Espirito Santo, Diana, and Nico Tassi. 2013. "Introduction." In *Making Spirits: Materiality and Transcendence in Contemporary Religions*, ed. Diana Espirito Santo and Nico Tassi, 1–30. London: I. B. Tauris.

Förster, Till. 1987. *Glänzend wie Gold: Gebguss bei den Senufo Elfenbeinküste*. Berlin: Reimer Verlag.

Fowler, Chris. 2004. *The Archaeology of Personhood: An Anthropological Approach*. London: Routledge.

Fowler, Chris. 2010. "From Identity and Material Culture to Personhood and Materiality." In *The Oxford Handbook of Material Culture Studies*, ed. Dan Hicks and Mary C. Beaudry, 352–85. Oxford: Oxford University Press.

Garlake, Peter. 1990. *The Kingdoms of Africa*, 2nd ed. New York: Peter Bedrick.

Gell, Alfred. 1992. "The Technology of Enchantment and the Enchantment of Technology." In *Anthropology, Art, and Aesthetics*, ed. Jeremy Coote and Anthony Shelton, 40–67. Oxford: Blackwell.

Glaze, Anita J. 1975. "Woman Power and Art in a Senufo Village." *African Arts* 8 (3): 24–29, 64–66, 90. https://doi.org/10.2307/3334950.

Glaze, Anita J. 1978. "Senufo Ornament and Decorative Arts." *African Arts* 12 (1): 63–71, 107–8. https://doi.org/10.2307/3335384.

Glaze, Anita J. 1981. *Art and Death in a Senufo Village*. Bloomington: Indiana University Press.

Goody, Esther, and Jack Goody. 1996. "The Naked and the Clothed." In *The Cloth of Many Colored Silks: Papers on History and Society Ghanaian and Islamic in Honor of Ivor Wilks*, ed. John Hunwick and Nancy Lawler, 67–89. Evanston, IL: Northwestern University Press.

Gosden, Chris. 2005. "What Do Objects Want?" *Journal of Archaeological Method and Theory* 12 (3): 193–211. https://doi.org/10.1007/s10816-005-6928-x.

Guyer, Jane I. 2004. *Marginal Gains: Monetary Transactions in Atlantic Africa*. Chicago: University of Chicago Press.

Guyer, Jane I., and Samuel M. Eno Belinga. 1995. "Wealth in People as Wealth in Knowledge: Accumulation and Composition in Equatorial Africa." *Journal of African History* 36 (1): 91–120. https://doi.org/10.1017/S0021853700026992.

Haaland, Gunnar, Randi Haaland, and Suman Rijal. 2002. "The Social Life of Iron: A Cross-Cultural Study of Technological, Symbolic, and Social Aspects of Iron Making." *Anthropos* 97 (1): 35–54.

Hahn, Hans Peter. 1996. *Die materielle Kultur der Konkomba, Kabyè und Lamba n Nord-Togo: Ein regionaler Kulturvergleich*. Köln: Rüdiger Köppe Verlag.

Hahn, Hans Peter, and Hadas Weiss. 2013. "Introduction: Biographies, Travels, and Itineraries of Things." In *Mobility, Meaning, and Transformations of Things: Shifting Contexts of Material Culture through Time and Space*, ed. Hans Peter Hahn and Hadas Weiss, 1–14. Oxford: Oxbow Books.

Herbert, Eugenia W. 1984. *Red Gold of Africa: Copper in Precolonial History and Culture*. Madison: University of Wisconsin Press.

Herbert, Eugenia W. 1993. *Iron, Gender, and Power: Rituals of Transformation in African Societies*. Bloomington: Indiana University Press.

Hicks, Dan. 2010. "The Material-Cultural Turn: Event and Effect." In *The Oxford Handbook of Material Culture Studies*, ed. Dan Hicks and Mary C. Beaudry, 25–98. Oxford: Oxford University Press.

Houtman, Dick, and Birgit Meyer, eds. 2012. *Things. Religion, and the Question of Materiality*. New York: Fordham University Press. https://doi.org/10.5422/fordham/9780823239450.001.0001.

Ingold, Tim. 2000. *The Perception of the Environment: Essays on Livelihood, Dwelling, and Skill*. London: Routledge. https://doi.org/10.4324/9780203466025.

Ingold, Tim. 2007. "Materials against Materiality." *Archaeological Dialogues* 14 (1): 1–16. https://doi.org/10.1017/S1380203807002127.

Ingold, Tim. 2011. *Being Alive: Essays on Movement, Knowledge, and Description*. London: Routledge.

Ingold, Tim, and Elizabeth Hallam. 2007. "Creativity and Cultural Improvisation: An Introduction." In *Creativity and Cultural Improvisation*, ed. Elizabeth Hallam and Tim Ingold, 1–24. Oxford: Berg.

Insoll, Timothy. 2006. "Shrine Franchising and the Neolithic in the British Isles: Some Observations Based upon the Tallensi, Northern Ghana." *Cambridge Archaeological Journal* 16 (2): 223–38. https://doi.org/10.1017/S0959774306000138.

Insoll, Timothy. 2013. "The Archaeology of Ritual and Religions in Africa." In *The Oxford Handbook of African Archaeology*, ed. Peter Mitchell and Paul Lane, 163–75. Oxford: Oxford University Press. https://doi.org/10.1093/oxfordhb/978019 9569885.013.0012.

Insoll, Timothy, David A. Polya, Keldeep Bhan, Duncan Irving, and Kym Jarvis. 2004. "Towards an Understanding of the Carnelian Bead Trade from Western India to Sub-Saharan Africa: The Application of UV-LA-ICP-MS to Carnelian from Gujarat, India and West Africa." *Journal of Archaeological Science* 31 (8): 1161–73. https://doi.org/10.1016/j.jas.2004.02.007.

Joyce, Rosemary, and Susan Gillespie, eds. 2015. *Things in Motion: Object Itineraries in Anthropological Practice*. Santa Fe, NM: School for Advanced Research Press.

Keane, Webb. 2003. "Semiotics and the Social Analysis of Material Things." *Language and Communication* 23 (3–4): 409–25. https://doi.org/10.1016/S0271-5309(03)00010-7.

Keane, Webb. 2008. "The Evidence of the Senses and the Materiality of Religion." *Journal of the Royal Anthropological Institute* 14 (s1): S110–27. https://doi.org/10.1111 /j.1467-9655.2008.00496.x.

Keane, Webb. 2010. "Marked, Absent, Habitual: Approaches to Neolithic Religion at Çatalhöyük." In *Religion in the Emergence of Civilization: Çatalhöyük as a Case Study*, ed. Ian Hodder, 187–219. Cambridge: Cambridge University Press. https://doi.org/10.1017/CBO9780511761416.008.

Knappett, Carl. 2004. "The Affordances of Things: A Post-Gibsonian Perspective on the Relationality of Mind and Matter." In *Rethinking Materiality: The Engagement of Mind with the Material World*, ed. Elizabeth DeMarrais, Chris Gosden and Colin Renfrew, 43–51. Cambridge: McDonald Institute Monographs.

Knappett, Carl. 2011. *An Archaeology of Interaction: Network Perspectives on Material Culture and Society*. Oxford: Oxford University Press. https://doi.org/10.1093/acpro f:osobl/9780199215454.001.0001.

Kodesh, Neil. 2008. "Networks of Knowledge: Clanship and Collective Well-Being in Buganda." *Journal of African History* 49 (2): 197–216. https://doi.org/10.1017/S00 21853708003629.

Kopytoff, Igor. 1986. "The Cultural Biography of Things: Commodization as a Process." In *The Social Life of Things: Commodities in Cultural Perspective*, ed. Arjun

Appadurai, 64–91. Cambridge: Cambridge University Press. https://doi.org
/10.1017/CBO9780511819582.004.

Kröger, Franz. 2001. *Materielle Kultur und Traditionelles Handwerk bei den Bulsa (Nord Ghana), Teilband 1.* Münster: Lit Verlag.

Lemonnier, Pierre. 1992. *Elements for an Anthropology of Technology.* Museum of Anthropology, Anthropological Paper 88. Ann Arbor: University of Michigan.

Loren, Diana DiPaolo. 2010. *The Archaeology of Clothing and Bodily Adornment in Colonial America.* Gainesville: University of Florida Press.

Magnavita, Sonja. 2003. "The Beads of Kissi, Burkina Faso." *Journal of African Archaeology* 1 (1): 127–38. https://doi.org/10.3213/1612-1651-10005.

Mauss, Marcel. 1979 [1950]. *Sociology and Psychology: Essays.* Trans. Ben Brewster. London: Routledge and Kegan Paul.

McNaughton, Patrick. 1988. *The Mande Blacksmiths: Knowledge, Power, and Art in West Africa.* Bloomington: Indiana University Press.

Meskell, Lynn. 2005. "Introduction: Object Orientations." In *Archaeologies of Materiality*, ed. Lynn Meskell, 1–17. Oxford: Blackwell. https://doi.org/10.1002
/9780470774052.ch1.

Meyer, Birgit. 1999. *Translating the Devil: Religion and Modernity among the Ewe in Ghana.* Edinburgh: Edinburgh University Press.

Meyer, Birgit. 2012. "Religious and Secular, 'Spiritual' and 'Physical' in Ghana." In *What Matters? Ethnographies of Value in a Not So Secular Age*, ed. Courtney Bender and Ann Taves, 86–118. New York: Columbia University Press. https://doi.org/10
.7312/columbia/9780231156851.003.0004.

Meyer, Birgit, and Dick Houtman. 2012. "Introduction: Material Religion—How Things Matter." In *Things: Religion and the Question of Materiality*, ed. Dick Houtman and Birgit Meyer, 1–23. New York: Fordham University Press.
https://doi.org/10.5422/fordham/9780823239450.003.0001.

Munn, Nancy D. 1983. "Gawan Kula: Spatiotemporal Control and the Symbolism of Influence." In *The Kula: New Perspectives on Massim Exchange*, ed. Jerry W. Leach and Edmund Leach, 277–308. Cambridge: Cambridge University Press.

Norman, Neil L. 2014. "Sacred Vortices of the African Atlantic World: Materiality of the Accumulative Aesthetic in the Hueda Kingdom, 1650–1727 CE." In *Materialities of Ritual in the Black Atlantic*, ed. Akinwumi Ogundiran and Paula Saunders, 47–67. Bloomington: Indiana University Press.

Norman, Neil L., and Kenneth G. Kelly. 2004. "Landscape Politics: The Serpent Ditch and the Rainbow in West Africa." *American Anthropologist* 106 (1): 98–110.
https://doi.org/10.1525/aa.2004.106.1.98.

Ogundiran, Akinwumi. 2002. "Of Small Things Remembered: Beads, Cowries, and Cultural Translations of the Atlantic Experience in Yorubaland." *International Journal of African Historical Studies* 35 (2–3): 427–57. https://doi.org/10.2307/3097620.

Ogundiran, Akinwumi. 2014. "Cowries and Rituals of Self-Realization in the Yoruba Region, ca. 1600–1860." In *Materialities of Ritual in the Black Atlantic*, ed. Akinwumi Ogundiran and Paula Saunders, 68–86. Bloomington: Indiana University Press.

Ogundiran, Akinwumi, and Paula Saunders. 2014. "On the Materiality of Black Atlantic Rituals." In *Materialities of Ritual in the Black Atlantic*, ed. Akinwumi Ogundiran and Paula Saunders, 1–27. Bloomington: Indiana University Press.

Owusu-Ansah, David. 1991. *Islamic Talismanic Tradition in Nineteenth-Century Asante: African Studies*, vol. 21. Lewiston, NY: Edwin Mellen.

Parish, Jane. 1999. "The Dynamics of Witchcraft and Indigenous Shrines among the Akan." *Africa: Journal of the International Africa Institute* 69 (3): 426–47. https://doi.org/10.2307/1161216.

Parker, John. 2004. "Witchcraft, Anti-Witchcraft, and Trans-Regional Ritual Innovation in Early Colonial Ghana: Sakrabundi and Aberewa, 1889–1910." *Journal of African History* 45 (3): 393–420. https://doi.org/10.1017/S0021853704 00951X.

Pauketat, Timothy R. 2013. "Bundles of/in/as Time." In *Big Histories, Human Lives: Tackling Problems of Scale in Archaeology*, ed. John Robb and Timothy R. Pauketat, 35–56. Santa Fe, NM: School for Advanced Research Press.

Pietz, William. 1985. "The Problem of the Fetish, I." *Res: Anthropology and Aesthetics* 9: 5–17. https://doi.org/10.1086/RESv9n1ms20166719.

Pietz, William. 1987. "The Problem of the Fetish, II: The Origin of the Fetish." *Res: Anthropology and Aesthetics* 13: 23–45. https://doi.org/10.1086/RESv13n1ms20166762.

Pietz, William. 1988. "The Problem of the Fetish, III: Bosman's Guinea and the Enlightenment Theory of Fetishism." *Res: Anthropology and Aesthetics* 16: 105–24. https://doi.org/10.1086/RESv16n1ms20166805.

Pietz, William. 1995. "The Spirit of Civilization: Blood Sacrifice and Monetary Debt." *Res: Anthropology and Aesthetics* 28: 23–38. https://doi.org/10.1086/RESv28n1ms201 66927.

Rattray, Robert S. 1927. *Religion and Art in Ashanti*. London: Oxford University Press.

Richard, François. 2010. "Re-Charting Atlantic Encounters: Object Trajectories and Histories of Value in the Siin (Senegal) and Senegambia." *Archaeological Dialogues* 17 (1): 1–27. https://doi.org/10.1017/S1380203810000036.

Robb, John. 2015. "What Do Things Want? Object Design as a Middle Range Theory of Material Culture." In *The Materiality of Everyday Life*, ed. Lisa Overholtzer and Cynthia Robin, 166–80. Archeological Papers of the American Anthropological

Association. Arlington, VA: American Anthropological Association. https://doi
.org/10.1111/apaa.12069.

Roddick, Andrew P., and Ann B. Stahl. 2016. "Knowledge in Motion: An
Introduction." In *Knowledge in Motion: Constellations of Learning across Time
and Place*, ed. Andrew P. Roddick and Ann B. Stahl, 3–35. Tucson: University of
Arizona Press.

Schildkrout, Enid, and Curtis A. Keim. 1990. *African Reflections: Art from
Northeastern Zaire*. Seattle: University of Washington Press.

Schmidt, Peter R. 1997. *Iron Technology in East Africa: Symbolism, Science, and
Archaeology*. Bloomington: Indiana University Press.

Schmidt, Peter R. 2009. "Tropes, Materiality, and Ritual Embodiment of African
Iron Smelting Furnaces as Human Figures." *Journal of Archaeological Method and
Theory* 16 (3): 262–82. https://doi.org/10.1007/s10816-009-9065-0.

Schoenbrun, David. 2016. "Pythons Worked: Constellating Communities of Practice
with Conceptual Metaphor in Northern Lake Victoria, ca. 800 to 1200 CE." In
*Knowledge in Motion: Making Communities and Constellations of Practice across Time
and Place*, ed. Andrew P. Roddick and Ann B. Stahl, 216–46. Tucson: University of
Arizona Press.

Stahl, Ann B. 1993. "Concepts of Time and Approaches to Analogical Reasoning in
Historical Perspective." *American Antiquity* 58 (2): 235–60. https://doi.org/10.2307
/281967.

Stahl, Ann B. 2001. *Making History in Banda: Anthropological Visions of Africa's Past*.
Cambridge: Cambridge University Press. https://doi.org/10.1017/CBO
9780511489600.

Stahl, Ann B. 2002. "Colonial Entanglements and the Practices of Taste: An
Alternative to Logocentric Approaches." *American Anthropologist* 104 (3): 827–45.
https://doi.org/10.1525/aa.2002.104.3.827.

Stahl, Ann B. 2007. "Entangled Lives: The Archaeology of Daily Life in the Gold
Coast Hinterlands, AD 1400–1900." In *Archaeology of Atlantic Africa and the
African Diaspora*, ed. Akinwumi Ogundiran and Toyin Falola, 49–76. Bloomington:
Indiana University Press.

Stahl, Ann B. 2008. "Dogs, Pythons, Pots, and Beads: The Dynamics of Shrines
and Sacrificial Practices in Banda, Ghana, AD 1400–1900." In *Memory Work: The
Materiality of Depositional Practice*, ed. Barbara Mills and William Walker, 159–86.
Santa Fe, NM: School of Advanced Research Press.

Stahl, Ann B. 2010. "Material Histories." In *The Oxford Handbook of Material Culture
Studies*, ed. Dan Hicks and Mary C. Beaudry, 148–70. Oxford: Oxford University
Press.

Stahl, Ann B. 2013. "Archaeological Insights into Aesthetic Communities of Practice in the Western Volta Basin." *African Arts* 46 (3): 54–67. https://doi.org/10.1162/A FAR_a_00088.

Stahl, Ann B. 2015a. "Circulations through Worlds Apart: Georgian and Victorian England in an African Mirror." In *Materializing Colonial Encounters: Archaeologies of African Experience*, ed. François G. Richard, 71–94. New York: Springer. https://doi.org/10.1007/978-1-4939-2633-6_3.

Stahl, Ann B. 2015b. "Metal Working and Ritualization: Negotiating Change through Improvisational Practice in Banda, Ghana, AD 1300–1650." In *The Materiality of Everyday Life*, ed. Lisa Overholtzer and Cynthia Robin, 53–71. Archeological Papers of the American Anthropological Society. Arlington, VA: American Anthropological Society.

Stahl, Ann B. 2015c. "The Transactional Dynamics of Surplus in Landscapes of Enslavement: Scalar Perspectives from Interstitial West Africa." In *Surplus: The Politics of Production and the Strategies of Everyday Life*, ed. Christopher T. Morehart and Kristin De Lucia, 267–306. Boulder: University Press of Colorado. https://doi.org/10.5876/9781607323808.c011.

Stahl, Ann B. 2016. "Complementary Crafts: The Dynamics of Multicraft Production in Banda, Ghana." In *Gendered Labor in Specialized Economies: Archaeological Perspectives on Male and Female Work*, ed. Sophia E. Kelly and Traci Ardren, 159–88. Boulder: University Press of Colorado. https://doi.org/10.5876/9781607324836.c006.

Steiner, Christopher B. 1985. "Another Image of Africa: Toward an Ethnohistory of European Cloth Marketed in West Africa, 1873–1960." *Ethnohistory* 32 (2): 91–110. https://doi.org/10.2307/482329.

Taves, Ann, and Courtney Bender. 2012. "Introduction: Things of Value." In *What Matters? Ethnographies of Value in a Not So Secular Age*, ed. Courtney Bender and Ann Taves, 1–33. New York: Columbia University Press.

Trapido, Joe. 2013. "Forms of Fetishism in Kinshasa: Historical Insights and Contemporary Practices." In *Making Spirits: Materiality and Transcendence in Contemporary Religions*, ed. Diana Espirito Santo and Nico Tassi, 205–28. London: I. B. Tauris.

Warnier, Jean-Pierre. 2007. *The Pot-King: The Body and Technologies of Power*. Leiden: Brill. https://doi.org/10.1163/ej.9789004152175.i-325.

Warnier, Jean-Pierre. 2009. "Technology as Efficacious Action on Objects . . . and Subjects." *Journal of Material Culture* 14 (4): 459–70. https://doi.org/10.1177/13591835 09345944.

Warnier, Jean-Pierre. 2011. "Bodily/Material Culture and the Fighter's Subjectivity." *Journal of Material Culture* 16 (4): 359–75. https://doi.org/10.1177/1359183511424840.

Warnier, Jean-Pierre. 2012. "Afterword: On Technologies of the Subject, Material Culture, Castes, and Value." In *Metals in Mandara Mountains Society and Culture*, ed. Nicholas David, 327–41. Trenton, NJ: Africa World Press.

Warnier, Jean-Pierre. 2013. "The Sacred King, Royal Containers, Alienable Material Contents, and Value in Contemporary Cameroon." In *Mobility, Meaning, and the Transformation of Things*, ed. Hans Peter Hahn and Hadas Weiss, 50–62. Oxford: Oxbow Books.

Wells, Peter S. 2012. *How Ancient Europeans Saw the World: Vision, Patterns, and the Shaping of the Mind in Prehistoric Times*. Princeton, NJ: Princeton University Press. https://doi.org/10.1515/9781400844777.

Wenger, Etienne. 1998. *Communities of Practice: Learning, Meaning, and Identity*. Cambridge: Cambridge University Press. https://doi.org/10.1017/CBO9780511 803932.

Werness, Hope B. 2006. *The Continuum Encyclopedia of Animal Symbolism in Art*. New York: Continuum Press.

Wylie, Alison. 2002. *Thinking from Things*. Berkeley: University of California Press.

Zedeño, Maria Nieves. 2008. "Bundled Worlds: The Roles and Interactions of Complex Objects from the North American Plains." *Journal of Archaeological Method and Theory* 15 (4): 362–78. https://doi.org/10.1007/s10816-008-9058-4.

10

Imagine the scene: archaeologists gathered in a wind-swept corner of the British countryside have excavated a spectacular Bronze Age burial, accompanied by numerous grave goods, and are giving a summary of their findings to members of the local press. At this juncture a commonplace trope is drawn upon: the individual buried is described as a person of great significance on the basis of the quantity and quality of the grave goods. One case in point is the discovery in 2002 of an individual in Amesbury, Wiltshire (Fitzpatrick 2011:5)—dubbed for the media the "Amesbury Archer"—who is described as "one of the most lavishly furnished bell beaker burials yet found in Europe" (Fitzpatrick 2011:208). This trope—reading significance from the grave goods that accompany burials—is so ingrained in archaeological thinking that we see not only off-the-cuff declarations to the media but the formalization of these ideas in archaeological theory. In the past, archaeological analyses of mortuary practices have assumed fixed and readable identities for the dead; processual reconstructions of social organization from mortuary variability data were founded on this fundamental principle (e.g., Binford 1971; Brown 1971; Saxe 1971; Tainter 1975). This concept has been thoroughly critiqued, particularly for the British Bronze Age (Parker Pearson 1999; Fowler 2004), and both authors have played a role in this discussion (Brück 2004; Jones 2002).

Archaeological thinking concerning mortuary practices is now well developed, and, as a discipline, we are

Finding Objects,
Making Persons

Fossils in British Early
Bronze Age Burials

Joanna Brück
and Andrew Meirion Jones

DOI: 10.5876/9781607327479.c010

acutely aware of the relationship between the archaeologist-as-interpreter and excavated mortuary assemblages (Fowler 2013), so why do we still so often see grave goods as a direct reflection of the social status of deceased individuals? This is not an easy question to answer, but we suspect it may result from the fact that Early Bronze Age mortuary practices are one of the few instances in British archaeology where we can observe a closed context containing a burial and accompanying grave goods (the other obvious example is Anglo-Saxon burials, where similar assumptions are at play; Williams 2006). Here, we question the simplistic assumption that the key role of grave goods is to communicate an individual's status, focusing on one category of grave good in particular—fossils—that allows us to critically rethink such simplistic formulations of individual identity.

In this chapter we examine a group of burials dating to the later part of the British Early Bronze Age (ca. 1900–1500 BC). Single (and occasionally multiple) burials in earthen barrows accompanied by a suite of grave goods, including fossils, are typical of this period (Woodward 2000). Since the earliest antiquarian investigations of barrows, the Early Bronze Age dead have been burdened with a variety of different representational loads: they have variously been understood to represent druids (Colt Hoare 1812), shamans (Piggott 1962; Woodward 2000), and individuals (e.g., Shennan 1975) but perhaps most commonly chiefly elites (Piggott 1938; Renfrew 1974). The artifacts that accompany these burials, including highly decorated pottery, copper daggers, and ornaments of gold, amber, jet, and other materials, have been read as "prestige goods" (Bradley 1984:68–95) or "symbols of power" (Clarke et al. 1985). More recently, they have been described as an example of "supernatural power dressing" (Sheridan 2008; Sheridan and Davis 2002). Such terms evoke the "go-getting" individuals of the Reagan-Thatcher era and highlight the Western sensibilities that underpin our assumptions regarding identity and personhood in this period of prehistory.

Two issues are at stake here that we wish to question: the tacit and comfortable assumptions that Euro-American notions of individuality existed in prehistoric Britain (see also Fowler 2004) and that burial assemblages can be simply read as representing status and prestige for the person buried. Both notions are underpinned by the implied assertion that contemporary Euro-American ontologies are universal, with assumed distinctions between person and world and between active subject and inert object, so that grave goods are viewed as nothing more than passive reflections of the power and wealth of the deceased.

PERSONS AND NETWORKS

One way we can question the universality of contemporary notions of the person is by examining how personhood is constituted in other historical contexts. Chris Fowler has pursued this strategy in a number of important publications (Fowler 2004, 2010, 2016). Fowler (2004:23–52) argues that persons are often considered composites made up of a variety of different substances, including mind, body, and soul. He takes a comparative approach to the composite person, delineating a variety of ways of being a person in a series of different ethnographic and historical situations, and identifies dividuality, partibility, and permeability as key aspects of the composite self. We are sympathetic to this kind of approach and have previously explored these ideas in relation to Early Bronze Age burials (Brück 2004; Jones 2002, forthcoming).

Another strategy we have previously pursued is to recognize the significance of material practices in the performance of personhood (Brück 2004; Jones 2002). Our work draws on the pioneering approaches of John Chapman and Bisserka Gaydarska (Chapman 2000; Chapman and Gaydarska 2007). Chapman and Gaydarska emphasize the importance of the twin practices of fragmentation and accumulation—practices that serve to relate, connect, or enchain people together as they divide up (fragment) or bring together (accumulate) materials in different ways. These kinds of practices imply the relational forms of personhood of the kind discussed by Fowler (though they may also be found in contexts where individual modes of personhood are practiced). We find these kinds of approaches extremely fruitful (see also papers in Alberti et al. 2013; Watts 2013). While we applaud previous discussions of the problems we have raised above, which have identified relational forms of personhood in prehistory as an antidote to the rampant characterization of prehistoric burials as representative of Euro-American individuals, in this chapter we wish to ask: Can we go further than this? Is it possible to move beyond the assertion of prehistoric personhood as relational? Is it possible to provide a more detailed picture of relationality?

FOSSILS IN EARLY BRONZE AGE BURIALS

In this chapter we attempt to explore these questions by examining the occurrence of fossils in British Early Bronze Age burials. Fossils are an unusual category of grave good (Leeming 2015), but it is evident that they cannot simply be interpreted as "prestige goods" or indices of status, and they remind us that Early Bronze Age people's understanding of their place in the world was surely different from our own. As we shall see below, the discovery of fossils in mortuary contexts requires us to reconsider some of the fundamental dualisms on which contemporary Western models of the individual are based. It calls into question the perceived boundaries between subject and object, self and other, and culture and nature and hints that landscapes and their constituent elements were sedimented into Early Bronze Age forms of personhood. Concepts of the individual familiar from our own cultural context presuppose that the human self is set apart from (and is superior to) the natural world, including inanimate objects (Morris 1991), but the examples we discuss suggest that this was not so in the Early Bronze Age.

Even in the contemporary Western world, however, the superiority of the human subject has increasingly been called into question. A number of authors have argued for a post-humanism that displaces humans from their central position and recognizes that humans occupy a world that intersects with other agencies—animal, vegetal, and environmental (e.g., Braidotti 2013; Coole and Frost 2010; Olsen 2010). Ethnographic studies of the relationship between people and environment indicate that the "natural" world is often understood to have what we would consider "cultural" origins (the product of ancestral acts, for example) and that plants, animals, and other natural phenomena are persons who engage in particular forms of social relationships with humans (e.g., Descola 1996). As we shall see, the presence of natural and modified fossils in Early Bronze Age barrows and mortuary deposits, along with the production of fossil skeuomorphs, suggests that fossils may have been viewed as crafted objects linked to earlier ancestral periods and, as such, were cosmologically charged. The treatment and deposition of fossils in Early Bronze Age burials call conventional concepts of agency and the "individual" into question, suggesting that agency was not considered solely a property of the human subject or indeed an intrinsic attribute of particular beings. Instead, it was relationally constituted in the spaces of intersubjective engagement among people, places, and things.

In the course of research for this chapter, we identified seventeen sites where fossils were deposited as grave goods or deliberately incorporated in some other way into a burial monument. These included crinoids, belemnites, ammonites, echinoids, and fossil sponges. The majority of sites are in southern and eastern England, particularly Wiltshire, Dorset, Kent, and East Yorkshire, where fossils commonly occur in the local Chalk geology and in other strata of Cretaceous and Jurassic age. Yet the way these objects were incorporated into the graves suggests that they held particular social significance. Perhaps the most extraordinary example of such a discovery is that recorded by Worthington G. Smith in 1887 on the Dunstable Downs in Bedfordshire

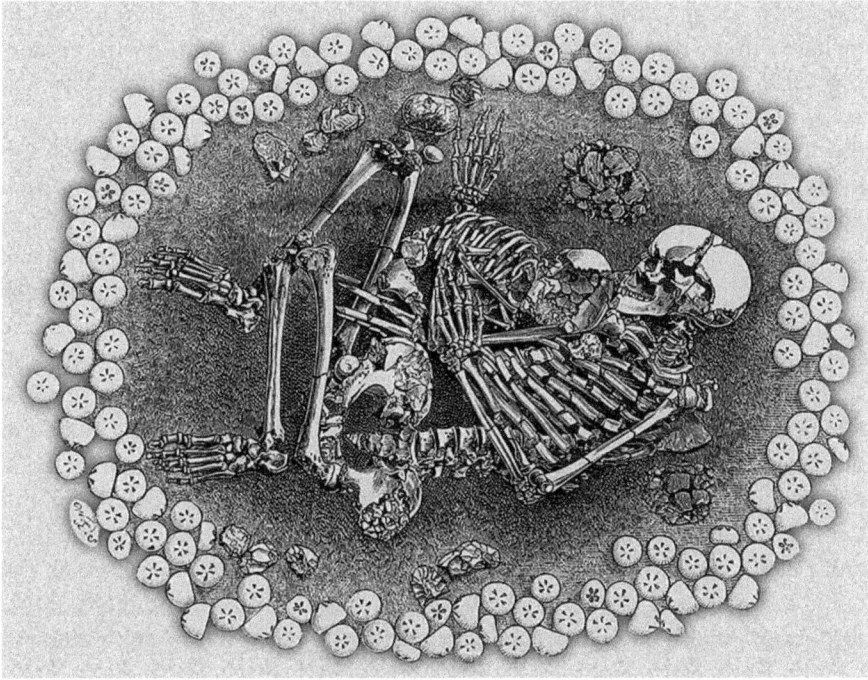

FIGURE 10.1. *Inhumation burial of a young adult female and child with echinoids from the Dunstable Downs, Bedfordshire. Source: Smith 1894:frontispiece.*

(Smith 1894; figure 10.1). Smith was not present when the burial was first uncovered, so precise contextual information is not available; however, enough is known to suggest that fossils were deliberately included as an important component of the mortuary deposit. The grave was found beneath an earthen barrow and contained the bodies of a young woman and a child around five years old (Smith 1894:334–38). The woman was laid on her right-hand side in a crouched position, and she was "clasping the almost perished relics" of the child. In and around the grave were approximately 200 fossil echinoids (*Ananchytes ovatus* and *Micraster coranguinum*), and Smith's reconstruction drawing reproduced in figure 10.1 suggests that these may originally have formed a ring around the burial. Other finds from the grave included a quartz pebble, a pottery vessel, animal bone, and a large quantity of worked flint.

The Dunstable example is unusual for the number of fossils it contained and the way they appear to have been arranged around the body, though we must treat this burial with caution: it is possible that the numbers of fossils may have been exaggerated (Leeming 2015:19). In contrast, other burials tend to include a much smaller number of fossils. Details of their depositional context suggest that, in general, fossils were incorporated into Early Bronze Age burials in one of two key ways. In many cases, particularly in southern England, they comprised elements of composite necklaces—objects whose beads were made of fossils and other natural materials with interesting properties such as amber, shale, jet, and shell, alongside manufactured materials such as faience. The primary inhumation burial of an adult female at Arreton Down, Isle of Wight, was accompanied by one segmented faience bead, three beads of chalk, and another five fossil beads—four of *Porosphaera globularis*, a late Cretaceous sponge, and the fifth made from a fragment of unidentified fossil shell (Alexander et al. 1960). The well-known central inhumation of a possible female from the Manton barrow (also known as Preshute G1a) in Wiltshire produced an extraordinary array of objects (Cunnington 1907). These included a grape cup (a type of small ceramic vessel we discuss further below) behind the head; a copper alloy dagger, 3 copper alloy awls, 1 shale bead, 1 stone bead, and 1 chalk bead in front of the feet; a possible ceramic lip plug close to the chin; and a second dagger with an amber pommel, a gold-mounted amber disc, a gold-mounted halberd pendant (a miniature version of a contemporary Central European weapon), a shale bead decorated with gold bands, 150 other shale beads, 5 other amber beads, and a single fossil crinoid bead, all behind the head and shoulders. The excavators state that the beads were not around the neck of the body but lay in a series of rows over one another, indicating that they remained strung together on deposition.

It is evident from this that the precise location of objects—including fossils—in the grave was very carefully choreographed. The positioning and association of objects hint at the construction of relational narratives of identity. The crouched inhumation of an adult near Minster in Kent (Anon. 2007) was accompanied by a jet armlet, an amber bead, and a second bead of polished fossil sponge with a dentalium shell placed through it—a striking and deliberate act of connection and assemblage. Barrow G61a at Amesbury in Wiltshire produced a number of burials, including a cremation burial in a rectangular grave (Ashbee 1985; figure 10.2). The cremation burial (an adult of indeterminate sex) had been arranged in a clearly defined pear-shaped heap. A small ceramic vessel containing an amber bead, fossil crinoid, and two flint flakes was placed upright at the tapering end of this deposit. An amber-colored beaver incisor was found standing against the pot. Under the pot there was a bronze awl and seven additional beads of amber, faience, red steatite, and cowrie shell. Such careful acts of juxtaposition spoke of links between the living

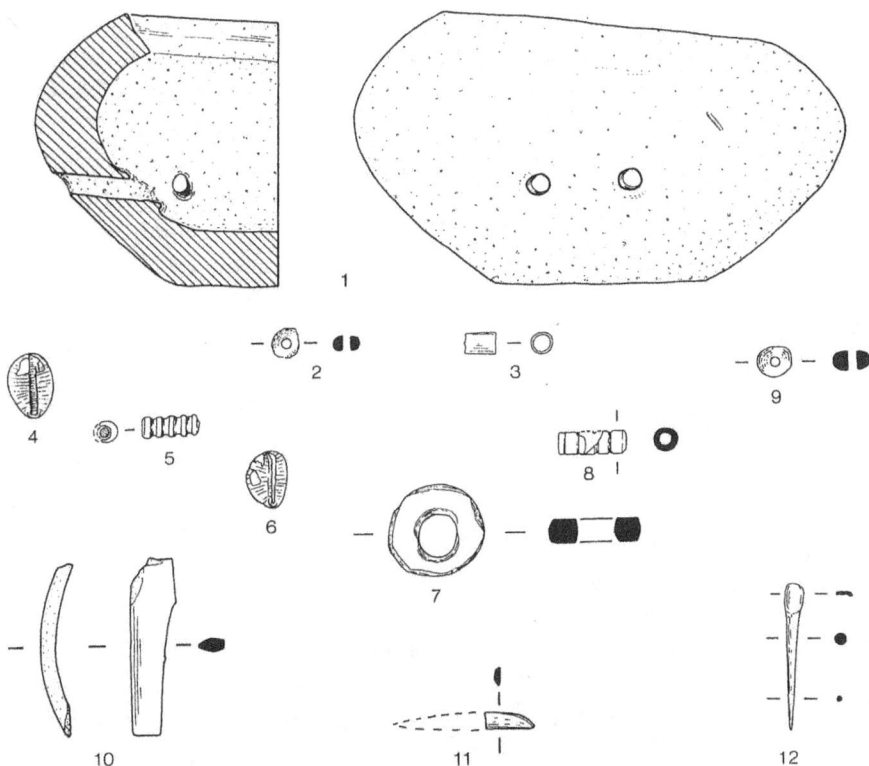

FIGURE 10.2. *Grave goods accompanying the cremation burial from Amesbury G61a (Ashbee 1985:fig. 39). 1: miniature vessel; 2 and 9: amber beads; 3: crinoid; 4 and 6: cowrie shells; 5 and 8: segmented faience beads; 7: quoit-shaped bead of steatite; 10: beaver's incisor; 11: bronze fragment; 12: bronze awl.*

and the dead, referencing particular activities and locating fossils in networks of association that defined the place of the dead in the social world.

In many of these cases, fossils are found with materials that may have been considered to have magical powers. Ann Woodward (2002) and Alison Sheridan and Mary Davis (2002) have pointed out that amber and jet—materials that were frequently used in the composite necklaces found in southern England—have unusual properties. Both are electrostatic and, unlike other materials of geological origin, they float, can be burned, and are warm to the touch; amber also gives off a distinctive resinous smell when burned. Likewise, the luminous and reflective characteristics of gold and the luster of shell may have been considered to confer animacy to objects made from these materials

(Conneller 2011; Saunders 2011). If so, then Early Bronze Age composite necklaces should not be viewed as decorative trappings. They were not merely a reflection of the wealth and status of their owner but served as potent items in their own right (Woodward 2000:116–19). The role of these necklaces was not simply to adorn the living and the dead but to impart certain qualities and powers to those who wore them. Yet such powers were not intrinsic to these objects but must be understood in relational terms. It was their positioning within a particular network of materials, activities, practices, and relationships that made them effective, as indicated in the literal "stringing together" of beads of different materials into necklaces.

This theme of juxtaposition emerges again in our second group of finds, mainly from northern England: fossils that appear to have formed an element of collections of unusual natural objects. Perhaps the best example comes from Langton in north Yorkshire (Greenwell 1877:138–39). Here, under a barrow, was the inhumation burial of an elderly woman lying on her right side with her head to the southwest. In front of her waist was a small group of objects, lying close together as if they had originally been contained in a bag. They included three copper alloy awls, a worked boar's tusk, a worked beaver's tooth, a pierced animal tooth fragment, a pierced nerita shell, three cowrie shells, a fragment of dentalium shell, a fish vertebra, a jet bead, and a fragment of fossil belemnite. In Scandinavia, similar collections of "odd" items found in a number of Bronze Age burials have been interpreted as the toolkits of shamans or other religious specialists (e.g., Glob 1974:116; Kaul 1998:16–20). It is certainly possible that these were collections of magical objects owned and used by the deceased during life, but they might also have been brought together specifically for the funeral rite or been gifts from mourners. Whatever the case, it seems likely that these were viewed as powerful things whose particular properties made them effective elements of the social world. Some of the items from Langton were pierced and may have been worn on the body or displayed in other important locations, perhaps because they were thought to have apotropaic powers. We would therefore argue that in the British Early Bronze Age, items we would regard today as inert, "natural" objects were considered to have agency.

The process of assembly that resulted in these interesting groups of objects—necklaces in the south and bags of special items in the north—is worth exploring further. The bundles documented among indigenous American groups in the nineteenth century and more recently provide a potentially useful parallel (Pauketat 2013a, 2013b; Zedeño 2008). These were collections of important sacred objects, often kept carefully wrapped. Bundles were considered to be powerful and animate; some were regarded as persons and even as ancestors. Their constituent elements spoke of the histories of their caretaker-guardians and the groups to whom they belonged. The opening of bundles, addition of new items, and intergenerational transfer were all hedged with ritual, as such acts of disclosure and transformation could result in dramatic changes to existing social relationships.

The process of citation (Jones 2007, 2012) involved in the creation of bundles can help illuminate the social role of similar assemblages in the Bronze Age. The choice of certain objects—those that evoked memories of places, people, and events—and their juxtaposition with other objects created narratives through which particular forms of identity could be constituted. The source of some of these materials has been investigated. For instance, Bronze Age amber is thought to have come from the Baltic, although some may have been found on the beaches of northeast England (Beck and Shennan 1991), while jet and shale objects are known to derive from particular geological deposits on the Yorkshire and Dorset coasts, respectively (Sheridan and Davis 2002). The shells also traveled some distance; most of the burials examined here were at least 20 or 30 miles from the sea. Animal bones may have referenced more local landscape settings, calling to mind significant people, activities, and relationships, although items such as beavers' teeth may have spoken of other qualities—the ability to move with ease between land and water, for example, or "human" characteristics, such as the capacity to build structures and alter the landscape (see Woodward 2000:118; Hill 2011). As such, the materials incorporated into Early Bronze Age assemblages spoke of different landscape contexts and material properties—the familiar and the foreign, fire and water, land and sea, aboveground and belowground—as well as specific social practices and the relations they sustained (Goldhahn 2012).

Interestingly, the fossils themselves are all from local or near-local sources. Fossils such as ammonites, belemnites, crinoids, and echinoids are common in Jurassic and Cretaceous strata, including the Chalk on which most of these sites are located. The inhumation burial of an adult male at Rudston in East Yorkshire, for example, produced an ammonite fragment, which had been placed in front of his face (Greenwell 1877:249). This burial is located on the Chalk, and the ammonite is unlikely to have come from far away. At Painsthorpe Wold in the same county, a group of objects, including a beaver's incisor, fossil *Gryphaea arcuata*, flint borer, knife and flake, and a lump of decayed organic matter, were lying together in front of the chest of an adult female inhumation (Mortimer 1905:132; figure 10.3). This burial, too, is located on the Chalk. However, *Gryphaea arcuata* fossils do not occur here;

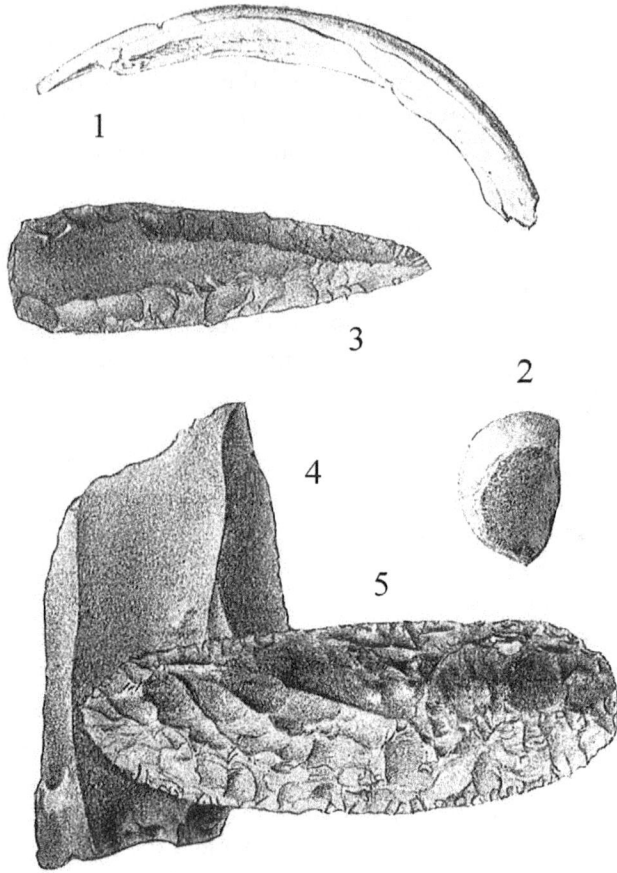

FIGURE 10.3. *Group of objects placed in front of the chest of the adult female inhumation burial in grave C, barrow 98, Painsthorpe Wold (Mortimer 1905:plate 41). 1: beaver's incisor; 2: fossil Gryphaea arcuata; 3: flint borer; 4: flint flake; 5: flint knife.*

they are found in another, very specific horizon in the local stratigraphy, the Lower Lias shales a few hundred meters to the west. It is interesting to consider in what context these and other fossils would have been encountered during the Early Bronze Age. Tilling the soil for the production of crops, sourcing flint for tools, building barrows, and digging pits for the deposition of event-marking or place-making materials are perhaps the most likely activities to have resulted in the discovery of fossils. In this sense, then, fossils were already bound into particular junctures of space, time, and memory as soon as they were unearthed.

As such, the assemblages of interesting objects and materials of which fossils formed a part acted as a means of "mapping" the world and its constituent relationships. They evoked places, events, and practices and—in the case of the necklaces at least—literally strung them together to create relational narratives of identity (Barrett 1994:121–22). The arresting colors of materials such as jet and amber (Jones 2002) may have called to mind origin myths or other cosmological references, while other chains of association linked materials and people across both space and time. Woodward (2002) and Sheridan and Davis (2002) have noted that jet, shale, and amber beads were often old on deposition, suggesting that they may have been heirlooms. Fossils and other "natural" items were also curated. For instance, the ammonite fragment from the burial at Rudston (Greenwell 1877:249) was worn, and Paul Ashbee (1985) suggests that the beaver's incisor from Amesbury G61a described above may also have been old when it was placed in the grave. It is easy to suggest that these were powerful and significant objects, curated over many years. Yet agency was not intrinsic to these items (or their owners) but emerged in the generative potential of juxtaposition. So, too, the forms of identity created in the interstices of such networks were not fixed but were constituted in performances of collection, arrangement, and disassembly (Jones 2012). As such, these assemblages of special objects were not solely about connection but also dealt with disruption; items such as fossils and materials such as amber and jet allowed people to encounter and engage with boundaries between land and water, familiar and exotic, surface and depth (cf. Randsborg 1993:124). These were collections of objects that evoked particular cosmographies, and it is therefore no surprise that they were incorporated into narratives of the social world.

Certainly, the evidence discussed here suggests that other conceptual boundaries—notably, that between nature and culture—central to Western post-Enlightenment philosophy were articulated quite differently and were almost certainly not recognized as such in the British Early Bronze Age. In particular, the way fossils and similar items were encountered, incorporated, and manipulated speaks of a different way of understanding the natural world. As we have seen, fossils are just one of a range of what we would today consider inert natural materials to be included as grave goods during this period. Unworked quartz pebbles are another material often found in Early Bronze Age burials. For example, the cremated remains of a young adult male from a ring cairn at Holmesfield, Brown Edge, near Totley in Derbyshire was accompanied by four pieces of struck flint and a single quartz pebble (Radley 1966), while a quartz pebble, bone pommel, and bone toggle found in the cremation deposit in cist I at Beech Hill House, Coupar Angus, Perthshire, were all burned, suggesting they had accompanied the deceased onto the pyre (Stevenson 1995:204). Like amber and jet, quartz has unusual properties; it sparkles in the sunlight and emits a bright white spark—triboluminescence—when struck. These potent qualities are undoubtedly one reason why it was so often incorporated in the monuments and graves of the Neolithic and Early Bronze Age (e.g., Darvill 2002; Bradley 2005). Other interesting "natural" materials were also deposited in Early Bronze Age graves. A cremation burial from Stockbridge Down in Hampshire produced a series of quoit-shaped beads made from fragments of stalactite from caves in the Mendip Hills 50 miles to the west (Stone and Gray Hill 1940; Sheridan and Shortland 2003). The discovery in caves of human remains, complete pots, and other votive deposits dating to this period suggests that these were considered otherworldly and liminal locations (Chamberlain 2012), places where strange rocky formations evoke the flow of water, just as fossils resemble other "frozen" animate entities. The deposition of beads made from stalactites would have provided one way of appropriating and re-contextualizing some of the power of these places.

Fossils, too, clearly elicited considerable interest when they were encountered. A pond barrow at Down Farm on Cranborne Chase in Dorset was sited so that its center point lay directly above a large, earth-fast ammonite (Martin Green, personal communication, 2013; figure 10.4). Occasionally, fossils were deliberately incorporated into flint artifacts during the knapping process. Barrow C44 at Driffield in East Yorkshire had been disturbed prior to excavation, but finds included a barbed-and-tanged arrowhead containing a fossil Terebratulid of a type that John Mortimer (1905:289) tells us is rarely found in this area; the maker of this object may have been responding to the particular visual and textural properties of this piece of flint.

The extent to which Early Bronze Age people worked, manipulated, or transformed fossils and similar objects is also worth considering. Often, they were used in their "natural" state; the fossil sea sponge (*Porosphera globularis*) from the middle ditch of a triple-ditch round barrow at Haynes Farm, Eyethorne, Kent, had a natural perforation to the center (Parfitt 2004), while the segments of crinoid stem that accompanied a cremation burial from a barrow at Chilcompton in Somerset formed naturally perforated cylinders that were probably used as beads (David Mullin and Jodie Lewis, personal communication, 2014). In these cases, the "natural" world produced items that resembled crafted objects. We cannot say how they were thought to have come into being, although they were perhaps considered to have been made

FIGURE 10.4. *Earth-fast ammonite at the center of the pond barrow at Down Farm.*
Courtesy, Martin Green.

by nonhuman others, such as spirits or ancestors. If so, then they may have
been seen as possessing some of the powers of those beings, agentive qualities
in some ways analogous to the curative and apotropaic properties thought to
have been held by fossils in more recent times. During the Middle Ages, fossils were termed thunderstones, fairy loaves, snakestones, and devil's toenails,
among other things. In more recent times, folk traditions in many parts of
northwest Europe view fossils as powerful artifacts that could prevent milk
from turning sour, ensure that a child was not taken by fairies, or protect a
home from lightning (Oakley 1965; McNamara 2007).

In other cases, fossils from Bronze Age contexts have been altered. The
bead of fossil sponge from the inhumation burial near Minster in Kent
(Anon. 2007) mentioned above had been polished, while the cremation burial
of a child from Blake's Firs, Easton Down, near Allington in Wiltshire was
accompanied by two quoit-shaped beads of sandstone, one shale barrel bead,
and a pierced fragment of belemnite (Ride 2001). The shells, teeth, and other

"natural" items from the Langton grave described above were in some cases worked and pierced and in other cases left unmodified. In the Early Bronze Age, then, the boundary between naturally made and culturally made objects was hazy, if it was drawn at all; the "objects" of the natural world were not lacking in social meaning and agency but were part of dense networks of relational associations that gave them particular potency.

ECHINOIDS AND ACCESSORY CUPS

We now consider the relationship between "made" and "natural" objects in more detail, focusing in particular on artifacts that resemble fossils. The creation of fossil skeuomorphs hints that fossils themselves may have been considered crafted objects, fashioned by ancestors or other mythical beings in the past. Moreover, the skeuomorphic character of certain Early Bronze Age grave goods speaks of the significance of networks of meaning like those described above; the character of both persons and objects was constituted in relational terms. A skeuomorph is an artifact that has been made to resemble another. Skeuomorphs are usually crafted from different materials than the objects they mimic but retain visual references to structural or functional aspects of the originals. Such artifacts illuminate the ways humans strive to understand the world relative to objects and practices that are already familiar. The act of producing skeuomorphs may also have been thought to imbue those objects with the qualities and powers of other things. The similarities between the decorative schemes applied to Early Bronze Age funerary ceramics and basketry have long been recognized (e.g., Manby 1995), and flint copies of copper alloy daggers have also become a renewed focus of discussion in recent years (Frieman 2012).

Interestingly, similar relationships can be discerned between fossils and other categories of Early Bronze Age grave goods. Fossils procured from local chalk and flint deposits provided templates for skeuomorphic forms. There are, for example, remarkable formal similarities among fossil crinoid stems, segmented faience fusiform beads (Sheridan and Shortland 2003), and shale and jet disc beads. The crinoid from Preshute G1a was strikingly similar in shape and size to the shale beads with which it was found (Cunnington 1907:8–9). Such items may have been seen as beads fashioned by the ancestors; in northern England, crinoids were known as "St. Cuthbert's beads" in the Middle Ages and were strung together to make rosaries (Lane and Ausich 2001). The use of faience to make skeuomorphs of crinoids is interesting. Sand—the main ingredient of faience—comes from the shoreline, much like shells, amber, jet, and shale. The production process for faience involves combining sand, fire, and water, a cosmogenic act that elides the cultural and natural worlds. It is possible that fossils were considered to have been crafted in a similar way in the mythical past by ancestors or other supernatural beings. By replicating that process and by wearing faience beads on the body, Bronze Age communities could harness the generative potential of a range of significant materials.

Other types of fossil skeuomorphs can also be identified. Nicholas Thomas (2005:26) draws our attention to a miniature cup from the central grave in barrow 2, Snail Down, Wiltshire. He suggests that this resembles in form and decoration the fossil sea urchin, or echinoid, *Micraster coraginium*, commonly found in the Upper Chalk geology. The vessel is a simple square-sided cup form decorated with pointed-tooth comb decorations (Longworth 2005:166). These form a series of linear decorations running vertically down the body of the pot and closely resemble the tuberceles of a fossil echinoid. Tuberceles are the sockets on the surface of the sea urchin that articulate with the spines. They are especially prominent in fossil specimens, as the spines are no longer in existence. These tuberceles cover the circumference of the sea urchin in a series of vertical lines radiating out from the peristome, or mouth, of the animal.

We find Thomas's observation intriguing and would like to explore it further in relation to other examples of miniature cups found in Early Bronze Age mortuary contexts, specifically the peculiar variants known as "grape cups." This class of vessel is decorated with a series of appliquéd balls with a grape-like appearance and is particularly common in regions dominated by Cretaceous Chalk geology. Firsthand analysis of examples in the Devizes Museum allowed us to examine in detail the manufacture of grape cups. Where the "grapes" had fallen out or been removed, it was possible to work out how these pots were decorated. The appliquéd balls were inserted into a series of small divots that cover the surface of the pot, creating the grape-like appearance. A good example is the vessel from Windmill Hill (Annable and Simpson 1964:nos. 234–35, 49). The articulation between the small holes on the surface and the balls of clay inserted into these holes is similar to the articulation between the tuberceles and spines of echinoids. Indeed, the appliquéd balls of clay covering the grape cups radiate over the surface of the pot in exactly the same way as the spines of a sea urchin (figure 10.5a and b). Given the common appearance of fossil sea urchins in the Upper Chalk geology and the fact that this is a particularly regional form of highly decorated miniature cup, it is possible that these fossils offered a template for the manufacture of the vessels.

Such skeuomorphs highlight relationships of similarity; properties of materials were drawn on and modeled from one context to another (cf.

A

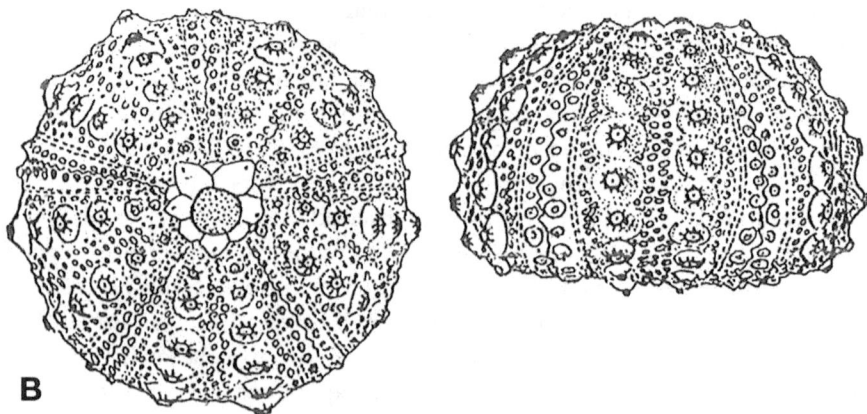

B

FIGURE 10.5. *Grape cup from Upton Lovell barrow G2e (photo Andrew Jones) alongside a drawing of an echinoid typical of the Purbeck Group of south-central England (Arkell 1947:fig. 29).*

Conneller 2013). The peculiar forms of fossils were mimicked in a range of materials, including clay and faience. The forms of fossils were also crafted and physically *incorporated* into other things—worked into beads and used as elements of composite necklaces or, at Down Farm, forming the earth-fast centerpiece of a pond barrow. Skeuomorphs underpin the relational and performative character of meaning making and underline the argument presented here that Early Bronze Age grave goods were not simply indices of wealth and prestige. Instead, these objects were relational agents within dense networks of meaning that highlight the permeability of the boundary between made and found objects and call into question any attempt to separate "culture" and "nature."

HUMAN-FOSSIL RELATIONS IN THE
BRITISH EARLY BRONZE AGE

What do these examples of the use of fossils in the British Early Bronze Age tell us about people's relationships with the environment? Did they view them as specimens of extinct animal or plant species, as we do today, or as curious components of the underlying local geology? As Richard Bradley (1998) has previously pointed out, we cannot expect prehistoric peoples to have encountered natural specimens like fossils in the same way we do today, with detailed knowledge of science (geology); this understanding only began to emerge in the late eighteenth and nineteenth centuries. Yet Early Bronze Age metalworkers would have been familiar with the principle of casting. This process of rendering one material in the form of another is very similar to the formation of fossils. As casts of once-living things, fossils may have been perceived as crafted objects rather than natural specimens and for this reason may have been selected and incorporated into the lives of Bronze Age people.

Chantal Conneller (2011) offers an illuminating discussion of the working of fossils during the Magdalenian and Aurignacian periods of the French Upper Palaeolithic. At the Grotte de Trilobite, Arcy-sur-Cure, Yonne, France, trilobite fossils were pierced for suspension while a beetle-like form was also carved in stone, suggesting a material response to the forms of beetle-like trilobites. At the Grottes de Jaurias, Girone, and Isturitz, Basse-Pyrénées, France, there is evidence for the working of fossil bones of *Halitherium* (an extinct species of Eocene dugong). Conneller argues that these bones were procured and worked precisely because they were unusual and were recognized as the bones of a strange animal species. She suggests that during the Palaeolithic, fossils may have been viewed as spirit animals emerging from stone, emphasizing the mutability and animacy of what we consider to be an inert material; and she compares the use of fossils to the depiction of animals in cave art: "In cave art, animals were glimpsed in the process of trying to emerge and the act of painting intentionally brought them forth. Fossils, by contrast, lay hidden within the flint or chalk, and it was often the act of procurement or of flintknapping that would inadvertently reveal them" (Conneller 2011:98). The appearance of fossils and their resemblance to known phenomena seem to have been particularly important, for example, the formal similarities between trilobites and beetles; these properties of formal similarity seem to have been drawn upon during the Upper Palaeolithic. The extent to which fossils were recognized as similar in form to living marine animals in either the Palaeolithic or the Bronze Age is, of course, unknown but remains an intriguing question. However, the juxtaposition of Early Bronze Age fossils with bones, teeth, shells, and magical materials such as amber suggests that they may have been viewed as "things" with similar animate properties or with similar origins in once-living beings.

BARROWS AS ASSEMBLAGES

We have considered particular grave groups as assemblages and emphasized parallels with North American practices of bundling (Pauketat 2013a; Zedeño 2008). While we are not arguing that there are precise and fixed parallels between our material and the practice of bundling as described by Timothy Pauketat and Maria Nieves Zedeño, we believe the principles of assembling and assemblage (commonly witnessed in bundle making) are worth further scrutiny in relation to the composition of Early Bronze Age barrows (see also Jones 2012:126–36 for a related argument).

Native American bundles were powerful because the potent materials they contained were gathered together and brought into relation with each other (Pauketat 2013a, 2013b; see also Chapman 2000). A similar argument can be made for the collections of materials from which barrows were built and of which fossils were a component in the British Early Bronze Age. In thinking about how these materials were assembled, it is important that we consider each element of the assemblage. As we remarked at the beginning of this chapter, traditional accounts have tended to define specific identities for the dead buried in Early Bronze Age barrows. Arguably, this is a legacy of antiquarian practices of barrow excavation that tended to focus on the burials themselves at the expense of the architecture of the barrow (Last 2007). A consequence of this is that the dead tend to be analytically cauterized from the barrows in which they are buried. This is mistaken. When we examine barrow assemblages without the shackles of Euro-American ontologies, we begin to realize that they are ontologically complex assemblages (Jones 2012, forthcoming) composed of human and animal bone, chalk, earth, stone, turf, and a variety of other materials including fossils, each of which may have had specific meanings based on, for example, origin, color, or technical properties. From this perspective we might think of barrows as highly charged and architecturally complex assemblages.

In such a context, fossils take on a particular significance. They emerge from the earth and in this form might have been incorporated into barrow architecture. Smaller fossils might have been added to necklace assemblages, as their properties of color and shape resonated with other materials used in bead manufacture. In the most striking cases, fossil forms were drawn upon to make skeuomorphs in clay and faience. The Early Bronze Age person was ontologically entangled with and related to these curious elements of the earth, grounding the individual in the local geology, from which fossils were derived and the materials that made up barrows were excavated. Rather than "power dressing," the various elements of the grave assemblage and the barrow situated the person in narratives of belonging and genealogy. In effect, the fossils allow the agency of the natural world to be enfolded within the personhood of the individual buried. In Pauketat's (2013b) terms, these deposits are not only bundles of time but also of space.

CONCLUSION

Fossils are curious and powerful materials brought from the earth, inadvertently encountered while building earthen barrows, digging for flint, and during other projects. They were drawn upon to make skeuomorphs in clay and faience, they were deposited in assemblages of special objects, and they were one of a number of heterogeneous materials incorporated into barrows during (and sometimes after) their construction (see also Jones forthcoming). Fossils in these contexts are not simply worked but are *worked into* barrow construction. There is a family resemblance between skeuomorphism as a process and processes of physical incorporation during the Early Bronze Age, with fossils included as elements of necklaces and similar collections of special objects, added to the suite of objects with the burial, and incorporated in the physical makeup of barrow architecture itself. How and for what reason(s) were these physical properties articulated and incorporated together? We raise the possibility that the process of bronze casting and the formation of fossils share physical similarities, and both may have been viewed as crafted objects in and of the ancestral past. In each of these cases, fossils were not treated as symbols or symbolic equivalents; rather, they were drawn upon because of their physical properties, as physical equivalences.

The deposition of fossils in mortuary contexts allows us to counter anachronistic narratives that conjure Early Bronze Age burials as settings in which the expression of individual status and wealth was the primary concern. Such finds clearly cannot be described as prestige goods; nor were they particularly "exotic" or visually striking objects. Instead, they were a significant component of practices that involved the "bundling" of materials and things. We have noted that materials such as jet, amber, and quartz may have been assembled in these contexts because of their animate qualities and suggest here that this may also have been the case for the selective incorporation of fossils. These "natural" specimens were incorporated into assemblages at various different scales, from the intimacy of the grave itself to the architectural structure of the mortuary monument. The processes of juxtaposition, accumulation, and disjuncture located both the living and the dead in cosmological schemes that described the order of things in relational terms. The arrangement around the body of objects and materials that invoked different places and practices was part of a narrative that mapped the social world but also embedded the person in an assemblage of material agents. We argue these were animate material agents that played transformative roles in mortuary ritual, their particular qualities and powers drawn out in the practices of production and consumption in which humans and other beings were engaged. They speak of the social significance of the "natural" world and the grounding of social identity in place.

The shared properties of made and unmade objects indicate that generative potential was located not solely in the human realm; skeuomorphic relationships between fossils and artifacts such as faience beads and grape cups suggest that ontological distinctions were not framed in terms of "culture" versus "nature" but more in terms of the equivalence of forms. Indeed, the formation or "crafting" of objects such as fossils (perhaps in the ancestral past) and their reworking hints that the dichotomies that underpin the individualizing ideologies of the modern Western world—culture/nature, subject/object, animate/inanimate—did not form a recognizable element of Bronze Age cosmographies. Fossils are but one of many curious materials that demonstrate the potency of the natural world and hint at forms of personhood and ontology very different from those familiar from our own cultural context.

ACKNOWLEDGMENTS

We are grateful to Peter Brück for information on the likely sources of the fossils discussed in this chapter and to Martin Green for the photograph of the ammonite at Down Farm. AMJ is particularly grateful to Paul Reilly, Louisa Minkin, and Ian Dawson for discussions about fossils and skeuomorphs.

REFERENCES CITED

Alberti, Benjamin, Andrew Meirion Jones, and Joshua Pollard. 2013. *Archaeology after Interpretation: Returning Materials to Archaeological Theory*. Walnut Creek, CA: Left Coast.

Alexander, John, Paul C. Ozanne, and Audrey Ozanne. 1960. "Report of the Investigation of a Round Barrow on Arreton Down, Isle of Wight." *Proceedings of the Prehistoric Society* 26: 263–302. https://doi.org/10.1017/S0079497X00016339.

Annable, F. Ken, and Derek D.A. Simpson. 1964. *Guide Catalogue of the Neolithic and Bronze Age Collections in Devizes Museum*. Devizes: Wiltshire Archaeological and Natural History Society.

Anon. 2007. "Interim Reports on Recent Work Carried Out by the Canterbury Archaeological Trust." *Archaeologia Cantiana* 127: 321–32.

Arkell, William J. 1947. *The Geology of the Country around Weymouth, Swanage, Corfe, and Lulworth*. London: Memoir of the Geological Survey of Great Britain.

Ashbee, Paul. 1985. "The Excavation of Amesbury Barrows 58, 61a, 61, 72." *Wiltshire Archaeological and Natural History Magazine* 79: 39–91.

Barrett, John C. 1994. *Fragments from Antiquity: An Archaeology of Social Life in Britain, 2900–1200 BC*. Oxford: Blackwell.

Beck, Curt W., and Stephen Shennan. 1991. *Amber in Prehistoric Britain*. Oxford: Oxbow Books.

Binford, Lewis R. 1971. "Mortuary Practices: Their Study and Potential." In *Approaches to the Social Dimensions of Mortuary Practices*, ed. James Brown, 6–29. Memoir of the Society for American Archaeology 25. Washington, DC: Society for American Archaeology.

Bradley, Richard. 1984. *The Social Foundations of Prehistoric Britain: Themes and Variations in the Archaeology of Power*. London: Longman.

Bradley, Richard. 1998. "Ruined Buildings, Ruined Stones: Enclosures, Tombs, and Natural Places in the Neolithic of South-West England." *World Archaeology* 30 (1): 13–22. https://doi.org/10.1080/00438243.1998.9980394.

Bradley, Richard. 2005. *The Moon and the Bonfire: An Investigation of Three Stone Circles in North-East Scotland*. Edinburgh: Society of Antiquaries of Scotland.

Braidotti, Rosi. 2013. *The Posthuman*. Cambridge: Polity.

Brown, James. 1971. "The Dimensions of Status in the Burials at Spiro." In *Approaches to the Social Dimensions of Mortuary Practices*, ed. James Brown, 92–112. Memoir of the Society for American Archaeology 25. Washington, DC: Society for American Archaeology.

Brück, Joanna. 2004. "Material Metaphors: The Relational Construction of Identity in Early Bronze Age Burials in Ireland and Britain." *Journal of Social Archaeology* 4 (3): 307–33. https://doi.org/10.1177/1469605304046417.

Chamberlain, Andrew. 2012. "Caves and the Funerary Landscape of Prehistoric Britain." In *Sacred Darkness: A Global Perspective on the Ritual Use of Caves*, ed. Holley Moyes, 81–86. Boulder: University Press of Colorado.

Chapman, John. 2000. *Fragmentation in Archaeology*. London: Routledge.

Chapman, John, and Bisserka Gaydarska. 2007. *Parts and Wholes: Fragmentation in Prehistoric Context*. Oxford: Oxbow.

Clarke, David V., Trevor G. Cowie, and Andrew Foxon. 1985. *Symbols of Power at the Time of Stonehenge*. Edinburgh: Her Majesty's Stationary Office.

Colt Hoare, Richard. 1812. *The Ancient History of Wiltshire*, vol. 1. London: William Miller.

Conneller, Chantal. 2011. *An Archaeology of Materials: Substantial Transformations in Early Prehistoric Europe*. London: Routledge.

Conneller, Chantal. 2013. "Deception and (Mis)representation: Skeuomorphs, Materials, and Forms." In *Archaeology after Interpretation: Returning Materials to Archaeological Theory*, ed. Benjamin Alberti, Andrew Meirion Jones, and Joshua Pollard, 119–33. Walnut Creek, CA: Left Coast.

Coole, Diana, and Samantha Frost. 2010. *New Materialisms: Ontology, Agency, and Politics*. Durham, NC: Duke University Press. https://doi.org/10.1215/9780822392996.

Cunnington, Maud E. 1907. "Notes on the Opening of a Bronze Age Barrow at Manton, Near Marlborough." *Wiltshire Archaeological and Natural History Magazine* 35: 1–20.

Darvill, Tim. 2002. "White on Blonde: Quartz Pebbles and the Use of Quartz at Neolithic Monuments in the Isle of Man and Beyond." In *Colouring the Past: The Significance of Colour in Archaeological Research*, ed. Andrew Meirion Jones and Gavin MacGregor, 73–91. Oxford: Berg.

Descola, Philippe. 1996. *In the Society of Nature: A Native Ecology in Amazonia*. Cambridge: Cambridge University Press. https://doi.org/10.4324/9780203451069.

Fitzpatrick, Andrew P. 2011. *The Amesbury Archer and the Boscombe Bowmen: Bell Beaker Burials at Boscombe Down, Amesbury, Wiltshire*. Salisbury: Wessex Archaeology.

Fowler, Chris. 2004. *An Archaeology of Personhood*. London: Routledge.

Fowler, Chris. 2010. "Relational Personhood as a Subject of Anthropology and Archaeology: Comparative and Complementary Analyses." In *Archaeology and Anthropology: Understanding Similarity, Exploring Difference*, ed. Duncan Garrow and Tom Yarrow, 137–59. Oxford: Oxbow.

Fowler, Chris. 2013. *The Emergent Past: A Relational Realist Archaeology of Early Bronze Age Mortuary Practices*. Oxford: Oxford University Press.

Fowler Chris. 2016. "Relational Personhood Revisited." *Cambridge Archaeological Journal* 26 (3): 397–412.

Frieman, Catherine. 2012. *Innovation and Imitation: Stone Skeuomorphs of Metal from 4th–2nd Millennia BC Northwest Europe*. Oxford: Archaeopress.

Glob, Peter V. 1974. *The Mound People: Danish Bronze-Age Man Preserved*. Ithaca, NY: Cornell University Press.

Goldhahn, Joakim. 2012. "On War and Memory and the Memory of War: The Middle Bronze Age Burial from Hvidegarden on Zealand in Denmark Revisited." In *N-TAG Ten: Proceedings of the 10th Nordic TAG Conference at Stiklestad, Norway, 2009*, ed. Ragnhild Berge, Marek Jasinski, and Kalle Sognnes, 237–50. Oxford: British Archaeological Reports.

Greenwell, William. 1877. *British Barrows: A Record of the Examination of Sepulchral Mounds in Various Parts of England*. Oxford: Clarendon.

Hill, Erica. 2011. "Animals as Agents: Hunting Ritual and Relational Ontologies in Prehistoric Alaska and Chukotka." *Cambridge Archaeological Journal* 21 (3): 407–26. https://doi.org/10.1017/S0959774311000448.

Jones, Andrew Meirion. 2002. "A Biography of Colour: Colour, Material Histories, and Personhood in Early Bronze Age Britain." In *Colouring the Past: The Significance of Colour in Archaeological Research*, ed. Andrew Meirion Jones and Gavin Macgregor, 159–74. Oxford: Berg.

Jones, Andrew Meirion. 2007. *Memory and Material Culture*. Cambridge: Cambridge University Press. https://doi.org/10.1017/CBO9780511619229.

Jones, Andrew Meirion. 2012. *Prehistoric Materialities: Becoming Material in Prehistoric Britain and Ireland*. Oxford: Oxford University Press. https://doi.org/10.1093/acprof:osobl/9780199556427.001.0001.

Jones, Andrew Meirion. Forthcoming. "Assembling the Dead: Assemblage, Process, and Syncreticism in the British Chalcolithic and Early Bronze Age." In *Syncreticism and Creolisation in Archaeology*, ed. Timothy Clack. Oxford: Oxford University Press.

Kaul, Flemming. 1998. *Ships on Bronzes: A Study in Bronze Age Religion and Iconography*. Copenhagen: National Museum of Denmark.

Lane, N. Gary, and William Ausich. 2001. "The Legend of St. Cuthberts Beads: A Palaeontological and Geological Perspective." *Folklore* 112: 65–87.

Last, Jonathan. 2007. "Beyond the Grave: New Perspectives on Barrows." In *Beyond the Grave: New Perspectives on Barrows*, ed. Jonathan Last, 1–13. Oxford: Oxbow.

Leeming, Peter. 2015. "'Also Found . . . (Not Illustrated) . . .': The Curious Case of the Missing Magical Fossils." In *The Materiality of Magic: An Artifactual Investigation into Ritual Practices and Popular Beliefs*, ed. Ceri Houlbrook and Natalie Armitage, 15–22. Oxford: Oxbow Books.

Longworth, Ian A. 2005. "Collared Urns, Food Vessels, and Accessory Cups from the Barrows." In *Snail Down, Wiltshire: The Bronze Age Barrow Cemetery and Related Earthworks, in the Parishes of Collingborne Ducis and Collingborne Kingston Excavations 1953, 1955, and 1957*, ed. Nicholas Thomas, 165–71. Monograph 3. Devizes: Wiltshire Archaeological and Natural History Society.

Manby, Terence G. 1995. "Skeuomorphism: Some Reflections of Leather, Wood, and Basketry in Early Bronze Age Pottery." In *Unbaked Urns of Rudely Shape: Essays on British and Irish Pottery for Ian Longworth*, ed. Ian Kinnes and Gillian Varndell, 81–88. Oxford: Oxbow.

McNamara, Kenneth. 2007. "Shepherds' Crowns, Fairy Loaves, and Thunderstones: The Mythology of Fossil Echinoids in England." In *Myth and Geology*, ed. Luigi Piccardi and Bruce Masse, 279–94. London: Geological Society. https://doi.org/10.1144/GSL.SP.2007.273.01.22.

Morris, Brian. 1991. *Western Conceptions of the Individual*. Oxford: Berg.

Mortimer, John R. 1905. *Forty Years' Researches in British and Saxon Burial Mounds of East Yorkshire*. London: A. Brown and Sons.

Oakley, Kenneth. 1965. "Folklore of Fossils." *Antiquity* 39 (154): 117–25. https://doi.org/10.1017/S0003598X00031641.

Olsen, Bjørnar. 2010. *In Defense of Things: Archaeology and the Ontology of Objects*. Lanham, MD: Altamira.

Parfitt, Keith. 2004. "A Round Barrow near Haynes Farm, Eyethorne." *Archaeologia Cantiana* 124: 397–415.

Parker Pearson, Michael. 1999. *The Archaeology of Death and Burial*. Stroud: Sutton.

Pauketat, Timothy R. 2013a. *An Archaeology of the Cosmos*. London: Routledge.

Pauketat, Timothy R. 2013b. "Bundles of/in/as Time." In *Big Histories, Human Lives: Tackling Problems of Scale in Archaeology*, ed. John Robb and Timothy R. Pauketat, 35–56. Santa Fe, NM: School for Advanced Research Press.

Piggott, Stuart. 1938. "The Early Bronze Age in Wessex." *Proceedings of the Prehistoric Society* 4 (1): 52–106. https://doi.org/10.1017/S0079497X00021137.

Piggott, Stuart. 1962. "From Salisbury Plain to South Siberia." *Wiltshire Archaeological and Natural History Magazine* 58: 93–97.

Radley, Jeffrey. 1966. "A Bronze Age Ring-Work on Totley Moor and Other Bronze Age Ring-Works in the Pennines." *Archaeological Journal* 123 (1): 1–26. https://doi .org/10.1080/00665983.1966.11077397.

Randsborg, Klavs. 1993. "Kivik: Archaeology and Iconography." *Acta Archaeologica* 64 (1): 1–149.

Renfrew, A. Colin. 1974. "Beyond a Subsistence Economy: The Evolution of Social Organisation in Europe." In *Reconstructing Complex Societies*, ed. Charlotte B. Moore, 69–85. Cambridge, MA: MIT Press.

Ride, David. 2001. "The Excavation of a Cremation Cemetery of the Bronze Age and a Flint Cairn at Easton Down, Allington, Wiltshire, 1983–1995." *Wiltshire Archaeological and Natural History Magazine* 94: 161–76.

Saunders, Nicholas. 2011. "Shimmering Worlds: Brilliance, Power, and Gold in Pre-Columbian Panama." In *To Capture the Sun: Gold of Ancient Panama*, ed. John W. Hoopes, Jeffrey Quilter, Nicholas Saunders, and Richard G. Cooke, 78–113. Tulsa, OK: Gilcrease Museum, University of Tulsa.

Saxe, Arthur A. 1971. "Social Dimensions of Mortuary Practices in a Mesolithic Population from Wadi Halfa, Sudan." In *Approaches to the Social Dimensions of Mortuary Practices*, ed. John Brown, 39–57. Memoir of the Society for American Archaeology 25. Washington, DC: Society for American Archaeology.

Shennan, Susan. 1975. "The Social Organisation at Branç." *Antiquity* 49 (196): 279–88. https://doi.org/10.1017/S0003598X00070319.

Sheridan, Alison. 2008. "Towards a Fuller, More Nuanced Narrative of Chalcolithic and Early Bronze Age Britain 2500–1500 BC." *Bronze Age Review* 1: 57–78.

Sheridan, Alison, and Mary Davis. 2002. "Investigating Jet and Jet-Like Artefacts from Prehistoric Scotland: The National Museums of Scotland Project." *Antiquity* 76 (293): 812–25. https://doi.org/10.1017/S0003598X00091298.

Sheridan, Alison, and Andrew Shortland. 2003. "Supernatural Power-Dressing." *British Archaeology* 30: 18–23.

Smith, Worthington G. 1894. *Man, the Primeval Savage: His Haunts and Relics from the Hill-Tops of Bedfordshire to Blackwall*. London: Edward Stanford.

Stevenson, Sylvia. 1995. "The Excavation of a Kerbed Cairn at Beech Hill House, Coupar Angus, Perthshire." *Proceedings of the Society of Antiquaries of Scotland* 125: 197–235.

Stone, John F.S., and N. Gray Hill. 1940. "A Round Barrow on Stockbridge Down, Hampshire." *Antiquaries Journal* 20 (1): 39–51. https://doi.org/10.1017/S00035 8150004556X.

Tainter, Joseph R. 1975. "Social Inference and Mortuary Practices: An Experiment in Numerical Classification." *World Archaeology* 7 (1): 1–15. https://doi.org/10.1080/004 38243.1975.9979617.

Thomas, Nicholas. 2005. *The Bronze Age Barrow Cemetery and Related Earthworks, in the Parishes of Collingborne Ducis and Collingborne Kingston Excavations 1953, 1955, and 1957.* Monograph 3. Devizes: Wiltshire Archaeological and Natural History Society.

Watts, Christopher. 2013. *Relational Archaeologies: Humans, Animals, and Things.* London: Routledge.

Williams, Howard 2006. *Death and Memory in Early Medieval Britain.* Cambridge: Cambridge University Press.

Woodward, Ann. 2000. *British Barrows: A Matter of Life and Death.* Stroud: Tempus.

Woodward, Ann. 2002. "Beads and Beakers: Heirlooms and Relics in the British Early Bronze Age." *Antiquity* 76 (294): 1040–47. https://doi.org/10.1017/S0003598 X00091845.

Zedeño, Maria Nieves. 2008. "Bundled Worlds: The Roles and Interactions of Complex Objects from the North American Plains." *Journal of Archaeological Method and Theory* 15 (4): 362–78. https://doi.org/10.1007/s10816-008-9058-4.

11

Relational Matters of Being

Personhood and Agency in Archaeology

Eleanor Harrison-Buck

This volume presents a diverse set of case studies that highlight the context-based, regional variability of personhood and agency worldwide. Yet a number of shared themes also emerge. One theme I explore here is agency and personhood as generative and mutually constituted processes; and the chapters in this volume, alongside other examples from both archaeological and ethnographic contexts, provide some insightful case studies. The volume as a whole offers important contributions to key areas of contemporary theory in studies of agency and personhood, some of which are reviewed below. These studies provide a critical examination of the so-called material turn, analytically engaging with relational perspectives grounded in ontological archaeology (see Alberti 2016).

I conclude this chapter with a critical look at the so-called new ontological realism (Alberti 2016; Gabriel 2015; Thomas 2015), discussing some of the current trends and shortcomings of the radical theory of ontological alterity. In its strictest sense, this approach privileges non-discursive materiality and a wholesale rejection of discursive cognitivism, suggesting that they are necessarily at odds and mutually exclusive. Despite attempts to eradicate Cartesian dualisms, I argue that this "all-or-nothing" approach has only furthered the mind/body gap in some current post-humanist studies of ontological archaeology. Instead of an "all-or-nothing" paradigm that opposes discursive and non-discursive knowledge, I suggest that scholars consider embodied

DOI: 10.5876/9781607327479.c011

cognition as "conversively co-creative" (sensu Brill de Ramírez 2007:22). This alternative, conversive form of embodied cognition suggests that epistemologies and ontologies exist among all societies across the globe but vary significantly because people interact with their physical world in markedly different ways.

AGENTIVE (NON-)PERSONS AND SOME FALSE DIVIDES

For some scholars, relational perspectives offer a replacement for traditional practice and agency-based theories for understanding personhood. For instance, John Robb (2010:494) notes that "agency is not a characteristic of individuals but of relationships; it is the socially reproductive quality of action within social relationships." This definition of agency implies that all agents are inherently social beings or persons (human or otherwise). Yet the case studies in this volume suggest that agents and persons are not necessarily synonymous. Erica Hill makes the important distinction that while many things have agency (the ability to act), not all of them possess the capacity for *reciprocity*—an ability to engage in social relationships with mutual respect—a defining trait for personhood in most animistic societies. These agents are considered non-persons or what Morten Pedersen (2001:415–16) might refer to as "asocial entities." To constitute personhood in some societies, an agent must have "the ability to elicit a response and to be a social other" (Eberl 2013:3). Therefore, agency is perhaps better defined more broadly as having the "capacity for action" (Robb 2010:493), whereas a *social* agent engages similarly to a *relational* person with a capacity to interact and intra-act.

Among the proto- and early historic Eskimo living along the Bering Sea coast examined by Hill in chapter 2, agential non-persons are identified based on their unpredictable and uncontrolled behavior, which includes acts of cannibalism. On the surface, these non-persons resemble relations among Amazonian groups that Philippe Descola (1996:94) describes as animic predation, which he characterizes as the inverse of reciprocity. Yet the comparison ends there. Carlos Fausto (2007:500) further describes such "predatory relations" among Amazonian groups, whereby an animal or human body or aspects of its vitality are captured and in some cases eaten by certain cannibalistic/carnivorous groups. Fausto (2007) clarifies distinctions between agents and persons in Amazonia, indicating first that not everything has agency (it is unequally distributed and hierarchical) and second that humans and animals hold a mutual predatory relationship and that their state of personhood is defined by "two modes of consumption: one, cooked, whose objective is strictly alimentary, and another, raw, whose goal is the appropriation of the victim's animistic capacities" (Fausto 2007:504). In other words, in this context both humans and (hunted) animals are treated as persons; it is in the act of consuming that their role(s) as subject may (or may not) shift to that of object, effectively blurring the body/soul opposition. The Amazonian and Eskimo case studies show that agency and personhood are not fixed or universal categories and highlight the regional and contextual variability that exists in this case between two different "animistic" societies (see Sahlins 2014 for a recent critique of the fourfold differentiation of animism, totemism, analogism, and naturalism outlined in Descola's [2013] ontological scheme).

Traditionally, scholars present models that emphasize human dominance over the natural world, but these reconstructions tend to obscure the ontological proximity of humans and animals and their mutually constituted relationship (Ingold 1996, 2000). For instance, indigenous hunters often view the hunt as a direct expression of their relationship with their prey, crediting their success to the animal's willing self-sacrifice rather than to their own (human) superiority or technological mastery over the animal (McNiven 2013:99). In many cases hunting practices blur not only the divide between body and soul but also human-animal distinctions. Some post-humanists argue that "ultimately, the power to alter webs of relationships derives not *from* people (or even from other organisms, places, things, or other relational 'nodes') but *from the relations themselves*" (Pauketat and Alt, chapter 4, original emphasis). Yet Pauketat and Alt conclude that these two perspectives on human history are not mutually exclusive but in a relational world are mutually co-creative and arise through a generative process (see further below).

Some see relational perspectives of personhood as an extension of post-processual thought, specifically in its rejection of the universal scientific truths espoused by the ecological functionalism of the processual movement (see Thomas 2015:1288). Yet the interpretive theory of post-processualism (first challenged by phenomenology in the 1990s) stands in stark contrast to contemporary ontological theory (Alberti 2016:164; Thomas 2015:1288). The former decodes (representational) meaning, while the latter codes (relational) performance or decorum—that is, both conscious and unconscious ways of being and doing. This distinction is highlighted by Brück and Jones in their study of British Early Bronze Age burials and grave goods, traditionally interpreted as social status indicators of the interred. Brück and Jones argue that such grave goods may constitute alternative ontological forms of Bronze Age personhood, which emphasize a human-landscape relationship rather than strictly the human individual "set apart from (and . . . superior to) the natural world" (Brück and Jones, chapter 10). The nature-culture divide—looking at nature as something "acted upon" by culture as a civilizing or progressive move—represents a pervasive "master narrative" grounded in Western epistemology (Borić 2013:49).

Another false divide in Western thought that has been maintained in economic anthropology is the alienable-inalienable divide (see Graeber 2001; Kopytoff 1986). Maria Nieves Zedeño, Wendi Field Murray, and Kaitlyn Chandler (chapter 5) revisit and further unpack this sharp dichotomy, examining materials including native feathers and European dyes, which would normally be characterized as inalienable and alienable, respectively. Yet in the context of painting and bundling, their object "itineraries" (sensu Joyce and Gillespie 2015) converge as a "relational node" (sensu Ingold 2007) and exemplify what Zedeño and colleagues describe as the inalienable-commodity-inalienable continuum (see also Kopytoff 1986). The same fluid continuum could also be applied to Howey's discussion in chapter 3 of European-derived copper kettles interred by the Mi'kmaq as grave goods in burials from northeastern North America. Throughout their route of circulation, objects can transition from alienable to inalienable and in some cases back again. This continuum is reminiscent of Bill Brown's (2001:4) discussion of an object's "flow within the circuits of production and distribution, consumption and exhibition." This circulation has no beginning or end, only temporary stoppages, knots, or nodes (Joyce and Gillespie 2015:3). In such instances, the "experiential qualities and other flows or movements of substances, materials, and phenomena ... become attached, entangled, or associated with others and, in the process, define not only people but other organisms, things, places, and the like" (Pauketat and Alt, chapter 4).

AGENCY AS GENERATIVE ACTION IN RELATIONAL SOCIETIES: CRAFTING PERSONS

Agency as generative action is what brings things to life. John Barrett (2014:69) makes the important point that if we define agency as simply a causal reaction between two relational objects, "this claim only renders agency as a force or quality identified as a 'product of material engagement,' which neither is specific enough for our purposes nor clarifies what, if anything, instigates such an engagement (another agency?)." A causal reaction can be considered agency (a seed pod that falls *on* the ground), but this action alone is insufficient to (re)generate another life force until it forms a relation or mutual interdependency (breaks apart and reseeds *in* the ground). A mutual constitution of being is a necessary component of relational personhood. Mutually constitutive relations are the generative acts (the social agency) that produce things in the world, whether those things are human offspring or crafted objects (see Hendon, chapter 7).

If we are to say that some *thing* has animate agency or a life force, it seems logical to conclude that it must have been created/generated/born similar to any other biological *thing*. While agency is characterized as a "product of material engagement" (Malafouris 2008a:34), in many instances to qualify as a relational person a social agent must also demonstrate the capacity to carry forth its own generative acts involving one or more other relations to co-produce new life into being. How one defines this continuum or "life cycle" (in a thing or a human) will vary based on ontological perspective. Likewise, how one defines person-hood also varies. While a baby is brought into being as an animate or sentient agent through a generative act, for some societies, such as the Aztec, the child is not considered a person until he or she undergoes a series of birthing and bathing rituals that imbue the child with vital life forces (Eberl 2013; Joyce 2000). In these instances, the child is seen as a precious raw material whose personhood is shaped through these and other rituals of socialization.

Often, the production of personhood goes hand in hand with the marking of gender roles and sexual divisions. To be a person requires the capacity to regenerate life; therefore, social agents (persons) are necessarily gendered beings. Extending this capacity that exists for all biological things (humans, plants, animals, and other living organisms) to inanimate things helps explain why some societies view crafting as a sexual act between humans and gendered object-beings. For example, in some African societies iron-smelting furnaces are gendered female and these "technological artifacts" are given bodily features, including clay breasts and vaginal openings, penetrated by male smelters with penis-like blow pipes (Schmidt 2009). Together, the smelter-furnace (person-object) relation is a reciprocal engagement seen as a male-female sexual act that is reproductive, together generating iron object-beings. The generative fluxes of these sexual mates are mutually constituted—the smelter needs the furnace as much as the furnace needs the smelter to produce.

Rather than a one-way process of engagement, it is the mutual work or co-production between relational beings that defines their personhood, and through their generative act of production an animacy or life force is spawned. The sharp divide between subject and object dissolves. Christopher Witmore (2007) calls this a *symmetrical* process. Julia Hendon (2010) emphasizes inter-subjectivity in this process. Following this logic, the vitality accorded to African iron bangles and rings examined by Ann Stahl (chapter 9) might be transferred to these objects during the (re)productive process. According to Peter Schmidt

(2009:263), those with the power to transform metal vis-à-vis the iron-smelting furnace not only held procreative power but also served as protectors and curative agents and could induce "medicinal curing, magical protections, and ancestral appeasement." Stahl's findings suggest that iron adornments were also capable of extending a form of protective power to the wearer as well as to the shrines they adorned as offerings. Rather than an inherent agency, the efficacious power of the iron jewelry may be the result of its reciprocal engagement and ability to act back on another relational being, effectively "restoring [it] to the *generative* fluxes of the world of materials in which [it] came into being and [continues] to subsist" (Ingold 2011:29, emphasis added).

The construction and decoration of marine transport canoes among the Torres Strait Islanders described by Ian McNiven (chapter 8) highlights another example of production as a generative act. Two types of gendered wood are smeared with bodily fluids, including blood, female discharge, and seminal fluid; their mixing is suggestive of sexual intercourse (Munn 1986:140; see also Tambiah 1983). The production process includes a suite of ritual actions, including the decoration of the prowboard with anthropomorphic features, effectively transforming the canoe into an animate (social) agent. Yet it is their capacity to interact with the water—as seaworthy object-beings— that sustains their status as relational persons. This example highlights "the ontological concept of assemblage, concerned with examining the changing character and affect of materials as they shift from one grouping and set of relationships to another" (Jones and Alberti 2013:31).

Julia Hendon in chapter 7 describes how crafting in ancient Mesoamerica was not merely a means to an end but a social interaction that formed a relationship between crafter and the raw materials being formed. She argues that it was through this engagement that crafted objects (and tools) became agents with the potential for personhood. Hendon notes that the "crafter's sense of self develops *in part* through enskillment" (emphasis added), a process in which the craftperson becomes increasingly proficient in the manipulation of raw materials and the tools of the trade. In a more radical post-humanist approach, Benjamin Alberti (2014:119) suggests that for some societies in which natural and cultural processes are not distinguished, skill cannot be attributed exclusively to the human body and must be more broadly conceived. This might explain why fossils could have been seen as crafted objects rather than simply as natural specimens curated by humans during the British Early Bronze Age (Brück and Jones, chapter 10). Alberti (2014:120) inverts the normative logic of enskillment, arguing that the technical action applied to raw material (with or without tools) is not the only gauge of skill "in a context in which skilled action was considered natural and all natural acts [were] considered potentially skilled." Hendon would not characterize skilled action as "natural" but does emphasize its supernatural elements, noting that in ancient Mesoamerica an animate life force was housed within both craftspersons and their tools; as such, both were sources of potent agency.

Despite their differences in approach, both Hendon and Alberti come to a similar conclusion that what was efficacious and communicative was the practice of production; the finished product itself is not what lends an object its potency and meaning but rather, it is the relations that form through the creative process. Viewed in this way, skilled action is a co-creative and generative act, bringing forth qualities and properties within both crafters and their tools in the transformation of raw material. Similarly, Looper (chapter 6) argues that for the ancient Maya, qualities and properties of both human and other-than-human agency and personhood were brought forth through numerous types of material transformations. He describes how for the Maya, physical and sensuous properties of objects were conjoined with performative acts, which included speaking or incantation. "By cutting and inscribing shells (and other media) with hieroglyphic texts, the ancient Maya allowed these materials to 'speak,' which was understood to be a manifestation of agency and liveliness" (Looper, chapter 6). In this case, the crafting of a shell trumpet and the production of scribal art did not merely produce a finely crafted object but served as a generative act that transformed an inanimate object into a breathing and speaking social agent with qualities of personhood.

PERSONHOOD AS NATURE OR NURTURE? ONTOLOGICAL DIFFERENCE AND ESSENTIALIST CLAIMS

Recent trends in anthropology advocate a theory of ontological difference, with some considering the possibility of multiple worlds rather than multiple worldviews (Alberti et al. 2011; Alberti and Marshall 2009; Henare et al. 2007; Holbraad 2009). The consideration of ontological difference, whether multiple worlds or multiple worldviews, has prompted a reconsideration of the constitution of personhood, which has had a profound impact on our archaeological reconstructions. Oliver Harris and John Robb (2012:668–69) suggest that by envisioning multiple, mutually exclusive ontologies, this creates a "closed" ontology whereby different groups would never be able to communicate and understand one another in circumstances of contact, which historically we know is not the case (see also Robb and Harris 2013). Rather than multiple ontologies, Mario Blaser (2013:552) prefers the term *ontological multiplicity* because it recasts ontology as a performance or enactment, as opposed to a foundational claim or essentialist fact about how the world operates.

In current postmodern theory, it would seem that anti-essentialist episte-mology has been taken to an extreme, wherein any universal truths about the world cannot be reasoned (Fahlander 2012:111). Even reason itself is not uni-versal (Latour 2013). This radical postmodernist critique emerged as a result of the deep-seated bias in anthropology born out of European colonization, where reason and rational thought were considered to be exclusive to Western societies and irrationality was associated with the (uncivilized) people of non-Western societies (Fowles 2013:9, citing Brück 1999). This perspective is per-haps seen as a progressive move on the part of postmodern theory, but this radical position appears to ignore the fact that some essentialist claims can be made—namely, that reason is universal in the sense that all humans share this capacity (Ingold 1996:26). Cognitive science indicates that reason "arises from the nature of our brains, bodies, and bodily experience" and that its structure is controlled by the same neural and cognitive mechanisms that allow us to perceive our surroundings and move about the landscape (Lakoff and Johnson 1999:4). Reason does not comprise some disembodied philosophy developed exclusively by Europeans during the Enlightenment, but neither is it some transcendental component of the universe (see Lakoff and Johnson 1999:4–7). It is both embodied mind and bodily experience that directly shapes the struc-ture of reason and makes sense of the world in which one lives. This explains the lack of a singular, shared rational trajectory among all societies across the globe (Latour 2013:66) and why "everyone's actions are performed for reasons that are, from the actor's perspective, entirely reasonable" (Fowles 2013:9).

Much of the current postmodern scholarship in archaeology applies a prac-tice-based phenomenological approach to the construction of relational person-hood that is grounded in non-discursive, bodily performed experience. In many studies, personhood as a relational constitution of being is seen as a learned condition, somewhat like acquiring hunting skills generation after generation (cf. Ingold 1996). The aim is to avoid any essentialist claims, but in doing so postmodern scholars also tend to ignore any innate ontogenetic contribution in the shaping of personhood. Notably, child psychology and psychobiology stud-ies suggest that relational personhood is ontologically prior to social learning. Referencing work of Colwyn Trevarthen (1980), João Pina-Cabral (2016:249) concludes that we are all relational beings; beginning as babies, we are in the company of others and are always plurally co-habiting the world. In this so-called basic mind (cf. Hutto and Myin 2013), "each human being starts his or her personal ontogeny—his or her path of being—inside human contagion"

(Pina-Cabral 2016:248). Neurodevelopment studies of both children and young nonhuman mammals living outside such contagion in non-relational environments—where physical and emotional connections with caregivers are severely lacking—have shown that such situations have lasting damage on cognitive capacities, suggesting that non-relational conditions are simply not conducive for the survival of humans or nonhumans (Perry 2002).

Thus, aside from the unfortunate cases of severe neglect and isolation, the vast majority of humans and nonhumans are relationally constituted at birth and therefore are inherently social beings whose personhood is shaped by intersubjective bodily experience, making the debate between Western individual versus non-Western dividual a moot point. Starting with relational intersubjectivity as a fundamental and indispensable condition of all personhood, it is from here that people discover their individual selves and learn through embodied reasoning appropriate ways of being—what I call ontological decorum—in the world in which they live and move about. In his discussion of human personhood, Chris Fowler's (2004) keen observation still resonates, that every human being has some degree of self-awareness or individuality as well as relational-awareness or dividuality, but how these aspects define the self varies (see also Fowler 2016). We cannot say someone is strictly a relational dividual with attentional animacy or a bounded individual with intentional agency (sensu Ingold 2013) without creating a "closed" and universalized ontology that often leads to falsely dichotomizing Western and non-Western cultures (see recent discussions by Fowles 2013; Harris and Robb 2012; Wilkinson 2013).

Many scholars focused on relational or ontological archaeology are "[engaging] with indigenous ideas as theories to reconfigure archaeological concepts and practice" (Alberti 2016:163). Alberti (2016) observes that while approaches to ontological archaeology vary—from Latourian perspectives to the "perspectivisms" of Viveiros de Castro—what these scholars share in common is their focus on alterity. Yet as I argue below, not all of these scholars seem to share the same radical approach to alterity as the new ontological realists (e.g., Fowles 2013). According to Alberti (2016:172), "If ontology is what 'is,' then alterity is the part of what others say what 'is' that does not make sense to us." In other words, ontology is "doing" and alterity is the "saying" or "thinking." The latter is typically characterized as discursive knowledge that resides in the cognitive or conceptual realm of the mind. Yet Alberti (2016:173) makes it clear that ontological alterity in archaeology strictly entails the "nondiscursitivy of things," suggesting that we are dealing with just the "doings" of the past (sensu Fowles 2013). This is part of the archaeological realist's concerted move away from discursive knowledge—the abstract, conceptual, and cognitive mind—as an interpretative or representational approach of a "knowing subject" (Jones and Alberti 2013). Instead, the realist's focus of attention is strictly on the non-discursive—the "performed body knowledge" (Budden and Sofaer 2009:203). The implication here is that the interpreting act of a knowing subject is the stuff of modernist objectivist science (à la Latour 1993). This "school" of onto-logical alterity, according to Alberti (2016:166), "[is] united in [its] questioning of the ability of modern Cartesian substance ontology—the view that the world is divided into two types of substance, extended matter and thought—to explain the material world fully."

Alberti (2016) and others gloss the term *alterity* as difference or otherness, but the term derives from the Latin word *alter*, meaning "other (of two)." Therefore, among realists, ontological alterity in its strictest sense is an "all-or-nothing" paradigm; it implies that you are not simply dealing with a slightly different version but with something else altogether. This is what Alberti and others (2011) mean when they refer to multiple worlds rather than multiple worldviews (see also Henare et al. 2007). However, by its very nature, ontologi-cal alterity can only be revealingly discussed from the perspective of the other world, that is, from the position of a "knowing subject" who has a precon-ceived conscious awareness of the other reality. Therefore, despite their con-certed efforts, realists will never be able to shake the position of a "knowing subject" because knowing what is different is apparently a necessary precursor for identifying alterity in the other world.

Another problem I see with the "all-or-nothing" approach to ontological alterity (when understood in its strictest sense) is that this reality appears to be formed through emotional attentiveness devoid of any rational mind or inten-tional way of being. This is what Timothy Ingold (2013) is suggesting when he privileges attentional vitality or animacy over intentional agency. If the latter is a "structuring force of the modern constitution on our habits of thought" (Ingold 2013:247), then when did this structuring force change? And how do we reconcile descendent communities who are seeking to reconnect with their ancestral past and who straddle these two "worlds"? This is the paradox set in motion by the new ontological realism, which offers insightful critical think-ing but whose "all-or-nothing" perspective becomes deeply problematic and unacceptable if followed to its logical conclusion.

THE THINKING BODY AND THE DOING MIND

Despite attempts to eradicate Cartesian dualisms, the movement of new ontological realism radicalizes the "great divides" (sensu Fowles 2010) and perpetuates the mind-body split with their wholesale rejection of the so-called modern substance ontology and their "all-or-nothing" approach to alterity. Their notion of reason and rational thought as (mis-)appropriated by the Modern Objectivists has been inspired by Bruno Latour (1993), whose work has been hugely influential on this group of scholars, especially his actor-network theory (ANT). In my estimation, Latour's general emphasis on matter has served to sideline thought among his post-humanist followers. For instance, Latour (2013:66) concludes that rational ve6rediction does not stem from a universal truth (Reason with a capital R) but must be defined "within a network that is proper to that network"; "once it has been deprived of its conditions of exercise" it loses meaning and, by extension, its rationality. When considering this perspective, it is perhaps not surprising why those who follow Latour might be inclined to privilege matter over mind and the conditions of bodily experience. Yet in this same context Latour (2013:66) himself states unequivocally: "To understand rationally any situation whatsoever is at once to unfold its network and define its preposition, the interpretive key in which it has to be grasped ([NET-PRE])." In essence, Latour is echoing what scientists studying embodied cognition have been saying for some time (see Lakoff and Johnson 1999): that our reality or ontology is recursively shaped by both the material conditions or networks in which the body moves about [NET] and our embodied minds [PRE]. Latour (2013:58) concludes that if you take the latter away, "you will understand nothing" of the networks you are traversing. In other words, "Any adequate account of meaning and rationality must give a central place to [the] embodied and imaginative structure of understanding by which we grasp our world" (Johnson 2013:xiii; see also Pina-Cabral 2016:249).

Archaeologists engaged in ontological realism seem to embrace a form of "radical embodied cognition" (sensu Pina-Cabral 2016) in that they reject any representationalist formulations—materialization of abstract beliefs and ideas as mental constructs or symbolic language standing as an intermediary between the observing subject and the objects of the physical world. Archaeological realists would argue that instead of intermediaries standing for or representing to the mind the objects of the physical world as discursive knowledge, materialization of matter itself arrives as non-discursive knowledge and is strictly a bodily performed experience always in a process of becoming (e.g., Alberti 2012; Lucas 2012; Jones and Alberti 2013). A primary aim of ontological realism has been to dissolve the "Cartesian separation between the thinking body and doing mind" (Budden and Sofaer 2009:203–4, citing Knappett 2005:5). While ontological realists often cite philosophers of embodied cognition, like Martin Heidegger or Maurice Merleau-Ponty, they rarely critically engage with the neuroscience evidence that supports embodied cognition (for some exceptions, see Malafouris 2008b, 2013). Yet this work has also contributed a great deal to turning on its head much of the twentieth-century philosophy espousing Cartesian dualisms.

According to Mark Johnson (2013), the mind-body gap can be understood as one that exists "between our cognitive, conceptual, formal, or rational side in contrast with our bodily, perceptual, material, and emotional side" (Johnson 2013: xxv). Post-humanists of the new ontological realism tend to privilege the latter assemblage, reflecting their roots in phenomenology. Yet the rejection of the former assemblage may also be a vestige of post-processualism and its concerted efforts to reject Western rationalist objectivism. As Sandy Budden and Joanna Sofaer (2009:204) suggest: "One way forward in this dilemma is to explore the role of non-discursive knowledge in relation to discursive knowledge, rather than treat them as opposite and incompatible notions. Discursive and non-discursive knowledge are complementary as both are needed in order to understand 'the making up of people' (Hacking 2004). The 'making up of people' is articulated through the interactions between abstract classifications and concrete actions."

Neuroscience studies of embodied cognition lend support to this notion of complementarity, demonstrating that the nature of all abstract conceptual constructs and metaphorical cognition is not separate from bodily experience but is fundamentally linked to aspects of our sensory-motor experience (Lakoff and Johnson 1999; Meteyard et al. 2012). This is what Johnson (2013) means by the embodied mind; the mind is not only connected to the body but bodily experience directly influences the mind in a mutually constitutive manner.

The neuroscience evidence suggests that the figurative language of metaphorical thinking is not merely abstract conceptual content separate from the body but is based on a physiology of emotions that forms in the mind through numerous sensory and motor systems grounded in bodily action (Johnson 2013; Lakoff and Johnson 1999). This suggests that all humans use non-discursive body knowledge *in combination with* discursive thinking to make sense of the world in which they live. Instead of an "all-or-nothing" paradigm that opposes discursive and non-discursive knowledge, we might consider embodied cognition as "conversively co-creative" (sensu Brill de Ramírez 2007:22). This alternative, conversive form of embodied cognition suggests that epistemologies and ontologies exist among all societies across the globe but vary significantly because people interact with their physical world in markedly different ways. For instance, the annual solar cycle is something many past and present societies have relied on to track time, but through the use of the clock this embodied cognition has become increasingly more abstract and is now primarily discursive knowledge compared to prehistoric times when the path of the sun was tracked through observations in the landscape, which relied more heavily on non-discursive bodily experience. The physical world in terms of the earth's rotation around the sun has remained the same, but our interaction with the physical world has changed and become less "attentional" (sensu Ingold 2013). Just as every person has different degrees of individual and relational awareness (Fowler 2004, 2016), so, too, does every person have the capacity and, indeed, varying degrees of intentional and attentional awareness; how these aspects vary depends on the person's interactions with the physical world. Lambros Malafouris (2013) takes this form of embodied cognition one step further in his Material Engagement Theory (MET), arguing that, like figurative language, the materials derived from the physical world are extensions of these cognitive processes (see also Malafouris 2008b).

Traditionally, anthropologists tend to couch reasoning in terms of conscious decision-making (rational choices) based on lifelong acquired learning, but this is a product of our training as observers who reconstruct past realities (ontological multiplicities) based on material evidence (Jones and Sibbesson 2013:155–56). While a relational ontology largely draws on the shared experiences and environments in which a body directly engages, much of this learning and reasoning according to cognitive scientists is "not completely conscious and almost unconscious" (Lakoff and Johnson 1999:4). This is what practice theorists who follow Pierre Bourdieu (1977) and his concept of "habitus" would argue: that the habitual practices and material representations that "create an intelligible, common-sense world imbued with meaning" are generated by both bodily practice and an embodied mind that is largely unconscious (Knapp and van Dommelen 2008:22).

"The mind is not merely embodied, but embodied in such a way that our conceptual systems draw largely upon commonalities of our bodies and of the environments we live in" (Lakoff and Johnson 1999:5–6). In this vein, posthumanists like Fowler and Harris (2015:138) conclude that materials in the Neolithic West Kennett chambered tomb "had the capacity to engage with people and evoke meaning and emotional resonance—they were potent." The embodied minds and bodies of the Neolithic inhabitants who shared the West Kennett chambered tomb were no doubt key contributors to this enduring place in the landscape through their ongoing and expanding relations. Yet in this particular case study, the agency of other-than-humans—from grave goods to dirt to dead bodies—seemingly overshadows the role of human agency and leaves us wondering (like the post-processualists before us) whether human intentionality and innovation had anything to do with the construction of the tomb. These scholars conclude, "The technologies of the time, such as pottery, *allowed* people to draw a connection between bodies, pots and the monument itself" (Fowler and Harris 2015:138, emphasis added).

Some now will only consider the process of materialization of matter itself for understanding truth and will not consider the materialization of abstract beliefs and ideas for fear of being interpretative (representationalist) and essentialist (e.g., Lucas 2012; see Alberti 2016 for further discussion of ontological realism and relativism). This prompts the question, have we taken post-humanism and such neo-materialist approaches too far? Characterizing relational persons (whether human or nonhuman) as "particles" or "waves" (e.g., Fowler and Harris 2015, à la Barad 2003, 2007) highlights their physical matter of being but seems to ignore their mental properties—as if an object-body is capable of operating outside of an embodied mind. The challenge we face goes beyond simply bridging the gap between mind and body; it requires us to invert our logic by considering the relationship of the body *in* the mind (sensu Johnson 2013; see also Malafouris 2013), as intra-related entities akin to Latour's NET-PRE model. One is a roadmap for the other to follow using both intention and attention (sensu Ingold 2013), depending on how one's relational sense of being and thinking is attuned as one moves through the world around him or her.

The "social skin" (Turner 1980) of both human and other-than-human beings is more than an inscribed body or "point of articulation between an interior self and an exterior society" (Joyce 2005:144) but is a performative, ongoing transition (sensu Butler 1990, 1993) of intra-related and mutually informing physical and mental properties of matter and thought (sensu Barad 2007). To truly reject Cartesian or "substance dualism," we must consider bodily experience—the perceptual, material, and emotional—operating *inside* the embodied cognitive, conceptual, formal, and rational mind (sensu Johnson 2013:xxv). From this perspective, we are more inclined to approach the physical and mental properties of matter and thought as symmetrical and mutually dependent constitutive relations, balancing human and nonhuman agency as relational persons in our archaeological theory and practice. The contributions in this volume demonstrate the strength of this "conversive" approach in studies of ontological archaeology, where both thinking and doing are co-creative conditions in the formation of agency, materiality, and personhood.

REFERENCES CITED

Alberti, Benjamin. 2012. "Cut, Pinch, and Pierce: Image as Practice among the Early Formative La Candelaria, First Millennium AD, Northwest Argentina." In *Encountering Imagery: Materialities, Perceptions, Relations*, ed. Ing-Marie Back Danielsson, Fredrik Fahlander, and Yiva Sjöstrand, 13–28. Stockholm: Stockholm University.

Alberti, Benjamin. 2014. "Designing Body-Pots in the Formative La Candelaria Culture, Northwest Argentina." In *Making and Growing: Anthropological Studies of Organisms and Artefacts*, ed. Elizabeth Hallam and Tim Ingold, 107–25. London: Routledge.

Alberti, Benjamin. 2016. "Archaeologies of Ontology." *Annual Review of Anthropology* 45 (1): 163–79. https://doi.org/10.1146/annurev-anthro-102215-095858.

Alberti, Benjamin, Severin Fowles, Martin Holbraad, Yvonne Marshall, and Christopher Witmore. 2011. "'Worlds Otherwise': Archaeology, Anthropology, and Ontological Difference." *Current Anthropology* 52 (6): 896–912. https://doi.org/10.1086/662027.

Alberti, Benjamin, and Yvonne Marshall. 2009. "Animating Archaeology: Local Theories and Conceptually Open-Ended Methodologies." *Cambridge Archaeological Journal* 19 (3): 344–56. https://doi.org/10.1017/S0959774309000535.

Barad, Karen. 2003. "Posthumanist Performativity: How Matter Comes to Matter." *Signs* 28 (3): 801–31. https://doi.org/10.1086/345321.

Barad, Karen. 2007. *Meeting the Universe Halfway: Quantum Physics and the Entanglement of Matter and Meaning*. Durham, NC: Duke University Press. https://doi.org/10.1215/9780822388128.

Barrett, John C. 2014. "The Material Constitution of Humanness." *Archaeological Dialogues* 21 (1): 65–74. https://doi.org/10.1017/S1380203814000105.

Blaser, Mario. 2013. "Ontological Conflicts and the Stories of Peoples in Spite of Europe: Toward a Conversation on Political Ontology." *Current Anthropology* 54 (5): 547–68. https://doi.org/10.1086/672270.

Borić, Dusan. 2013. "Theater of Predation: Beneath the Skin of Gobekli Tepe Images." In *Relational Archaeologies: Humans, Animals, Things*, ed. Christopher Watts, 42–64. London: Routledge.

Bourdieu, Pierre. 1977. *Outline of a Theory of Practice*. Cambridge: Cambridge University Press. https://doi.org/10.1017/CBO9780511812507.

Brill de Ramírez, Susan Berry. 2007. *Native American Life-History Narratives: Colonial and Postcolonial Navajo Ethnography*. Albuquerque: University of New Mexico Press.

Brown, Bill. 2001. "Thing Theory." *Critical Inquiry* 28 (1): 1–22. https://doi.org/10.1086/449030.

Brück, Joanna. 1999. "Ritual and Rationality: Some Problems of Interpretation in European Archaeology." *European Journal of Archaeology* 12 (1): 313–44.

Budden, Sandy, and Joanna Sofaer. 2009. "Non-Discursive Knowledge and the Construction of Identity: Potters, Potting, and Performance at the Bronze Age Tell of Sz'azhalombatta, Hungary." *Cambridge Archaeological Journal* 19 (2): 203–20. https://doi.org/10.1017/S0959774309000274.

Butler, Judith. 1990. *Gender Trouble: Feminism and the Subversion of Identity.* New York: Routledge.

Butler, Judith. 1993. *Bodies That Matter: On the Discursive Limits of "Sex."* New York: Routledge.

Descola, Philippe. 1996. "Constructing Natures: Symbolic Ecology and Social Practice." In *Nature and Society: Anthropological Perspectives,* ed. Philippe Descola and Gísli Pálsson, 82–102. New York: Routledge. https://doi.org/10.4324/978 0203451069_chapter_5.

Descola, Philippe. 2013. *Beyond Nature and Culture.* Trans. Janet Lloyd. Chicago: University of Chicago Press.

Eberl, Markus. 2013. "Nourishing Gods: Birth and Personhood in Highland Mexican Codices." *Cambridge Archaeological Journal* 3: 1–23.

Fausto, Carlos. 2007. "Feasting on People: Eating Animals and Humans in Amazonia." *Current Anthropology* 48 (4): 497–530. https://doi.org/10.1086/518298.

Fahlander, Fredrik. 2012. "Are We There Yet? Archaeology and the Postmodern in the New Millennium." *Current Swedish Archaeology* 20: 109–29.

Fowler, Chis. 2004. *The Archaeology of Personhood: An Anthropological Approach.* London: Routledge.

Fowler, Chis. 2016. "Relational Personhood Revisited." *Cambridge Archaeological Journal* 26 (3): 397–412. https://doi.org/10.1017/S0959774316000172.

Fowler, Chris, and Oliver J.T. Harris. 2015. "Enduring Relations: Exploring a Paradox of New Materialism." *Journal of Material Culture* 20 (2): 127–48. https://doi.org/10 .1177/1359183515577176.

Fowles, Severin M. 2010. "Animist/Analyst." Paper presented at the Annual Meeting of the Theoretical Archaeology Group, Brown University, Providence, RI, April 30–May 2.

Fowles, Severin M. 2013. *An Archaeology of Doings: Secularism and the Study of Pueblo Religion.* Santa Fe, NM: School for Advanced Research Press.

Gabriel, Markus. 2015. *Fields of Sense: A New Realist Ontology.* Edinburgh: Edinburgh University Press.

Graeber, David. 2001. *Toward an Anthropological Theory of Value: The False Coin of Our Own Dreams.* New York: Palgrave. https://doi.org/10.1057/9780312299064.

Hacking, Ian. 2004. "Between Michel Foucault and Erving Goffman: Between Discourse in the Abstract and Face-to-Face Interaction." *Economy and Society* 33 (3): 277–302. https://doi.org/10.1080/0308514042000225671.

Harris, Oliver J.T., and John Robb. 2012. "Multiple Ontolgies and the Problem of the Body in History." *American Anthropologist* 114 (4): 668–79. https://doi.org/10.1111/j.1548-1433.2012.01513.x.

Henare, Amiria, Martin Holbraad, and Sari Wastell. 2007. *Thinking through Things: Theorising Artefacts Ethnographically*. New York: Routledge.

Hendon, Julia A. 2010. *Houses in a Landscape: Memory and Everyday Life in Mesoamerica*. Durham, NC: Duke University Press.

Holbraad, Martin. 2009. "Ontology, Ethnography, Archaeology: An Afterword on the Ontography of Things." *Cambridge Archaeological Journal* 19 (3): 431–41. https://doi.org/10.1017/S0959774309000614.

Hutto, Daniel, and Erik Myin. 2013. *Radicalizing Enactivism: Basic Minds without Content*. Cambridge: MIT Press.

Ingold, Timothy. 1996. "The Optimal Forager and Economic Man." In *Nature and Society: Anthropological Perspectives*, ed. Philipe Descola and Gísli Pálsson, 25–44. New York: Routledge.

Ingold, Timothy. 2000. *The Perception of the Environment: Essays on Livelihood, Dwelling, and Skill*. London: Routledge. https://doi.org/10.4324/9780203466025.

Ingold, Timothy. 2007. "Materials against Materiality." *Archaeological Dialogues* 14 (1): 1–16. https://doi.org/10.1017/S1380203807002127.

Ingold, Timothy. 2011. *Being Alive: Essays on Movement, Knowledge, and Description*. London: Routledge.

Ingold, Timothy. 2013. "The Maze and the Labyrinth: Reflections of a Fellow-Traveler." In *Relational Archaeologies: Humans, Animals, Things*, ed. Christopher Watts, 245–49. London: Routledge.

Johnson, Mark. 2013. *The Body in the Mind: The Bodily Basis of Meaning, Imagination, and Reason*, 2nd ed. Chicago: University of Chicago Press.

Jones, Andrew Meirion, and Benjamin Alberti. 2013. "Introduction: Archaeology after Interpretation." In *Archaeology after Interpretation: Returning Materials to Archaeological Theory*, ed. Benjamin Alberti, Andrew Meirion Jones, and Joshua Pollard, 15–42. Walnut Creek, CA: Left Coast.

Jones, Andrew Meirion, and Emilie Sibbesson. 2013. "Archaeological Complexity: Materials, Multiplicity, and the Transitions to Agriculture in Britain." In *Archaeology after Interpretation: Returning Materials to Archaeological Theory*, ed. Benjamin Alberti, Andrew Meirion Jones, and Joshua Pollard, 151–72. Walnut Creek, CA: Left Coast.

Joyce, Rosemary A. 2000. "Girling the Girl and Boying the Boy: The Production of Adulthood in Ancient Mesoamerica." *World Archaeology* 31 (3): 473–83.

Joyce, Rosemary A. 2005. "Archaeology of the Body." *Annual Review of Anthropology* 34 (1): 139–58. https://doi.org/10.1146/annurev.anthro.33.070203 .143729.

Joyce, Rosemary A., and Susan D. Gillespie, eds. 2015. *Things in Motion: Object Itineraries in Anthropological Practice*. Santa Fe, NM: School for Advanced Research Press.

Knapp, A. Bernard, and Petere van Dommelen. 2008. "Past Practices: Rethinking Individuals and Agents in Archaeology." *Cambridge Archaeological Journal* 18 (1): 15–34. https://doi.org/10.1017/S0959774308000024.

Knappett, Carl. 2005. *Thinking through Material Culture: An Interdisciplinary Perspective*. Philadelphia: University of Pennsylvania Press. https://doi.org/10 .9783/9780812202496.

Kopytoff, Igor. 1986. "The Cultural Biography of Things: Commoditization as a Process." In *The Social Life of Things: Commodities in Cultural Perspective*, ed. Arjun Appadurai, 64–91. Cambridge: Cambridge University Press.

Lakoff, George, and Mark Johnson. 1999. *Philosophy in the Flesh: The Embodied Mind and Its Challenge to Western Thought*. New York: Basic Books.

Latour, Bruno. 1993. *We Have Never Been Modern*. Cambridge: Harvard University Press.

Latour, Bruno. 2013. *An Inquiry into Modes of Existence: An Anthropology of the Moderns*. Trans. Catherine Porter. Paris: Editions La Decouverte.

Lucas, Gavin. 2012. *Understanding the Archaeological Record*. Cambridge: Cambridge University Press.

Malafouris, Lambros. 2008a. "At the Potter's Wheel: An Argument for Material Agency." In *Material Agency: Towards a Non-Anthropocentric Approach*, ed. Carl Knappett and Lambros Malafouris, 19–36. New York: Springer. https://doi.org/10 .1007/978-0-387-74711-8_2.

Malafouris, Lambros. 2008b. "Beads for a Plastic Mind: The 'Blind Man's Stick' (BMS) Hypothesis and the Active Nature of Material Culture." *Cambridge Archaeological Journal* 18 (3): 401–14. https://doi.org/10.1017/S0959774308000449.

Malafouris, Lambros. 2013. *How Things Shape the Mind: A Theory of Material Engagement*. Cambridge: MIT Press.

McNiven, Ian. 2013. "Between the Living and the Dead: Relational Ontologies and the Ritual Dimensions of Dugong Hunting across Torres Strait." In *Archaeologies of Relationality: Humans, Animals, Things*, ed. Christoher Watts, 97–116. London: Routledge.

Meteyard, Lotte, Sara Rodriguez Cuadrado, Bahador Bahrami, and Gabriella Vigliocco. 2012. "Coming of Age: A Review of Embodiment and the Neuroscience of Semantics." *Cortex* 48 (7): 788–804. https://doi.org/10.1016/j.cortex.2010.11.002.

Munn, Nancy D. 1986. *The Fame of Gawa: A Symbolic Study of Value Transformation in a Massim (Papua New Guinea) Society*. Cambridge: Cambridge University Press.

Pedersen, Morten A. 2001. "Totemism, Animism, and North Asian Indigenous Ontologies." *Journal of the Royal Anthropological Institute* 7 (3): 411–27. https://doi.org/10.1111/1467-9655.00070.

Perry, Bruce D. 2002. "Childhood Experience and the Expression of Genetic Potential: What Childhood Neglect Tells Us about Nature and Nurture." *Brain and Mind* 3 (1): 79–100. https://doi.org/10.1023/A:1016557824657.

Pina-Cabral, João. 2016. "Brazilian Serialities: Personhood and Radical Embodied Cognition." *Current Anthropology* 57 (3): 247–60. https://doi.org/10.1086/686300.

Robb, John. 2010. "Beyond Agency." *World Archaeology* 42 (4): 493–520. https://doi.org/10.1080/00438243.2010.520856.

Robb, John, and Oliver J.T. Harris. 2013. *The Body in History: Europe from the Palaeolithic to the Future*. Cambridge: Cambridge University Press.

Sahlins, Marshall. 2014. "On the Ontological Scheme of *Beyond Nature and Culture*." *HAU: Journal of Ethnographic Theory* 4 (1): 281–90. https://doi.org/10.14318/hau4.1.013.

Schmidt, Peter R. 2009. "Tropes, Materiality, and Ritual Embodiment of African Iron Smelting Furnaces as Human Figures." *Journal of Archaeological Method and Theory* 16 (3): 262–82. https://doi.org/10.1007/s10816-009-9065-0.

Tambiah, Stanley J. 1983. "On Flying Witches and Flying Canoes: The Coding of Male and Female Values." In *The Kula: New Perspectives on Massim Exchange*, ed. Jerry W. Leach and Edmund Leach, 171–200. Cambridge: Cambridge University Press.

Thomas, Julien. 2015. "The Future of Archaeological Theory." *Antiquity* 89 (348): 1287–96. https://doi.org/10.15184/aqy.2015.183.

Trevarthen, Colwyn. 1980. "The Foundations of Human Intersubjectivity: Development of Interpersonal and Cooperative Understanding in Infants." In *The Social Foundations of Language and Thought: Essays in Honour of J. S. Bruner*, ed. David R. Olson, Jerome S. Bruner, and George A. Miller, 316–42. New York: Norton.

Turner, Terence S. 1980. "The Social Skin." In *Not Work Alone: A Cross-Cultural View of Activities Superfluous to Survival*, ed. Jeremy Cherfas and Roger Lewin, 112–140. London: Temple Smith.

Wilkinson, Darryl. 2013. "The Emperor's New Body: Personhood, Ontology, and the Inka Sovereign." *Cambridge Archaeological Journal* 23 (3): 417–32. https://doi.org/10 .1017/S0959774313000541.

Witmore, Christopher L. 2007. "Symmetrical Archaeology: Excerpts of a Manifesto." *World Archaeology* 39 (4): 546–62. https://doi.org/10.1080/00438240701679411.

Contributors

Susan M. Alt
Anthropology Department
Indiana University, Bloomington
Student Building 130, 701 E. Kirkwood Avenue
Bloomington, IN 47405-7100
susalt@indiana.edu

Joanna Brück
Department of Anthropology and Archaeology
University of Bristol
Office 2N12
43 Woodland Road
Clifton, Bristol BS8 1UU
joanna.bruck@bristol.ac.uk

Kaitlyn Chandler
Randi Korn and Associates, Inc.
2417B Mount Vernon Avenue
Alexandria, VA 22301
chandler@randikorn.com

Eleanor Harrison-Buck
Department of Anthropology
University of New Hampshire
Huddleston Hall 311
Durham, NH 03824
e.harrison-buck@unh.edu

Julia A. Hendon
Department of Anthropology
Gettysburg College
Campus Box 2985
Gettysburg, PA 17325
jhendon@gettysburg.edu

ERICA HILL
Social Sciences Department
University of Alaska Southeast
11066 Auke Lake Way
Juneau, AK 99801
edhill@alaska.edu

MEGHAN C. L. HOWEY
Department of Anthropology
University of New Hampshire
Huddleston Hall 313
Durham, NH 03824
meghan.howey@unh.edu

ANDREW MEIRION JONES
Department of Archaeology
Faculty of Humanities
University of Southampton
Highfield
Southampton SO17 1BF
United Kingdom
amj@soton.ac.uk

MATTHEW LOOPER
Department of Art and Art History
California State University, Chico
Ayres Hall 107
Chico, CA 95929-0820
mlooper@csuchico.edu

IAN J. MCNIVEN
Monash Indigenous Centre
Monash University
Room S824, Menzies Building
20 Chancellors Walk
Clayton, Victoria 3800
Australia

WENDI FIELD MURRAY
School of Anthropology
University of Arizona
Emil W. Haury Building
Tucson, AZ 85721
wfmurray@email.arizona.edu

TIMOTHY R. PAUKETAT
Department of Anthropology
University of Illinois at
Champaign-Urbana
109 Davenport Hall
607 S. Mathews Avenue
M/C 148
Urbana, IL 61801
pauketat@illinois.edu

ANN B. STAHL
Department of Anthropology
University of Victoria
Cornett Building, Room B228
3800 Finnerty Road
Victoria BC V8P 5C2
stahlann@uvic.ca

MARÍA NIEVES ZEDEÑO
BARA, School of Anthropology
University of Arizona
Emil W. Haury Building, Room 316B
Tucson, AZ 85721
mzedeno@email.arizona.edu

228(n3); defining Personhood in, 158–59, 198–99; of mortuary practices, 237–38; ontological multiplicities, 269–70

Arikara, birds and, 105, 109, 117

Arreton Down (Isle of Wight), burials at, 242

art historians, on agency of images, 128–29

Asante empire, 206, 226

asocial entities, 13, 264

assemblage converter, Cahokia as, 91

Assiniboine, birds and, 105, 109, 113, 114

Astor-Aguilera, Miguel Angel, 127, 150, 151, 152, 158, 159

Atlantic trade, and West Africa, 204, 205, 208

Augustine, Stephen, 63

Aurignacian period, 253

autonomous action, autonomy, of canoes, 169, 171–72

Aztecs: children becoming persons, 153–54, 267; souls, 152

Baikal, Lake, dog and wolf burials at, 31

Bakongo, 139, 140, 141

Banda, 227(n1); glass bead trade, 205–6; ornaments, 17, 197, 208–15; ritual contexts and objects, 216–25; serpentine symbolism in, 225–26

Banda Research Project (BRP), 207–9

bangles, Banda, 208, 209–11, 217, 221–23, 226, 267

Barad, Karen, 5

barrows: as bundled assemblages, 254–55; grave goods in, 242–43, 247, 250; pond, 248, 249, 253

Basques, 51, 52, 53–54, 57

Basse-Pyrénées, Grotte de, 253

beads: in Early Bronze Age burials, 242, 249; in Ngre Kataa shrines, 224–25; St. Cuthbert's, 250–51; stalactite, 248; West African trade in, 205–6, 220

bears, heads of, 37

bear-trapping pits, 110

Beaver Bundle, 113, 117

Beech Hill House (Perthshire), Bronze Age burials in, 248

beings, 4; agential, 34, 266; agential non-person, 40–41; animacy of, 152–53

Belize, speaking objects at, 132

belugas, as animal persons, 35

Bering Sea, 14; hunter-gatherers on, 32–33

betelnut, 173

big men, canoes as, 174–75

binding, 127

Bird-David, Nurit, 10

bird knowledge, 100, 108; rights and practices, 109–10

bird parts/objects: in ceremonial paraphernalia, 106, 109; as commodities, 113–15; ceremonial use of, 111–13

birds, 108; agency of, 15–16; characteristics of, 105–6; as gods and spirits, 106–7; personhood, 104–5; social roles, 100, 101; trade in, 114–15, 117

Black Elk, on sweat baths, 81

Blackfeet Indian Reservation, eagle-trapping pits on, 110

Blackfoot, 11, 12, 107, 108, 109, 119; birds and, 105, 116, 117, 118; eagle feathers used by, 111–15; eagle trapping, 110–11

Bladder Festival, 37

Blake's Firs (Easton Down, Wiltshire), Bronze Age cremation burials, 249–50

Blaser, Mario, 269

blood, sap as, 177

boat houses, Melanesian canoes in, 175

bodies, 17, 174

bodily modification, West Africa, 204

Boigu, 178

Bomai, 189, 190

bones, eagle, 109, 113

Borgia Codex, 153–54, 156

Bourdieu, Pierre, 275

Bowdich, T. Edward, 206

bows, canoe, 178–81

breath, breathing, 134, 140; ensouled, 137–38

Brill de Ramírez, Susan Berry, 7, 12, 263

Brings-down-the-Sun, eagle feather trade and, 114–15

British, 18; in Maritime provinces, 52, 54

Bronze Age, 237; fossils in, 255–56; mortuary practices, 238, 239–50; object bundles, 244–45

Brown, Bill, 12

Brown, Linda, 19

Brown Old Man, 115

BRP. *See* Banda Research Project

Bruwan (canoe), 183, *184*

Budden, Sandy, 275

bullroarers, and waking up canoes, 178, 186

bundle holders, eagle trapping by, 110

bundles, 13, 204; bird materials in, 16, 108, 117,

118; Bronze Age barrows as, 254–55; and eagle feathers, 111, 112–13; ritual treatment of, 11–12; sacred Bronze Age, 244–45; as social persons, 77–78

bundling, 7, 8, 77, 200–201, 202; Banda ornaments, 17–18; Banda shrines, 221–25; Bronze Age barrows, 254–55

burials, burial practices, 30, 31, 81; British Bronze Age, 18, 237–38, 239–50, 265; copper kettles in, 56–61; Mi'kmaq, 15, 66–67; seal, *38*

Burkina Faso, glass beads in, 205

Cabot, John, 53

caches: Eskimo hunting, 37, 39; in Maya sites, 159

Caddoans, 85

Cahokia, 15, 73, 79; maize cultivation at, 85–86; mortuary ritual, 90–91; mound construction at, 81–82; pottery at, 82–83; rebuilding of, 79–80; shell use, 88–*89*; sweat baths, 80–81; water symbolism at, 89–90

Cahokia grid, 80

calumet pipes, 111

cannibalism, 41; by agential non-persons, 34, 40, 42; in mutual predatory relationships, 264–65

canoes, 17, 268; anthropomorphization and zoomorphization of, 178–82; dismemberment and dispersal of, 186–87; Melanesian, 171–75; naming, 185–86; as object-beings, 168–69, 187–88; predatorization of, 182–85; sentience of, 188–89; Torres Strait, 167–69, 176–78

caribou, as persons, 36

carnelian beads, in Banda sites, 224–25, 226

castaways, in Torres Straits, 188, 189, 190

Caste War, 127

casts, fossils as, 253, 255–56

caves, fossils from, 253

Catlin, George, paintings by, *107*

Ceibal, 131, 140

cemeteries, organization of, 30

ceremonial paraphernalia, bird parts as, 109

Cerro Palenque, termination deposits, 158–59

Ch'a Chaak (Thunderstorm), 156

Chalk, fossils from, 245–46

Chalmers, James, 177

charms: Islamic, 206; hunting magic, 183–85

Chiapas, animate objects in, 157

chieftancy, Banda, 205

Chilcompton (Somerset), Early Bronze Age burials in, 248

childbirth, Mesoamerican concepts, 153, 154

children: agency of, 30; becoming persons, 153–54, 267; burial practices and, 31, 62; personhood of, 270–71

Chimaltenango/Chimbal, 149

Christianity, in Maritime Provinces, 66

Chukotka, 31, 35–36, 37, 43

circular buildings, at Cahokia, 80, 81

Cleveland shell plaque, imagery and inscriptions on, 134–38, 140, 141

Codex Mendoza, 154

codices, Maya, 16–17

co-essences, 151, 152

cognitive science, 270

Colonial period, in Maritime provinces, 15, 51–54, 55

colonization, colonialism, 149; French, 54, 66–67

color symbolism, 55

Comalapa, 139

commodities, 118; bird feathers as, 113–15; and personhood, 102–5

communication: by birds, 105–6; inalienable goods, 103–4; Maya visual, 16–17; object-human, 11–12

compositional practices, 200–201; Banda shrines, 217, 221–22

conchs (*Strombus* spp.), 140; inscriptions and, 134–38; as musical instruments, 132–33

consciousness, of objects, 13–14

conservation, of inalienable possessions, 103

Contact period, 16; Maritime provinces, 51–52

cooking pots, in Maya creation stories, 156–57

Copán, speech inscriptions at, 131–32

Copán valley, household archaeology in, 158–59

copper, symbolic power of, 55

copper alloys: Banda ornaments, 211, *212*, 214, 27, 220, 222, 226; Saharan trade in, 204–5

copper kettles, 15, 51, 55; as grave goods, 56–61, 266; life forces of, 61–62; as relations, 66, 67

corn. *See* maize

cosmogenesis, faience production and, 251

cosmography, Early Bronze Age, 247
cosmology: Cahokia, 80; hunter-gatherer, 32–33; Mesoamerican, 150–51; Mi'kmaq, 57, 63; Missouri River groups, 117–18
cowrie shells, Banda ornaments, 208
crafted objects, fossils as, 253
crafting, 7; fossil skeuomorphs, 240, 248–49; implements used in, 148–49, 155–58; in Mesoamerica, 268, 269
creation stories: Kluskap in, 63–64; Mandan, 111; Maya, 156–57
crinoids, 248; mimics of, 250–51
crosses, with souls, 127
Crow, birds and, 105, 109, 117
Crow-Has-Water Society Bundle, 113
cults, Torres Strait, 188–89
cultural relativism, 198

Dalles, the, eagle feather trade, 114
Dauan, 187
Dauar, 187
dead, in Torres Straits, 190
deaths, of Melanesian canoes, 174
decision-making, conscious, 275
decommissioning, of Cahokia structures, 81
deer, in Maya art, 134
deities. *See* gods
Deleuze, Gilles, 73, 76
Denys, Nicolas, 60, 66
depositional practices, Maya, 158–59
Descola, Philippe: 264; socialized naturalism, 6
design, 202; and response, 201
destiny, in Mesoamerica, 150–51
dialogue, 12, 16, 36
Dibi (Dibiri Island), 177
disabled, care for, 31
diseases, European, 62
dismemberment, of Torres Strait canoes, 186–87
dispersal, of Torres Strait canoes, 186–87
display, of icons, 103–4
dividual, dividuality, 9, 271
divination, 7, 214, 222
divine, and objects, 141
dogai, 181
dogs, 31; at Banda sites, 203–4, 211, 220, 222; as sacrificial animals, 215–16, 223
Dorset, jet and shale from, 245

Down Farm (Dorset), pond barrow, 248, *249*, 253
Dresden Codex, 156
dress, and personhood, 204
Driffield (East Yorkshire), Barrow C44, 248
drums, speaking, 132, *134*
dugongs: Torres Straits relationships with, 42, 175, 178, 182–83; Upper Palaeolithic use of, 253
Dunstable Downs (Bedfordshire), Early Bronze Age burials, 240–42
dyes, in Plains bundles, 16, 117

eagle feathers: as commodities, 113–15; gifts of, 111–13; valuation system, 119–20
eagle lodges, 106
eagle medicine, 110
Eagle Protection act, 110
eagle rights, 109–10
eagle tipi lodge, 111
eagle trapping, 106; and horse trade, 114–15; techniques, 110–11
Early Bronze Age, 18; fossil-human relationships, 253–55, 268; fossil skeuomorphs in, 250–53; magical powers in, 243–44; mortuary practices, 238, 239–50; personhood, 265–66
ear spools, 138
echinoids: in Early Bronze Age burials, *241*–42; skeuomorphs of, 251–53
ecological psychology, 201
ecology, visual, 201, 203, 205
effigies, Kaqchikel Maya use of, 139–40
elites, Maya, 138
embodied cognition, 264, 274
embodiment, 174, 275
Emerald Acropolis, 80
empathy, 34, 35
enchantment, 11, 201
Endangered Species Act, 110
England, Early Bronze Age burials in, 240–50
entanglement, 15, 76; in hunter-gatherer cosmology, 32–33; of maize farming, 87–88
epistemology, postmodern, 20
Erub, 189
Eskimo, 31, 33; agency and personhood, 14–15, 43; agential nonpersons, 39–41, 264, 265; persons, 34–39; reciprocity, 41–42

hearth fires, with souls, 127
Hidatsa, birds and, 105, 107, 109, 110, 117
hieroglyphic inscriptions: Maya, 16, 190, 134–38; speeches of gods and, 131–32
Hodder, Ian, 8
hoes, agency of, 157
Holbraad, Martin, 13
Holmesfield, Brown Edge (Derbyshire), ring cairn at, 247–48
Hopps (Pictou) site, *53*; copper kettles in, 57–59
horses: burial of, 31; and eagle feather trade, 114–15
households, depositional contexts, 158–59
houses, with souls, 127
Hudson Bay Company, bird use and trade, 113–14, 117
hulls, canoe, 181–82
Hummingbird Vase (Tikal), 131, *132*
hunter-gatherers, 10, 265; personhood and agency, 31
hunting, 7, 10, 137, 265; Eskimo, 14, 34–35, 42; reciprocity in, 35–36; Torres Strait Islanders, 175, 178, 182–86
hunting magic, Torres Strait, 183–85

iconography, agency and, 130
icons, display of, 103–4
identities, identity, 7, 9; formation of, 55, 105; social, 152, 256
illusionism, power of, 139
images, agency of, 128–29
implements, 154; crafting, 155–58; household, 158–59; personhood of, 148–49
inalienable goods/possessions, 118, 119; commoditization of, 100–101; communication of, 103–4; reciprocity and, 102–3
Incas, 139
India, carnelian beads from, 224
infants, agency of, 30, 153
Ingold, Timothy: on agency and animacy, 4, 129, 272; on meshwork, 8, 75–76
Iniskim Bundle, 113
injured, care for, 31
inorganic substances, 75, 77
inscription, 170
intentionalization, intentionality, 170; of canoes, 169, 171–72, 190–91
interactive dispositions, 103

interdependency, of relationships, 10, 14
interpretive theory, 265
inua, 36, 37
Inuit, Greenland, 43
Inupiaq Eskimo, 14, 37; hunting behavior, 34–35; wild babies, 30, 40
Inupiat, 36, 40, 41, 43
inversion, death as, 62
invocations, Banda, 197
Ipisia, 177
Ipiutak site, on Cape Krusenstern, *39*
iron, 267, 268; in Banda culture, 208, 209–11, *212*, 217, 220; in Ngre Kataa shrines, 221–22
Islam, and West African amulets, 206
isolation, social, 43
Isturitz, Grotte de, 253
itineraries, object-based, 3
Itqiirpak, 41
Ixoc Ahaua deities, 158

jade, jadite, 130, 137, 140
Jaurias, Grotte de, 253
jet, Bronze Age use, 243, 245, 256
Jewel Jaguar, Lord, 134
Johnson, Mark, 274–276

Kachina masks, as transformative objects, 104
Kaqchikel Maya, 127; effigy use, 139–40
Kaurareg, canoes, 183, 185–86
Kent, Early Bronze Age burials, 242
kettles: copper trade, 15, 51, 55; as grave goods, 56–60, 266; life forces of, 61–62; mutilation of, 60–61; in mythology, 63–65; as relations, 66, 67
K'iche' Maya, 157
Kipp, Darrell, 117
Kiriwina Island, 171
Kissi sites, 205
Kiwai, 176, 178
KK. *See* Kuulo Kataa
Kluskap, 63–64, 65
Kluskap's Kettle. *See* Ooteomul
knowledge, 8, 36, 109; of ritual behaviors, 14–15; transfer of, 108, 118–19
Krusenstern, Cape, seal skull cache, 37, *39*
kula canoes, 186; life histories of, 171–73
kula exchange, 200
Kulkalgal, 188–89

red birds, Plains trade in, 115
reincarnation, 106
relational ontologies, 29, 30, 73, 78; Eskimo, 42; Mi'kmaq, 65–66
relationships, 15, 75; conversive, 7–8; Eskimo, 34–35; mutual predatory, 264–65; subject-object, 12–13; interdependency of, 10, 14; power of, 72–73
relatives, relations: copper kettles as, 15, 57, 62; Mi'kmaq, 65–66; other-than-human, 51–52, 67
religion, 200
remora, as canoe decoration, 183, *184*
respect, in Eskimo relationships, 34, 37
response, design and, 201
restraint, in Eskimo Social relationships, 34
rhizome, rhizomization, 76; in Mississippian culture, 73, 75, 90
ring cairns, Bronze Age burials in, 247–48
rings: Banda, 208, 209–11, *212*, 213(table), 214, 217, 222, 226, 267
ritual contexts, Banda, 216–25
ritualization, of canoe parts, 186–87
rituals, 200, 267; Banda ornamentation and, 205–6; canoe life cycle, 171–73, 174, 175, 177–78, 185–86; Eskimo hunting, 34–35; metallurgy and, 220–22; of sacred objects, 11–12; at West African shrines, 207, 223
Rudston (Yorkshire), Bronze Age burials at, 245, 247

sacred bundles, as social persons, 77–78. *See also* bundles
sacrifices, dog, 215–16, 223
Saguane, 177
Sahara, and West African trade, 204–5
Sahlins, Marshall, 9
saints, images of, 126
Salmon River (Nova Scotia), copper-kettle burial in, 59
salt, with souls, 127
Santa Rita Murals, musical instruments on, 132, *133*
Santee Sioux, eagle feather use in, 111
Santiago Atitlan, weaving in, 157–58
Santiago Chimaltenango, 149
sap, as blood, 177
sarup, 188, 189, 190
Saskatchewan, eagle-trapping pits in, 110

Scandinavia, in Bronze Age burials, 244
scarification, West African, 204
sculptural materials, with divine essences, 130
sculpture, West African, 204
sea, as liminal, 190; as spiritscape, 189
seals: as persons, 34, 35, 36; treatment of remains, 37–39
sea urchin (*Micraster coraginium*), skeuomorphs of, 251, *252*, 253
Selawik, 41
self, selfhood, in Mesoamerica, 150, 151
self-sacrifice, of animals, 10, 34
semiotic forms, pythons as, 225
semiotic processes, 202
sentience, 170; of Torres Strait canoes, 169, 188–89
Senufo, 203, 214, 228(n5)
serpents: African symbolism, 214–15, 225–26; speech scrolls, 138
Seven Blind Brothers, canoe of, 190
sewing, Eskimo hunting and, 34
sexual divisions, 267
shaking tents, 80
shale, Bronze Age objects of, 245
shallop, Mi'kmaq use of, 54
shamans, Eskimo, 34
sharing, Eskimo, 34, 35–36
shells, 102; in Banda contexts, 220; as canoe decorations, 173, 178; Mississippian use of, 73, 81–*89*; speaking, 132–33, 134–38, 140
shipwrecks, Torres Straits, 189
shrines, 80; Banda, 17, 197, 217–20; as compositions/bundles, 201, 204; Mississippian, 81–82; West African, 207, 221–25, 228(n5)
Sigai, 188–89
signification, of objects, 127–28
silver production, in Guanajuato, 103
Sisilha, 131
skeuomorphs, fossil, 240, 248–49, 250–53
slaving, 204
social actors, social action, 6, 126, 149, 167, 170, 202
social hierarchy, inalienable possessions and, 119
sociality, 8, 42
social relations, 75, 100, 128, 130, 169, 189; gifts and commodities, 102–5; with things, 199–200; Torres Straits canoes, 187–88

Ulúa River valley (Lower), household archaeology in, 158–59
Upper Palaeolithic, fossil use, 253–54
Upton Lovell barrow, grape cup from, *252*

Vakuta Island, canoe manufacture in, 172–73
value systems: inalienable goods in, 100–101; Missouri River tribes, 117, 119–20
Vanuatu, outrigger canoes, 174–75
Varney culture/tradition, 84; Maize growing, 85, 88; in Mississippi Valley, 86–87, 91–92
vases, speaking, 131, *132*
vision quests, bird knowledge, 108
visual ecology, 201, 203, 205
Viveiros de Castro, Eduardo, on perspectivism, 6
Volta River basin, 199; dogs and pythons in, 203–4

Wabad (Wabuda) Island, canoe trees from, 176, 177
Wabanaki, 52, *53*
waga (seagoing canoes), 171–72
Waiat spirit-beings, 187
Wakanda, 77
Wala Island, outrigger canoes, 174–75
Walker, William, 19
walrus, as persons, 34, 35, 36
war bonnets, feathers used in, 111–*12*
Waruksti, 77
Watanabe, John, 149
water, 75, 76, 81; and maize growing, 87–88; in Mississippian culture, 73, 89–90
waterfowl, Plains tribes and, 117
water temples, at Cahokia, 80

ways of knowing, 11. *See also* knowledge
wealth: British Bronze Age, 238; shell as, 135–36
weaving, Maya concepts of, 154, 156, 157–58
well-being, 197, 199
West Africa, 197, 198, 267; shrines, 207, 221–23; trade networks, 204–6. *See also* Banda
West Kennett, Neolithic chambered tombs in, 275–76
whales, 189; as persons, 34, 35, 36
whistles, 113, 132
wild babies, 30, 34, 40, 42
Windmill Hill, grape cup from, 251
Witmore, Christopher, 5, 267
wolves, personhood of, 31
women, behavior during hunts, 34, 35
wood, in Maya culture, 130
wooden people, in Maya creation, 156–57
woodpeckers, trade in, 115
worldview, hunter-gatherer, 32–33
writing, Maya hieroglyphic, 16

Yonne (France), cave sites in, 253
York Factory, 114
Yorkshire, jet and shale in, 245
yua, 36
Yucatan, nonhuman agents in, 127, 131, 157
Yucatec Maya, 154
Yukaghir, 35
Yupiit, Central, 36, 40, 41, 43
Yup'ik, 14, 34, 35, 37

Zinacanteco Tzotzil Maya, souls, 126–27, 152
zoomorphism, zoomorphization, of canoes, 169, 173, 178–82

www.ingramcontent.com/pod-product-compliance
Lightning Source LLC
Chambersburg PA
CBHW070911030426
42336CB00014BA/2374